C000103958

THE
POETICAL WORKS
OF
WILLIAM WORDSWORTH

THE

Poetical Works

OF

WILLIAM WORDSWORTH

EVENING VOLUNTARIES
ITINERARY POEMS OF 1833
POEMS OF SENTIMENT AND REFLECTION
SONNETS DEDICATED TO LIBERTY
AND ORDER
MISCELLANEOUS POEMS
INSCRIPTIONS
SELECTIONS FROM CHAUCER
POEMS REFERRING TO THE PERIOD OF
OLD AGE
EPITAPHS AND ELEGIAC PIECES
ODE: INTIMATIONS OF IMMORTALITY

Edited from the manuscripts
with
textual and critical notes
by
E. DE SELINCOURT
and
HELEN DARBISHIRE

OXFORD
AT THE CLARENDON PRESS

OXFORD
UNIVERSITY PRESS

Great Clarendon Street, Oxford OX2 6DP
United Kingdom

Oxford University Press is a department of the University of Oxford.
It furthers the University's objective of excellence in research, scholarship,
and education by publishing worldwide. Oxford is a registered trade mark of
Oxford University Press in the UK and in certain other countries

Copyright Oxford University Press 1940

The moral rights of the author have been asserted

First published 1940

Published in the United States of America by Oxford University Press
198 Madison Avenue, New York, NY 10016, United States of America

British Library Cataloguing in Publication Data
Data available

Library of Congress Cataloging in Publication Data
Data available

ISBN 978-0-19-811827-5 Volume I
ISBN 978-0-19-811828-2 Volume II
ISBN 978-0-19-811829-9 Volume III
ISBN 978-0-19-811830-5 Volume IV
ISBN 978-0-19-811831-2 Volume V
ISBN 978-0-19-254152-9 Five volume set

PREFACE

THIS volume, comprising the remainder of Wordsworth's shorter poems, contains a considerable proportion of his later work, notably the *Evening Voluntaries*—perhaps the best example of his mature style, *Memorials of the Tour of 1833*, and two late Sonnet-sequences; but also some of his most characteristic early work in *Poems of Sentiment and Reflection* and *Poems referring to the Period of Old Age*. The great *Ode, Intimations of Immortality* &c., stands significantly at the end.

Appendix A gives the surviving portions of his translations of Virgil, of which only a fragment has hitherto been published; Appendix B contains Poems and Verses of various periods, either never printed by Wordsworth or not included in his final edition of 1849–50. I have reserved unpublished passages of blank verse which have kinship with *The Prelude* and *The Excursion* for the Appendix to Vol. V which will contain *The Excursion*.

In following Wordsworth's final text I have made a few corrections, in most cases supported by the manuscripts: *vide Poems of Sentiment and Reflection*, XXVI, 46 (p. 98); *Sonnets upon the Punishment of Death*, I, 10 (p. 135); *Miscellaneous Poems*, VII, 27 (p. 161); *The Cuckoo and the Nightingale*, 28 (p. 218); *Troilus and Cressida*, 118 and 138 (p. 232). But the most important emendation, sanctioned by Wordsworth's own hand, is in the *Ode, Intimations of Immortality* at line 69 (*vide* text p. 281 and note p. 466).

I am indebted to Professor H. W. Garrod and Professor D. Nichol Smith for help in tracing the Latin verses ascribed to T. Warton (Appendix B. VIII).

I wish to express my gratitude to Mr. E. H. W. Meyerstein for his generosity in trusting me with the *Longman* manuscript of *Poems of 1807* for prolonged study. Finally I tender my warm thanks to my friend, Sir Humphrey Milford, for lending his expert eye to the scrutiny of my proofs.

H. D.

July 1947.

TABLE OF ABBREVIATIONS, ETC., USED IN THE *APPARATUS CRITICUS* AND NOTES

W. or W. W. William Wordsworth.

D. W. Dorothy Wordsworth.

Dora W. Dora Wordsworth.

M. H. or M. W. Mary Wordsworth.

S. H. Sara Hutchinson.

H. C. R. Henry Crabb Robinson.

E. Q. Edward Quillinan.

M. *Memoirs of W. W.*, by Christopher Wordsworth.

E.L. *The Early Letters of W. W. and D. W.* Oxford, 1935.

M.Y. *The Letters of W. W. and D. W. Middle Years* (1806–1820), 2 vols. Oxford, 1937.

L.Y. *The Letters of W. W. and D. W. Later Years* (1821–50), 3 vols. Oxford, 1939.

C.R. The Correspondence of Henry Crabb Robinson with the Wordsworth Circle, ed. Edith J. Morley, 1927.

I. F. The notes dictated by W. W. to Isabella Fenwick in 1843.

O.E.D. The Oxford English Dictionary.

L.B. *Lyrical Ballads*, 1798, 1800, 1802, 1805.

1807. *Poems in Two Volumes*, 1807.

Vol. of 1835. *Yarrow Revisited and other Poems.*

Vol. of 1842. *Poems chiefly of Early and Late Years.*

1815, 1820, &c. Collective editions published in 1815, 1820, &c.

K. Professor William Knight, editor of W. W.'s *Poetical Works*, 8 vols. 1896.

Dowden. Professor Edward Dowden, editor of W. W.'s *Poetical Works*, 7 vols. 1892–3.

Hutchinson. Mr. Thomas Hutchinson, editor of the Oxford Wordsworth, The *Lyrical Ballads* (1798) 1898, and the *Poems in Two Volumes* (1807) 1897.

L. *Longman MSS.* Manuscripts of the *Lyrical Ballads* (1800–5) and of *Poems in Two Volumes*, 1807, now in the British Museum, formerly in the possession of Mr. T. Norton Longman, then in that of Mr. E. H. W. Meyerstein.

C. Variants from a copy of W.'s Poetical Works, 1836–7, formerly in the possession of Lord Coleridge, used by W. for correction and re-drafting of his text, now in the Royal Library at Windsor.

MS. M. A manuscript of Poems included for the most part in

Poems in Two Volumes, 1807, transcribed probably in March, 1804, *v.* E. de S., *The Prelude*, p. xx.

MS. 101. A large folio note-book in use from 1820 onwards, in which poems have been transcribed by D. W., M. W., S. H., and Dora W., and in which W. himself has written drafts of poems in process of composition. It has been possible to deduce identity of date for certain poems on the same or adjacent pages from similarity of ink and handwriting and the placing and sequence of drafts.

MS. 92. A quarto note-book containing transcriptions of Poems intended for the *Poems chiefly of Early and Late Years*, published in 1842.

MS. 1, MS. 2, &c., in *Apparatus Criticus* indicate variants from first draft, second draft, &c., of manuscript text of the particular poem.

MS. C^l. Christabel note-book, used between 1798 and 1800.

MS. 18^a. Notebook used between 1798 and 1800 (versions generally later than those in MS. C^l).

MS. G.B. MSS. from the George Beaumont Collection, now in Pierpont Morgan Library, New York.

[ ] indicates a word or words missing from the manuscript.

Words enclosed in [ ] represent a reading from another MS. or printed text: words enclosed in ( ) a reading from the same MS.

17/18 lines found in a manuscript or printed text between line 17 and line 18.

CONTENTS

MISCELLANEOUS POEMS

INSCRIPTIONS

EPITAPHS AND ELEGIAC PIECES

APPENDIX A

APPENDIX B

EVENING VOLUNTARIES

I

[Composed 1832.—Published 1835.]

CALM is the fragrant air, and loth to lose
Day's grateful warmth, tho' moist with falling dews.
Look for the stars, you'll say that there are none;
Look up a second time, and, one by one,
You mark them twinkling out with silvery light,   5
And wonder how they could elude the sight!
The birds, of late so noisy in their bowers,
Warbled a while with faint and fainter powers,
But now are silent as the dim-seen flowers:
Nor does the village Church-clock's iron tone   10
The time's and season's influence disown;
Nine beats distinctly to each other bound
In drowsy sequence—how unlike the sound
That, in rough winter, oft inflicts a fear
On fireside listeners, doubting what they hear!   15
The shepherd, bent on rising with the sun,
Had closed his door before the day was done,
And now with thankful heart to bed doth creep,
And joins his little children in their sleep.
The bat, lured forth where trees the lane o'ershade,   20
Flits and reflits along the close arcade;
The busy dor-hawk chases the white moth

I. MS. 1 *has the title* "Twilight by the side of Grasmere Lake"
1–2 A twofold sleep the mountain tops (slumber the huge hills) partake
    High in the air and deep within the (in the still) lake   MS. 1
8 *not in* MS. 1   9 Are hushed and silent . . .   MS. 1, *which goes on at l.* 27
11 The night-calm's soothing influence   MS.
16–29 *An earlier draft runs:*
    The Labourer wont to rise at break of day
    Has closed his door, and from the public way
    The sound of hoof or wheel is heard no more;
    One boat there was, but it has touched the shore,
    That was the last dip of its slackened oar.
17–21 Has closed his door, the bat her flight begun
    Through the dim air of evening, slow to lose
    Its grateful warmth, though moist with falling dews. MS. 2
19 joins   1837: join   1835
20–1 The flitting Bat here thrids a close arcade
    Of pollard oaks forth tempted by the shade. MS. 3
22 The busy   1837: Far-heard the   1835

With burring note, which Industry and Sloth
Might both be pleased with, for it suits them both.
A stream is heard—I see it not, but know   25
By its soft music whence the waters flow:
Wheels and the tread of hoofs are heard no more;
One boat there was, but it will touch the shore
With the next dipping of its slackened oar;
Faint sound, that, for the gayest of the gay,   30
Might give to serious thought a moment's sway,
As a last token of man's toilsome day!

II
ON A HIGH PART OF THE COAST OF CUMBERLAND
Easter Sunday, April 7.

THE AUTHOR'S SIXTY-THIRD BIRTHDAY
[Composed April 7, 1833.—Published 1835.]

THE Sun, that seemed so mildly to retire,
Flung back from distant climes a streaming fire,
Whose blaze is now subdued to tender gleams,
Prelude of night's approach with soothing dreams.
Look round;—of all the clouds not one is moving;   5
'Tis the still hour of thinking, feeling, loving.
Silent, and stedfast as the vaulted sky,
The boundless plain of waters seems to lie:—
Comes that low sound from breezes rustling o'er
The grass-crowned headland that conceals the shore?   10
No; 'tis the earth-voice of the mighty sea,
Whispering how meek and gentle he *can* be!

  Thou Power supreme! who, arming to rebuke
Offenders, dost put off the gracious look,
And clothe thyself with terrors like the flood   15

25-6 *not in* MS. *or* 1835   30 Sound that for tripping elves and
goblins gay MS.
II. *No title in* 1835: "Seaside, Moresby" MS.   7 vaulted] concave MS.
8 Th' illimitable ocean MS.   9 sound] voice MS.   10 The cliff
high raised above the unseen shore? MS.
13-15 Dread Power of Powers *etc.* MS. 2
        Father, who when thy justice *must* rebuke
        The sinner . . .
        And execute thy purpose MS. 1

Of ocean roused into his fiercest mood,
Whatever discipline thy Will ordain
For the brief course that must for me remain;
Teach me with quick-eared spirit to rejoice
In admonitions of thy softest voice! 20
Whate'er the path these mortal feet may trace,
Breathe through my soul the blessing of thy grace,
Glad, through a perfect love, a faith sincere
Drawn from the wisdom that begins with fear,
Glad to expand; and, for a season, free 25
From finite cares, to rest absorbed in Thee!

III

(BY THE SEA-SIDE)

[Composed March–April 1833.—Published 1835.]

THE sun is couched, the sea-fowl gone to rest,
And the wild storm hath somewhere found a nest;
Air slumbers—wave with wave no longer strives,
Only a heaving of the deep survives,
A tell-tale motion! soon will it be laid, 5
And by the tide alone the water swayed.
Stealthy withdrawings, interminglings mild
Of light with shade in beauty reconciled—
Such is the prospect far as sight can range,
The soothing recompence, the welcome change. 10
Where now the ships that drove before the blast,
Threatened by angry breakers as they passed;
And by a train of flying clouds bemocked;
Or, in the hollow surge, at anchor rocked
As on a bed of death? Some lodge in peace, 15
Saved by His care who bade the tempest cease;
And some, too heedless of past danger, court
Fresh gales to waft them to the far-off port;
But near, or hanging sea and sky between,
Not one of all those wingèd powers is seen, 20

17–19 Author and Life of all things! blest are they
        Who, pacing needfully the world's broad way
        Have learned with MSS.
21–4 *not in* MSS. 1, 2
III. (BY THE SEA-SIDE)] Composed by the seaside at Moresby. After
a Storm MS.

Seen in her course, nor 'mid this quiet heard;
Yet oh! how gladly would the air be stirred
By some acknowledgment of thanks and praise,
Soft in its temper as those vesper' lays
Sung to the Virgin while accordant oars   25
Urge the slow bark along Calabrian shores;
A sea-born service through the mountains felt
Till into one loved vision all things melt:
Or like those hymns that soothe with graver sound
The gulfy coast of Norway iron-bound;   30
And, from the wide and open Baltic, rise
With punctual care, Lutherian harmonies.
Hush, not a voice is here! but why repine,
Now when the star of eve comes forth to shine
On British waters with that look benign?   35
Ye mariners, that plough your onward way,
Or in the haven rest, or sheltering bay,
May silent thanks at least to God be given
With a full heart; "our thoughts are *heard* in heaven!"

IV

[Composed 1834.—Published 1835.]

Not in the lucid intervals of life
That come but as a curse to party-strife;
Not in some hour when Pleasure with a sigh
Of languor puts his rosy garland by;
Not in the breathing-times of that poor slave   5
Who daily piles up wealth in Mammon's cave—
Is Nature felt, or can be; nor do words,
Which practised talent readily affords,
Prove that her hand has touched responsive chords;

28 Till] While MS.   38–9 silent . . . *heard*] *silent* . . . heard MS., 1835
IV. 1–19 Alas, for them who crave impassioned strife
          How few the lucid intervals of life;
          When lonely Nature's finer issues hit
          The brain's perceptions, for the heart are fit;
          With meekness sensibilities abide
          That do but rarely visit stormy pride,
          Full oft the powers of genius are confined
          By chains which round herself she dares to wind. MS. 1
5 Not in the respite of Ambition's slave MS. 2
7–11   Do lonely Nature's finer issues move
          The soul to rapture or the heart to love. MS. 2

Nor has her gentle beauty power to move   10
With genuine rapture and with fervent love
The soul of Genius, if he dare to take
Life's rule from passion craved for passion's sake;
Untaught that meekness is the cherished bent
Of all the truly great and all the innocent.   15
 But who *is* innocent ? By grace divine,
Not otherwise, O Nature! we are thine,
Through good and evil thine, in just degree
Of rational and manly sympathy.
To all that Earth from pensive hearts is stealing,   20
And Heaven is now to gladdened eyes revealing,
Add every charm the Universe can show
Through every change its aspects undergo—
Care may be respited, but not repealed;
No perfect cure grows on that bounded field.   25
Vain is the pleasure, a false calm the peace,
If He, through whom alone our conflicts cease,
Our virtuous hopes without relapse advance,
Come not to speed the Soul's deliverance;
To the distempered Intellect refuse   30
His gracious help, or give what we abuse.

V

(BY THE SIDE OF RYDAL MERE)

[Composed 1834.—Published 1835.]

THE linnet's warble, sinking towards a close,
Hints to the thrush 'tis time for their repose;
The shrill-voiced thrush is heedless, and again
The monitor revives his own sweet strain;
But both will soon be mastered, and the copse   5
Be left as silent as the mountain-tops,

12 dare 1837: dares 1835 15 Of minds unselfish and benevolent. MS. 2
20–31 Add all that Earth from human sight is stealing
  To all that heaven is at this hour revealing,
  What does it serve for pleasure or for peace
  If he who can alone the Soul release
  From bonds, for her deliverance refuse
  His signet, or his mercy we abuse. MS. 2
24 A respite only can those medicines yield MS. 1
V. 5–12 But a few minutes more of fading light
  Will leave the whole copse voiceless, ere the night

Ere some commanding star dismiss to rest
The throng of rooks, that now, from twig or nest,
(After a steady flight on home-bound wings,
And a last game of mazy hoverings   10
Around their ancient grove) with cawing noise
Disturb the liquid music's equipoise.

O Nightingale! Who ever heard thy song
Might here be moved, till Fancy grows so strong
That listening sense is pardonably cheated   15
Where wood or stream by thee was never greeted.
Surely, from fairest spots of favoured lands,
Were not some gifts withheld by jealous hands,
This hour of deepening darkness here would be
As a fresh morning for new harmony;   20
And lays as prompt would hail the dawn of Night:
A *dawn* she has both beautiful and bright,
When the East kindles with the full moon's light;
Not like the rising sun's impatient glow
Dazzling the mountains, but an overflow   25
Of solemn splendour, in mutation slow.

Wanderer by spring with gradual progress led,
For sway profoundly felt as widely spread;
To king, to peasant, to rough sailor, dear,
And to the soldier's trumpet-wearied ear;   30
How welcome wouldst thou be to this green Vale
Fairer than Tempe! Yet, sweet Nightingale!

By some commanding star to silent rest
Dismiss the rooks that now from bough or nest
In yon old grove disturb with cawing noise
The liquid music's [easy ?] equipoise. MS.
14 Will have it here, and truth receive no wrong MS.   15 That . . .
is] And . . . be MS.
16–18 Alas when all our Choristers have retreated
       These hills by thy low voice (In vales that by thy voice) are never
           greeted
       Surely if Nature from most . . .
       Held not some favor back with . . . MS.
19 deepening darkness] gathering shadows MS.   20 new] thy MS.
24–6 *not in* MS., 1835
27–8 Heart-thrilling Bird mid Eastern roses bred
       For empire deeply *etc.* MS.
31–41 Whether thou givest or withhold'st thy lay
       Be ours to walk content with Nature's way,

From the warm breeze that bears thee on, alight
At will, and stay thy migratory flight;
Build, at thy choice, or sing, by pool or fount,   35
Who shall complain, or call thee to account?
The wisest, happiest, of our kind are they
That ever walk content with Nature's way,
God's goodness—measuring bounty as it may;
For whom the gravest thought of what they miss,   40
Chastening the fulness of a present bliss,
Is with that wholesome office satisfied,
While unrepining sadness is allied
In thankful bosoms to a modest pride.

VI

[Composed 1834.—Published 1835.]

SOFT as a cloud is yon blue Ridge—the Mere
Seems firm as solid crystal, breathless, clear,
And motionless; and, to the gazer's eye,
Deeper than ocean, in the immensity
Of its vague mountains and unreal sky!   5
But, from the process in that still retreat,
Turn to minuter changes at our feet;
Observe how dewy Twilight has withdrawn
The crowd of daisies from the shaven lawn,
And has restored to view its tender green,   10
That, while the sun rode high, was lost beneath their
     dazzling sheen.
—An emblem this of what the sober Hour
Can do for minds disposed to feel its power!
Thus oft, when we in vain have wish'd away
The petty pleasures of the garish day,   15
Meek eve shuts up the whole usurping host
(Unbashful dwarfs each glittering at his post)

While at all times and seasons what we miss
Tempers the fulness of a loving bliss, MS.
VI. 8 Observe] But mark MS.
13-14 Like office can this sober shadowy hour
     Perform for hearts *etc.*
The MS. also preserves ll. 8-19 as a separate (chiefly octosyllabic) poem:
     The dewy evening has withdrawn
     The daisies from the shaven lawn
     And has restored its tender green
     Lost while the sun was up beneath their dazzling sheen.

And leaves the disencumbered spirit free
To reassume a staid simplicity.

'Tis well—but what are helps of time and place,   20
When wisdom stands in need of nature's grace;
Why do good thoughts, invoked or not, descend,
Like Angels from their bowers, our virtues to befriend;
If yet To-morrow, unbelied, may say,
"I come to open out, for fresh display,   25
The elastic vanities of yesterday?"

VII

[Composed 1834.—Published 1835.]

THE leaves that rustled on this oak-crowned hill,
And sky that danced among those leaves, are still;
Rest smooths the way for sleep; in field and bower
Soft shades and dews have shed their blended power
On drooping eyelid and the closing flower;   5
Sound is there none at which the faintest heart
Might leap, the weakest nerve of superstition start;
Save when the Owlet's unexpected scream
Pierces the ethereal vault; and ('mid the gleam
Of unsubstantial imagery, the dream,   10
From the hushed vale's realities, transferred
To the still lake) the imaginative Bird
Seems, 'mid inverted mountains, not unheard.

Grave Creature!—whether, while the moon shines bright
On thy wings opened wide for smoothest flight,   15

Like office can this sober hour
Perform for hearts that feel its power
When we in vain have wished away
The garish pleasures of broad day
While each stood glittering at his post.
Meek eventide shuts up the whole usurping host
And leaves the humble spirit free
To reassume its own simplicity.

18 the groundwork of our nature free MS.
VII. MS. *has the title* "Twilight"   1–2 Ceased is the rustling . . . The
sky . . . is still MS.
3–5 Advancing slowly from the faded West
    Sleep treads a way prepared for him by Rest. MS.
7 superstition] fancy MS.   8 at intervals the Owlet's scream MS.

Thou art discovered in a roofless tower,
Rising from what may once have been a lady's bower;
Or spied where thou sitt'st moping in thy mew
At the dim centre of a churchyard yew;
Or from a rifted crag or ivy tod   20
Deep in a forest, thy secure abode,
Thou giv'st, for pastime's sake, by shriek or shout,
A puzzling notice of thy whereabout—
May the night never come, nor day be seen,
When I shall scorn thy voice or mock thy mien!   25

   In classic ages men perceived a soul
Of sapience in thy aspect, headless Owl!
Thee Athens reverenced in the studious grove;
And near the golden sceptre grasped by Jove,
His Eagle's favourite perch, while round him sate   30
The Gods revolving the decrees of Fate,
Thou, too, wert present at Minerva's side:
Hark to that second larum!—far and wide
The elements have heard, and rock and cave replied.

VIII

[Composed June 8, 1802.—Published 1807; omitted from edd. 1815–32; republished 1835.]

This *Impromptu* appeared, many years ago, among the Author's poems, from which, in subsequent editions, it was excluded. It is reprinted at the request of the Friend in whose presence the lines were thrown off.

   THE sun has long been set,
     The stars are out by twos and threes,
   The little birds are piping yet
     Among the bushes and trees;
   There's a cuckoo, and one or two thrushes,   5
   And a far-off wind that rushes,
   And a sound of water that gushes,
   And the cuckoo's sovereign cry
   Fills all the hollow of the sky.

16 encountered in a moon-lit MS.
19/20 Or in a glimmering Barn when thou dost chuse
    (Wishing the Sun good speed) to mope and muse MS.
20 Or watch for food; or from an ivy tod MS.
23/4 Or hast been robbed of liberty and joy
    The drooping Captive of a thoughtless boy MS.
VIII. 6 And a noise of MSS., 1807   7 With a noise of MSS., 1807

Who would go "parading"   10
In London, and "masquerading,"
On such a night of June
With that beautiful soft half-moon,
And all these innocent blisses ?
On such a night as this is!   15

IX

COMPOSED UPON AN EVENING OF EXTRA-ORDINARY SPLENDOUR AND BEAUTY

[Composed summer, 1817.—Published 1820.]

I

HAD this effulgence disappeared
With flying haste, I might have sent,
Among the speechless clouds, a look
Of blank astonishment ;
But 'tis endued with power to stay,   5
And sanctify one closing day,
That frail Mortality may see—
What is ?—ah no, but what *can* be!
Time was when field and watery cove
With modulated echoes rang,   10
While choirs of fervent Angels sang
Their vespers in the grove ;
Or, crowning, star-like, each some sovereign height,
Warbled, for heaven above and earth below,
Strains suitable to both.—Such holy rite,   15
Methinks, if audibly repeated now

11 and "masquerading" 1807: "and masquerading" 1835–50
13/14 With what the breathless Lake is feeling
        And what the dewy air to peace dismisses,
        With all that Earth from pensive hearts is stealing
        And Heaven to gladdened eyes revealing, MSS.
IX. Composed during a sunset of transcendent Beauty, in the summer of
1817. MS. Evening Ode, (Composed *etc. as text*) 1820   6 sanctify]
solemnize MS.
11–12 Of harp and voice while Angels sang
        Amid the umbrageous grove MS.
13 *so* 1832: Or, ranged like stars along some MS., 1820–7
15–18 . . . Ye sons of Light,
        If such communion were repeated now
        Nor harp nor Seraph's voice could move
        Sublimer rapture, holier love MS.

From hill or valley, could not move
Sublimer transport, purer love,
Than doth this silent spectacle—the gleam—
The shadow—and the peace supreme!   20

II

No sound is uttered,—but a deep
And solemn harmony pervades
The hollow vale from steep to steep,
And penetrates the glades.
Far-distant images draw nigh,   25
Called forth by wondrous potency
Of beamy radiance, that imbues
Whate'er it strikes with gem-like hues!
In vision exquisitely clear,
Herds range along the mountain side;   30
And glistening antlers are descried;
And gilded flocks appear.
Thine is the tranquil hour, purpureal Eve!
But long as god-like wish, or hope divine,
Informs my spirit, ne'er can I believe   35
That this magnificence is wholly thine!
—From worlds not quickened by the sun
A portion of the gift is won;
An intermingling of Heaven's pomp is spread
On grounds which British shepherds tread!   40

III

And, if there be whom broken ties
Afflict, or injuries assail,
Yon hazy ridges to their eyes
Present a glorious scale,
Climbing suffused with sunny air,   45
To stop—no record hath told where!

21 What though no sound be heard, a deep MS.   30 range] graze
MS.   37 not quickened] unquicken'd MS.
41-9 And if they wish for smooth escape
    From grief and this terrestrial vale,
    Yon hazy (mountain) ridges take (rocks and clouds present) the shape
    Of stairs a gradual scale,
    By which the fancy might ascend
    And with those happy spirits blend
    Whose motions smitten with glad awe
    By night the dreaming Patriarch saw
    Wings *etc.* MS.

And tempting Fancy to ascend,
And with immortal Spirits blend!
—Wings at my shoulders seem to play;
But, rooted here, I stand and gaze   50
On those bright steps that heavenward raise
Their practicable way.
Come forth, ye drooping old men, look abroad,
And see to what fair countries ye are bound!
And if some traveller, weary of his road,   55
Hath slept since noon-tide on the grassy ground,
Ye Genii! to his covert speed;
And wake him with such gentle heed
As may attune his soul to meet the dower
Bestowed on this transcendent hour!   60

                    IV

Such hues from their celestial Urn
Were wont to stream before mine eye,
Where'er it wandered in the morn
Of blissful infancy.
This glimpse of glory, why renewed ?   65
Nay, rather speak with gratitude;
For, if a vestige of those gleams
Survived, 'twas only in my dreams.
Dread Power! whom peace and calmness serve
No less than Nature's threatening voice,   70
If aught unworthy be my choice,
From THEE if I would swerve;
Oh, let Thy grace remind me of the light
Full early lost, and fruitlessly deplored;
Which, at this moment, on my waking sight   75
Appears to shine, by miracle restored;

---

49 shoulders 1837: shoulder 1820–32   53 Come from your doors ye old
men MS.   57–8 covert speed . . . heed] couch repair . . . care MS.
61–3 Whence but from some celestial Urn
      Those colours, wont to meet my eye
      Where'er I MS.
62 mine 1837: my 1820–32
69–70 whom storms and darkness serve. The thunder or the still small
voice MS.

My soul, though yet confined to earth,
Rejoices in a second birth!
—'Tis past, the visionary splendour fades;
And night approaches with her shades.   80

Note—The multiplication of mountain-ridges, described at the com-
mencement of the third Stanza of this Ode as a kind of Jacob's Ladder,
leading to Heaven, is produced either by watery vapours, or sunny haze;—
in the present instance by the latter cause. Allusions to the Ode entitled
"Intimations of Immortality" pervade the last Stanza of the foregoing
Poem.

X

COMPOSED BY THE SEA-SHORE

[Composed 1833.—Published 1842.]

WHAT mischief cleaves to unsubdued regret,
How fancy sickens by vague hopes beset;
How baffled projects on the spirit prey,
And fruitless wishes eat the heart away,
The Sailor knows; he best, whose lot is cast   5
On the relentless sea that holds him fast
On chance dependent, and the fickle star
Of power, through long and melancholy war.
O sad it is, in sight of foreign shores,
Daily to think on old familiar doors,   10
Hearths loved in childhood, and ancestral floors;
Or, tossed about along a waste of foam,
To ruminate on that delightful home
Which with the dear Betrothèd *was* to come;
Or came and was and is, yet meets the eye   15
Never but in the world of memory;
Or in a dream recalled, whose smoothest range
Is crossed by knowledge, or by dread, of change,
And if not so, whose perfect joy makes sleep
A thing too bright for breathing man to keep.   20
Hail to the virtues which that perilous life
Extracts from Nature's elemental strife;
And welcome glory won in battles fought
As bravely as the foe was keenly sought.
But to each gallant Captain and his crew   25
A less imperious sympathy is due,

X. 1–8 *not in* MS.   20 Too bright for mortal Creature long to
keep MS.

Such as my verse now yields, while moonbeams play
On the mute sea in this unruffled bay;
Such as will promptly flow from every breast,
Where good men, disappointed in the quest   30
Of wealth and power and honours, long for rest;
Or, having known the splendours of success,
Sigh for the obscurities of happiness.

XI
[Composed February 25, 1841.—Published 1842.]

THE Crescent-moon, the Star of Love,
　　Glories of evening, as ye there are seen
　　With but a span of sky between—
　　Speak one of you, my doubts remove,
Which is the attendant Page and which the Queen?   5

XII
TO THE MOON
COMPOSED BY THE SEASIDE,—ON THE COAST OF CUMBERLAND
[Composed 1835.—Published 1837.]

WANDERER! that stoop'st so low, and com'st so near
To human life's unsettled atmosphere;
Who lov'st with Night and Silence to partake,
So might it seem, the cares of them that wake;
And, through the cottage-lattice softly peeping,   5
Dost shield from harm the humblest of the sleeping;
What pleasure once encompassed those sweet names
Which yet in thy behalf the Poet claims,
An idolizing dreamer as of yore!—
I slight them all; and, on this sea-beat shore   10
Sole-sitting, only can to thoughts attend
That bid me hail thee as the SAILOR'S FRIEND;
So call thee for heaven's grace through thee made known
By confidence supplied and mercy shown,
When not a twinkling star or beacon's light   15
Abates the perils of a stormy night;
And for less obvious benefits, that find

XI. 1 Crescent-] setting MS.   2–3 Bright Pair! with but a span of
sky between MSS.
XII. *For* MS. *draft v. notes, p.* 398.

Their way, with thy pure help, to heart and mind ;
Both for the adventurer starting in life's prime ;
And veteran ranging round from clime to clime, 20
Long-baffled hope's slow fever in his veins,
And wounds and weakness oft his labour's sole remains.

The aspiring Mountains and the winding Streams,
Empress of Night! are gladdened by thy beams ;
A look of thine the wilderness pervades, 25
And penetrates the forest's inmost shades ;
Thou, chequering peaceably the minster's gloom,
Guid'st the pale Mourner to the lost one's tomb ;
Canst reach the Prisoner—to his grated cell
Welcome, though silent and intangible !— 30
And lives there one, of all that come and go
On the great waters toiling to and fro, .
One, who has watched thee at some quiet hour
Enthroned aloft in undisputed power,
Or crossed by vapoury streaks and clouds that move 35
Catching the lustre they in part reprove—
Nor sometimes felt a fitness in thy sway
To call up thoughts that shun the glare of day,
And make the serious happier than the gay ?

Yes, lovely Moon! if thou so mildly bright 40
Dost rouse, yet surely in thy own despite,
To fiercer mood the frenzy-stricken brain,
Let me a compensating faith maintain ;
That there's a sensitive, a tender, part
Which thou canst touch in every human heart, 45
For healing and composure.—But, as least
And mightiest billows ever have confessed
Thy domination ; as the whole vast Sea
Feels through her lowest depths thy sovereignty ;
So shines that countenance with especial grace 50
On them who urge the keel her *plains* to trace
Furrowing its way right onward. The most rude,
Cut off from home and country, may have stood—
Even till long gazing hath bedimmed his eye,
Or the mute rapture ended in a sigh— 55
Touched by accordance of thy placid cheer,
With some internal lights to memory dear,

Or fancies stealing forth to soothe the breast
Tired with its daily share of earth's unrest,—
Gentle awakenings, visitations meek;   60
A kindly influence whereof few will speak,
Though it can wet with tears the hardiest cheek.

And when thy beauty in the shadowy cave
Is hidden, buried in its monthly grave;
Then, while the Sailor, 'mid an open sea   65
Swept by a favouring wind that leaves thought free,
Paces the deck—no star perhaps in sight,
And nothing save the moving ship's own light
To cheer the long dark hours of vacant night—
Oft with his musings does thy image blend,   70
In his mind's eye thy crescent horns ascend,
And thou art still, O Moon, that SAILOR'S FRIEND!

XIII

TO THE MOON

(RYDAL)

[Composed 1835.—Published 1837.]

QUEEN of the stars!—so gentle, so benign,
That ancient Fable did to thee assign,
When darkness creeping o'er thy silver brow
Warned thee these upper regions to forego,
Alternate empire in the shades below—   5
A Bard, who, lately near the wide-spread sea
Traversed by gleaming ships, looked up to thee
With grateful thoughts, doth now thy rising hail
From the close confines of a shadowy vale.
Glory of night, conspicuous yet serene,   10
Nor less attractive when by glimpses seen
Through cloudy umbrage, well might that fair face,
And all those attributes of modest grace,
In days when Fancy wrought unchecked by fear,
Down to the green earth fetch thee from thy sphere,   15
To sit in leafy woods by fountains clear!

XIII. 1-4 Queen of the Stars, as bright as when of yore
        Whole nations knelt thy presence to adore
        Thou to whom Fable gave (Truth loved thee so)
        When thou [wert] doomed these regions *etc.* MS.

O still belov'd (for thine, meek Power, are charms
That fascinate the very Babe in arms,
While he, uplifted towards thee, laughs outright,
Spreading his little palms in his glad Mother's sight)   20
O still belov'd, once worshipped! Time, that frowns
In his destructive flight on earthly crowns,
Spares thy mild splendour; still those far-shot beams
Tremble on dancing waves and rippling streams
With stainless touch, as chaste as when thy praise   25
Was sung by Virgin-choirs in festal lays;
And through dark trials still dost thou explore
Thy way for increase punctual as of yore,
When teeming Matrons—yielding to rude faith
In mysteries of birth and life and death   30
And painful struggle and deliverance—prayed
Of thee to visit them with lenient aid.
What though the rites be swept away, the fanes
Extinct that echoed to the votive strains;
Yet thy mild aspect does not, cannot, cease   35
Love to promote and purity and peace;
And Fancy, unreproved, even yet may trace
Faint types of suffering in thy beamless face.

Then, silent Monitress! let us—not blind
To worlds unthought of till the searching mind   40
Of Science laid them open to mankind—
Told, also, how the voiceless heavens declare
God's glory; and acknowledging thy share
In that blest charge; let us—without offence
To aught of highest, holiest, influence—   45
Receive whatever good 'tis given thee to dispense.
May sage and simple, catching with one eye
The moral intimations of the sky,
Learn from thy course, where'er their own be taken,
"To look on tempests, and be never shaken;"   50
To keep with faithful step the appointed way
Eclipsing or eclipsed, by night or day,
And from example of thy monthly range
Gently to brook decline and fatal change;
Meek, patient, stedfast, and with loftier scope,   55
Than thy revival yields, for gladsome hope!

XIV

TO LUCCA GIORDANO

[Composed February 11, 1846.—Published 1850.]

GIORDANO, verily thy Pencil's skill
Hath here portrayed with Nature's happiest grace
The fair Endymion couched on Latmos-hill;
And Dian gazing on the Shepherd's face
In rapture,—yet suspending her embrace,   5
As not unconscious with what power the thrill
Of her most timid touch his sleep would chase,
And, with his sleep, that beauty calm and still.
O may this work have found its last retreat
Here in a Mountain-bard's secure abode,   10
One to whom, yet a School-boy, Cynthia showed
A face of love which he in love would greet,
Fixed, by her smile, upon some rocky seat;
Or lured along where green-wood paths he trod.

RYDAL MOUNT, 1846.

XV

[Composed June 10, 1846.—Published 1850.]

WHO but is pleased to watch the moon on high
Travelling where she from time to time enshrouds
Her head, and nothing loth her Majesty
Renounces, till among the scattered clouds
One with its kindling edge declares that soon   5
Will reappear before the uplifted eye
A Form as bright, as beautiful a moon,
To glide in open prospect through clear sky.
Pity that such a promise e'er should prove
False in the issue, that yon seeming space   10
Of sky should be in truth the stedfast face
Of a cloud flat and dense, through which must move
(By transit not unlike man's frequent doom)
The Wanderer lost in more determined gloom.

XIV. TO LUCCA GIORDANO] *Upon a picture brought from Italy by my Son,
which, together with its Companions, now hangs at Rydal Mount* MS.
XV. 1–2 Who but has watched the Queen of Night on high
       Travelling where ever and anon she shrouds MS.
8 To glide] Gliding MS.
13–14 The Wanderer lost in more enduring gloom
       Delusive lot; how like Man's frequent doom! MS.

XVI

[Composed January 10, 1846.—Published 1850.]

WHERE lies the truth ? has Man, in wisdom's creed,
A pitiable doom; for respite brief
A care more anxious, or a heavier grief ?
Is he ungrateful, and doth little heed
God's bounty, soon forgotten ; or indeed,   5
Must Man, with labour born, awake to sorrow
When Flowers rejoice and Larks with rival speed
Spring from their nests to bid the Sun good morrow ?
They mount for rapture as their songs proclaim
Warbled in hearing both of earth and sky ;   10
But o'er the contrast wherefore heave a sigh ?
Like those aspirants let us soar—our aim,
Through life's worst trials, whether shocks or snares,
A happier, brighter, purer Heaven than theirs.

XVI. 4–6 Ungrateful is he taking little heed
      Of bounty soon forgotten ? or indeed
      Is not Man made to mourn, must wake to sorrow MS. 1
6 Who but must fear that he may wake to sorrow, *corr. to* Who that lies
down, and may not wake *etc.* MS. 2   9 as] ; this MSS.   11 heave a]
should we MS. 1

POEMS

COMPOSED OR SUGGESTED DURING A TOUR, IN THE SUMMER
OF 1833

[Except when otherwise stated, composed in 1833.—Published in 1835.]

Having been prevented by the lateness of the season, in 1831, from visiting
Staffa and Iona, the author made these the principal objects of a short
tour in the summer of 1833, of which the following Series of Poems is a
Memorial. The course pursued was down the Cumberland river Derwent,
and to Whitehaven; thence (by the Isle of Man, where a few days were
passed) up the Frith of Clyde to Greenock, then to Oban, Staffa, Iona;
and back towards England, by Loch Awe, Inverary, Loch Goil-head,
Greenock, and through parts of Renfrewshire, Ayrshire, and Dumfries-
shire, to Carlisle, and thence up the river Eden, and homewards by
Ullswater.

I

ADIEU, Rydalian Laurels! that have grown
And spread as if ye knew that days might come
When ye would shelter in a happy home,
On this fair Mount, a Poet of your own,
One who ne'er ventured for a Delphic crown   5
To sue the God; but, haunting your green shade
All seasons through, is humbly pleased to braid
Ground-flowers, beneath your guardianship, self-sown.
Farewell! no Minstrels now with harp new-strung
For summer wandering quit their household bowers;   10
Yet not for this wants Poesy a tongue
To cheer the Itinerant on whom she pours
Her spirit, while he crosses lonely moors,
Or musing sits forsaken halls among.

II

WHY should the Enthusiast, journeying through this Isle,
Repine as if his hour were come too late?

POEMS COMPOSED *ETC.* 1845: SONNETS . . . TOUR IN SCOTLAND
ETC. 1835–43
I. 5 a Delphic] fame's deathless MS.
5–6 One who to win your emblematic crown
Aspires not, but frequenting *etc.*
Who dares not sue the God for your bright crown
Of deathless leaves, but haunting *etc.* K
7 delights fresh wreaths to braid K
II. 1–3 The Enthusiast, wandering through this favoured Isle
Seeks not his pleasure in an age too late
From many an ivied tower enthroned in state MS.

Not unprotected in her mouldering state,
Antiquity salutes him with a smile,
'Mid fruitful fields that ring with jocund toil,   5
And pleasure-grounds where Taste, refined Co-mate
Of Truth and Beauty, strives to imitate,
Far as she may, primeval Nature's style.
Fair Land! by Time's parental love made free,
By Social Order's watchful arms embraced;   10
With unexampled union meet in thee,
For eye and mind, the present and the past;
With golden prospect for futurity,
If that be reverenced which ought to last.

III

THEY called Thee MERRY ENGLAND, in old time;
A happy people won for thee that name
With envy heard in many a distant clime;
And, spite of change, for me thou keep'st the same
Endearing title, a responsive chime   5
To the heart's fond belief; though some there are
Whose sterner judgments deem that word a snare
For inattentive Fancy, like the lime
Which foolish birds are caught with. Can, I ask,
This face of rural beauty be a mask   10
For discontent, and poverty, and crime;
These spreading towns a cloak for lawless will?
Forbid it, Heaven!—and MERRY ENGLAND still
Shall be thy rightful name, in prose and rhyme!

IV

TO THE RIVER GRETA, NEAR KESWICK

GRETA, what fearful listening! when huge stones
Rumble along thy bed, block after block:
Or, whirling with reiterated shock,

5 jocund] happy MS.
9–11 Fair land of Mountains mid thy guardian sea
    By social Order faithfully embraced
    So long, with matchless etc.
14 so 1845: If what is rightly reverenced may last. MS., 1835–43
III. 7 Observers stern, who MS.   9–10 Can . . . be a] Is . . . a mere
MS.   13 and 1837: that 1835   14 Shall 1837: May 1835

Combat, while darkness aggravates the groans:
But if thou (like Cocytus from the moans   5
Heard on his rueful margin) thence wert named
The Mourner, thy true nature was defamed,
And the habitual murmur that atones
For thy worst rage, forgotten. Oft as Spring
Decks, on thy sinuous banks, her thousand thrones,   10
Seats of glad instinct and love's carolling,
The concert, for the happy, then may vie
With liveliest peals of birth-day harmony:
To a grieved heart the notes are benisons.

V

TO THE RIVER DERWENT

[Composed ?.—Published 1819.]

AMONG the mountains were we nursed, loved Stream!
Thou near the eagle's nest—within brief sail,
I, of his bold wing floating on the gale,
Where thy deep voice could lull me! Faint the beam
Of human life when first allowed to gleam   5
On mortal notice.—Glory of the vale,
Such thy meek outset, with a crown, though frail,
Kept in perpetual verdure by the steam
Of thy soft breath!—Less vivid wreath entwined
Nemean victor's brow; less bright was worn,   10
Meed of some Roman chief—in triumph borne
With captives chained; and shedding from his car
The sunset splendours of a finished war
Upon the proud enslavers of mankind!

VI

IN SIGHT OF THE TOWN OF COCKERMOUTH

(Where the Author was born, and his Father's remains are laid.)

A POINT of life between my Parents' dust,
And yours, my buried Little-ones! am I;
And to those graves looking habitually

IV. 7 true] glad MS.
11 Seats of glad] For joyous MS.
V. 1 nursed] born MS.   10 Nemean] The Isthmian MS.: Nemæan
1819–50
VI. On the Sight of Cockermouth Church MS.

In kindred quiet I repose my trust.
Death to the innocent is more than just,   5
And, to the sinner, mercifully bent;
So may I hope, if truly I repent
And meekly bear the ills which bear I must:
And You, my Offspring! that do still remain,
Yet may outstrip me in the appointed race,   10
If e'er, through fault of mine, in mutual pain
We breathed together for a moment's space,
The wrong, by love provoked, let love arraign,
And only love keep in your hearts a place.

VII

ADDRESS FROM THE SPIRIT OF COCKERMOUTH CASTLE

"THOU look'st upon me, and dost fondly think,
Poet! that, stricken as both are by years,
We, differing once so much, are now Compeers,
Prepared, when each has stood his time, to sink
Into the dust. Erewhile a sterner link   5
United us; when thou, in boyish play,
Entering my dungeon, didst become a prey
To soul-appalling darkness. Not a blink
Of light was there;—and thus did I, thy Tutor,
Make thy young thoughts acquainted with the grave; 10
While thou wert chasing the wing'd butterfly
Through my green courts; or climbing, a bold suitor,
Up to the flowers whose golden progeny
Still round my shattered brow in beauty wave."

VIII

NUN'S WELL, BRIGHAM

THE cattle crowding round this beverage clear
To slake their thirst, with reckless hoofs have trod
The encircling turf into a barren clod;
Through which the waters creep, then disappear,
Born to be lost in Derwent flowing near;   5
Yet, o'er the brink, and round the limestone cell
Of the pure spring (they call it the "Nun's Well,"

VII. CASTLE] *Castle To the Author* MS.
VIII. 4 And tho' the infant waters disappear MS.

Name that first struck by chance my startled ear)
A tender Spirit broods—the pensive Shade
Of ritual honours to this Fountain paid　　　　　　　10
By hooded Votaresses with saintly cheer;
Albeit oft the Virgin-mother mild
Looked down with pity upon eyes beguiled
Into the shedding of "too soft a tear."

IX

TO A FRIEND

On the banks of the Derwent.

[Composed probably January 1834.]

PASTOR and Patriot!—at whose bidding rise
These modest walls, amid a flock that need,
For one who comes to watch them and to feed,
A fixed Abode—keep down presageful sighs.
Threats, which the unthinking only can despise,　　　　5
Perplex the Church; but be thou firm,—be true
To thy first hope, and this good work pursue,
Poor as thou art. A welcome sacrifice
Dost Thou prepare, whose sign will be the smoke
Of thy new hearth; and sooner shall its wreaths,　　　10
Mounting while earth her morning incense breathes,
From wandering fiends of air receive a yoke,
And straightway cease to aspire, than God disdain
This humble tribute as ill-timed or vain.

X

MARY QUEEN OF SCOTS

Landing at the mouth of the Derwent, Workington.

DEAR to the Loves, and to the Graces vowed,
The Queen drew back the wimple that she wore;
And to the throng, that on the Cumbrian shore
Her landing hailed, how touchingly she bowed!

11 votaresses 1837: Votaries 1835
IX. 4 presageful] foreboding MSS.　　　9 To Him who dwells in Heaven
MSS.
X. 3–4 *So* 1837:
. . . how touchingly she bowed
That hailed her landing on the Cumbrian shore MS., 1835

And like a Star (that, from a heavy cloud   5
Of pine-tree foliage poised in air, forth darts,
When a soft summer gale at evening parts
The gloom that did its loveliness enshroud)
She smiled; but Time, the old Saturnian Seer,
Sighed on the wing as her foot pressed the strand,   10
With step prelusive to a long array
Of woes and degradations hand in hand—
Weeping captivity, and shuddering fear
Stilled by the ensanguined block of Fotheringay!

XI

STANZAS

SUGGESTED IN A STEAMBOAT OFF SAINT BEES' HEADS, ON THE
COAST OF CUMBERLAND

IF Life were slumber on a bed of down,
Toil unimposed, vicissitude unknown,
Sad were our lot: no hunter of the hare
Exults like him whose javelin from the lair
Has roused the lion; no one plucks the rose,   5
Whose proffered beauty in safe shelter blows
'Mid a trim garden's summer luxuries,
With joy like his who climbs, on hands and knees,
For some rare plant, yon Headland of St. Bees.

This independence upon oar and sail,   10
This new indifference to breeze or gale,
This straight-lined progress, furrowing a flat lea,
And regular as if locked in certainty—
Depress the hours. Up, Spirit of the storm!
That Courage may find something to perform;   15
That Fortitude, whose blood disdains to freeze

5 And like . . . heavy 1840: Bright as . . . sombre MS., 1835–7
6 High poised in air, of pine-tree foliage, darts MS.   9 Seer 1835–43:
seer 1845
11–14 Thence forth he saw a long and long array
    Of miserable seasons . . .
    . . . pallid fear
    And last *etc.* MS.
XI. 6–7 That mid smooth pathway in a garden blows
        For easy-minded men itself at ease MS. 2
14 Depress] Deaden MS. 2

At Danger's bidding, may confront the seas,
Firm as the towering Headlands of St. Bees.

Dread cliff of Baruth! *that* wild wish may sleep,
Bold as if men and creatures of the Deep   20
Breathed the same element; too many wrecks
Have struck thy sides, too many ghastly decks
Hast thou looked down upon, that such a thought
Should here be welcome, and in verse enwrought:
With thy stern aspect better far agrees   25
Utterance of thanks that we have past with ease,
As millions thus shall do, the Headlands of St. Bees.

Yet, while each useful Art augments her store,
What boots the gain if Nature should lose more?
And Wisdom, as she holds a Christian place   30
In man's intelligence sublimed by grace?
When Bega sought of yore the Cumbrian coast,
Tempestuous winds her holy errand cross'd:
She knelt in prayer—the waves their wrath appease;
And, from her vow well weighed in Heaven's decrees,   35
Rose, where she touched the strand, the Chantry of St.
      Bees.

"Cruel of heart were they, bloody of hand,"
Who in these Wilds then struggled for command;
The strong were merciless, without hope the weak;
Till this bright Stranger came, fair as day-break,   40
And as a cresset true that darts its length
Of beamy lustre from a tower of strength;
Guiding the mariner through troubled seas,
And cheering oft his peaceful reveries,
Like the fixed Light that crowns yon Headland of St.Bees.

To aid the Votaress, miracles believed   46
Wrought in men's minds, like miracles achieved;

28 Much has Art gained thus linking shore with shore MS. 2   30 as
she holds 1845: that once held 1835–43   33 A wild sea-storm MS. 2
33/4 As high and higher heaved the billows, faith
      Grew with them, mightier than the powers of death. 1835
34 Kneeling...that storm she did appease MS.   46 In those rude ages MS. 2
46–8 Dread Cliff of Baruth, thus thy ancient claim
      Gave way at length to Bega's softened name
      She too hath been obscured, but verse shall tell MS. 1

So piety took root; and Song might tell
What humanizing virtues near her cell
Sprang up, and spread their fragrance wide around;   50
How savage bosoms melted at the sound
Of gospel-truth enchained in harmonies
Wafted o'er waves, or creeping through close trees,
From her religious Mansion of St. Bees.

When her sweet Voice, that instrument of love,   55
Was glorified, and took its place, above
The silent stars, among the angelic quire,
Her chantry blazed with sacrilegious fire,
And perished utterly; but her good deeds
Had sown the spot, that witnessed them, with seeds   60
Which lay in earth expectant, till a breeze
With quickening impulse answered their mute pleas,
And lo! a *statelier* pile, the Abbey of St. Bees.

There are the naked clothed, the hungry fed;
And Charity extendeth to the dead   65
Her intercessions made for the soul's rest
Of tardy penitents; or for the best
Among the good (when love might else have slept,
Sickened, or died) in pious memory kept:
Thanks to the austere and simple Devotees,   70
Who, to that service bound by venial fees,
Keep watch before the altars of St. Bees.

Are not, in sooth, their Requiems sacred ties
Woven out of passion's sharpest agonies,
Subdued, composed, and formalized by art,   75
To fix a wiser sorrow in the heart?

49 near 1837: round 1835
56–61 Had long held concord in the Quires above
Her altars sank, crushed by an impious hand,
And Pagan rites once more defiled the land,
But might not kill her memory: her good deeds
Flourished no longer, but had scattered seeds
That in the ground lay patient, till a breeze MS. 1
56–9 Had long been tuned, the silent stars above
In blissful concert with *etc. as text*
Her chantry perished in devouring fire
Launched out of Pagan hands MS. 2
64 are 1837: were 1835   65 extendeth 1837: extended 1835   66
Her prayers and masses MS. 2   69 Sickened,] Languished. C   73
Are 1837: Were 1835

The prayer for them whose hour is past away
Says to the Living, profit while ye may!
A little part, and that the worst, he sees
Who thinks that priestly cunning holds the keys   80
That best unlock the secrets of St. Bees.

Conscience, the timid being's inmost light,
Hope of the dawn and solace of the night,
Cheers these Recluses with a steady ray
In many an hour when judgment goes astray.   85
Ah! scorn not hastily their rule who try
Earth to despise, and flesh to mortify;
Consume with zeal, in wingèd ecstasies
Of prayer and praise forget their rosaries,
Nor hear the loudest surges of St. Bees.   90

Yet none so prompt to succour and protect
The forlorn traveller, or sailor wrecked
On the bare coast; nor do they grudge the boon
Which staff and cockle hat and sandal shoon
Claim for the pilgrim: and, though chidings sharp   95
May sometimes greet the strolling minstrel's harp,
It is not then when, swept with sportive ease,
It charms a feast-day throng of all degrees,
Brightening the archway of revered St. Bees.

How did the cliffs and echoing hills rejoice   100
What time the Benedictine Brethren's voice,
Imploring, or commanding with meet pride,
Summoned the Chiefs to lay their feuds aside,
And under one blest ensign serve the Lord
In Palestine. Advance, indignant Sword!   105
Flaming till thou from Panym hands release
That Tomb, dread centre of all sanctities
Nursed in the quiet Abbey of St. Bees.

But look we now to them whose minds from far
Follow the fortunes which they may not share.   110

77–8 is . . . Says 1837: was . . . Said 1835
100–1 How did the Mountain echoes with glad choice
        Of syllables take up the Brethren's MS. 2
108/9 On, Champions, on!—But mark! the passing Day
        Submits her intercourse to milder sway, 1835
109 so 1837: With high and low whose busy thoughts from far 1835
109–12 Meanwhile for High and Low the passing Day

While in Judea Fancy loves to roam,
She helps to make a Holy-land at home:
The Star of Bethlehem from its sphere invites
To sound the crystal depth of maiden rights;
And wedded Life, through scriptural mysteries,   115
Heavenward ascends with all her charities,
Taught by the hooded Celibates of St. Bees.

Nor be it e'er forgotten how by skill
Of cloistered Architects, free their souls to fill
With love of God, throughout the Land were raised   120
Churches, on whose symbolic beauty gazed
Peasant and mail-clad Chief with pious awe;
As at this day men seeing what they saw,
Or the bare wreck of faith's solemnities,
Aspire to more than earthly destinies;   125
Witness yon Pile that greets us from St. Bees.

Yet more; around those Churches, gathered Towns
Safe from the feudal Castle's haughty frowns;
Peaceful abodes, where Justice might uphold
Her scales with even hand, and culture mould   130
The heart to pity, train the mind in care
For rules of life, sound as the Time could bear.
Nor dost thou fail, thro' abject love of ease,
Or hindrance raised by sordid purposes,
To bear thy part in this good work, St. Bees.   135

Who with the ploughshare clove the barren moors,
And to green meadows changed the swampy shores?
Thinned the rank woods; and for the cheerful grange
Made room where wolf and boar were used to range?
Who taught, and showed by deeds, that gentler chains   140
Should bind the vassal to his lord's domains?

Submits its intercourse to milder sway
     The Knight who in Judea may not roam
     Can find or make his Holy-land *etc*. MS. 2
118–35 *om*. 1835–43   119 Architects ... souls] builders ... hearts
C   120 were for his worship raised C   121 For worship structures on whose beauty C   123 men] we C   125 Uplift our hearts
for blissful (May lift the heart to heavenly *corr. to* blissful) C
136–9 Mountains of Caupland what delight was yours
     When plough invaded at your feet the moors,
     When hatchets thinned the forests, and the grange
     Appeared *etc*. MS. 2

The thoughtful Monks, intent their God to please,
For Christ's dear sake, by human sympathies
Poured from the bosom of thy Church, St. Bees!

But all availed not; by a mandate given   145
Through lawless will the Brotherhood was driven
Forth from their cells; their ancient House laid low
In Reformation's sweeping overthrow.
But now once more the local Heart revives,
The inextinguishable Spirit strives.   150
Oh may that Power who hushed the stormy seas,
And cleared a way for the first Votaries,
Prosper the new-born College of St. Bees!

Alas! the Genius of our age, from Schools
Less humble, draws her lessons, aims, and rules.   155
To Prowess guided by her insight keen
Matter and Spirit are as one Machine;
Boastful Idolatress of formal skill
She in her own would merge the eternal will:
Better, if Reason's triumphs match with these,   160
Her flight before the bold credulities
That furthered the first teaching of St. Bees.[1]

XII

IN THE CHANNEL, BETWEEN THE COAST OF CUMBERLAND AND THE ISLE OF MAN

RANGING the heights of Scawfell or Blackcomb,
In his lone course the Shepherd oft will pause,
And strive to fathom the mysterious laws

[1] See "Excursion," seventh part; and "Ecclesiastical Sketches," second part, near the beginning.

151-3 Albeit upheld by milder energies
          Than hers who cleared her way thro' stormy seas
          By might of Faith.—God prosper thee, St. Bees MS. 2
158-9 Elate with [?] and mechanic skill
          She ponders not the laws of Soul and Will MS. 2
156-9 Would merge, Idolatress of formal skill,
          In her own systems God's Eternal Will.
          To her despising faith in things unseen
          Matter and Spirit are as one Machine. MS. Letter 1844 and C
158-9 She sinks, Idolatress of formal skill,
          In her own systems God's eternal will. MS. Letter 1842
159/60 Expert to move in paths that Newton trod,
          From Newton's Universe would banish God MS. 2, 1835

By which the clouds, arrayed in light or gloom,
On Mona settle, and the shapes assume   5
Of all her peaks and ridges. What he draws
From sense, faith, reason, fancy, of the cause,
He will take with him to the silent tomb.
Or by his fire, a child upon his knee,
Haply the untaught Philosopher may speak   10
Of the strange sight, nor hide his theory
That satisfies the simple and the meek,
Blest in their pious ignorance, though weak
To cope with Sages undevoutly free.

XIII

AT SEA OFF THE ISLE OF MAN

BOLD words affirmed, in days when faith was strong
And doubts and scruples seldom teased the brain,
That no adventurer's bark had power to gain
These shores if he approached them bent on wrong;
For, suddenly up-conjured from the Main,   5
Mists rose to hide the Land—that search, though long
And eager, might be still pursued in vain.
O Fancy, what an age was *that* for song!
That age, when not by *laws* inanimate,
As men believed, the waters were impelled,   10
The air controlled, the stars their courses held;
But element and orb on *acts* did wait
Of *Powers* endued with visible form, instinct
With will, and to their work by passion linked.

XIV

DESIRE we past illusions to recal?
To reinstate wild Fancy, would we hide
Truths whose thick veil Science has drawn aside?
No,—let this Age, high as she may, instal
In her esteem the thirst that wrought man's fall,   5
The universe is infinitely wide;
And conquering Reason, if self-glorified,
Can nowhere move uncrossed by some new wall

XII. 9-10 Or haply with . . . That rude MS.   13 How blest is MS.
14 Sages] science MS.
XIII. 2 *not in* MS., 1835

Or gulf of mystery, which thou alone,
Imaginative Faith! canst overleap,   10
In progress toward the fount of Love,—the throne
Of Power whose ministers the records keep
Of periods fixed, and laws established, less
Flesh to exalt than prove its nothingness.

XV

ON ENTERING DOUGLAS BAY, ISLE OF MAN
"Dignum laude virum Musa vetat mori."

THE feudal Keep, the bastions of Cohorn,
Even when they rose to check or to repel
Tides of aggressive war, oft served as well
Greedy ambition, armed to treat with scorn
Just limits; but yon Tower, whose smiles adorn   5
This perilous bay, stands clear of all offence;
Blest work it is of love and innocence,
A Tower of refuge built for the else forlorn.
Spare it, ye waves, and lift the mariner,
Struggling for life, into its saving arms!   10
Spare, too, the human helpers! Do they stir
'Mid your fierce shock like men afraid to die?
No; their dread service nerves the heart it warms,
And they are led by noble HILLARY.[1]

XVI

BY THE SEA-SHORE, ISLE OF MAN

WHY stand we gazing on the sparkling Brine,
With wonder smit by its transparency,
And all-enraptured with its purity?—
Because the unstained, the clear, the crystalline,
Have ever in them something of benign;   5
Whether in gem, in water, or in sky,
A sleeping infant's brow, or wakeful eye
Of a young maiden, only not divine.

[1] See Note.

XIV. 12 *so* 1837: Of Power, whose ministering Spirits records keep   1835
XV. 1–2 The Citadels of Vauban and Cohorn
      Even when they rose with purpose MS.
4 Dark projects of Ambition, proud to scorn MS.   8 built for 1845:
to MS., 1835–43

Scarcely the hand forbears to dip its palm
For beverage drawn as from a mountain-well.   10
Temptation centres in the liquid Calm;
Our daily raiment seems no obstacle
To instantaneous plunging in, deep Sea!
And revelling in long embrace with thee.[1]

XVII

ISLE OF MAN

A YOUTH too certain of his power to wade
On the smooth bottom of this clear bright sea,
To sight so shallow, with a bather's glee,
Leapt from this rock, and but for timely aid
He, by the alluring element betrayed,   5
Had perished. Then might Sea-nymphs (and with sighs
Of self-reproach) have chanted elegies
Bewailing his sad fate, when he was laid
In peaceful earth: for, doubtless, he was frank,
Utterly in himself devoid of guile;   10
Knew not the double-dealing of a smile;
Nor aught that makes men's promises a blank,
Or deadly snare: and He survives to bless
The Power that saved him in his strange distress.

XVIII

ISLE OF MAN

DID pangs of grief for lenient time too keen,
Grief that devouring waves had caused—or guilt
Which they had witnessed, sway the man who built
This Homestead, placed where nothing could be seen,
Nought heard, of ocean troubled or serene?   5

[1] The sea-water on the coast of the Isle of Man is singularly pure and beautiful.

XVI. 14 revelling] wantoning MS.
XVII. 4-8 *so* 1837:
         ... and surely, had not aid
         Been near, must soon have breathed out life, betrayed
         By fondly trusting to an element
         Fair, and to others more than innocent;
         Then had sea-nymphs sung dirges for him laid MS., 1835
5 He] Here C
XVIII. ISLE OF MAN *so* 1837: THE RETIRED MARINE OFFICER, ISLE OF MAN
1835   1 Did 1837: Not MS., 1835   2 or 1837: nor MS., 1835
3 sway 1837: swayed MS., 1835   5 serene. MS., 1835
917.17 IV   D

A tired Ship-soldier on paternal land,
That o'er the channel holds august command,
The dwelling raised,—a veteran Marine.
He, in disgust, turned from the neighbouring sea
To shun the memory of a listless life   10
That hung between two callings. May no strife
More hurtful here beset him, doomed though free,
Self-doomed, to worse inaction, till his eye
Shrink from the daily sight of earth and sky!

XIX

BY A RETIRED MARINER
(A Friend of the Author.)

FROM early youth I ploughed the restless Main,
My mind as restless and as apt to change;
Through every clime and ocean did I range,
In hope at length a competence to gain;
For poor to Sea I went, and poor I still remain.   5
Year after year I strove, but strove in vain,
And hardships manifold did I endure,
For Fortune on me never deign'd to smile;
Yet I at last a resting-place have found,
With just enough life's comforts to procure,   10
In a snug Cove on this our favoured Isle,
A peaceful spot where Nature's gifts abound;
Then sure I have no reason to complain,
Though poor to Sea I went, and poor I still remain.

XX

AT BALA-SALA, ISLE OF MAN
(Supposed to be written by a Friend.)

BROKEN in fortune, but in mind entire
And sound in principle, I seek repose
Where ancient trees this convent-pile enclose,[1]
In ruin beautiful. When vain desire

[1] Rushen Abbey.

_____

6 A tired MS., 1835, 1845: No,—a   1837–43
8–10   —Fantastic slave of spleen
    He sought by shunning thus the neighbouring sea
    Refuge from memory K
9 He 1845: Who . . . 1835–43: The weary Man C
XIX. 12 Where all the requisites of life abound MS.
XX. 1 in mind] of mind MS.

Intrudes on peace, I pray the eternal Sire 5
To cast a soul-subduing shade on me,
A grey-haired, pensive, thankful Refugee;
A shade—but with some sparks of heavenly fire
Once to these cells vouchsafed. And when I note
The old Tower's brow yellowed as with the beams 10
Of sunset ever there, albeit streams
Of stormy weather-stains that semblance wrought,
I thank the silent Monitor, and say
"Shine so, my aged brow, at all hours of the day!"

XXI

TYNWALD HILL

ONCE on the top of Tynwald's formal mound
(Still marked with green turf circles narrowing
Stage above stage) would sit this Island's King,
The laws to promulgate, enrobed and crowned;
While, compassing the little mound around, 5
Degrees and Orders stood, each under each:
Now, like to things within fate's easiest reach,
The power is merged, the pomp a grave has found.
Off with yon cloud, old Snafell! that thine eye
Over three Realms may take its widest range; 10
And let, for them, thy fountains utter strange
Voices, thy winds break forth in prophecy,
If the whole State must suffer mortal change,
Like Mona's miniature of sovereignty.

XXII

DESPOND who will—*I* heard a voice exclaim,
"Though fierce the assault, and shatter'd the defence,
It cannot be that Britain's social frame,
The glorious work of time and providence,

8-9 such sparks of holy fire
As once were cherished here MS.
11 albeit] and know that K
XXI. 1-3 Time was when on the top of yon small mound
(Still marked with circles duly narrowing
Each above each) K
4 Sate 'mid the assembled people (Would sit by solemn usage) robed and
crowned K   5 little] grassy K   9 yon cloud] those clouds K
XXII. 1 Clear voices from pure worlds of hope exclaim MS.

Before a flying season's rash pretence   5
Should fall; that She, whose virtue put to shame,
When Europe prostrate lay, the Conqueror's aim,
Should perish, self-subverted. Black and dense
The cloud is; but brings *that* a day of doom
To Liberty? Her sun is up the while,   10
That orb whose beams round Saxon Alfred shone:
Then laugh, ye innocent Vales! ye Streams, sweep on,
Nor let one billow of our heaven-blest Isle
Toss in the fanning wind a humbler plume."

XXIII

IN THE FRITH OF CLYDE, AILSA CRAG

(During an Eclipse of the Sun, July 17.)

SINCE risen from ocean, ocean to defy,
Appeared the Crag of Ailsa, ne'er did morn
With gleaming lights more gracefully adorn
His sides, or wreathe with mist his forehead high:
Now, faintly darkening with the sun's eclipse,   5
Still is he seen, in lone sublimity,
Towering above the sea and little ships;
For dwarfs the tallest seem while sailing by,
Each for her haven; with her freight of Care,
Pleasure, or Grief, and Toil that seldom looks   10
Into the secret of to-morrow's fare;
Though poor, yet rich, without the wealth of books,
Or aught that watchful Love to Nature owes
For her mute Powers, fix'd Forms, or transient Shows.

XXIV

ON THE FRITH OF CLYDE

(In a Steamboat.)

ARRAN! a single-crested Teneriffe,
A St. Helena next—in shape and hue,
Varying her crowded peaks and ridges blue;
Who but must covet a cloud-seat, or skiff
Built for the air, or wingèd Hippogriff?   5

5 Before a season's calculating sense MS.   10 Her] The *corr. to* Our
MS.   13 our] this MS.
XXIII. IN THE FRITH *etc*. 1835 Ailsa Crag, between 5 o'clock and 6 in the
morning of the seventh of July, an eclipse of the Sun commencing MS.
14 or 1837: and 1835

That he might fly, where no one could pursue,
From this dull Monster and her sooty crew;
And, as a God, light on thy topmost cliff.
Impotent wish! which reason would despise
If the mind knew no union of extremes,   10
No natural bond between the boldest schemes
Ambition frames and heart-humilities.
Beneath stern mountains many a soft vale lies,
And lofty springs give birth to lowly streams.

XXV

ON REVISITING DUNOLLY CASTLE
[See former Series, Vol. iii, p. 268.]

THE captive Bird was gone;—to cliff or moor
Perchance had flown, delivered by the storm;
Or he had pined, and sunk to feed the worm:
Him found we not: but, climbing a tall tower,
There saw, impaved with rude fidelity   5
Of art mosaic, in a roofless floor,
An Eagle with stretched wings, but beamless eye—
An Eagle that could neither wail nor soar.
Effigy of the Vanished—(shall I dare
To call thee so?) or symbol of fierce deeds   10
And of the towering courage which past times
Rejoiced in—take, whate'er thou be, a share,
Not undeserved, of the memorial rhymes
That animate my way where'er it leads!

XXVI

THE DUNOLLY EAGLE

NOT to the clouds, not to the cliff, he flew;
But when a storm, on sea or mountain bred,
Came and delivered him, alone he sped
Into the castle-dungeon's darkest mew.

XXIV. 8 as   1837: like   1835
XXV. 5–6 Espied in rude mosaic effigy
          Set in a roofless Chamber's pavement floor MS.
9 *so* 1837: Effigies of the Vanished 1835: Shade of the poor Departed
MS.
10–12 *so* 1837:
                                . . . past times,
          That towering courage, and the savage deeds
          Those times were proud of, take Thou too a share,   1835

Now, near his master's house in open view   5
He dwells, and hears indignant tempests howl,
Kennelled and chained. Ye tame domestic fowl,
Beware of him! Thou, saucy cockatoo,
Look to thy plumage and thy life!—The roe,
Fleet as the west wind, is for *him* no quarry;   10
Balanced in ether he will never tarry,
Eyeing the sea's blue depths. Poor Bird! even so
Doth man of brother man a creature make
That clings to slavery for its own sad sake.

XXVII
WRITTEN IN A BLANK LEAF OF
MACPHERSON'S OSSIAN
[Composed 1824.—Published 1827.]

OFT have I caught, upon a fitful breeze,
Fragments of far-off melodies,
With ear not coveting the whole,
A part so charmed the pensive soul:
While a dark storm before my sight   5
Was yielding, on a mountain height
Loose vapours have I watched, that won
Prismatic colours from the sun;
Nor felt a wish that heaven would show
The image of its perfect bow.   10
What need, then, of these finished Strains?
Away with counterfeit Remains!
An abbey in its lone recess,
A temple of the wilderness,
Wrecks though they be, announce with feeling   15
The majesty of honest dealing.
Spirit of Ossian! if imbound
In language thou may'st yet be found,
If aught (intrusted to the pen
Or floating on the tongues of men,   20
Albeit shattered and impaired)
Subsist thy dignity to guard,
In concert with memorial claim
Of old grey stone, and high-born name
That cleaves to rock or pillared cave   25

XXVI. 7 domestic] villatic MS.
XXVII. 1 upon a   1832: from   1827

Where moans the blast, or beats the wave,
Let Truth, stern arbitress of all,
Interpret that Original,
And for presumptuous wrongs atone ;—
Authentic words be given, or none!   30

Time is not blind ;—yet He, who spares
Pyramid pointing to the stars,
Hath preyed with ruthless appetite
On all that marked the primal flight
Of the poetic ecstasy   35
Into the land of mystery.
No tongue is able to rehearse
One measure, Orpheus! of thy verse ;
Musæus, stationed with his lyre
Supreme among the Elysian quire,   40
Is, for the dwellers upon earth,
Mute as a lark ere morning's birth.
Why grieve for these, though past away
The music, and extinct the lay ?
When thousands, by severer doom,   45
Full early to the silent tomb
Have sunk, at Nature's call ; or strayed
From hope and promise, self-betrayed ;
The garland withering on their brows ;
Stung with remorse for broken vows ;   50
Frantic—else how might they rejoice ?
And friendless, by their own sad choice!

Hail, Bards of mightier grasp! on you
I chiefly call, the chosen Few,
Who cast not off the acknowledged guide,   55
Who faltered not, nor turned aside ;
Whose lofty genius could survive
Privation, under sorrow thrive ;
In whom the fiery Muse revered .
The symbol of a snow-white beard,   60
Bedewed with meditative tears
Dropped from the lenient cloud of years.

Brothers in soul! though distant times
Produced you nursed in various climes,
Ye, when the orb of life had waned,   65
A plenitude of love retained:

Hence, while in you each sad regret
By corresponding hope was met,
Ye lingered among human kind,
Sweet voices for the passing wind;   70
Departing sunbeams, loth to stop,
Though smiling on the last hill-top!
Such to the tender-hearted maid
Even ere her joys begin to fade;
Such, haply, to the rugged chief   75
By fortune crushed, or tamed by grief;
Appears, on Morven's lonely shore,
Dim-gleaming through imperfect lore,
The Son of Fingal; such was blind
Maeonides of ampler mind;   80
Such Milton, to the fountain-head
Of glory by Urania led!

XXVIII

CAVE OF STAFFA

WE SAW, but surely, in the motley crowd,
Not One of us has felt the far-famed sight;
How *could* we feel it? each the other's blight,
Hurried and hurrying, volatile and loud.
O for those motions only that invite   5
The Ghost of Fingal to his tuneful Cave
By the breeze entered, and wave after wave
Softly embosoming the timid light!
And by *one* Votary who at will might stand
Gazing and take into his mind and heart,   10
With undistracted reverence, the effect
Of those proportions where the almighty hand
That made the worlds, the sovereign Architect,
Has deigned to work as if with human Art!

XXIX

CAVE OF STAFFA

(After the Crowd had departed.)

THANKS for the lessons of this Spot—fit school
For the presumptuous thoughts that would assign
Mechanic laws to agency divine;

XXVIII. 2 *felt* MS., 1835
XXIX. After the crowd *etc.* 1845: *not in* 1835–43

And, measuring heaven by earth, would overrule
Infinite Power. The pillared vestibule,   5
Expanding yet precise, the roof embowed,
Might seem designed to humble man, when proud
Of his best workmanship by plan and tool.
Down-bearing with his whole Atlantic weight
Of tide and tempest on the Structure's base,   10
And flashing to that Structure's topmost height,
Ocean has proved its strength, and of its grace
In calms is conscious, finding for his freight
Of softest music some responsive place.

XXX

CAVE OF STAFFA

YE shadowy Beings, that have rights and claims
In every cell of Fingal's mystic Grot,
Where are ye ? Driven or venturing to the spot,
Our fathers glimpses caught of your thin Frames,
And, by your mien and bearing, knew your names;   5
And they could hear *his* ghostly song who trod
Earth, till the flesh lay on him like a load,
While he struck his desolate harp without hopes or aims.
Vanished ye are, but subject to recal;
Why keep *we* else the instincts whose dread law   10
Ruled here of yore, till what men felt they saw,
Not by black arts but magic natural!
If eyes be still sworn vassals of belief,
Yon light shapes forth a Bard, that shade a Chief.

XXXI

FLOWERS ON THE TOP OF THE PILLARS AT THE ENTRANCE
OF THE CAVE

HOPE smiled when your nativity was cast,
Children of Summer! Ye fresh Flowers that brave
What Summer here escapes not, the fierce wave,
And whole artillery of the western blast,
Battering the Temple's front, its long-drawn nave   5
Smiting, as if each moment were their last.
But ye, bright Flowers, on frieze and architrave

11 *so* 1837: flashing upwards to its MS., 1835
XXX. 11 *saw* MS., 1835

Survive, and once again the Pile stands fast:
Calm as the Universe, from specular towers
Of heaven contemplated by Spirits pure   10
With mute astonishment, it stands sustained
Through every part in symmetry, to endure,
Unhurt, the assault of Time with all his hours,
As the supreme Artificer ordained.

XXXII

IONA

On to Iona!—What can she afford
To *us* save matter for a thoughtful sigh,
Heaved over ruin with stability
In urgent contrast ? To diffuse the Word
(Thy Paramount, mighty Nature! and Time's Lord)   5
Her Temples rose, 'mid pagan gloom; but why,
Even for a moment, has our verse deplored
Their wrongs, since they fulfilled their destiny ?
And when, subjected to a common doom
Of mutability, those far-famed Piles   10
Shall disappear from both the sister Isles,
Iona's Saints, forgetting not past days,
Garlands shall wear of amaranthine bloom,
While heaven's vast sea of voices chants their praise.

XXXIII

IONA

(Upon Landing.)

How sad a welcome! To each voyager
Some ragged child holds up for sale a store
Of wave-worn pebbles, pleading on the shore
Where once came monk and nun with gentle stir,

XXXI. 11–12 *so* 1840:
          Suns and their systems, diverse yet sustained
          In symmetry, and fashioned to endure, MS., 1835–8
13 the worst assaults of hostile Powers C   14 Artificer] Geometer MS.
XXXII. 9–11 And when the wonders of the Sister Isles
          Shall disappear, sharing the common doom,
          To the last remnant of the several Piles MS.
XXXIII. 1–3 *so* 1837: With earnest look, to every voyager *etc. as text (but*
his *for* a *in* l. 2) 1835
          With outstretched hands, round every voyager
          Press ragged children, each to supplicate
          A price for wave-worn pebbles on his plate, MS.

Blessings to give, news ask, or suit prefer.   5
Yet is yon neat trim church a grateful speck
Of novelty amid the sacred wreck
Strewn far and wide. Think, proud Philosopher!
Fallen though she be, this Glory of the west,
Still on her sons the beams of mercy shine;   10
And "hopes, perhaps more heavenly bright than thine,
A grace by thee unsought and unpossest,
A faith more fixed, a rapture more divine
Shall gild their passage to eternal rest."

XXXIV

THE BLACK STONES OF IONA

[See Martin's *Voyage among the Western Isles.*]

HERE on their knees men swore: the stones were black,
Black in the people's minds and words, yet they
Were at that time, as now, in colour grey.
But what is colour, if upon the rack
Of conscience souls are placed by deeds that lack   5
Concord with oaths? What differ night and day
Then, when before the Perjured on his way
Hell opens, and the heavens in vengeance crack
Above his head uplifted in vain prayer
To Saint, or Fiend, or to the Godhead whom   10
He had insulted—Peasant, King, or Thane?
Fly where the culprit may, guilt meets a doom;
And, from invisible worlds at need laid bare,
Come links for social order's awful chain.

XXXV

HOMEWARD we turn. Isle of Columba's Cell,
Where Christian piety's soul-cheering spark
(Kindled from Heaven between the light and dark
Of time) shone like the morning-star, farewell!—
And fare thee well, to Fancy visible,   5
Remote St. Kilda, lone and loved sea-mark

6 Yet is 1837: But see MS., 1835   7 the 1837: this MS., 1835   8 *so*
1837: Nay spare thy scorn, haughty MS., 1835
XXXV. 5-6 *so* 1837:
              Remote St. Kilda, art thou visible?
              No—but farewell to thee, beloved sea-mark   1835

For many a voyage made in her swift bark,
When with more hues than in the rainbow dwell
Thou a mysterious intercourse dost hold,
Extracting from clear skies and air serene,   10
And out of sun-bright waves, a lucid veil,
That thickens, spreads, and, mingling fold with fold,
Makes known, when thou no longer canst be seen,
Thy whereabout, to warn the approaching sail.

XXXVI

GREENOCK
Per me si va nella Città dolente.

WE have not passed into a doleful City,
We who were led to-day down a grim dell,
By some too boldly named "the Jaws of Hell:"
Where be the wretched ones, the sights for pity?
These crowded streets resound no plaintive ditty:—   5
As from the hive where bees in summer dwell,
Sorrow seems here excluded; and that knell,
It neither damps the gay, nor checks the witty.
Alas! too busy Rival of old Tyre,
Whose merchants Princes were, whose decks were thrones; 10
Soon may the punctual sea in vain respire
To serve thy need, in union with that Clyde
Whose nursling current brawls o'er mossy stones,
The poor, the lonely, herdsman's joy and pride.

XXXVII

"THERE!" said a Stripling, pointing with meet pride
Towards a low roof with green trees half concealed,
"Is Mosgiel Farm; and that's the very field
Where Burns ploughed up the Daisy." Far and wide
A plain below stretched seaward, while, descried   5

5–10 Adieu, remote St. Kilda, visible
        To Fancy only, a beloved sea-mark
        For many etc. as text
        Adieu to thee, and all that with thee dwell
        Simplest of humankind. Fair to behold
        Thou art, extracting from clear skies serene MS.
7 her swift   1837: Fancy's 1835
12 That spreads, and intermingling MS.   14 to guide the passing
sail MS.
XXXVI. 9 so 1837: Too busy Mart! thus fared it with old Tyre MS., 1835
XXXVII. MS. gives the title Burns' Daisy

Above sea-clouds, the Peaks of Arran rose;
And, by that simple notice, the repose
Of earth, sky, sea, and air, was vivified.
Beneath "the random *bield* of clod or stone"
Myriads of daisies have shone forth in flower   10
Near the lark's nest, and in their natural hour
Have passed away; less happy than the One
That, by the unwilling ploughshare, died to prove
The tender charm of poetry and love.

XXXVIII
THE RIVER EDEN, CUMBERLAND

EDEN! till now thy beauty had I viewed
By glimpses only, and confess with shame
That verse of mine, whate'er its varying mood,
Repeats but once the sound of thy sweet name:
Yet fetched from Paradise that honour came,   5
Rightfully borne; for Nature gives thee flowers
That have no rivals among British bowers;
And thy bold rocks are worthy of their fame.
Measuring thy course, fair Stream! at length I pay
To my life's neighbour dues of neighbourhood;   10
But I have traced thee on thy winding way
With pleasure sometimes by this thought restrained—
For things far off we toil, while many a good
Not sought, because too near, is never gained.

XXXIX
MONUMENT OF MRS. HOWARD
(by Nollekens),
In Wetheral Church, near Corby, on the banks of the Eden.

STRETCHED on the dying Mother's lap, lies dead
Her new-born Babe; dire ending of bright hope!
But Sculpture here, with the divinest scope
Of luminous faith, heavenward hath raised that head
So patiently; and through one hand has spread   5
A touch so tender for the insensate Child—
(Earth's lingering love to parting reconciled,

XXXVIII. 13 *so* 1845: That things far off are toiled for, while a good MS.,
1835-8: That for things *etc. as text*   1840-3   14 never 1840: seldom
MS., 1835-8
XXXIX. 2 ending 1845: issue MS., 1835-43   3-4 with so divine a
scope Embodies truth, MS.

Brief parting, for the spirit is all but fled)—
That we, who contemplate the turns of life
Through this still medium, are consoled and cheered; 10
Feel with the Mother, think the severed Wife
Is less to be lamented than revered;
And own that Art, triumphant over strife
And pain, hath powers to Eternity endeared.

XL

SUGGESTED BY THE FOREGOING

TRANQUILLITY! the sovereign aim wert thou
In heathen schools of philosophic lore;
Heart-stricken by stern destiny of yore
The Tragic Muse thee served with thoughtful vow;
And what of hope Elysium could allow 5
Was fondly seized by Sculpture, to restore
Peace to the Mourner. But when He who wore
The crown of thorns around his bleeding brow
Warmed our sad being with celestial light,
Then Arts, which still had drawn a softening grace 10
From shadowy fountains of the Infinite,
Communed with that Idea face to face:
And move around it now as planets run,
Each in its orbit round the central Sun.

XLI

NUNNERY

THE floods are roused, and will not soon be weary;
Down from the Pennine Alps[1] how fiercely sweeps
CROGLIN, the stately Eden's tributary!

[1] The chain of Crossfell.

10 consoled] inspired MS.
XL. *No title in* 1835   1 the sovereign] prime end and *corr. to* the paramount MS.   3 In quest of thee did Science dive and soar MS.
5–6 And Sculpture fondly laboured to endow (strove to re-endow)
    Man with lost rights and honour to restore MS.
7 *so* 1838: Peace to the Mourner's [his troubled MS.] soul, but He who
wore 1835–7
8–9 *so* 1840:
    The crown of thorns had from a bleeding brow
    Through our sad being shed his glorious light 1838; 1835–7 *as text
but* his glorious *for* celestial.   9 Brought doubted Immortality to light
corr. to Poured thro' the mists of being (bewildering mists a) glorious light MS.
12–13 Were urged and found to move with steadier pace
    Along their courses as the *etc.* MS.

He raves, or through some moody passage creeps
Plotting new mischief—out again he leaps   5
Into broad light, and sends, through regions airy,
That voice which soothed the Nuns while on the steeps
They knelt in prayer, or sang to blissful Mary.
That union ceased: then, cleaving easy walks
Through crags, and smoothing paths beset with danger,   10
Came studious Taste; and many a pensive stranger
Dreams on the banks, and to the river talks.
What change shall happen next to Nunnery Dell?
Canal, and Viaduct, and Railway, tell!

XLII
STEAMBOATS, VIADUCTS, AND RAILWAYS

MOTIONS and Means, on land and sea at war
With old poetic feeling, not for this,
Shall ye, by Poets even, be judged amiss!
Nor shall your presence, howsoe'er it mar
The loveliness of Nature, prove a bar   5
To the Mind's gaining that prophetic sense
Of future change, that point of vision, whence
May be discovered what in soul ye are.
In spite of all that beauty may disown
In your harsh features, Nature doth embrace   10
Her lawful offspring in· Man's art; and Time,
Pleased with your triumphs o'er his brother Space,
Accepts from your bold hands the proffered crown
Of hope, and smiles on you with cheer sublime.

XLIII
THE MONUMENT COMMONLY CALLED LONG MEG AND HER DAUGHTERS, NEAR THE RIVER EDEN
[Composed 1821.—Published 1822; ed. 1827.]

A WEIGHT of awe, not easy to be borne,
Fell suddenly upon my Spirit—cast
From the dread bosom of the unknown past,

XLI. 6-8 Seeking in vain broad light, and regions airy
          But with that voice which once high on the steeps
          Mingled with vespers, sung to blissful Mary MS.
XLIII. 1 awe] woe MS. *corr.*   easy] easily MS.
2-7 Hath sometimes fallen on my bosom cast
                    corr. to
          And loth to be removed is sometimes cast

When first I saw that family forlorn.
Speak Thou, whose massy strength and stature scorn   5
The power of years—pre-eminent, and placed
Apart, to overlook the circle vast—
Speak, Giant-mother! tell it to the Morn
While she dispels the cumbrous shades of Night;
Let the Moon hear, emerging from a cloud;   10
At whose behest uprose on British ground
That Sisterhood, in hieroglyphic round
Forth-shadowing, some have deemed, the infinite
The inviolable God, that tames the proud![1]

XLIV

LOWTHER

Lowther! in thy majestic Pile are seen
Cathedral pomp and grace, in apt accord
With the baronial castle's sterner mien;
Union significant of God adored,
And charters won and guarded by the sword   5
Of ancient honour; whence that goodly state
Of polity which wise men venerate,
And will maintain, if God his help afford.
Hourly the democratic torrent swells;

[1] See Note.

Upon my bosom from the unknown past
When I beheld that sisterhood forlorn
With [And] Her sole standing among yellow corn
In fearless height preeminent and placed
As if to overlook the circle vast MSS.
4 family 1837: Sisterhood 1822–32   5 Speak Thou 1837: And Her
1827–32 And Her whose strength and stature seem to scorn 1822   8
Speak giant mother to the dawning morn MS. 1
9–11 Let the moon hear, emerging from a cloud
          The truth disclosed to guide our steps aright
          Or be at least the mystery unbound MS. 1, MS. 2 *as text but l.* 11 The
truths disclosed, the mystery unbound
11–13 *so* 1837; *so* 1827–32, *but l.* 12 Thy progeny *for* That Sisterhood;
          When, how, and wherefore, rose on British ground
          That wondrous Monument, whose mystic round
          Forth shadows, some have deemed, to mortal sight 1822
XLIV. *No title in* 1835; Lowther Castle MS.
1–2 in thy magnificence are seen
          Shapes of cathedral pomp that well accord MS.
9 Hourly] But high MS.

For airy promises and hopes suborned   10
The strength of backward-looking thoughts is scorned.
Fall if ye must, ye Towers and Pinnacles,
With what ye symbolise; authentic Story
Will say, Ye disappeared with England's Glory!

XLV

TO THE EARL OF LONSDALE

"Magistratus indicat virum."

LONSDALE! it were unworthy of a Guest,
Whose heart with gratitude to thee inclines,
If he should speak, by fancy touched, of signs
On thy Abode harmoniously imprest,
Yet be unmoved with wishes to attest   5
How in thy mind and moral frame agree
Fortitude, and that Christian Charity
Which, filling, consecrates the human breast.
And if the Motto on thy 'scutcheon teach
With truth, "THE MAGISTRACY SHOWS THE MAN;"   10
That searching test thy public course has stood;
As will be owned alike by bad and good,
Soon as the measuring of life's little span
Shall place thy virtues out of Envy's reach.[1]

XLVI

THE SOMNAMBULIST

[Composed 1828 ?.—Published 1835.]

LIST, ye who pass by Lyulph's Tower[2]
    At eve; how softly then
Doth Aira-force, that torrent hoarse,
    Speak from the woody glen!

[1] See Note.

[2] A pleasure-house built by the late Duke of Norfolk upon the banks of Ullswater. FORCE is the word used in the Lake District for Waterfall.

XLV. 2–7 One chiefly well aware how much he owes
             To thy regard, to speak in verse or prose
             Of types and signs harmoniously imprest
             On thy Abode, neglecting to attest
             That in thy Mansion's Lord as well agree
             Meekness and strength and Christian charity MS.
9–11   And if, as thy armorial bearings teach,
             "The Magistracy indicates the Man,"
             That test thy life triumphantly has stood; MS.
XLVI. 1 'Tis sweet to stand by MSS.   4 Speak] Sound MSS.

Fit music for a solemn vale!
   And holier seems the ground
To him who catches on the gale
The spirit of a mournful tale,
   Embodied in the sound.

Not far from that fair site whereon   10
   The Pleasure-house is reared,
As story says, in antique days
   A stern-brow'd house appeared;
Foil to a Jewel rich in light
   There set, and guarded well;   15
Cage for a Bird of plumage bright,
Sweet-voiced, nor wishing for a flight
   Beyond her native dell.

To win this bright Bird from her cage,
   To make this Gem their own,   20
Came Barons bold, with store of gold,
   And Knights of high renown;
But one She prized, and only one;
   Sir Eglamore was he;
Full happy season, when was known,   25
Ye Dales and Hills! to you alone
   Their mutual loyalty—

Known chiefly, Aira! to thy glen,
   Thy brook, and bowers of holly;
Where Passion caught what Nature taught,   30
   That all but love is folly;
Where Fact with Fancy stooped to play;
   Doubt came not, nor regret—
To trouble hours that winged their way,
As if through an immortal day   35
   Whose sun could never set.

But in old times Love dwelt not long
   Sequester'd with repose;
Best throve the fire of chaste desire,

5–7 To rudest shepherd of the vale
   The spot seems fairy ground;
   For he can catch upon the gale MSS.
8 a mournful] an ancient MSS.   19 bright] sweet MSS.   26 Dales]
streams MSS.   27 Their true love's sanctity MS.   28–36 *not*
in MSS.   37 old times] that age MSS.

Fanned by the breath of foes.   40
"A conquering lance is beauty's test,
    And proves the Lover true;"
So spake Sir Eglamore, and pressed
The drooping Emma to his breast,
    And looked a blind adieu.   45

They parted.—Well with him it fared
    Through wide-spread regions errant;
A knight of proof in love's behoof,
    The thirst of fame his warrant:
And She her happiness can build   50
    On woman's quiet hours;
Though faint, compared with spear and shield,
The solace beads and masses yield,
    And needlework and flowers.

Yet blest was Emma when she heard   55
    Her Champion's praise recounted;
Though brain would swim, and eyes grow dim,
    And high her blushes mounted;
Or when a bold heroic lay
    She warbled from full heart;   60
Delightful blossoms for the *May*
Of absence! but they will not stay,
    Born only to depart.

Hope wanes with her, while lustre fills
    Whatever path he chooses;   65
As if his orb, that owns no curb,
    Received the light hers loses.
He comes not back; an ampler space
    Requires for nobler deeds;
He ranges on from place to place,   70
Till of his doings is no trace,
    But what her fancy breeds.

His fame may spread, but in the past
    Her·spirit finds its centre;
Clear sight She has of what he was,   75
    And that would now content her.

<hr>

40 When fanned by MSS.   57 brain . . . eyes] her brain . . . her eyes
MS.

"Still is he my devoted Knight?"
  The tear in answer flows;
Month falls on month with heavier weight;
Day sickens round her, and the night   80
  Is empty of repose.

In sleep She sometimes walked abroad,
  Deep sighs with quick words blending,
Like that pale Queen whose hands are seen
  With fancied spots contending;   85
But *she* is innocent of blood,—
  The moon is not more pure
That shines aloft, while through the wood
She thrids her way, the sounding Flood
  Her melancholy lure!   90

While 'mid the fern-brake sleeps the doe,
  And owls alone are waking,
In white arrayed, glides on the Maid
  The downward pathway taking,
That leads her to the torrent's side   95
  And to a holly bower;
By whom on this still night descried?
By whom in that lone place espied?
  By thee, Sir Eglamore!

A wandering Ghost, so thinks the Knight,   100
  His coming step has thwarted,
Beneath the boughs that heard their vows,
  Within whose shade they parted.
Hush, hush, the busy Sleeper see!
  Perplexed her fingers seem,   105
As if they from the holly tree
Green twigs would pluck, as rapidly
  Flung from her to the stream.

What means the Spectre? Why intent
  To violate the Tree,   110

77–8 "No more, perchance, my own true Knight
    He is"—that phantom grows; MSS.
82 In troubled sleep she walked MSS.   95–6 Nor stopped till near
. . . She reached MSS.   99 By thee] The Knight MSS.
102–3 On ground that heard their plighted vows,
    The ground on which MSS.

Thought Eglamore, by which I swore
   Unfading constancy?
Here am I, and to-morrow's sun,
   To her I left, shall prove
That bliss is ne'er so surely won   115
As when a circuit has been run
   Of valour, truth, and love.

So from the spot whereon he stood,
   He moved with stealthy pace;
And, drawing nigh, with his living eye,   120
   He recognised the face;
And whispers caught, and speeches small,
   Some to the green-leaved tree,
Some muttered to the torrent-fall;—
"Roar on, and bring him with thy call;   125
   I heard, and so may He!"

Soul-shattered was the Knight, nor knew
   If Emma's Ghost it were,
Or boding Shade, or if the Maid
   Her very self stood there.   130
He touched; what followed who shall tell?
   The soft touch snapped the thread
Of slumber—shrieking back she fell,
And the Stream whirled her down the dell
   Along its foaming bed.   135

In plunged the Knight!—when on firm ground
   The rescued Maiden lay,
Her eyes grew bright with blissful light,
   Confusion passed away;
She heard, ere to the throne of grace   140
   Her faithful Spirit flew,
His voice—beheld his speaking face;
And, dying, from his own embrace,
   She felt that he was true.

So was he reconciled to life: 145
   Brief words may speak the rest;

122 caught] heard MSS.
129-30 Or if the Maid by sleep betrayed
   In very life stood there. MSS.
136-46 In plunged the Knight!—he strove in vain
   Brief words *etc.* MSS.

Within the dell he built a cell,
　　And there was Sorrow's guest;
In hermits' weeds repose he found,
　　From vain temptations free;　　　　　　　　　　　150
Beside the torrent dwelling—bound
By one deep heart-controlling sound,
　　And awed to piety.

Wild stream of Aira, hold thy course,
　　Nor fear memorial lays,　　　　　　　　　　　　155
Where clouds that spread in solemn shade,
　　Are edged with golden rays!
Dear art thou to the light of heaven,
　　Though minister of sorrow;
Sweet is thy voice at pensive even;　　　　　　　　160
And thou, in lovers' hearts forgiven,
　　Shalt take thy place with Yarrow!

XLVII

TO CORDELIA M———
Hallsteads, Ullswater.

Not in the mines beyond the western main,
You say, Cordelia, was the metal sought,
Which a fine skill, of Indian growth, has wrought
Into this flexible yet faithful Chain;
Nor is it silver of romantic Spain;　　　　　　　　5
But from our loved Helvellyn's depths was brought,
Our own domestic mountain. Thing and thought
Mix strangely; trifles light, and partly vain,
Can prop, as you have learnt, our nobler being:
Yes, Lady, while about your neck is wound　　　　10
(Your casual glance oft meeting) this bright cord,
What witchery, for pure gifts of inward seeing,
Lurks in it, Memory's Helper, Fancy's Lord,
For precious tremblings in your bosom found!

XLVIII

Most sweet it is with unuplifted eyes
To pace the ground, if path be there or none,

158 to] in MS.
XLVII. 2 *so* 1845: You tell me, Delia! 1835–43　　　5–6 *so* 1845: Spain
You say, but from Helvellyn's 1835–43
XLVIII. *Title* CONCLUSION 1835–43

While a fair region round the traveller lies
Which he forbears again to look upon;
Pleased rather with some soft ideal scene, 5
The work of Fancy, or some happy tone
Of meditation, slipping in between
The beauty coming and the beauty gone.
If Thought and Love desert us, from that day
Let us break off all commerce with the Muse: 10
With Thought and Love companions of our way,
Whate'er the senses take or may refuse,
The Mind's internal heaven shall shed her dews
Of inspiration on the humblest lay.

POEMS OF
SENTIMENT AND REFLECTION

I

EXPOSTULATION AND REPLY

[Composed 1798.—Published 1798.]

"WHY, William, on that old grey stone,
Thus for the length of half a day,
Why, William, sit you thus alone,
And dream your time away?

"Where are your books?—that light bequeathed   5
To Beings else forlorn and blind!
Up! up! and drink the spirit breathed
From dead men to their kind.

"You look round on your Mother Earth,
As if she for no purpose bore you;   10
As if you were her first-born birth,
And none had lived before you!"

One morning thus, by Esthwaite lake,
When life was sweet, I knew not why,
To me my good friend Matthew spake,   15
And thus I made reply:

"The eye—it cannot choose but see;
We cannot bid the ear be still;
Our bodies feel, where'er they be,
Against or with our will.   20

"Nor less I deem that there are Powers
Which of themselves our minds impress;
That we can feed this mind of ours
In a wise passiveness.

"Think you, 'mid all this mighty sum   25
Of things for ever speaking,
That nothing of itself will come,
But we must still be seeking?

"—Then ask not wherefore, here, alone,
Conversing as I may,   30
I sit upon this old grey stone,
And dream my time away."

II
THE TABLES TURNED

AN EVENING SCENE ON THE SAME SUBJECT
[Composed 1798.—Published 1798.]

Up! up! my Friend, and quit your books;
Or surely you'll grow double:
Up! up! my Friend, and clear your looks;
Why all this toil and trouble?

The sun, above the mountain's head,   5
A freshening lustre mellow
Through all the long green fields has spread,
His first sweet evening yellow.

Books! 'tis a dull and endless strife:
Come, hear the woodland linnet,   10
How sweet his music! on my life,
There's more of wisdom in it.

And hark! how blithe the throstle sings!
He, too, is no mean preacher:
Come forth into the light of things,   15
Let Nature be your Teacher.

She has a world of ready wealth,
Our minds and hearts to bless—
Spontaneous wisdom breathed by health,
Truth breathed by cheerfulness.   20

One impulse from a vernal wood
May teach you more of man,
Of moral evil and of good,
Than all the sages can.

Sweet is the lore which Nature brings;   25
Our meddling intellect
Mis-shapes the beauteous forms of things:—
We murder to dissect.

Enough of Science and of Art;
Close up those barren leaves;   30
Come forth, and bring with you a heart
That watches and receives.

II. 1–4 *so* 1820: ll. 1–2 *and* 3–4 *transposed* 1798–1815   14 He, too, is
1815   And he is 1798–1805   30 those 1837: these 1798–1832

III
LINES WRITTEN IN EARLY SPRING
[Composed 1798.—Published 1798.]

I HEARD a thousand blended notes,
While in a grove I sate reclined,
In that sweet mood when pleasant thoughts
Bring sad thoughts to the mind.

To her fair works did Nature link   5
The human soul that through me ran;
And much it grieved my heart to think
What man has made of man.

Through primrose tufts, in that green bower,
The periwinkle trailed its wreaths;   10
And 'tis my faith that every flower
Enjoys the air it breathes.

The birds around me hopped and played,
Their thoughts I cannot measure:—
But the least motion which they made,   15
It seemed a thrill of pleasure.

The budding twigs spread out their fan,
To catch the breezy air;
And I must think, do all I can,
That there was pleasure there.   20

If this belief from heaven be sent,
If such be Nature's holy plan,
Have I not reason to lament
What man has made of man?

IV
A CHARACTER
[Composed probably September or October, 1800.—Published 1800.]

I MARVEL how Nature could ever find space
For so many strange contrasts in one human face:
There's thought and no thought, and there's paleness and bloom
And bustle and sluggishness, pleasure and gloom.

III. 9 green 1837 sweet 1798–1832
21–2 so 1837: If I these thoughts may not prevent,
            If such be of my creed the plan 1798–1815: 1820 as 1837 but
in 21 is for be; 21 From Heaven if this belief be sent 1827–32
IV. 2 so 1837: For all the expression (the things and the nothings) you see
in his MS. C*l*: For the weight and the levity seen in his 1800 MS. 18*a*.
4 sluggishness] indolence MS.

There 's weakness, and strength both redundant and vain;   5
Such strength as, if ever affliction and pain
Could pierce through a temper that 's soft to disease,
Would be rational peace—a philosopher's ease.

There 's indifference, alike when he fails or succeeds,
And attention full ten times as much as there needs;   10
Pride where there 's no envy, there 's so much of joy;
And mildness, and spirit both forward and coy.

There 's freedom, and sometimes a diffident stare
Of shame scarcely seeming to know that she 's there,
There 's virtue, the title it surely may claim,   15
Yet wants heaven knows what to be worthy the name.

This picture from nature may seem to depart,
Yet the Man would at once run away with your heart;
And I for five centuries right gladly would be
Such an odd such a kind happy creature as he.   20

V
TO MY SISTER
[Composed 1798.—Published 1798.]

It is the first mild day of March:
Each minute sweeter than before,
The redbreast sings from the tall larch
That stands beside our door.

There is a blessing in the air,   5
Which seems a sense of joy to yield
To the bare trees, and mountains bare,
And grass in the green field.

My sister! ('tis a wish of mine)
Now that our morning meal is done,   10
Make haste, your morning task resign;
Come forth and feel the sun.

7–8 Could pierce through his temper as soft as a fleece
Would surely be fortitude, sister of peace. MS. C*l*.
9–12, 13–16 *transposed in* MS.
17 *so* 1837 This picture, you say, has nor nature nor art MS.; What a
picture! 'tis drawn without nature or art 1800 This sketch 'tis a thing
which you do not approve
18 Yet the man would at once run away with your love MS. C*l*.
V. 9 My] Dear C

Edward will come with you ;—and, pray,
Put on with speed your woodland dress ;
And bring no book: for this one day   15
We'll give to idleness.

No joyless forms shall regulate
Our living calendar:
We from to-day, my Friend, will date
The opening of the year.   20

Love, now a universal birth,
From heart to heart is stealing,
From earth to man, from man to earth:
—It is the hour of feeling.

One moment now may give us more   25
Than years of toiling reason:
Our minds shall drink at every pore
The spirit of the season.

Some silent laws our hearts will make,
Which they shall long obey: 30
We for the year to come may take
Our temper from to-day.

And from the blessed power that rolls
About, below, above,
We'll frame the measure of our souls: 35
They shall be tuned to love.

Then come, my Sister! come, I pray,
With speed put on your woodland dress ;
And bring no book: for this one day
We'll give to idleness.   40

VI
SIMON LEE
THE OLD HUNTSMAN
With an incident in which he was concerned.
[Composed 1798.—Published 1798.]

In the sweet shire of Cardigan,
Not far from pleasant Ivor-hall,
An old Man dwells, a little man,—
'Tis said he once was tall.

26 *so* 1837: Than fifty years of reason   1798–1832   29 will   1820 may
1798–1815

Full five-and-thirty years he lived   5
A running huntsman merry;
And still the centre of his cheek
Is red as a ripe cherry.

No man like him the horn could sound,
And hill and valley rang with glee   10
When Echo bandied, round and round,
The halloo of Simon Lee.
In those proud days, he little cared
For husbandry or tillage;
To blither tasks did Simon rouse   15
The sleepers of the village.

He all the country could outrun,
Could leave both man and horse behind;
And often, ere the chase was done,
He reeled, and was stone-blind.   20
And still there's something in the world
At which his heart rejoices;
For when the chiming hounds are out,
He dearly loves their voices!

But, oh the heavy change!—bereft   25
Of health, strength, friends, and kindred, see!

VI. 1–56 *so* 1837

1.

In the sweet shire of Cardigan,
Not far from pleasant Ivor-hall,
An old man dwells, a little man,
I've heard he once was tall.
Of years he has upon his back,
No doubt, a burthen weighty;
He says he is three score and ten,
But others say he's eighty.

2.

A long blue livery-coat has he,
That's fair behind, and fair before;
Yet, meet him where you will, you
   see
At once that he is poor.
Full five and twenty years he lived
A running huntsman merry;
And, though he has but one eye left,
His cheek is like a cherry.

3.

No man like him the horn could
   sound,
And no man was so full of glee;
To say the least, four counties round
Had heard of Simon Lee;
His master's dead, and no one now
Dwells in the hall of Ivor;
Men, dogs, and horses, all are dead;
He is the sole survivor.

4.

His hunting feats have him bereft
Of his right eye, as you may see:
And then, what limbs those feats
   have left
To poor old Simon Lee!
He has no son, he has no child,
His wife, an aged woman,
Lives with him, near the waterfall,
Upon the village common.

Old Simon to the world is left
In liveried poverty.
His Master 's dead,—and no one now
Dwells in the Hall of Ivor;   30
Men, dogs, and horses, all are dead;
He is the sole survivor.

And he is lean and he is sick;
His body, dwindled and awry,
Rests upon ankles swoln and thick;   35
His legs are thin and dry.
One prop he has, and only one,
His wife, an aged woman,
Lives with him, near the waterfall,
Upon the village Common.   40

Beside their moss-grown hut of clay,
Not twenty paces from the door,
A scrap of land they have, but they
Are poorest of the poor.
This scrap of land he from the heath   45
Enclosed when he was stronger;
But what to them avails the land
Which he can till no longer?

5.

And he is lean and he is sick,
His little body 's half awry
His ancles they are swoln and thick;
His legs are thin and dry.
When he was young he little knew
Of husbandry, or tillage;
And now he 's forced to work
    though weak,
—The weakest in the village.

6.

He all the country could outrun,
Could leave both man and horse
    behind;
And often, ere the race was done,
He reeled and was stone blind.
And still there 's something in the
    world
At which his heart rejoices;
For when the chiming hounds are
    out,
He dearly loves their voices!

7.

Old Ruth works out of doors with
    him,
And does what Simon cannot do;
For she, not over stout of limb,
Is stouter of the two.
And though you with your utmost
    skill
From labour could not wean them,
Alas! 'tis very little, all
Which they can do between them.

8.

Beside their moss-grown hut of clay,
Not twenty paces from the door,
A scrap of land they have, but they
Are poorest of the poor.
This scrap of land he from the heath
Enclosed when he was stronger;
But what avails the land to them,
When they can till no longer?

1798: *for variants between* 1798 *and* 1843 *v. notes* p. 413

Oft, working by her Husband's side,
Ruth does what Simon cannot do;   50
For she, with scanty cause for pride,
Is stouter of the two.
And, though you with your utmost skill
From labour could not wean them,
'Tis little, very little—all   55
That they can do between them.

Few months of life has he in store
As he to you will tell,
For still, the more he works, the more
Do his weak ankles swell.   60
My gentle Reader, I perceive
How patiently you've waited,
And now I fear that you expect
Some tale will be related.

O Reader! had you in your mind   65
Such stores as silent thought can bring,
O gentle Reader! you would find
A tale in every thing.
What more I have to say is short,
And you must kindly take it: 70
It is no tale; but, should you think,
Perhaps a tale you'll make it.

One summer-day I chanced to see
This old Man doing all he could
To unearth the root of an old tree,   75
A stump of rotten wood.
The mattock tottered in his hand;
So vain was his endeavour,
That at the root of the old tree
He might have worked for ever.   80

"You're overtasked, good Simon Lee,
Give me your tool," to him I said;
And at the word right gladly he
Received my proffered aid.

60 *so* 1815: His poor old ancles swell   1798–1805
63 *so* 1820: And I'm afraid *etc.*   1798–1815   70 *so* 1820: I hope you'll
etc.   1798–1815   75 *so* 1815: About the root *etc.*   1798–1805

I struck, and with a single blow   85
The tangled root I severed,
At which the poor old Man so long
And vainly had endeavoured.

The tears into his eyes were brought,
And thanks and praises seemed to run   90
So fast out of his heart, I thought
They never would have done.
—I've heard of hearts unkind, kind deeds
With coldness still returning;
Alas! the gratitude of men   95
Hath oftener left me mourning.

VII
WRITTEN IN GERMANY
ON ONE OF THE COLDEST DAYS OF THE CENTURY
[Composed 1799.—Published 1800.]

'The Reader must be apprised that the Stoves in North Germany generally
have the impression of a galloping horse upon them, this being part of
the Brunswick Arms.

A PLAGUE on your languages, German and Norse!
Let me have the song of the kettle;
And the tongs and the poker, instead of that horse
That gallops away with such fury and force
On this dreary dull plate of black metal.   5

See that Fly,—a disconsolate creature! perhaps
A child of the field or the grove;
And, sorrow for him! the dull treacherous heat
Has seduced the poor fool from his winter retreat,
And he creeps to the edge of my stove.   10

Alas! how he fumbles about the domains
Which this comfortless oven environ!
He cannot find out in what track he must crawl,

96 Hath   1820: Has   1798–1815
VII. 1 plague on   1820: fig for   1800–15
5/6 Our earth is no doubt made of excellent stuff;
     But her pulses beat slower and slower:
     The weather in Forty was cutting and rough,
     And then, as Heaven knows, the Glass stood low enough;
     And *now* it is four degrees lower. 1800–15
6 See that   1820: Here's a   1800–15

Now back to the tiles, then in search of the wall,
And now on the brink of the iron. 15

Stock-still there he stands like a traveller bemazed:
The best of his skill he has tried;
His feelers, methinks, I can see him put forth
To the east and the west, to the south and the north,
But he finds neither guide-post nor guide. 20

His spindles sink under him, foot, leg, and thigh!
His eyesight and hearing are lost;
Between life and death his blood freezes and thaws;
And his two pretty pinions of blue dusky gauze
Are glued to his sides by the frost. 25

No brother, no mate has he near him—while I
Can draw warmth from the cheek of my Love;
As blest and as glad, in this desolate gloom,
As if green summer grass were the floor of my room,
And woodbines were hanging above. 30

Yet, God is my witness, thou small helpless Thing!
Thy life I would gladly sustain
Till summer come up from the south, and with crowds
Of thy brethren a march thou should'st sound through the clouds,
And back to the forests again! 35

VIII
A POET'S EPITAPH
[Composed 1799.—Published 1800.]

ART thou a Statist in the van
Of public conflicts trained and bred?
—First learn to love one living man;
Then may'st thou think upon the dead.

A Lawyer art thou?—draw not nigh! 5
Go, carry to some fitter place
The keenness of that practised eye,
The hardness of that sallow face.

14 then in search of 1837: and now back to 1800–32   19 to the South
1827: and the South 1800–20   21 His 1845: See! his 1800–20; How his
1827–37   26 mate 1827: Friend 1800–20
VIII. 1 Statist 1837: Statesman 1800–32   2 conflicts 1837: business
1800–32   6 fitter 1820: other 1800–15
7–8 *so* 1820: The hardness of thy coward eye,
          The falsehood of thy sallow face.   1800–15

Art thou a Man of purple cheer ?
A rosy Man, right plump to see ?   10
Approach ; yet, Doctor, not too near,
This grave no cushion is for thee.

Or art thou one of gallant pride,
A Soldier and no man of chaff ?
Welcome !—but lay thy sword aside,   15
And lean upon a peasant's staff.

Physician art thou ?—one, all eyes,
Philosopher !—a fingering slave,
One that would peep and botanize
Upon his mother's grave ?   20

Wrapt closely in thy sensual fleece,
O turn aside,—and take, I pray,
That he below may rest in peace,
Thy ever-dwindling soul, away !

A Moralist perchance appears ;   25
Led, Heaven knows how ! to this poor sod :
And he has neither eyes nor ears ;
Himself his world, and his own God ;

One to whose smooth-rubbed soul can cling
Nor form, nor feeling, great or small ;   30
A reasoning, self-sufficing thing,
An intellectual All-in-all !

Shut close the door ; press down the latch ;
Sleep in thy intellectual crust ;
Nor lose ten tickings of thy watch   35
Near this unprofitable dust.

But who is He, with modest looks,
And clad in homely russet brown ?
He murmurs near the running brooks
A music sweeter than their own.   40

13 *so* 1820: Art thou a man *etc.* 1800–15   24 *so* 1837: Thy pinpoint
of a soul, 1800–5: That abject thing, thy soul 1815–32   30 or 1837:
nor 1800–32   31 self-sufficing 1800, 1815–50: self-sufficient 1802–5

He is retired as noontide dew,
Or fountain in a noon-day grove;
And you must love him, ere to you
He will seem worthy of your love.

The outward shows of sky and earth,   45
Of hill and valley, he has viewed;
And impulses of deeper birth
Have come to him in solitude.

In common things that round us lie
Some random truths he can impart,—   50
The harvest of a quiet eye
That broods and sleeps on his own heart.

But he is weak; both Man and Boy,
Hath been an idler in the land;
Contented if he might enjoy   55
The things which others understand.

—Come hither in thy hour of strength;
Come, weak as is a breaking wave!
Here stretch thy body at full length;
Or build thy house upon this grave.   60

IX
TO THE DAISY
[Composed 1802.—Published 1807.]

BRIGHT Flower! whose home is everywhere,
Bold in maternal Nature's care,
And all the long year through the heir
    Of joy and sorrow;
Methinks that there abides in thee   5
Some concord with humanity,
Given to no other flower I see
    The forest thorough!

Is it that Man is soon deprest?
A thoughtless Thing! who, once unblest,   10
Does little on his memory rest,

IX. 1–3 Confiding Flower, by Nature's care
       Made bold,—who, lodging here or there,
       Art all the long year through the heir   1837 *only*
2 *so* 1843: A Pilgrim bold in Nature's care 1807–32   3 And oft, 1827-32
4 and 1850: or 1807–45   6 Communion with humanity 1837 *only*
9 *so* 1807–20; 1837: And wherefore? Man is soon deprest; 1827–32

Or on his reason,
And Thou would'st teach him how to find
A shelter under every wind,
A hope for times that are unkind   15
    And every season?

Thou wander'st the wide world about,
Uncheck'd by pride or scrupulous doubt,
With friends to greet thee, or without,
    Yet pleased and willing;   20
Meek, yielding to the occasion's call,
And all things suffering from all,
Thy function apostolical
    In peace fulfilling.

X

MATTHEW
[Composed 1799.—Published 1800.]

In the School of ———— is a tablet, on which are inscribed, in gilt letters,
the Names of the several persons who have been Schoolmasters there
since the foundation of the School, with the time at which they entered
upon and quitted their office. Opposite to one of those Names the Author
wrote the following lines.

IF Nature, for a favourite child,
In thee hath tempered so her clay,
That every hour thy heart runs wild,
Yet never once doth go astray,

Read o'er these lines; and then review   5
This tablet, that thus humbly rears
In such diversity of hue
Its history of two hundred years.

—When through this little wreck of fame,
Cipher and syllable! thine eye   10
Has travelled down to Matthew's name,
Pause with no common sympathy.

And, if a sleeping tear should wake,
Then be it neither checked nor stayed:
For Matthew a request I make   15
Which for himself he had not made.

17–24 *not in* 1827–32
X. MATTHEW 1837: Lines written on a tablet in a School   1800

Poor Matthew, all his frolics o'er,
Is silent as a standing pool;
Far from the chimney's merry roar,
And murmur of the village school.   20

The sighs which Matthew heaved were sighs
Of one tired out with fun and madness;
The tears which came to Matthew's eyes
Were tears of light, the dew of gladness.

Yet, sometimes, when the secret cup   25
Of still and serious thought went round,
It seemed as if he drank it up—
He felt with spirit so profound.

—Thou soul of God's best earthly mould!
Thou happy Soul! and can it be   30
That these two words of glittering gold
Are all that must remain of thee?

XI
THE TWO APRIL MORNINGS
[Composed 1799.—Published 1800.]

WE walked along, while bright and red
Uprose the morning sun;
And Matthew stopped, he looked, and said,
"The will of God be done!"

A village schoolmaster was he,   5
With hair of glittering grey;
As blithe a man as you could see
On a spring holiday.

And on that morning, through the grass,
And by the steaming rills,   10
We travelled merrily, to pass
A day among the hills.

"Our work," said I, "was well begun,
Then, from thy breast what thought,
Beneath so beautiful a sun,   15
So sad a sigh has brought?"

24 dew   1815: oil   1800–5   32 to thee?   1805 *only*

A second time did Matthew stop;
And fixing still his eye
Upon the eastern mountain-top,
To me he made reply: 20

"Yon cloud with that long purple cleft
Brings fresh into my mind
A day like this which I have left
Full thirty years behind.

"And just above yon slope of corn   25
Such colours, and no other,
Were in the sky, that April morn,
Of this the very brother.

"With rod and line I sued the sport
Which that sweet season gave,   30
And, to the churchyard come, stopped short
Beside my daughter's grave.

"Nine summers had she scarcely seen,
The pride of all the vale;
And then she sang;—she would have been   35
A very nightingale.

"Six feet in earth my Emma lay;
And yet I loved her more,
For so it seemed, than till that day
I e'er had loved before.   40

"And, turning from her grave, I met,
Beside the churchyard yew,
A blooming Girl, whose hair was wet
With points of morning dew.

"A basket on her head she bare;   45
Her brow was smooth and white:
To see a child so very fair,
It was a pure delight!

XI. 25–8 *so* 1802: And on that slope of springing corn
                    The self-same crimson hue
                    Fell from the sky that April morn,
                    The same which now I view! 1800
29–30 *so* 1815: . . . my silent sport
                 I plied by Derwent's wave, 1800–5
31 *so* 1837: And coming to the church, 1800–32

"No fountain from its rocky cave
E'er tripped with foot so free;   50
She seemed as happy as a wave
That dances on the sea.

"There came from me a sigh of pain
Which I could ill confine;
I looked at her, and looked again: 55
And did not wish her mine!"

Matthew is in his grave, yet now,
Methinks, I see him stand,
As at that moment, with a bough
Of wilding in his hand.   60

XII
THE FOUNTAIN
A CONVERSATION
[Composed 1799.—Published 1800.]

WE talked with open heart, and tongue
Affectionate and true,
A pair of friends, though I was young,
And Matthew seventy-two.

We lay beneath a spreading oak,   5
Beside a mossy seat;
And from the turf a fountain broke,
And gurgled at our feet.

"Now, Matthew!" said I, "let us match
This water's pleasant tune   10
With some old border-song, or catch
That suits a summer's noon;

"Or of the church-clock and the chimes
Sing here beneath the shade,
That half-mad thing of witty rhymes   15
Which you last April made!"

In silence Matthew lay, and eyed
The spring beneath the tree;
And thus the dear old Man replied,
The grey-haired man of glee: 20

59 a 1827: his 1800–15
XII. 9 *so* 1820: Now, Matthew, let us try to match 1800–15

"No check, no stay, this Streamlet fears;
How merrily it goes!
'Twill murmur on a thousand years,
And flow as now it flows.

"And here, on this delightful day,   25
I cannot choose but think
How oft, a vigorous man, I lay
Beside this fountain's brink.

"My eyes are dim with childish tears,
My heart is idly stirred,   30
For the same sound is in my ears
Which in those days I heard.

"Thus fares it still in our decay:
And yet the wiser mind
Mourns less for what age takes away   35
Than what it leaves behind.

"The blackbird amid leafy trees,
The lark above the hill,
Let loose their carols when they please,
Are quiet when they will.   40

"With Nature never do *they* wage
A foolish strife; they see
A happy youth, and their old age
Is beautiful and free:

"But we are pressed by heavy laws;   45
And often, glad no more,
We wear a face of joy, because
We have been glad of yore.

"If there be one who need bemoan
His kindred laid in earth,   50
The household hearts that were his own;
It is the man of mirth.

"My days, my Friend, are almost gone,
My life has been approved,

21 *so* 1837: Down to the vale this water steers 1800–32
20/21 Down to the vale with eager speed
      Behold this streamlet run,
      From subterranean bondage freed,
      And glittering in the sun. C
21 No guide it needs, no check it fears C   37 amid leafy   1837: in
the summer   1800–32   38 above   1837: upon   1800–32

And many love me; but by none   55
Am I enough beloved."

"Now both himself and me he wrongs,
The man who thus complains!
I live and sing my idle songs
Upon these happy plains;   60

"And, Matthew, for thy children dead
I'll be a son to thee!"
At this he grasped my hand, and said,
"Alas! that cannot be."

We rose up from the fountain-side;   65
And down the smooth descent
Of the green sheep-track did we glide;
And through the wood we went;

And, ere we came to Leonard's rock,
He sang those witty rhymes   70
About the crazy old church-clock,
And the bewildered chimes.

XIII
PERSONAL TALK
[Composed ?.—Published 1807.]

I

I AM not One who much or oft delight
To season my fireside with personal talk,—
Of friends, who live within an easy walk,
Or neighbours, daily, weekly, in my sight:
And, for my chance-acquaintance, ladies bright,   5
Sons, mothers, maidens withering on the stalk,
These all wear out of me, like Forms, with chalk
Painted on rich men's floors, for one feast-night.
Better than such discourse doth silence long,
Long, barren silence, square with my desire;   10
To sit without emotion, hope, or aim,
In the loved presence of my cottage-fire,
And listen to the flapping of the flame,
Or kettle whispering its faint undersong.

63 my hand 1815: his hands MS., 1800-5
XIII. 3 Of 1815: About MS., 1807   12 *so* 1815: By my half-kitchen,
my half-parlour fire MS., 1807   14 kettle 1827: kettle, 1807-20

II

"Yet life," you say, "is life; we have seen and see,   15
And with a living pleasure we describe;
And fits of sprightly malice do but bribe
The languid mind into activity.
Sound sense, and love itself, and mirth and glee
Are fostered by the comment and the gibe."   20
Even be it so: yet still among your tribe,
Our daily world's true Worldlings, rank not me!
Children are blest, and powerful; their world lies
More justly balanced; partly at their feet,
And part far from them:—sweetest melodies   25
Are those that are by distance made more sweet;
Whose mind is but the mind of his own eyes,
He is a Slave; the meanest we can meet!

III

Wings have we,—and as far as we can go
We may find pleasure: wilderness and wood,   30
Blank ocean and mere sky, support that mood
Which with the lofty sanctifies the low.
Dreams, books, are each a world; and books, we know,
Are a substantial world, both pure and good:
Round these, with tendrils strong as flesh and blood,   35
Our pastime and our happiness will grow.
There find I personal themes, a plenteous store,
Matter wherein right voluble I am,
To which I listen with a ready ear;
Two shall be named, pre-eminently dear,—   40
The gentle Lady married to the Moor;
And heavenly Una with her milk-white Lamb.

IV

Nor can I not believe but that hereby
Great gains are mine; for thus I live remote
From evil-speaking; rancour, never sought,   45
Comes to me not; malignant truth, or lie.

37–40 *so* 1827: There do I find a never-failing store
                    Of personal themes, and such as I love best;
                    Matter *etc.*
                    Two will I mention, dearer than the rest;   MS., 1807–20

Hence have I genial seasons, hence have I
Smooth passions, smooth discourse, and joyous thought:
And thus from day to day my little boat
Rocks in its harbour, lodging peaceably.   50
Blessings be with them—and eternal praise,
Who gave us nobler loves, and nobler cares—
The Poets, who on earth have made us heirs
Of truth and pure delight by heavenly lays!
Oh! might my name be numbered among theirs,   55
Then gladly would I end my mortal days.

XIV

ILLUSTRATED BOOKS AND NEWSPAPERS
[Composed 1846.—Published 1850.]

DISCOURSE was deemed Man's noblest attribute,
And written words the glory of his hand;
Then followed Printing with enlarged command
For thought—dominion vast and absolute
For spreading truth, and making love expand.   5
Now prose and verse sunk into disrepute
Must lacquey a dumb Art that best can suit
The taste of this once-intellectual Land.
A backward movement surely have we here,
From manhood—back to childhood; for the age—   10
Back towards caverned life's first rude career.
Avaunt this vile abuse of pictured page!
Must eyes be all in all, the tongue and ear
Nothing? Heaven keep us from a lower stage!

XV

TO THE SPADE OF A FRIEND
(AN AGRICULTURIST)
Composed while we were labouring together in his pleasure-ground.
[Composed (probably) 1806.—Published 1807.]

SPADE! with which Wilkinson hath tilled his lands,
And shaped these pleasant walks by Emont's side,
Thou art a tool of honour in my hands;
I press Thee, through the yielding soil, with pride.

48 discourse] desires MS.
XIV. 11 Backward as far as Egypt's oldest year MS.

Rare master has it been thy lot to know;   5
Long hast Thou served a man to reason true;
Whose life combines the best of high and low,
The labouring many and the resting few;

Health, meekness, ardour, quietness secure,
And industry of body and of mind;   10
And elegant enjoyments, that are pure
As nature is;—too pure to be refined.

Here often hast Thou heard the Poet sing
In concord with his river murmuring by;
Or in some silent field, while timid spring   15
Is yet uncheered by other minstrelsy.

Who shall inherit Thee when death has laid
Low in the darksome cell thine own dear lord?
That man will have a trophy, humble Spade!
A trophy nobler than a conqueror's sword.   20

If he be one that feels, with skill to part
False praise from true, or, greater from the less,
Thee will he welcome to his hand and heart,
Thou monument of peaceful happiness!

He will not dread with Thee a toilsome day—   25
Thee his loved servant, his inspiring mate!
And, when Thou art past service, worn away,
No dull oblivious nook shall hide thy fate.

His thrift thy uselessness will never scorn;
An *heir-loom* in his cottage wilt Thou be:—   30
High will he hang thee up, well pleased to adorn
His rustic chimney with the last of Thee!

XV. 8 labouring 1837: toiling 1807–32   9 *so* 1827: Health, quiet,
meekness, ardour, hope secure 1807–20   20 *so* 1815: More noble than
the noblest warrior's sword. 1807
25–6 *so* 1837: With thee he will not dread a toilsome day,
              His powerful servant *etc.* 1807–32
28 *so* 1837: Thee a surviving soul shall consecrate. 1807–32
29 usefulness 1807 *and* 1832   31 *so* 1837: . . . up, and will adorn
1807–32

XVI

A NIGHT THOUGHT

[Composed ?.—Published 1837 (*The Tribute: edited by Lord Northampton*);
vol. of 1842.]

Lo! where the Moon along the sky
Sails with her happy destiny;
Oft is she hid from mortal eye
    Or dimly seen,
But when the clouds asunder fly   5
    How bright her mien!

Far different we—a froward race,
Thousands though rich in Fortune's grace
With cherished sullenness of pace
    Their way pursue,   10
Ingrates who wear a smileless face
    The whole year through.

If kindred humours e'er would make
My spirit droop for drooping's sake,
From Fancy following in thy wake,   15
    Bright ship of heaven!
A counter impulse let me take
    And be forgiven.

XVII

INCIDENT

CHARACTERISTIC OF A FAVOURITE DOG

[Composed 1805.—Published 1807.]

On his morning rounds the Master
Goes to learn how all things fare;
Searches pasture after pasture,
Sheep and cattle eyes with care;

XVI. 1-2 The moon that sails along the sky
        Moves with a happy destiny, *The Tribute*
   6/7 Not flagging when the winds all sleep,
        Not hurried onward, when they sweep
        The bosom of th' aetherial deep,
        Not turned aside,
        She knows an even course to keep,
        Whate'er betide. *The Tribute*
7 **Perverse are we** *etc. The Tribute*

And, for silence or for talk,   5
He hath comrades in his walk;
Four dogs, each pair of different breed,
Distinguished two for scent, and two for speed.

See a hare before him started!
—Off they fly in earnest chase;   10
Every dog is eager-hearted,
All the four are in the race:
And the hare whom they pursue,
Knows from instinct what to do;
Her hope is near: no turn she makes;   15
But, like an arrow, to the river takes.

Deep the river was, and crusted
Thinly by a one night's frost;
But the nimble Hare hath trusted
To the ice, and safely crost;   20
She hath crost, and without heed
All are following at full speed,
When, lo! the ice, so thinly spread,
Breaks—and the greyhound, DART, is over-head!

Better fate have PRINCE and SWALLOW—   25
See them cleaving to the sport!
MUSIC has no heart to follow,
Little MUSIC, she stops short.
She hath neither wish nor heart,
Hers is now another part: 30
A loving creature she, and brave!
And fondly strives her struggling friend to save.

From the brink her paws she stretches,
Very hands as you would say!
And afflicting moans she fetches,   35
As he breaks the ice away.
For herself she hath no fears,—
Him alone she sees and hears,—
Makes efforts with complainings; nor gives o'er
Until her fellow sinks to re-appear no more.   40

XVII. 14 Knows from 1837: Hath an 1807–32   32 fondly strives
1815: doth her best 1807   39–40 ... efforts with ... sinks to re-appear
1837: ... efforts and ... sank, [sunk 1807–15] and re-appear'd 1807–32

XVIII

TRIBUTE

TO THE MEMORY OF THE SAME DOG

[Composed 1805.—Published 1807.]

LIE here, without a record of thy worth,
Beneath a covering of the common earth!
It is not from unwillingness to praise,
Or want of love, that here no Stone we raise;
More thou deserv'st; but *this* man gives to man,   5
Brother to brother, *this* is all we can.
Yet they to whom thy virtues made thee dear
Shall find thee through all changes of the year:
This Oak points out thy grave; the silent tree
Will gladly stand a monument of thee.   10

We grieved for thee, and wished thy end were past;
And willingly have laid thee here at last:
For thou hadst lived till every thing that cheers
In thee had yielded to the weight of years;
Extreme old age had wasted thee away,   15
And left thee but a glimmering of the day;
Thy ears were deaf, and feeble were thy knees,—
I saw thee stagger in the summer breeze,
Too weak to stand against its sportive breath,
And ready for the gentlest stroke of death.   20
It came, and we were glad; yet tears were shed;
Both man and woman wept when thou wert dead;
Not only for a thousand thoughts that were,
Old household thoughts, in which thou hadst thy share;
But for some precious boons vouchsafed to thee,   25
Found scarcely anywhere in like degree!
For love, that comes wherever life and sense
Are given by God, in thee was most intense;
A chain of heart, a feeling of the mind,

XVIII. *Before l.* 1. Lie here sequester'd: be this little mound
                    For ever thine, and be it holy ground! 1807–20
2 Beneath a 1827: Beneath the 1807–20
5–6   that Man gives to Man
    The Brother to the Brother—all we can L
11 *so* 1837: I pray'd for thee, and that thy end were past 1807–15; 1820–32
as text but I *for* We
27–8 *so* 1837: For love, that comes to all; the holy sense,
                    Best gift of God *etc.* 1807–32

A tender sympathy, which did thee bind　　30
Not only to us Men, but to thy Kind:
Yea, for thy fellow-brutes in thee we saw
A soul of love, love's intellectual law:—
Hence, if we wept, it was not done in shame;
Our tears from passion and from reason came,　　35
And, therefore, shalt thou be an honoured name!

XIX
FIDELITY
[Composed 1805.—Published 1807.]

A BARKING sound the Shepherd hears,
A cry as of a dog or fox;
He halts—and searches with his eyes
Among the scattered rocks:
And now at distance can discern　　5
A stirring in a brake of fern;
And instantly a dog is seen,
Glancing through that covert green.

The Dog is not of mountain breed;
Its motions, too, are wild and shy;　　10
With something, as the Shepherd thinks,
Unusual in its cry:
Nor is there any one in sight
All round, in hollow or on height;
Nor shout, nor whistle strikes his ear;　　15
What is the creature doing here?

It was a cove, a huge recess,
That keeps, till June, December's snow;
A lofty precipice in front,
A silent tarn[1] below!　　20
Far in the bosom of Helvellyn,
Remote from public road or dwelling,
Pathway, or cultivated land;
From trace of human foot or hand.

[1] Tarn is a *small* Mere or Lake, mostly high up in the mountains.

33 A soul 1837: The soul 1807–32
XIX. 7–8 *so* 1815–50 (*but* 1815 from *for* through)
　　From which immediately leaps out
　　A Dog, and yelping runs about MSS., 1807
23–4 And oft from month to month they say
　　No human being goes that way MS. *del.*

There sometimes doth a leaping fish 25
Send through the tarn a lonely cheer;
The crags repeat the raven's croak,
In symphony austere;
Thither the rainbow comes—the cloud—
And mists that spread the flying shroud; 30
And sunbeams; and the sounding blast,
That, if it could, would hurry past;
But that enormous barrier holds it fast.

Not free from boding thoughts, a while
The Shepherd stood; then makes his way 35
O'er rocks and stones, following the Dog
As quickly as he may;
Nor far had gone before he found
A human skeleton on the ground;
The appalled Discoverer with a sigh 40
Looks round, to learn the history.

From those abrupt and perilous rocks
The Man had fallen, that place of fear!

25 doth 1820: does MS., 1807   33 holds 1837: binds MSS.–1832
34 *so* 1815: Not knowing what to think   MSS.. 1807   36 *so* 1837:
Towards the Dog, o'er rocks and stones MSS.–1832   40 *so* 1815: Sad
sight! The Shepherd *etc.* MS., 1807
40–1   Sad sight! he leaves it, as it lies,
          Untouch'd and to the village hies. MSS.
41/2   A Company return'd forthwith;
          And mark what to their eyes was shewn!
          The raiment yet was on the bones,
          Although the flesh was gone;
          A raiment, though decay'd untorn;
          Such as the living Man had worn;
          As if the flesh, from day to day,
          Had perish'd by its own decay.

          How died he? This was quickly learn'd
          By proofs collected here and there;
          An angling rod which from the steep
          Hung midway in the air,
          A Hat, and, still on higher ground,
          Some needments in a kerchief bound;
          These did, with other proofs, make out
          The mournful story past all doubt. MSS.

42–9   From those abrupt and perilous rocks
          The Man had fallen, that place of fear!
          And signs and circumstances dawn'd

At length upon the Shepherd's mind
It breaks, and all is clear: 45
He instantly recalled the name,
And who he was, and whence he came;
Remembered, too, the very day
On which the Traveller passed this way.

But hear a wonder, for whose sake   50
This lamentable tale I tell!
A lasting monument of words
This wonder merits well.
The Dog, which still was hovering nigh,
Repeating the same timid cry,   55
This Dog, had been through three months' space
A dweller in that savage place.

Yes, proof was plain that, since the day
When this ill-fated Traveller died,
The Dog had watched about the spot,   60
Or by his master's side:

Till everything was clear;
They made discovery of his name,
And who he was, and whence he came,
And some could call to mind the day
When with his Dog he pass'd this way.

A youth he was, and come from far,
Yet, in this Country was well known
As one who wander'd through the hills
And loved to be alone.
With pencil and with angling rod
He went, and oft such places trod
That some had warn'd him to beware,
Who witness'd how he went and where. MSS.

50–1 *so* 1815: But hear a wonder now, for sake
            Of which this mournful Tale I tell   MSS., 1807
57/8   In the forlorn Abyss had lived:
            To this unfriendly spot had clung
            Exposed to sun and wind; and here
            Had she brought forth her Young,
            For of her helpless Offspring, one
            Was lying near the Skeleton;
            Which must (as its appearance told)
            Have lived till it was six weeks old. MSS.
59 *so* 1827: On which the Traveller (Young Man   MSS.) thus had died
MSS.–1820

How nourished here through such long time
He knows who gave that love sublime;
And gave that strength of feeling, great
Above all human estimate!   65

XX
ODE TO DUTY
[Composed 1804.—Published 1807.]

'Jam non consilio bonus, sed more eò perductus, ut non tantum rectè
facere possim, sed nisi rectè facere non possim."

STERN Daughter of the Voice of God!
O Duty! if that name thou love
Who art a light to guide, a rod
To check the erring, and reprove;
Thou, who art victory and law   5
When empty terrors overawe;
From vain temptations dost set free;
And calm'st the weary strife of frail humanity!

There are who ask not if thine eye
Be on them; who, in love and truth,   10
Where no misgiving is, rely
Upon the genial sense of youth;

XX. The motto *added* 1837 1–8 *not in* M
1–12 There are who tread a blameless way
   In purity, and love, and truth,
   Though resting on no better stay
   Than on the genial sense of youth: L *and cancel* 1807

2   Duty! if best that name thou love B
4–8 To chasten all things and reprove,
   Who breathest thy benign intents
   Among the senseless elements,
   And work'st in Creatures that are free
   By Reason, Choice, or Thought, thy highest ministry B
8 *so* 1815: From strife and from despair; a glorious ministry 1807
8/9 O'er earth, o'er heaven thy yoke is thrown
   All Natures thy behests obey:
   Man only murmurs; he alone
   In wilfulness rejects thy sway.
   Him empty terrors overawe
   And vain temptations are his law,
   He bids his better mind be dumb,
   And foresight does but breed remorse for times to come M, B
11 Without misgiving do rely M

Glad Hearts! without reproach or blot;
Who do thy work, and know it not:
Oh! if through confidence misplaced   15
They fail, thy saving arms, dread Power! around them cast.

Serene will be our days and bright,
And happy will our nature be,
When love is an unerring light,
And joy its own security.   20
And they a blissful course may hold
Even now, who, not unwisely bold,
Live in the spirit of this creed;
Yet seek thy firm support, according to their need.

13–24 Glad Hearts! without reproach or blot;
　　　Who do the right, and know it not:
　　　May joy be theirs while life shall last
　　　And may a genial sense remain, when Youth is past.

　　　Serene would be our days and bright;
　　　And happy would our Nature be;
　　　If Love were an unerring light;
　　　And joy its own security.
　　　And bless'd are they who in the main,
　　　This creed, even now, do entertain,
　　　Do in this spirit live; yet know
　　　That Man hath other hopes; strength which elsewhere must **grow.**
　　　　L *and cancel* 1807.

15, 16 May joy be theirs till they grow old
　　　　And if they fail do thou direct them and uphold M
　　　　May joy be theirs while life shall last
　　　　And Thou; if they should totter, teach them to stand fast: 1807–20:
　　　　Long may the kindly impulse last
　　　　But thou *etc. as* 1807–20, 1827–32
21–4 *so* 1845; *so* 1837 *but* find *for* seek:
　　　　And bless'd are they who in the main
　　　　This faith, even now, do entertain:
　　　　Live in the spirit of this creed;
　　　　Yet find that other strength according to their need.   1807–20
21–3 *as* 1845, 24 *as* 1807–20, 1827–32
　　　　And bless'd are they who, in the main,
　　　　This holy creed do entertain,
　　　　Yet even these may live to know
　　　　That they have hopes to seek, strength which elsewhere must
grow. M B

I, loving freedom, and untried;   25
No sport of every random gust,
Yet being to myself a guide,
Too blindly have reposed my trust:
And oft, when in my heart was heard
Thy timely mandate, I deferred   30
The task, in smoother walks to stray;
But thee I now would serve more strictly, if I may.

Through no disturbance of my soul,
Or strong compunction in me wrought,
I supplicate for thy control;   35
But in the quietness of thought:
Me this unchartered freedom tires;
I feel the weight of chance-desires:
My hopes no more must change their name,
I long for a repose that ever is the same.   40

[Yet not the less would I throughout
Still act according to the voice
Of my own wish; and feel past doubt
That my submissiveness was choice:
Not seeking in the school of pride   45
For "precepts over dignified",
Denial and restraint I prize
No farther than they breed a second Will more wise.]

25-32 I, loving freedom, and untried;
    No sport of every random gust,
    Yet being to myself a guide,
    Too blindly have reposed my trust;
    Resolv'd that nothing e'er should press
    Upon my present happiness
    I shov'd unwelcome tasks away:
    But henceforth I would serve; and strictly if I may.

    O Power of Duty! sent from God
    To enforce on earth his high behest,
    And keep us faithful to the road
    Which conscience hath pronounc'd the best:
    Thou, who art Victory and Law
    When empty terrors overawe;
    From vain temptations dost set free,
    From Strife, and from Despair, a glorious Ministry! L *and cancel* 1807.
29 And   1827: Full   1815-20   29-33 1807 *as* L 29-32   31 The task
imposed from day to day   1815-20   33 Through] From   M, and L *corr.*
to text   37 unchartered] perpetual   B, M, and L *corr. to* text   40
long] wish   M   41-8 *not in* 1815-50

Stern Lawgiver! yet thou dost wear
The Godhead's most benignant grace;   50
Nor know we anything so fair
As is the smile upon thy face:
Flowers laugh before thee on their beds
And fragrance in thy footing treads;
Thou dost preserve the stars from wrong;   55
And the most ancient heavens, through Thee, are fresh
    and strong.

To humbler functions, awful Power!
I call thee: I myself commend
Unto thy guidance from this hour;
Oh, let my weakness have an end!   60
Give unto me, made lowly wise,
The spirit of self-sacrifice;
The confidence of reason give;
And in the light of truth thy Bondman let me live!

XXI
CHARACTER OF THE HAPPY WARRIOR

[Composed December 1805 or January 1806.—Published 1807.

WHO is the happy Warrior? Who is he
That every man in arms should wish to be?
—It is the generous Spirit, who, when brought
Among the tasks of real life, hath wrought
Upon the plan that pleased his boyish thought: 5
Whose high endeavours are an inward light
That makes the path before him always bright:
Who, with a natural instinct to discern
What knowledge can perform, is diligent to learn;
Abides by this resolve, and stops not there,   10
But makes his moral being his prime care;
Who, doomed to go in company with Pain,
And Fear, and Bloodshed, miserable train!
Turns his necessity to glorious gain;
In face of these doth exercise a power   15
Which is our human nature's highest dower;
Controls them and subdues, transmutes, bereaves
Of their bad influence, and their good receives:

XXI. 2 That   1820: Whom   1807–15   5 boyish   1845: childish
1807–43   7 makes   1832: make   1807–27

By objects which might force the soul to abate
Her feeling, rendered more compassionate;   20
Is placable—because occasions rise
So often that demand such sacrifice;
More skilful in self-knowledge, even more pure,
As tempted more; more able to endure,
As more exposed to suffering and distress;   25
Thence, also, more alive to tenderness.
—'Tis he whose law is reason; who depends
Upon that law as on the best of friends;
Whence, in a state where men are tempted still
To evil for a guard against worse ill,   30
And what in quality or act is best
Doth seldom on a right foundation rest,
He labours good on good to fix, and owes
To virtue every triumph that he knows:
—Who, if he rise to station of command,   35
Rises by open means; and there will stand
On honourable terms, or else retire,
And in himself possess his own desire;
Who comprehends his trust, and to the same
Keeps faithful with a singleness of aim;   40
And therefore does not stoop, nor lie in wait
For wealth, or honours, or for worldly state;
Whom they must follow; on whose head must fall,
Like showers of manna, if they come at all:
Whose powers shed round him in the common strife,   45
Or mild concerns of ordinary life,
A constant influence, a peculiar grace;
But who, if he be called upon to face
Some awful moment to which Heaven has joined
Great issues, good or bad for human kind,   50
Is happy as a Lover; and attired
With sudden brightness, like a Man inspired;
And, through the heat of conflict, keeps the law
In calmness made, and sees what he foresaw;
Or if an unexpected call succeed,   55
Come when it will, is equal to the need:
—He who, though thus endued as with a sense
And faculty for storm and turbulence,
Is yet a Soul whose master-bias leans
33 *so* 1837: He fixes good on good alone,   1807–32

To homefelt pleasures and to gentle scenes;   60
Sweet images! which, whereso'er he be,
Are at his heart; and such fidelity
It is his darling passion to approve;
More brave for this, that he hath much to love:—
'Tis, finally, the Man, who, lifted high,   65
Conspicuous object in a Nation's eye,
Or left unthought-of in obscurity,—
Who, with a toward or untoward lot,
Prosperous or adverse, to his wish or not—
Plays, in the many games of life, that one   70
Where what he most doth value must be won:
Whom neither shape of danger can dismay,
Nor thought of tender happiness betray;
Who, not content that former worth stand fast,
Looks forward, persevering to the last,   75
From well to better, daily self-surpast:
Who, whether praise of him must walk the earth
For ever, and to noble deeds give birth,
Or he must fall, to sleep without his fame,
And leave a dead unprofitable name—   80
Finds comfort in himself and in his cause;
And, while the mortal mist is gathering, draws
His breath in confidence of Heaven's applause:
This is the happy Warrior; this is He
That every Man in arms should wish to be.   85

XXII
THE FORCE OF PRAYER[1]
OR,
THE FOUNDING OF BOLTON PRIORY
A TRADITION

[Composed 1807.—Published 1815 (4to, along with *The White Doe of Rylstone*); ed. 1815.]

" 𝔚𝔥𝔞𝔱 𝔦𝔰 𝔤𝔬𝔬𝔡 𝔣𝔬𝔯 𝔞 𝔟𝔬𝔬𝔱𝔩𝔢𝔰𝔰 𝔟𝔢𝔫𝔢? "
With these dark words begins my Tale;
And their meaning is, whence can comfort spring
When Prayer is of no avail?

---

[1] See "The White Doe of Rylstone."

---

79 *so* 1840; fall and sleep   1837: Or He must go to dust without
1807-32   85   That 1845:   Whom   1807-43
XXII. 2   The lady answer'd "endless sorrow"
               Her words are clear; but the Falconer's words

" 𝔚𝔥𝔞𝔱 𝔦𝔰 𝔤𝔬𝔬𝔡 𝔣𝔬𝔯 𝔞 𝔟𝔬𝔬𝔱𝔩𝔢𝔰𝔰 𝔟𝔢𝔫𝔢? "   5
The Falconer to the Lady said;
And she made answer "ENDLESS SORROW!"
For she knew that her Son was dead.

She knew it by the Falconer's words,
And from the look of the Falconer's eye;   10
And from the love which was in her soul
For her youthful Romilly.

—Young Romilly through Barden woods
Is ranging high and low;
And holds a greyhound in a leash,   15
To let slip upon buck or doe.

The pair have reached that fearful chasm,
How tempting to bestride!
For lordly Wharf is there pent in
With rocks on either side.   20

The striding-place is called THE STRID,
A name which it took of yore:
A thousand years hath it borne that name,
And shall a thousand more.

And hither is young Romilly come,   25
And what may now forbid
That he, perhaps for the hundredth time,
Shall bound across THE STRID?

He sprang in glee,—for what cared he
That the river was strong, and the rocks were steep?— 30
But the greyhound in the leash hung back,
And checked him in his leap.

The Boy is in the arms of Wharf,
And strangled by a merciless force;

Are a path that is dark to travel thorough.

These words I bring from the Banks of Wharf,
Dark words to front an antient tale; MS.
7 "endless sorrow"] as ye have heard MS.   11 soul] heart MS.   17
The pair 1820; And the pair MS., 1815
18–19 Where he who dares may stride
      Across the river Wharf, pent in MS.
25 hither] thither MS.

For never more was young Romilly seen   35
Till he rose a lifeless corse.

Now there is stillness in the vale,
And long, unspeaking, sorrow:
Wharf shall be to pitying hearts
A name more sad than Yarrow.   40

If for a Lover the Lady wept,
A solace she might borrow
From death, and from the passion of death:—
Old Wharf might heal her sorrow.

She weeps not for the wedding-day   45
Which was to be to-morrow:
Her hope was a further-looking hope,
And hers is a mother's sorrow.

He was a tree that stood alone,
And proudly did its branches wave;   50
And the root of this delightful tree
Was in her husband's grave!

Long, long in darkness did she sit,
And her first words were, "Let there be
In Bolton, on the field of Wharf,   55
A stately Priory!"

The stately Priory was reared;
And Wharf, as he moved along,
To matins joined a mournful voice,
Nor failed at even-song.   60

And the Lady prayed in heaviness
That looked not for relief!
But slowly did her succour come,
And a patience to her grief.

Oh! there is never sorrow of heart   65
That shall lack a timely end,
If but to God we turn, and ask
Of Him to be our friend!

39–40 Wharf has buried fonder hopes
      Than e'er were drown'd in Yarrow   MS.
42 solace] comfort   MS.

XXIII
A FACT, AND AN IMAGINATION
OR,

CANUTE AND ALFRED, ON THE SEA-SHORE

[Composed 1816.—Published 1820.]

THE Danish Conqueror, on his royal chair,
Mustering a face of haughty sovereignty,
To aid a covert purpose, cried—"O ye
Approaching Waters of the deep, that share
With this green isle my fortunes, come not where   5
Your Master's throne is set."—Deaf was the Sea;
Her waves rolled on, respecting his decree
Less than they heed a breath of wanton air.
—Then Canute, rising from the invaded throne,
Said to his servile Courtiers,—"Poor the reach,   10
The undisguised extent, of mortal sway!
He only is a King, and he alone
Deserves the name (this truth the billows preach)
Whose everlasting laws, sea, earth, and heaven obey."

This just reproof the prosperous Dane   15
Drew from the influx of the main,
For some whose rugged northern mouths would strain
At oriental flattery;
And Canute (fact more worthy to be known)
From that time forth did for his brows disown   20
The ostentatious symbol of a crown;
Esteeming earthly royalty
Contemptible as vain.

Now hear what one of elder days,
Rich theme of England's fondest praise,   25
Her darling Alfred, *might* have spoken;

XXIII. 6–8 *so* 1840 *but* had *for* heed:
 . . . Absurd decree!
 A mandate uttered to the foaming sea,
 Is to its motion less than wanton air MS.—1837
 The foaming sea Heard and rolled on respecting his decree
 Less than it heeds *etc. as text* C
19 which is worthier to be known MS. fact 1849: truth MS. 1820–45
23 as 1849: and 1820–45
26–7 Her darling Alfred might have taught
 The Sea, the prompter of his thought,
 Such words as these methinks he might have spoken
 To chear *etc.* MS.

To cheer the remnant of his host
When he was driven from coast to coast,
Distressed and harassed, but with mind unbroken:

"My faithful followers, lo! the tide is spent   30
That rose, and steadily advanced to fill
The shores and channels, working Nature's will
Among the mazy streams that backward went,
And in the sluggish pools where ships are pent:
And now, his task performed, the flood stands still,   35
At the green base of many an inland hill,
In placid beauty and sublime content!
Such the repose that sage and hero find;
Such measured rest the sedulous and good
Of humbler name; whose souls do, like the flood   40
Of Ocean, press right on; or gently wind,
Neither to be diverted nor withstood,
Until they reach the bounds by Heaven assigned."

XXIV

[Composed 1816.—Published 1820.]

"A LITTLE *onward lend thy guiding hand*
To these dark steps, a little further on!"
—What trick of memory to *my* voice hath brought
This mournful iteration? For though Time,
The Conqueror, crowns the Conquered, on this brow   5
Planting his favourite silver diadem,
Nor he, nor minister of his—intent
To run before him, hath enrolled me yet,
Though not unmenaced, among those who lean
Upon a living staff, with borrowed sight.   10
—O my own Dora, my belovèd child!
Should that day come—but hark! the birds salute
The cheerful dawn, brightening for me the east;

30 My Son, behold the [   ] of the tide MS.   35 his 1837: its MSS.,
1820–32   37 sublime] entire MSS.   39 sedulous] diligent MS.
XXIV. 8–9 To run before with too officious speed
                Casting a shadow on his Master's path
                Hath been permitted to enroll me yet
                Though *etc.* MS. *corr. to text*
11 *so* 1850: O my Antigone, beloved child! MS., 1820–45

For me, thy natural leader, once again
Impatient to conduct thee, not as erst   15
A tottering infant, with compliant stoop
From flower to flower supported; but to curb
Thy nymph-like step swift-bounding o'er the lawn,
Along the loose rocks, or the slippery verge
Of foaming torrents.—From thy orisons   20
Come forth; and, while the morning air is yet
Transparent as the soul of innocent youth,
Let me, thy happy guide, now point thy way,
And now precede thee, winding to and fro,
Till we by perseverance gain the top   25
Of some smooth ridge, whose brink precipitous
Kindles intense desire for powers withheld
From this corporeal frame; whereon who stands
Is seized with strong incitement to push forth
His arms, as swimmers use, and plunge—dread thought, 30
For pastime plunge—into the "abrupt abyss",
Where ravens spread their plumy vans, at ease!

And yet more gladly thee would I conduct
Through woods and spacious forests,—to behold
There, how the Original of human art,   35
Heaven-prompted Nature, measures and erects
Her temples, fearless for the stately work,
Though waves, to every breeze, its high-arched roof,
And storms the pillars rock. But we such schools
Of reverential awe will chiefly seek   40
In the still summer noon, while beams of light,
Reposing here, and in the aisles beyond
Traceably gliding through the dusk, recal
To mind the living presences of nuns;
A gentle, pensive, white-robed sisterhood,   45
Whose saintly radiance mitigates the gloom
Of those terrestial fabrics, where they serve,
To Christ, the Sun of righteousness, espoused.

19 The loose rocks, and along . . . edge MS.   34 spacious] wide-spread
MS.   37 Her sylvan temples, fearless for the work, MS.   45 gentle]
saintly MS.   46 Whose radiance mitigates the shady gloom MS.   47
fabrics] mansions MS.

Now also shall the page of classic lore,
To these glad eyes from bondage freed, again   50
Lie open; and the book of Holy Writ,
Again unfolded, passage clear shall yield
To heights more glorious still, and into shades
More awful, where, advancing hand in hand,
We may be taught, O Darling of my care!   55
To calm the affections, elevate the soul,
And consecrate our lives to truth and love.

XXV
ODE TO LYCORIS
MAY, 1817

[Composed May, 1817.—Published 1820.]

I

AN age hath been when Earth was proud
Of lustre too intense
To be sustained; and Mortals bowed
The front in self-defence.
Who *then*, if Dian's crescent gleamed,   5
Or Cupid's sparkling arrow streamed
While on the wing the Urchin played,
Could fearlessly approach the shade?
—Enough for one soft vernal day,
If I, a bard of ebbing time,   10
And nurtured in a fickle clime,
May haunt this hornèd bay;
Whose amorous water multiplies
The flitting halcyon's vivid dyes;

49-55 *So* 1827:
   Re-open now thy everlasting gates,
Thou Fane of Holy Writ! Ye classic Domes,
To these glad orbs from darksome bondage freed,
Unfold again your portals! Passage lies
Through you to heights more glorious still, and shades
More awful, where this Darling of my care,
Advancing with me hand in hand, may learn,
Without forsaking a too earnest world, 1820 *so* MS. *but for
last three lines*:
. . . where this Novice, of my hopes
The sunbeam, darling of my care, with whom
I now am free to enter hand in hand
Cheared by the sound of tuneful harps, may learn
Without forsaking . . .
57 our lives 1827: her life MS., 1820

And smooths her liquid breast—to show   15
These swan-like specks of mountain snow,
White as the pair that slid along the plains
Of heaven, when Venus held the reins!

II

In youth we love the darksome lawn
Brushed by the owlet's wing;   20
Then, Twilight is preferred to Dawn,
And Autumn to the Spring.
Sad fancies do we then affect,
In luxury of disrespect
To our own prodigal excess   25
Of too familiar happiness.
Lycoris (if such name befit
Thee, thee my life's celestial sign!)
When Nature marks the year's decline,
Be ours to welcome it;   30
Pleased with the harvest hope that runs
Before the path of milder suns;
Pleased while the sylvan world displays
Its ripeness to the feeding gaze;
Pleased when the sullen winds resound the knell   35
Of the resplendent miracle.

III

But something whispers to my heart
That, as we downward tend,
Lycoris! life requires an *art*
To which our souls must bend;   40
A skill—to balance and supply;
And, ere the flowing fount be dry,
As soon it must, a sense to sip,
Or drink, with no fastidious lip.
Then welcome, above all, the Guest   45
Whose smiles, diffused o'er land and sea,
Seem to recal the Deity
Of youth into the breast:

XXV. 15 her   1827: its   1820
31-2 *so* 1827: Pleased with the soil's requited cares;
                Pleased with the blue that ether wears;   1820
45-8 *so* 1827: Frank greeting, then, to that blithe Guest
                Diffusing smiles o'er land and sea
                To aid the vernal Deity
                Whose home is in the breast!   1820

May pensive Autumn ne'er present
A claim to her disparagement!   50
While blossoms and the budding spray
Inspire us in our own decay;
Still, as we nearer draw to life's dark goal,
Be hopeful Spring the favourite of the Soul!

XXVI
TO THE SAME

[Composed, as a whole, 1817.—Published 1820.]

ENOUGH of climbing toil!—Ambition treads
Here, as 'mid busier scenes, ground steep and rough,
Or slippery even to peril! and each step,
As we for most uncertain recompence
Mount toward the empire of the fickle clouds,   5
Each weary step, dwarfing the world below,
Induces, for its old familiar sights,
Unacceptable feelings of contempt,
With wonder mixed—that Man could e'er be tied,
In anxious bondage, to such nice array   10
And formal fellowship of petty things!
—Oh! 'tis the *heart* that magnifies this life,
Making a truth and beauty of her own;
And moss-grown alleys, circumscribing shades,
And gurgling rills, assist her in the work   15

XXVI. 2 As in the sphere of courts MS.; 'mid   1827: in   1820   3 *so*
1827: Oft perilous, always tiresome; MS., 1820   4–6 recompence . . .
step   1827: gain ascend Towards the clouds, 1820
4–10 . . . gain ascend,
        Dwindling, the old familiar world below
        Induces stealthy feelings of contempt
        With wonder, that our hearts could e'er be tied
        By anxious interest to such nice array   MS.
14–16 No, if she be not wanting to herself Do moss-grown . . . Less
efficaciously C
14–42 And low-brow'd cell and circumscribing shades
        Such as surround us here assist the work.
        Come let me see thee sink *etc.* MS. 1
15–42 Such as do now surround us, aid her more
        In the blest work than tower'd Palace high
        Far blazing as if built of fire: or pomp
        Of sea and land contending for regard
        Of the lone Shepherd on the mountain top
        While he perchance following some humble quest

More efficaciously than realms outspread,
As in a map, before the adventurer's gaze—
Ocean and Earth contending for regard.

The umbrageous woods are left—how far beneath!
But lo! where darkness seems to guard the mouth   20
Of yon wild cave, whose jaggèd brows are fringed
With flaccid threads of ivy, in the still
And sultry air, depending motionless.
Yet cool the space within, and not uncheered
(As whoso enters shall ere long perceive)—   25
By stealthy influx of the timid day
Mingling with night, such twilight to compose
As Numa loved; when, in the Egerian grot,
From the sage Nymph appearing at his wish,
He gained whate'er a regal mind might ask,   30
Or need, of counsel breathed through lips divine.

Long as the heat shall rage, let that dim cave
Protect us, there deciphering as we may
Diluvian records; or the sighs of Earth
Interpreting; or counting for old Time   35
His minutes, by reiterated drops,
Audible tears, from some invisible source
That deepens upon fancy—more and more
Drawn toward the centre whence those sighs creep forth
To awe the lightness of humanity.   40
Or, shutting up thyself within thyself,
There let me see thee sink into a mood
Of gentler thought, protracted till thine eye
Be calm as water when the winds are gone,
And no one can tell whither. Dearest Friend!   45

Of both is heedless. Rather, would I gaze
On a small flower, retaining at my feet
Its long-loved aspect than become the sport
Of transmutations taking more away
Than they can give in recompense. Rest here
And let me see thee sink etc. MS., 2
19–42 *so* 1827: Lo! there a dim Egerian grotto fringed
With ivy-twine, profusely from its brows
Dependant,—enter without further aim;
And let me *etc.* 1820
32–51 *For earlier drafts v. notes*   43 gentler 1827: quiet   1820

We two have known such happy hours together
That, were power granted to replace them (fetched
From out the pensive shadows where they lie)
In the first warmth of their original sunshine,
Loth should I be to use it: passing sweet   50
Are the domains of tender memory!

XXVII
SEPTEMBER, 1819
[Composed September, 1819.—Published 1820.]

THE sylvan slopes with corn-clad fields
Are hung, as if with golden shields,
Bright trophies of the sun!
Like a fair sister of the sky,
Unruffled doth the blue lake lie,   5
The mountains looking on.

And, sooth to say, yon vocal grove,
Albeit uninspired by love,
By love untaught to ring,
May well afford to mortal ear   10
An impulse more profoundly dear
Than music of the Spring.

For *that* from turbulence and heat
Proceeds, from some uneasy seat
In nature's struggling frame,   15
Some region of impatient life:
And jealousy, and quivering strife,
Therein a portion claim.

This, this is holy;—while I hear
These vespers of another year,   20
This hymn of thanks and praise,
My spirit seems to mount above
The anxieties of human love,
And earth's precarious days.

46 two   MSS.   1820–43: too   1845–50 happy] blissful   MSS.   51 tender]
pensive   MS.
XXVII. 2 as if with] that show like   MS.   7 vocal] tuneful   MS.

But list!—though winter storms be nigh,   25
Unchecked is that soft harmony:
There lives Who can provide
For all His creatures; and in Him,
Even like the radiant Seraphim,
These choristers confide.   30

XXVIII
UPON THE SAME OCCASION
[Composed September, 1819.—Published 1820.]

DEPARTING summer hath assumed
An aspect tenderly illumed,
The gentlest look of spring;
That calls from yonder leafy shade
Unfaded, yet prepared to fade,   5
A timely carolling.

No faint and hesitating trill,
Such tribute as to winter chill
The lonely redbreast pays!
Clear, loud, and lively is the din,   10
From social warblers gathering in
Their harvest of sweet lays.

Nor doth the example fail to cheer
Me, conscious that my leaf is sere,
And yellow on the bough:—   15
Fall, rosy garlands, from my head!
Ye myrtle wreaths, your fragrance shed
Around a younger brow!

Yet will I temperately rejoice;
Wide is the range, and free the choice   20
Of undiscordant themes;
Which, haply, kindred souls may prize
Not less than vernal ecstasies,
And passion's feverish dreams.

XXVIII. 6 timely] tuneful MS.
17–18 Your flowers, ye wreaths of myrtle shed,
    Ye cannot keep them now. MS.

For deathless powers to verse belong,   25
And they like Demi-gods are strong
On whom the Muses smile;
But some their function have disclaimed,
Best pleased with what is aptliest framed
To enervate and defile.   30

Not such the initiatory strains
Committed to the silent plains
In Britain's earliest dawn:
Trembled the groves, the stars grew pale,
While all-too-daringly the veil   35
Of nature was withdrawn!

Nor such the spirit-stirring note
When the live chords Alcæus smote,
Inflamed by sense of wrong;
Woe! woe to Tyrants! from the lyre   40
Broke threateningly, in sparkles dire
Of fierce vindictive song.

And not unhallowed was the page
By wingèd Love inscribed, to assuage
The pangs of vain pursuit;   45
Love listening while the Lesbian Maid
With finest touch of passion swayed
Her own Æolian lute.

O ye, who patiently explore
The wreck of Herculanean lore,   50
What rapture! could ye seize
Some Theban fragment, or unroll
One precious, tender-hearted, scroll
Of pure Simonides.

28 function] Patrons MS.
30/1 And surely of the (tuneful) industrious band
     Who spread along their native land (Whose filmy verse o'erspreads
        the land)
     The (With) snares of soft desire
     There are who might be taught to spurn
     The task, more clearly to discern,
     More nobly to aspire. MS.
47 With passion's fervent finger swayed MS.   54 pure] sweet MS.

That were, indeed, a genuine birth   55
Of poesy; a bursting forth
Of genius from the dust:
What Horace gloried to behold,
What Maro loved, shall we enfold?
Can haughty Time be just!   60

XXIX
MEMORY

[Composed 1823.—Published 1827.]

A PEN—to register; a key—
That winds through secret wards;
Are well assigned to Memory
By allegoric Bards.

As aptly, also, might be given   5
A Pencil to her hand;
That, softening objects, sometimes even
Outstrips the heart's demand;

That smoothes foregone distress, the lines
Of lingering care subdues,   10
Long-vanished happiness refines,
And clothes in brighter hues;

Yet, like a tool of Fancy, works
Those Spectres to dilate
That startle Conscience, as she lurks   15
Within her lonely seat.

O! that our lives, which flee so fast,
In purity were such,
That not an image of the past
Should fear that pencil's touch!   20

Retirement then might hourly look
Upon a soothing scene,
Age steal to his allotted nook
Contented and serene;

With heart as calm as lakes that sleep,   25
In frosty moonlight glistening;

58 gloried] boasted MS.

Or mountain rivers, where they creep
Along a channel smooth and deep,
To their own far-off murmurs listening.

XXX

[Composed 1829.—Published 1835.]

This Lawn, a carpet all alive
With shadows flung from leaves—to strive
   In dance, amid a press
Of sunshine, an apt emblem yields
Of Worldlings revelling in the fields   5
   Of strenuous idleness ;

Less quick the stir when tide and breeze
Encounter, and to narrow seas
   Forbid a moment's rest ;
The medley less when boreal Lights   10
Glance to and fro, like aery Sprites
   To feats of arms addrest !

Yet, spite of all this eager strife,
This ceaseless play, the genuine life
   That serves the stedfast hours,   15
Is in the grass beneath, that grows
Unheeded, and the mute repose
   Of sweetly-breathing flowers.

XXXI
HUMANITY

[Composed 1829.—Published 1835.]

The Rocking-stones, alluded to in the beginning of the following verses,
are supposed to have been used, by our British ancestors, both for
judicial and religious purposes. Such stones are not uncommonly found,
at this day, both in Great Britain and in Ireland.

What though the Accused, upon his own appeal
To righteous Gods when man has ceased to feel,
Or at a doubting Judge's stern command,
Before the Stone of Power no longer stand—

XXX. 5 worldling revellers   MSS.
XXXI. 1–8 What though dislodged by purer faith, no more
            White-vested Priests the hallowed Oak adore
            Nor Seer nor Judge consult the Stone of Power!   MS.

To take his sentence from the balanced Block,   5
As, at his touch, it rocks, or seems to rock;
Though, in the depths of sunless groves, no more
The Druid-priest the hallowed Oak adore;
Yet, for the Initiate, rocks and whispering trees
Do still perform mysterious offices!   10
And functions dwell in beast and bird that sway
The reasoning mind, or with the fancy play,
Inviting, at all seasons, ears and eyes
To watch for undelusive auguries:—
Not uninspired appear their simplest ways;   15
Their voices mount symbolical of praise—
To mix with hymns that Spirits make and hear;
And to fallen man their innocence is dear.
Enraptured Art draws from those sacred springs
Streams that reflect the poetry of things!   20
Where Christian Martyrs stand in hues portrayed,
That, might a wish avail, would never fade,
Borne in their hands the lily and the palm
Shed round the altar a celestial calm;
There, too, behold the lamb and guileless dove   25
Prest in the tenderness of virgin love
To saintly bosoms!—Glorious is the blending
Of right affections climbing or descending
Along a scale of light and life, with cares
Alternate; carrying holy thoughts and prayers   30
Up to the sovereign seat of the Most High;
Descending to the worm in charity;
Like those good Angels whom a dream of night
Gave, in the field of Luz, to Jacob's sight
All, while *he* slept, treading the pendent stairs   35

11–14 And still in beast and bird a function dwells,
      That, while we look and listen, sometimes tells
      Upon the heart, in more authentic guise
      Than Oracles, or wingèd Auguries,
      Spake to the Science of the ancient Wise. MS., 1835
16–17 Their voice ascends . . . Of hymns which blessèd Spirits   MS.
19–20 *not in* MS.   21 Where Martyrs stand, or soar,   MS.
22–3 That if a wish might save them, ne'er would fade
      The unspotted lilly, the victorious palm MS.
29   Along the scale of things, with ceaseless cares MS.
34–5 Showed to the Patriarch, not in banded flight,
      But, treading, while he slept, the MS.

Earthward or heavenward, radiant messengers,
That, with a perfect will in one accord
Of strict obedience, serve the Almighty Lord;
And with untired humility forbore
To speed their errand by the wings they wore.   40

What a fair world were ours for verse to paint,
If Power could live at ease with self-restraint!
Opinion bow before the naked sense
Of the great Vision,—faith in Providence;
Merciful over all his creatures, just   45
To the least particle of sentient dust;
But fixing by immutable decrees
Seedtime and harvest for his purposes!
Then would be closed the restless oblique eye
That looks for evil like a treacherous spy;   50
Disputes would then relax, like stormy winds
That into breezes sink; impetuous minds
By discipline endeavour to grow meek
As Truth herself, whom they profess to seek.
Then Genius, shunning fellowship with Pride,   55
Would braid his golden locks at Wisdom's side;
Love ebb and flow untroubled by caprice;
And not alone *harsh* tyranny would cease,
But unoffending creatures find release
From qualified oppression, whose defence   60
Rests on a hollow plea of recompence;
Thought-tempered wrongs, for each humane respect
Oft worse to bear, or deadlier in effect.
Witness those glances of indignant scorn
From some high-minded Slave, impelled to spurn   65
The kindness that would make him less forlorn;
Or, if the soul to bondage be subdued,
His look of pitiable gratitude!

Alas for thee, bright Galaxy of Isles,
Whose day departs in pomp, returns with smiles—   70
To greet the flowers and fruitage of a land,

38 serve   1845: served   1835–43   40 *so* 1837: The ready service of the
wings MS., 1835   45 his creatures   1840: existence   MS., 1835, 1837
45–7 Compationate to all that suffer, just
     In the end to every creature born of dust C
47–8 *not in* MS.   52 impetuous] and ardent MS.   70 Whose   1837:
Where   MS., 1835

As the sun mounts, by sea-born breezes fanned;
A land whose azure mountain-tops are seats
For Gods in council, whose green vales, retreats
Fit for the shades of heroes, mingling there   75
To breathe Elysian peace in upper air.

Though cold as winter, gloomy as the grave,
Stone-walls a prisoner make, but not a slave.
Shall man assume a property in man?
Lay on the moral will a withering ban?   80
Shame that our laws at distance still protect
Enormities, which they at home reject!
"Slaves cannot breathe in England"—yet that boast
Is but a mockery! when from coast to coast,
Though *fettered* slave be none, her floors and soil   85
Groan underneath a weight of slavish toil,
For the poor Many, measured out by rules
Fetched with cupidity from heartless schools,
That to an Idol, falsely called "the Wealth
Of Nations", sacrifice a People's health,   90
Body and mind and soul; a thirst so keen
Is ever urging on the vast machine
Of sleepless Labour, 'mid whose dizzy wheels
The Power least prized is that which thinks and feels.

Then, for the pastimes of this delicate age,   95
And all the heavy or light vassalage
Which for their sakes we fasten, as may suit
Our varying moods, on human kind or brute,
'Twere well in little, as in great, to pause,
Lest Fancy trifle with eternal laws.   100
Not from his fellows only man may learn
Rights to compare and duties to discern!
All creatures and all objects, in degree,
Are friends and patrons of humanity.
There are to whom the garden, grove, and field,   105
Perpetual lessons of forbearance yield;

81 still   1837: should   MS., 1835   83–4 *so* 1837: a proud boast! And
yet a mockery! if   MS., 1835   89 to a monstrous Idol called   C
91 The weal of body mind and soul; so keen
     A thirst is ever . . . C
101–4 *not in* MS.: *in* 1835 *they appear as a motto prefixed to the poem*

Who would not lightly violate the grace
The lowliest flower possesses in its place;
Nor shorten the sweet life, too fugitive,
Which nothing less than Infinite Power could give.   110

XXXII
[Composed 1846.—Published 1850.]

THE unremitting voice of nightly streams
That wastes so oft, we think, its tuneful powers,
If neither soothing to the worm that gleams
Through dewy grass, nor small birds hushed in bowers,
Nor unto silent leaves and drowsy flowers,—   5
That voice of unpretending harmony
(For who what is shall measure by what seems
To be, or not to be,
Or tax high Heaven with prodigality?)
Wants not a healing influence that can creep   10
Into the human breast, and mix with sleep
To regulate the motion of our dreams

XXXII. 1 unremitting...nightly] unsuspended...mountain MS.1   2
Where Nature seems to work with wasted powers MS.1; That calls the
breeze to modulate its powers MS.2   3 That voice that soothes, perchance
MS.1   4 dewy] summer, (dusky) MSS.   nor] and MSS.   5
And lulls at dewy eve the shutting flowers MS.1   6 *not in* MSS.
7 For] Yet MSS.
10–17 This has been known to mingle with the sleep (That voice, it has
           been known to mix with sleep)
       Of human kind, and regulate our dreams
       For kindly issues, as a knight too well (Once to how strange an issue
           he full well)
       Had learned, who scooped into a votive cell
       Yon rock impending from the shaggy steep
       That he in hermit's weeds therein might dwell
       For ever bound
       To the lone river's heart-controuling (spirit-soothing) sound (To one
           deep solemn)
       Why, let these words to simple Listeners tell. MS.1
       That voice by night with healing power can creep
       Into the human heart or mix with sleep,
       As knew of yore the hermit in his cell
       Scooped out from rocky steep
       As all with gratitude can tell
       Who at this day mid Cumbrian mountains dwell. MS.2
11 breast] heart MS.

For kindly issues—as through every clime
Was felt near murmuring brooks in earliest time;
As, at this day, the rudest swains who dwell   15
Where torrents roar, or hear the tinkling knell
Of water-breaks, with grateful heart could tell.

XXXIII
THOUGHTS ON THE SEASONS
[Composed 1829.—Published 1835.]

FLATTERED with promise of escape
    From every hurtful blast,
Spring takes, O sprightly May! thy shape,
    Her loveliest and her last.

Less fair is summer riding high   5
    In fierce solstitial power,
Less fair than when a lenient sky
    Brings on her parting hour.

When earth repays with golden sheaves
    The labours of the plough,   10
And ripening fruits and forest leaves
    All brighten on the bough;

What pensive beauty autumn shows,
    Before she hears the sound
Of winter rushing in, to close   15
    The emblematic round!

Such be our Spring, our Summer such;
    So may our Autumn blend
With hoary Winter, and Life touch,
    Through heaven-born hope, her end!   20

XXXIV
TO —

UPON THE BIRTH OF HER FIRST-BORN CHILD, MARCH, 1833

[Composed March, 1833.—Published 1835.]

"Tum porro puer, ut saevis projectus ab undis
Navita, nudus humi jacet," &c.—LUCRETIUS.

LIKE a shipwreck'd Sailor tost
By rough waves on a perilous coast,
Lies the Babe, in helplessness

XXXIII. THOUGHTS 1850: THOUGHT 1835–45

And in tenderest nakedness,
Flung by labouring Nature forth   5
Upon the mercies of the earth.
Can its eyes beseech ?—no more
Than the hands are free to implore:
Voice but serves for one brief cry;
Plaint was it ? or prophecy   10
Of sorrow that will surely come ?
Omen of man's grievous doom!

But, O Mother! by the close
Duly granted to thy throes;
By the silent thanks, now tending   15
Incense-like to Heaven, descending
Now to mingle and to move
With the gush of earthly love,
As a debt to that frail Creature,
Instrument of struggling Nature   20
For the blissful calm, the peace
Known but to this *one* release—
Can the pitying spirit doubt
That for human-kind springs out
From the penalty a sense   25
Of more than mortal recompence ?

As a floating summer cloud,
Though of gorgeous drapery proud,
To the sun-burnt traveller,
Or the stooping labourer,   30
Oft-times makes its bounty known
By its shadow round him thrown;
So, by chequerings of sad cheer,
Heavenly Guardians, brooding near,
Of their presence tell—too bright   35
Haply for corporeal sight!
Ministers of grace divine
Feelingly their brows incline
O'er this seeming Castaway
Breathing, in the light of day,   40
Something like the faintest breath
That has power to baffle death—
Beautiful, while very weakness
Captivates like passive meekness.

And, sweet Mother! under warrant 45
Of the universal Parent,
Who repays in season due
Them who have, like thee, been true
To the filial chain let down
From his everlasting throne, 50
Angels hovering round thy couch,
With their softest whispers vouch,
That—whatever griefs may fret,
Cares entangle, sins beset,
This thy First-born, and with tears 55
Stain her cheek in future years—
Heavenly succour, not denied
To the babe, whate'er betide,
Will to the woman be supplied!

Mother! blest be thy calm ease; 60
Blest the starry promises,—
And the firmament benign
Hallowed be it, where they shine!
Yes, for them whose souls have scope
Ample for a wingèd hope, 65
And can earthward bend an ear
For needful listening, pledge is here,
That, if thy new-born Charge shall tread
In thy footsteps, and be led
By that other Guide, whose light 70
Of manly virtues, mildly bright,
Gave him first the wished-for part
In thy gentle virgin heart;
Then, amid the storms of life
Presignified by that dread strife 75
Whence ye have escaped together,
She may look for serene weather;
In all trials sure to find
Comfort for a faithful mind;
Kindlier issues, holier rest, 80
Than even now await her prest,
Conscious Nursling, to thy breast!

XXXV
THE WARNING

A SEQUEL TO THE FOREGOING

[Composed 1833.—Published 1835.]

LIST, the winds of March are blowing;
Her ground-flowers shrink, afraid of showing
Their meek heads to the nipping air,
Which ye feel not, happy pair!
Sunk into a kindly sleep.   5
We, meanwhile, our hope will keep;
And if Time leagued with adverse Change
(Too busy fear!) shall cross its range,
Whatsoever check they bring,
Anxious duty hindering,   10
To like hope our prayers will cling.

Thus, while the ruminating spirit feeds
Upon the events of home as life proceeds,
Affections pure and holy in their source
Gain a fresh impulse, run a livelier course;   15
Hopes that within the Father's heart prevail,
Are in the experienced Grandsire's slow to fail;
And if the harp pleased his gay youth, it rings
To his grave touch with no unready strings,
While thoughts press on, and feelings overflow,   20
And quick words round him fall like flakes of snow.

Thanks to the Powers that yet maintain their sway,
And have renewed the tributary Lay,
Truths of the heart flock in with eager pace,
And FANCY greets them with a fond embrace;   25
Swift as the rising sun his beams extends
She shoots the tidings forth to distant friends;
Their gifts she hails (deemed precious, as they prove
For the unconscious Babe so prompt a love!)—
But from this peaceful centre of delight   30
Vague sympathies have urged her to take flight:
Rapt into upper regions, like the bee

XXXV. 11 like] that C   13 *so* 1837: Upon each home-event   1835
23 Lay,] Lay. 1835 *etc.*   29 so prompt a 1843: an unbelated 1835-7:
so prompt to   1840 *and* C
31/2 She rivals the fleet Swallow, making rings
    In the smooth lake where'er he dips his wings;   1835

That sucks from mountain heath her honey fee,
Or, like the warbling lark intent to shroud
His head in sunbeams or a bowery cloud,   35
She soars—and here and there her pinions rest
On proud towers, like this humble cottage, blest
With a new visitant, an infant guest—
Towers where red streamers flout the breezy sky
In pomp foreseen by her creative eye,   40
When feasts shall crowd the hall, and steeple bells
Glad proclamation make, and heights and dells
Catch the blithe music as it sinks and swells,
And harboured ships, whose pride is on the sea,
Shall hoist their topmost flags in sign of glee,   45
Honouring the hope of noble ancestry.

But who (though neither reckoning ills assigned
By Nature, nor reviewing in the mind
The track that was, and is, and must be, worn
With weary feet by all of woman born)—   50
Shall *now* by such a gift with joy be moved,
Nor feel the fulness of that joy reproved ?
Not He, whose last faint memory will command
The truth that Britain was his native land ;
Whose infant soul was tutored to confide   55
In the cleansed faith for which her martyrs died ;
Whose boyish ear the voice of her renown
With rapture thrilled ; whose Youth revered the crown
Of Saxon liberty that Alfred wore,
Alfred, dear Babe, thy great Progenitor!   60
—Not He, who from her mellowed practice drew
His social sense of just, and fair, and true ;
And saw, thereafter, on the soil of France
Rash Polity begin her maniac dance,
Foundations broken up, the deeps run wild,   65
Nor grieved to see (himself not unbeguiled)—
Woke from the dream, the dreamer to upbraid,
And learn how sanguine expectations fade
When novel trusts by folly are betrayed,—
To see Presumption, turning pale, refrain   70
From further havoc, but repent in vain,—

43 and   1837: or   1835

Good aims lie down, and perish in the road
Where guilt had urged them on with ceaseless goad,
Proofs thickening round her that on public ends
Domestic virtue vitally depends,   75
That civic strife can turn the happiest hearth
Into a grievous sore of self-tormenting earth.

Can such a One, dear Babe! though glad and proud
To welcome thee, repel the fears that crowd
Into his English breast, and spare to quake   80
Less for his own than for thy innocent sake?
Too late—or, should the providence of God
Lead, through dark ways by sin and sorrow trod,
Justice and peace to a secure abode,
Too soon—thou com'st into this breathing world;   85
Ensigns of mimic outrage are unfurled.
Who shall preserve or prop the tottering Realm?
What hand suffice to govern the state-helm?
If, in the aims of men, the surest test
Of good or bad (whate'er be sought for or profest)   90
Lie in the means required, or ways ordained,
For compassing the end, else never gained;
Yet governors and govern'd both are blind
To this plain truth, or fling it to the wind;
If to expedience principle must bow;   95
Past, future, shrinking up beneath the incumbent Now;
If cowardly concession still must feed

74–5 *so* 1840: Till undiscriminating Ruin swept
                    The Land, and Wrong perpetual vigil kept;
                    With proof before her that *etc.*   1835–7
76–7 1840: *not in* 1835, 1837:
                    And civic strife, by hourly calling forth
                    Mutual despite can turn the happiest hearth
                 ⎰ (Thanks to the coming phrase) into a hell on earth
                 ⎱ Into a rankling sore of self-tormented earth   C
81 *so* 1840: Not for his own, but   1835–7
82–4 Too late or sent too early, for fast bound
        To endless cycle good and ill turn round   MS.
83 dark   1840: blind   1835–7
88 How save the good old Ship whose luckless helm
88/9 A Pilot grasps that plays the tyrant's part
        Storm raising after storm with treacherous art
        If to confound the remnant of the crew
        Who yet are sane in mind in spirit true, MS.

The thirst for power in men who ne'er concede;
Nor turn aside, unless to shape a way
For domination at some riper day;   100
If generous Loyalty must stand in awe
Of subtle Treason, in his mask of law,
Or with bravado insolent and hard,
Provoking punishment, to win reward;
If office help the factious to conspire,   105
And they who *should* extinguish, fan the fire—
Then, will the sceptre be a straw, the crown
Sit loosely, like the thistle's crest of down;
To be blown off at will, by Power that spares it
In cunning patience, from the head that wears it.   110

Lost people, trained to theoretic feud!
Lost above all, ye labouring multitude!
Bewildered whether ye, by slanderous tongues
Deceived, mistake calamities for wrongs;
And over fancied usurpations brood,   115
Oft snapping at revenge in sullen mood;
Or, from long stress of real injuries fly
To desperation for a remedy;
In bursts of outrage spread your judgments wide,
And to your wrath cry out, "Be thou our guide;"   120
Or, bound by oaths, come forth to tread earth's floor
In marshalled thousands, darkening street and moor
With the worst shape mock-patience ever wore;
Or, to the giddy top of self-esteem
By Flatterers carried, mount into a dream   125
Of boundless suffrage, at whose sage behest
Justice shall rule, disorder be supprest,
And every man sit down as Plenty's Guest!
—O for a bridle bitted with remorse
To stop your Leaders in their headstrong course!   130
Oh may the Almighty scatter with His grace
These mists, and lead you to a safer place,
By paths no human wisdom can foretrace!
May He pour round you, from worlds far above
Man's feverish passions, His pure light of love,   135
That quietly restores the natural mien
To hope, and makes truth willing to be seen!

102 in 1837: with 1835
917.17 IV   I

Else shall your blood-stained hands in frenzy reap
Fields gaily sown when promises were cheap.—
Why is the Past belied with wicked art,   140
The Future made to play so false a part,
Among a people famed for strength of mind,
Foremost in freedom, noblest of mankind ?
We act as if we joyed in the sad tune
Storms make in rising, valued in the moon   145
Nought but her changes. Thus, ungrateful Nation!
If thou persist, and, scorning moderation,
Spread for thyself the snares of tribulation,
Whom, then, shall meekness guard ? What saving skill
Lie in forbearance, strength in standing still ?   150
—Soon shall the widow (for the speed of Time
Nought equals when the hours are winged with crime)
Widow, or wife, implore on tremulous knee,
From him who judged her lord, a like decree ;
The skies will weep o'er old men desolate :   155
Ye little-ones! Earth shudders at your fate,
Outcasts and homeless orphans——

But turn, my Soul, and from the sleeping pair
Learn thou the beauty of omniscient care!
Be strong in faith, bid anxious thoughts lie still ;   160
Seek for the good and cherish it—the ill
Oppose, or bear with a submissive will.

XXXVI

[Composed Dec. 5, 1832.—Published 1835.]

IF this great world of joy and pain
    Revolve in one sure track ;
If freedom, set, will rise again,
    And virtue, flown, come back ;
Woe to the purblind crew who fill   5
    The heart with each day's care ;
Nor gain, from past or future, skill
    To bear, and to forbear!

141–2 Why plays Futurity this shameless part
        To cheat MS.
XXXVI. 7 gain] learn MS.

XXXVII
THE LABOURER'S NOON-DAY HYMN
[Composed 1834.—Published 1835.]

Up to the throne of God is borne
The voice of praise at early morn,
And he accepts the punctual hymn
Sung as the light of day grows dim.

Nor will he turn his ear aside   5
From holy offerings at noontide.
Then here reposing let us raise
A song of gratitude and praise.

What though our burthen be not light,
We need not toil from morn to night;   10
The respite of the mid-day hour
Is in the thankful Creature's power.

Blest are the moments, doubly blest,
That, drawn from this one hour of rest,
Are with a ready heart bestowed   15
Upon the service of our God!

Each field is then a hallowed spot,
An altar is in each man's cot,
A church in every grove that spreads
Its living roof above our heads.   20

Look up to Heaven! the industrious Sun
Already half his race hath run;
He cannot halt nor go astray,
But our immortal Spirits may.

Lord! since his rising in the East,   25
If we have faltered or transgressed,
Guide, from thy love's abundant source,
What yet remains of this day's course:

Help with thy grace, through life's short day,
Our upward and our downward way;   30
And glorify for us the west,
Where we shall sink to final rest.

XXXVII. 17 *so* 1845: Why should we crave a   1835-43

XXXVIII
ODE

COMPOSED ON MAY MORNING

[Composed 1826.—Published 1835.]

WHILE from the purpling east departs
    The star that led the dawn,
Blithe Flora from her couch upstarts,
    For May is on the lawn.
A quickening hope, a freshening glee,   5
    Foreran the expected Power,
Whose first-drawn breath, from bush and tree,
    Shakes off that pearly shower.

All Nature welcomes Her whose sway
    Tempers the year's extremes;   10
Who scattereth lustres o'er noon-day,
    Like morning's dewy gleams;
While mellow warble, sprightly trill,
    The tremulous heart excite;
And hums the balmy air to still   15
    The balance of delight.

Time was, blest Power! when youths and maids
    At peep of dawn would rise,
And wander forth, in forest glades
    Thy birth to solemnize.   20
Though mute the song—to grace the rite
    Untouched the hawthorn bough,
Thy Spirit triumphs o'er the slight;
    Man changes, but not Thou!

Thy feathered Lieges bill and wings   25
    In love's disport employ;
Warmed by thy influence, creeping things
    Awake to silent joy:
Queen art thou still for each gay plant

XXXVIII. 8/9 *Here follows* XXXIX 17–24   MS.
9–11 What month can rival thee, sweet May,
    Tempering . . . And scattering . . .   MS.
11 And breathes a freshness o'er MS. 1   15 And a soothing hum prevails.
MS. 1   17 blest Power! when] when courtly MS.   18 peep] blush MSS.
19 in forest] blest Power! in   MS.

Where the slim wild deer roves; 30
And served in depths where fishes haunt
   Their own mysterious groves.

Cloud-piercing peak, and trackless heath,
   Instinctive homage pay;
Nor wants the dim-lit cave a wreath 35
   To honour thee, sweet May!
Where cities fanned by thy brisk airs
   Behold a smokeless sky,
Their puniest flower-pot-nursling dares
   To open a bright eye. 40

And if, on this thy natal morn,
   The pole, from which thy name
Hath not departed, stands forlorn
   Of song and dance and game;
Still from the village-green a vow 45
   Aspires to thee addrest,
Wherever peace is on the brow,
   Or love within the breast.

Yes! where Love nestles thou canst teach
   The soul to love the more; 50
Hearts also shall thy lessons reach
   That never loved before.
Stript is the haughty one of pride,
   The bashful freed from fear,
While rising, like the ocean-tide, 55
   In flows the joyous year.

Hush, feeble lyre! weak words refuse
   The service to prolong!
To yon exulting thrush the Muse
   Entrusts the imperfect song; 60
His voice shall chant, in accents clear,
   Throughout the live-long day,
Till the first silver star appear,
   The sovereignty of May.

33 trackless] desart MS.   34 homage] tribute MSS.
37–40 But most some little favorite nook
    That our own hands have drest
    Upon thy train delights to look
    And seems to love thee best. MSS. *v. To May XXXIX.* 45–8 *infra*
41 And what if on thy birthday MS.   53 The haughty Ones are stripped
MS.

XXXIX
TO MAY

[Composed 1826–34.—Published 1835.]

THOUGH many suns have risen and set
    Since thou, blithe May, wert born,
And Bards, who hailed thee, may forget
    Thy gifts, thy beauty scorn;
There are who to a birthday strain   5
    Confine not harp and voice,
But evermore throughout thy reign
    Are grateful and rejoice!

Delicious odours! music sweet,
    Too sweet to pass away!   10
Oh for a deathless song to meet
    The soul's desire—a lay
That, when a thousand years are told,
    Should praise thee, genial Power!
Through summer heat, autumnal cold,   15
    And winter's dreariest hour.

Earth, sea, thy presence feel—nor less,
    If yon ethereal blue
With its soft smile the truth express,
    The heavens have felt it too.   20
The inmost heart of man if glad
    Partakes a livelier cheer;
And eyes that cannot but be sad
    Let fall a brightened tear.

Since thy return, through days and weeks   25
    Of hope that grew by stealth,
How many wan and faded cheeks
    Have kindled into health!
The Old, by thee revived, have said,
    "Another year is ours;"   30
And wayworn Wanderers, poorly fed,
    Have smiled upon thy flowers.

XXXIX. 1 many] twelve bright MS.   5 birthday] natal MS.   11
meet] greet MS.   12 The soul's desire] Thy blest return MS.   17–
24 *not in* MS.   31–2 Perhaps the [And many a] poor man wanting
bread Has MS.

Who tripping lisps a merry song
   Amid his playful peers ?
The tender Infant who was long   35
   A prisoner of fond fears ;
But now, when every sharp-edged blast
   Is quiet in its sheath,
His Mother leaves him free to taste
   Earth's sweetness in thy breath.   40

Thy help is with the weed that creeps
   Along the humblest ground ;
No cliff so bare but on its steeps
   Thy favours may be found ;
But most on some peculiar nook   45
   That our own hands have drest,
Thou and thy train are proud to look,
   And seem to love it best.

And yet how pleased we wander forth
   When May is whispering, "Come !   50
Choose from the bowers of virgin earth
   The happiest for your home ;
Heaven's bounteous love through me is spread
   From sunshine, clouds, winds, waves,
Drops on the mouldering turret's head,   55
   And on your turf-clad graves !"

Such greeting heard, away with sighs
   For lilies that must fade,
Or "the rathe primrose as it dies
   Forsaken" in the shade !   60
Vernal fruitions and desires
   Are linked in endless chase ;
While, as one kindly growth retires,
   Another takes its place.

And what if thou, sweet May, hast known   65
   Mishap by worm and blight ;
If expectations newly blown
   Have perished in thy sight ;

51-2 In every bower of . . . Is built a happy   MS.   65-6 And if, sweet
May, thy hopes have known Mishap from   MS.

If loves and joys, while up they sprung,
    Were caught as in a snare ;   70
Such is the lot of all the young,
    However bright and fair.

Lo! Streams that April could not check
    Are patient of thy rule ;
Gurgling in foamy water-break,   75
    Loitering in glassy pool:
By thee, thee only, could be sent
    Such gentle mists as glide,
Curling with unconfirmed intent,
    On that green mountain's side.   80

How delicate the leafy veil
    Through which yon house of God
Gleams 'mid the peace of this deep dale
    By few but shepherds trod!
And lowly huts, near beaten ways,   85
    No sooner stand attired
In thy fresh wreaths, than they for praise
    Peep forth, and are admired.

Season of fancy and of hope,
    Permit not for one hour   90
A blossom from thy crown to drop,
    Nor add to it a flower!
Keep, lovely May, as if by touch
    Of self-restraining art,
This modest charm of not too much,   95
    Part seen, imagined part!

XL
LINES

SUGGESTED BY A PORTRAIT PROM THE PENCIL OF F. STONE

[Composed 1834.—Published 1835.]

BEGUILED into forgetfulness of care
Due to the day's unfinished task ; of pen
Or book regardless, and of that fair scene

72 The doom of all the   MS.   81 the] a   MS.   82 Through which
yon] To grace (Half hides) the   MS.   83 Hast thou renewed (Thy
network wov'n) in   MS.   93 So perfect now is that fine touch   MS.

In Nature's prodigality displayed
Before my window, oftentimes and long   5
I gaze upon a Portrait whose mild gleam
Of beauty never ceases to enrich
The common light; whose stillness charms the air,
Or seems to charm it, into like repose;
Whose silence, for the pleasure of the ear,   10
Surpasses sweetest music. There she sits
With emblematic purity attired
In a white vest, white as her marble neck
Is, and the pillar of the throat would be
But for the shadow by the drooping chin   15
Cast into that recess—the tender shade,
The shade and light, both there and everywhere,
And through the very atmosphere she breathes,
Broad, clear, and toned harmoniously, with skill
That might from nature have been learnt in the hour   20
When the lone shepherd sees the morning spread
Upon the mountains. Look at her, whoe'er
Thou be that, kindling with a poet's soul,
Hast loved the painter's true Promethean craft
Intensely—from Imagination take   25
The treasure,—what mine eyes behold see thou,
Even though the Atlantic ocean roll between.

A silver line, that runs from brow to crown
And in the middle parts the braided hair,
Just serves to show how delicate a soil   30
The golden harvest grows in; and those eyes,
Soft and capacious as a cloudless sky
Whose azure depth their colour emulates,
Must needs be conversant with upward looks,
Prayer's voiceless service; but now, seeking nought   35
And shunning nought, their own peculiar life
Of motion they renounce, and with the head
Partake its inclination towards earth
In humble grace, and quiet pensiveness
Caught at the point where it stops short of sadness.   40

Offspring of soul-bewitching Art, make me
Thy confidant! say, whence derived that air
Of calm abstraction? Can the ruling thought

23-4 Thou be that lov'st the Painter's subtle craft   MS.

Be with some lover far away, or one
Crossed by misfortune, or of doubted faith ?   45
Inapt conjecture! Childhood here, a moon
Crescent in simple loveliness serene,
Has but approached the gates of womanhood,
Not entered them; her heart is yet unpierced
By the blind Archer-god; her fancy free: 50
The fount of feeling, if unsought elsewhere,
Will not be found.
            Her right hand, as it lies
Across the slender wrist of the left arm
Upon her lap reposing, holds—but mark
How slackly, for the absent mind permits   55
No firmer grasp—a little wild-flower, joined
As in a posy, with a few pale ears
Of yellowing corn, the same that overtopped
And in their common birthplace sheltered it
Till they were plucked together; a blue flower   60
Called by the thrifty husbandman a weed;
But Ceres, in her garland, might have worn
That ornament, unblamed. The floweret, held
In scarcely conscious fingers, was, she knows,
(Her Father told her so) in youth's gay dawn   65
Her Mother's favourite; and the orphan Girl,
In her own dawn—a dawn less gay and bright,
Loves it, while there in solitary peace
She sits, for that departed Mother's sake.
—Not from a source less sacred is derived   70
(Surely I do not err) that pensive air
Of calm abstraction through the face diffused
And the whole person.
            Words have something told
More than the pencil can, and verily
More than is needed, but the precious Art   75
Forgives their interference—Art divine,
That both creates and fixes, in despite
Of Death and Time, the marvels it hath wrought.

Strange contrasts have we in this world of ours!
That posture, and the look of filial love   80
Thinking of past and gone, with what is left
Dearly united, might be swept away

From this fair Portrait's fleshly Archetype,
Even by an innocent fancy's slightest freak
Banished, nor ever, haply, be restored   85
To their lost place, or meet in harmony
So exquisite; but *here* do they abide,
Enshrined for ages. Is not then the Art
Godlike, a humble branch of the divine,
In visible quest of immortality,   90
Stretched forth with trembling hope ?—In every realm,
From high Gibraltar to Siberian plains,
Thousands, in each variety of tongue
That Europe knows, would echo this appeal;
One above all, a Monk who waits on God   95
In the magnific Convent built of yore
To sanctify the Escurial palace. He—
Guiding, from cell to cell and room to room,
A British Painter (eminent for truth
In character, and depth of feeling, shown   100
By labours that have touched the hearts of kings,
And are endeared to simple cottagers)—
Came, in that service, to a glorious work,
Our Lord's Last Supper, beautiful as when first
The appropriate Picture, fresh from Titian's hand,   105
Graced the Refectory: and there, while both
Stood with eyes fixed upon that masterpiece,
The hoary Father in the Stranger's ear
Breathed out these words:—"Here daily do we sit,
Thanks given to God for daily bread, and here   110
Pondering the mischiefs of these restless times,
And thinking of my Brethren, dead, dispersed,
Or changed and changing, I not seldom gaze
Upon this solemn Company unmoved
By shock of circumstance, or lapse of years,   115
Until I cannot but believe that they—
They are in truth the Substance, we the Shadows."

So spake the mild Jeronymite, his griefs
Melting away within him like a dream
Ere he had ceased to gaze, perhaps to speak: 120
And I, grown old, but in a happier land,

103 *so* 1837: Left not unvisited a MS., 1835   106-7 and . . . master-
piece] There while the eyes Of both upon that Masterpiece were fixed MS.

Domestic Portrait! have to verse consigned
In thy calm presence those heart-moving words:
Words that can soothe, more than they agitate;
Whose spirit, like the angel that went down   125
Into Bethesda's pool, with healing virtue
Informs the fountain in the human breast
Which by the visitation was disturbed.
——But why this stealing tear? Companion mute,
On thee I look, not sorrowing; fare thee well,   130
My Song's Inspirer, once again farewell![1]

XLI

THE FOREGOING SUBJECT RESUMED

[Composed 1834.—Published 1835.]

AMONG a grave fraternity of Monks,
For One, but surely not for One alone,
Triumphs, in that great work, the Painter's skill,
Humbling the body, to exalt the soul;
Yet representing, amid wreck and wrong   5
And dissolution and decay, the warm
And breathing life of flesh, as if already
Clothed with impassive majesty, and graced
With no mean earnest of a heritage
Assigned to it in future worlds. Thou, too,   10
With thy memorial flower, meek Portraiture!
From whose serene companionship I passed
Pursued by thoughts that haunt me still; thou also—
Though but a simple object, into light
Called forth by those affections that endear   15
Thy private hearth; though keeping thy sole seat
In singleness, and little tried by time,
Creation, as it were, of yesterday—

[1] The pile of buildings composing the palace and convent of San Lorenzo has, in common usage, lost its proper name in that of the *Escurial*, a village at the foot of the hill upon which the splendid edifice, built by Philip the Second, stands. It need scarcely be added that Wilkie is the painter alluded to.

124–30 *Added to* MS. *on separate sheet*   128 Which 1837: That 1835
131 And now, my Song's Inspirer, fare thee well. MS.
XLI. 4 MS. *omits*   5 Yet] By MS.   8–9 Clothed with a portion
of the inheritance MS.

With a congenial function art endued
For each and all of us, together joined   20
In course of nature under a low roof
By charities and duties that proceed
Out of the bosom of a wiser vow.
To a like salutary sense of awe
Or sacred wonder, growing with the power   25
Of meditation that attempts to weigh,
In faithful scales, things and their opposites,
Can thy enduring quiet gently raise
A household small and sensitive,—whose love,
Dependent as in part its blessings are   30
Upon frail ties dissolving or dissolved
On earth, will be revived, we trust, in heaven.[1]

XLII

[Composed August, 1844.—Published 1845.]

So fair, so sweet, withal so sensitive,
Would that the little Flowers were born to live,
Conscious of half the pleasure which they give;

That to this mountain-daisy's self were known
The beauty of its star-shaped shadow, thrown   5
On the smooth surface of this naked stone!

And what if hence a bold desire should mount
High as the Sun, that he could take account
Of all that issues from his glorious fount!

So might he ken how by his sovereign aid   10
These delicate companionships are made;
And how he rules the pomp of light and shade;

---

[1] In the class entitled "Musings", in Mr. Southey's Minor Poems, is one upon his own miniature Picture, taken in childhood, and another upon a landscape painted by Gaspar Poussin. It is possible that every word of the above verses, though similar in subject, might have been written had the author been unacquainted with those beautiful effusions of poetic sentiment. But, for his own satisfaction, he must be allowed thus publicly to acknowledge the pleasure those two Poems of his Friend have given him, and the grateful influence they have upon his mind as often as he reads them or thinks of them.

XLII. C *heads the poem* Suggested at noon on Loughrigg Fell *and alternatively* To the noontide Sun   1 fair and   C   6 Its sole companion on   C

And were the Sister-power that shines by night
So privileged, what a countenance of delight
Would through the clouds break forth on human sight!   15

Fond fancies! wheresoe'er shall turn thine eye
On earth, air, ocean, or the starry sky,
Converse with Nature in pure sympathy;

All vain desires, all lawless wishes quelled,
Be Thou to love and praise alike impelled,   20
Whatever boon is granted or withheld.

XLIII

UPON SEEING A COLOURED DRAWING OF THE BIRD OF PARADISE IN AN ALBUM

[Composed 1835–6.—Published 1837.]

WHO rashly strove thy Image to portray?
Thou buoyant minion of the tropic air;
How could he think of the live creature—gay
With a divinity of colours, drest
In all her brightness, from the dancing crest   5
Far as the last gleam of the filmy train
Extended and extending to sustain
The motions that it graces—and forbear
To drop his pencil! Flowers of every clime
Depicted on these pages smile at time;   10
And gorgeous insects copied with nice care
Are here, and likenesses of many a shell
Tossed ashore by restless waves,
Or in the diver's grasp fetched up from caves
Where sea-nymphs might be proud to dwell: 15
But whose rash hand (again I ask) could dare,
'Mid casual tokens and promiscuous shows,
To circumscribe this Shape in fixed repose;
Could imitate for indolent survey,

XLII. 16 turn] range MS.
16–17 Fond fancies! bred between a smile and sigh
　　　Do thou more wise, where'er thou turn'st thine eye   C
　　　(. . . wheresoe'er shall range thine eye
　　　Among the forms and powers of earth or sky)   C
19–20 A thankful heart, all lawless wishes quell'd,
　　　To joy, to praise, to love alike compell'd,   C

Perhaps for touch profane,   20
Plumes that might catch, but cannot keep, a stain;
And, with cloud-streaks lightest and loftiest, share
The sun's first greeting, his last farewell ray!

　Resplendent Wanderer! followed with glad eyes
Where'er her course; mysterious Bird!   25
To whom, by wondering Fancy stirred,
Eastern Islanders have given
A holy name—the Bird of Heaven!
And even a title higher still,
The Bird of God! whose blessed will   30
She seems performing as she flies
Over the earth and through the skies
In never-wearied search of Paradise—
Region that crowns her beauty with the name
She bears for *us*—for us how blest,   35
How happy at all seasons, could like aim
Uphold our Spirits urged to kindred flight
On wings that fear no glance of God's pure sight,
No tempest from his breath, their promised rest
Seeking with indefatigable quest   40
Above a world that deems itself most wise
When most enslaved by gross realities!

SONNETS
DEDICATED TO LIBERTY AND ORDER
I

COMPOSED AFTER READING A NEWSPAPER OF THE DAY
[Composed 1831.—Published 1835.]

"PEOPLE! your chains are severing link by link;
Soon shall the Rich be levelled down—the Poor
Meet them half way." Vain boast! for These, the more
They thus would rise, must low and lower sink
Till, by repentance stung, they fear to think;   5
While all lie prostrate, save the tyrant few
Bent in quick turns each other to undo,
And mix the poison, they themselves must drink.
Mistrust thyself, vain Country! cease to cry,
"Knowledge will save me from the threatened woe." 10
For, if than other rash ones more thou know,
Yet on presumptuous wing as far would fly
Above thy knowledge as they dared to go,
Thou wilt provoke a heavier penalty.

II

UPON THE LATE GENERAL FAST. MARCH, 1832
[Composed 1832.—Published 1832.]

RELUCTANT call it was; the rite delayed;
And in the Senate some there were who doffed
The last of their humanity, and scoffed
At providential judgments, undismayed
By their own daring. But the People prayed   5
As with one voice; their flinty heart grew soft
With penitential sorrow, and aloft
Their spirit mounted, crying, "God us aid!"
Oh that with aspirations more intense,
Chastised by self-abasement more profound,   10
This People, once so happy, so renowned
For liberty, would seek from God defence
Against far heavier ill, the pestilence
Of revolution, impiously unbound!

I. 9 Proud country fear the worst, though millions cry MS   12 And
yet from change to change MS.
II. 4 judgments 1838: judgment 1832–7   9–10 *so* 1837: with soul-
aspirings ... And heart-humiliations 1832   11 once 1837: long 1832

III

[Composed 1838.—Published: Sonnet-vol. of 1838.]

SAID Secrecy to Cowardice and Fraud,
Falsehood and Treachery, in close council met,
Deep under ground, in Pluto's cabinet,
"The frost of England's pride will soon be thawed;
Hooded the open brow that overawed   5
Our schemes; the faith and honour, never yet
By us with hope encountered, be upset;—
For once I burst my bands, and cry, applaud!"
Then whispered she, "The Bill is carrying out!"
They heard, and, starting up, the Brood of Night   10
Clapped hands, and shook with glee their matted locks;
All Powers and Places that abhor the light .
Joined in the transport, echoed back their shout,
Hurrah for——, hugging his ballot-box!

IV

[Composed 1838.—Published: Sonnet-vol. of 1838.]

BLEST Statesman He, whose Mind's unselfish will
Leaves him at ease among grand thoughts: whose eye
Sees that, apart from magnanimity,
Wisdom exists not; nor the humbler skill
Of Prudence, disentangling good and ill   5
With patient care. What tho' assaults run high,
They daunt not him who holds his ministry,
Resolute, at all hazards, to fulfil
Its duties;—prompt to move, but firm to wait,—
Knowing, things rashly sought are rarely found;   10
That, for the functions of an ancient State—
Strong by her charters, free because imbound,
Servant of Providence, not slave of Fate—
Perilous is sweeping change, all chance unsound.

III. 14 ——] Grote MS.
IV. 2 him 1842: her C and 1838   6 though 1838: if C   11 for
1838: in   14 "All change is perilous and all chance unsound" C

V

IN ALLUSION TO VARIOUS RECENT HISTORIES AND NOTICES OF
THE FRENCH REVOLUTION

[Composed ?.—Published: vol. of 1842.]

PORTENTOUS change when History can appear
As the cool Advocate of foul device;
Reckless audacity extol, and jeer
At consciences perplexed with scruples nice!
They who bewail not, must abhor, the sneer   5
Born of Conceit, Power's blind Idolater;
Or haply sprung from vaunting Cowardice
Betrayed by mockery of holy fear.
Hath it not long been said the wrath of Man
Works not the righteousness of God? Oh bend,   10
Bend, ye Perverse! to judgments from on High,
Laws that lay under Heaven's perpetual ban
All principles of action that transcend
The sacred limits of humanity.

VI

CONTINUED

[Composed ?.—Published: vol. of 1842.]

WHO ponders National events shall find
An awful balancing of loss and gain,
Joy based on sorrow, good with ill combined,
And proud deliverance issuing out of pain
And direful throes; as if the All-ruling Mind,   5
With whose perfection it consists to ordain
Volcanic burst, earthquake, and hurricane,
Dealt in like sort with feeble human kind
By laws immutable. But woe for him
Who thus deceived shall lend an eager hand   10
To social havoc. Is not Conscience ours,
And Truth, whose eye guilt only can make dim;
And Will, whose office, by divine command,
Is to control and check disordered Powers?

V. 1–2   can leer
         With prurient levity on foul device MS.

VII

CONCLUDED

[Composed ?.—Published: vol. of 1842.]

LONG-FAVOURED England! be not thou misled
By monstrous theories of alien growth,
Lest alien frenzy seize thee, waxing wroth,
Self-smitten till thy garments reek dyed red
With thy own blood, which tears in torrents shed   5
Fail to wash out, tears flowing ere thy troth
Be plighted, not to ease but sullen sloth,
Or wan despair—the ghost of false hope fled
Into a shameful grave. Among thy youth,
My Country! if such warning be held dear,   10
Then shall a Veteran's heart be thrilled with joy,
One who would gather from eternal truth,
For time and season, rules that work to cheer—
Not scourge, to save the People—not destroy.

VIII

[Composed 1839.—Published: vol. of 1842.]

MEN of the Western World! in Fate's dark book
Whence these opprobrious leaves of dire portent?
Think ye your British Ancestors forsook
Their native Land, for outrage provident;
From unsubmissive necks the bridle shook   5
To give, in their Descendants, freer vent
And wider range to passions turbulent,
To mutual tyranny a deadlier look?
Nay, said a voice, soft as the south wind's breath,
Dive through the stormy surface of the flood   10
To the great current flowing underneath;
Explore the countless springs of silent good;
So shall the truth be better understood,
And thy grieved Spirit brighten strong in faith.

VII. 9–11   If but one youth
          Thy Son, my Country! hold this warning dear
             . . . an old Man's heart MS.
VIII. 4 native Land] narrow Isle MS.   5 Think ye they fled
restraints they ill could brook MS.   9 voice more soft than Zephyr's
MS.   12 Explore] Think on MS. 1; Mark well MS. 2   13 be known
and understood MS.

IX

TO THE PENNSYLVANIANS

[Composed probably January or February, 1845.—Published 1845.]

DAYS undefiled by luxury or sloth,
Firm self-denial, manners grave and staid,
Rights equal, laws with cheerfulness obeyed,
Words that require no sanction from an oath,
And simple honesty a common growth—   5
This high repute, with bounteous Nature's aid,
Won confidence, now ruthlessly betrayed
At will, your power the measure of your troth!—
All who revere the memory of Penn
Grieve for the land on whose wild woods his name   10
Was fondly grafted with a virtuous aim,
Renounced, abandoned by degenerate Men
For state-dishonour black as ever came
To upper air from Mammon's loathsome den.

X

AT BOLOGNA, IN REMEMBRANCE OF THE LATE
INSURRECTIONS, 1837

I

[Composed probably 1837.—Published: vol. of 1842.]

AH why deceive ourselves! by no mere fit
Of sudden passion roused shall men attain
True freedom where for ages they have lain
Bound in a dark abominable pit,
With life's best sinews more and more unknit.   5
Here, there, a banded few who loathe the chain
May rise to break it: effort worse than vain
For thee, O great Italian nation, split
Into those jarring fractions.—Let thy scope
Be one fixed mind for all; thy rights approve   10
To thy own conscience gradually renewed;
Learn to make Time the father of wise Hope;
Then trust thy cause to the arm of Fortitude,
The light of Knowledge, and the warmth of Love.

X. 7 May strive to spurn MS.
9–10   Ere thou cope
          Uprisen, with baleful sway
corr. to   Thy first scope
          Be unity of mind MS.

XI

CONTINUED

II

[Composed probably 1837.—Published: vol. of 1842.]

HARD task! exclaim the undisciplined, to lean
On Patience coupled with such slow endeavour,
That long-lived servitude must last for ever,
Perish the grovelling few, who, prest between
Wrongs and the terror of redress, would wean   5
Millions from glorious aims. Our chains to sever
Let us break forth in tempest now or never!—
What, is there then no space for golden mean
And gradual progress?—Twilight leads to day,
And, even within the burning zones of earth,   10
The hastiest sunrise yields a temperate ray;
The softest breeze to fairest flowers gives birth:
Think not that Prudence dwells in dark abodes,
She scans the future with the eye of gods.

XII

CONCLUDED

III

[Composed probably 1837.—Published: vol. of 1842.]

As leaves are to the tree whereon they grow
And wither, every human generation
Is to the Being of a mighty nation,
Locked in our world's embrace through weal and woe;
Thought that should teach the zealot to forego   5
Rash schemes, to abjure all selfish agitation,
And seek through noiseless pains and moderation
The unblemished good they only can bestow.
Alas! with most, who weigh futurity
Against time present, passion holds the scales: 10
Hence equal ignorance of both prevails,
And nations sink; or, struggling to be free,
Are doomed to flounder on, like wounded whales
Tossed on the bosom of a stormy sea.

XIII

[Composed January or February, 1845.—Published 1845.]

YOUNG ENGLAND—what is then become of Old
Of dear Old England ? Think they she is dead,
Dead to the very name ? Presumption fed
On empty air! That name will keep its hold
In the true filial bosom's inmost fold   5
For ever.—The Spirit of Alfred, at the head
Of all who for her rights watch'd, toil'd and bled,
Knows that this prophecy is not too bold.
What—how! shall she submit in will and deed
To Beardless Boys—an imitative race,   10
The *servum pecus* of a Gallic breed ?
Dear Mother! if thou *must* thy steps retrace,
Go where at least meek Innocency dwells;
Let Babes and Sucklings be thy oracles.

XIV

[Composed ?.—Published: vol. of 1842.]

FEEL for the wrongs to universal ken
Daily exposed, woe that unshrouded lies;
And seek the Sufferer in his darkest den,
Whether conducted to the spot by sighs
And moanings, or he dwells (as if the wren   5
Taught him concealment) hidden from all eyes
In silence and the awful modesties
Of sorrow;—feel for all, as brother Men!
Rest not in hope want's icy chain to thaw
By casual boons and formal charities;   10
Learn to be just, just through impartial law;
Far as ye may, erect and equalise;
And, what ye cannot reach by statute, draw
Each from his fountain of self-sacrifice!

XIV. 9–10 *so* 1845: Feel for the Poor,—but not to still your qualms
                 By formal charity or dole of alms;   1842

SONNETS UPON THE PUNISHMENT OF DEATH

IN SERIES

[Composed 1839–40.—Published December, 1841 (*Quarterly Review*); vol. of 1842.]

I

SUGGESTED BY THE VIEW OF LANCASTER CASTLE (ON THE ROAD FROM THE SOUTH)

THIS Spot—at once unfolding sight so fair
Of sea and land, with yon grey towers that still
Rise up as if to lord it over air—
Might soothe in human breasts the sense of ill,
Or charm it out of memory; yea, might fill   5
The heart with joy and gratitude to God
For all his bounties upon man bestowed:
Why bears it then the name of "Weeping Hill"?
Thousands, as toward yon old Lancastrian Towers,
A prison's crown, along this way they pass'd   10
For lingering durance or quick death with shame,
From this bare eminence thereon have cast
Their first look—blinded as tears fell in showers
Shed on their chains; and hence that doleful name.

II

TENDERLY do we feel by Nature's law
For worst offenders: though the heart will heave
With indignation, deeply moved we grieve,
In afterthought, for Him who stood in awe
Neither of God nor man, and only saw,   5
Lost wretch, a horrible device enthroned
On proud temptations, till the victim groaned
Under the steel his hand had dared to draw.
But O, restrain compassion, if its course,
As oft befals, prevent or turn aside   10
Judgments and aims and acts whose higher source
Is sympathy with the unforewarned, who died
Blameless—with them that shuddered o'er his grave,
And all who from the law firm safety crave.

I. 10 pass'd] past   1842–50 *v.* note.

III

THE Roman Consul doomed his sons to die
Who had betrayed their country. The stern word
Afforded (may it through all time afford)
A theme for praise and admiration high.
Upon the surface of humanity   5
He rested not; its depths his mind explored;
He felt; but his parental bosom's lord
Was Duty,—Duty calmed his agony.
And some, we know, when they by wilful act
A single human life have wrongly taken,   10
Pass sentence on themselves, confess the fact,
And to atone for it, with soul unshaken
Kneel at the feet of Justice, and, for faith
Broken with all mankind, solicit death.

IV

Is *Death*, when evil against good has fought
With such fell mastery that a man may dare
By deeds the blackest purpose to lay bare—
Is Death, for one to that condition brought,
For him, or any one, the thing that ought   5
To be *most* dreaded? Lawgivers, beware,
Lest, capital pains remitting till ye spare
The murderer, ye, by sanction to that thought,
Seemingly given, debase the general mind;
Tempt the vague will tried standards to disown,   10
Nor only palpable restraints unbind,
But upon Honour's head disturb the crown,
Whose absolute rule permits not to withstand
In the weak love of life his least command.

III. 2 For treason to MS.   3 through all time] evermore MS.
4–6 A theme for general admiration high
    As just; the surface of humanity
    Deceived not him; MS.
8–14 Was reason; she had sat the cause to try
    And who could grieve if he whose wilful act
    A fellow creature's life has *etc.*
(*corr. to* Nor let us shrink from praise of one whose act
        With fixed aforethought malice life hath taken)
    Sitting himself in judgment of the fact
    Should be of all desire to live forsaken,
    (Pass sentence on himself with Soul unshaken)
    Yea, as a Being who has broken faith
    With the whole human race should covet (thirst for) death. MS.

V

Nᴏᴛ to the object specially designed,
Howe'er momentous in itself it be,
Good to promote or curb depravity,
Is the wise Legislator's view confined.
His Spirit, when most severe, is oft most kind;   5
As all Authority in earth depends
On Love and Fear, their several powers he blends,
Copying with awe the one Paternal mind.
Uncaught by processes in show humane,
He feels how far the act would derogate   10
From even the humblest functions of the State;
If she, self-shorn of Majesty, ordain
That never more shall hang upon her breath
The last alternative of Life or Death.

VI

Yᴇ brood of conscience—Spectres! that frequent
The bad man's restless walk, and haunt his bed—
Fiends in your aspect, yet beneficent
In act, as hovering Angels when they spread
Their wings to guard the unconscious Innocent—   5
Slow be the Statutes of the land to share
A laxity that could not but impair
Your power to punish crime, and so prevent.
And ye, Beliefs! coiled serpent-like about
The adage on all tongues, "Murder will out,"   10
How shall your ancient warnings work for good
In the full might they hitherto have shown,
If for deliberate shedder of man's blood
Survive not Judgment that requires his own?

VII

Bᴇғᴏʀᴇ the world had past her time of youth
While polity and discipline were weak,
The precept eye for eye, and tooth for tooth,
Came forth—a light, though but as of daybreak,
Strong as could then be borne. A Master meek   5
Proscribed the spirit fostered by that rule,

VII. 2 While yet the arm of polity was MS.   3 precept] maxim MS.
4–6 Came forth a glimmering (feeble) and imperfect streak
    The dawn of Justice. An Instructor meek
    And holy superseded the first rule;
corr. to Brought to mankind a better, purer

Patience *his* law, long-suffering *his* school,
And love the end, which all through peace must seek.
But lamentably do they err who strain
His mandates, given rash impulse to controul   10
And keep vindictive thirstings from the soul,
So far that, if consistent in their scheme,
They must forbid the State to inflict a pain,
Making of social order a mere dream.

VIII

Fɪᴛ retribution, by the moral code
Determined, lies beyond the State's embrace,
Yet, as she may, for each peculiar case
She plants well-measured terrors in the road
Of wrongful acts. Downward it is and broad,   5
And, the main fear once doomed to banishment,
Far oftener then, bad ushering worse event,
Blood would be spilt that in his dark abode
Crime might lie better hid. And, should the change
Take from the horror due to a foul deed,   10
Pursuit and evidence so far must fail,
And, guilt escaping, passion then might plead
In angry spirits for her old free range,
And the "wild justice of revenge" prevail.

VII. 8–14 But these Interpreters have yet to seek
        The Spirit, who, to the letter all too strict,
        Would place his blessed rules in domination
        Not only, as designed, o'er bursts of passion,
        And pains which passion's vengeance longs to inflict,
        But o'er the State's forbearance stretched to extremes
        Which for her stedfast reason are mere dreams. MS.1
9–14   . . . strain
        His mandates given to temper and control
        Private resentment, and to calm the soul
        Under all wrong, strain them to that extreme
        That would forbid the *State* to inflict a pain,
        Would make of social order a mere dream. MS.2
VIII. 1 by] to   MS.
2–9 Adjusted, ne'er was wisely thought the aim
        Of penal law; her humbler safer claim
        Is to plant obvious terrors in the road
        That points to guilty deeds. But is it trod?
        If fear were none of capital punishment
        The robber might give way to worse intent
        And blood be shed   MS.
10 Take from . . . foul] Abate . . . fatal MS.   11 so far must] must
oftener   MS.   13 In angry] With untaught MS.

IX

THOUGH to give timely warning and deter
Is one great aim of penalty, extend
Thy mental vision further and ascend
Far higher, else full surely shalt thou err.
What is a State? The wise behold in her   5
A creature born of time, that keeps one eye
Fixed on the statutes of Eternity,
To which her judgments reverently defer.
Speaking through Law's dispassionate voice the State
Endues her conscience with external life   10
And being, to preclude or quell the strife
Of individual will, to elevate
The grovelling mind, the erring to recal,
And fortify the moral sense of all.

X

OUR bodily life, some plead, that life the shrine
Of an immortal spirit, is a gift
So sacred, so informed with light divine,
That no tribunal, though most wise to sift
Deed and intent, should turn the Being adrift   5
Into that world where penitential tear
May not avail, nor prayer have for God's ear
A voice—that world whose veil no hand can lift
For earthly sight. "Eternity and Time,"
They urge, "have interwoven claims and rights   10
Not to be jeopardised through foulest crime:
The sentence rule by mercy's heaven-born lights."
Even so; but measuring not by finite sense
Infinite Power, perfect Intelligence.

XI

AH, think how one compelled for life to abide
Locked in a dungeon needs must eat the heart
Out of his own humanity, and part
With every hope that mutual cares provide;
And, should a less unnatural doom confide   5
In life-long exile on a savage coast,
Soon the relapsing penitent may boast

IX. 4 thou shalt   1842

Of yet more heinous guilt, with fiercer pride.
Hence thoughtful Mercy, Mercy sage and pure,
Sanctions the forfeiture that Law demands,   10
Leaving the final issue in *His* hands
Whose goodness knows no change, whose love is sure,
Who sees, foresees; who cannot judge amiss,
And wafts at will the contrite soul to bliss.

XII

SEE the Condemned alone within his cell
And prostrate at some moment when remorse
Stings to the quick, and, with resistless force,
Assaults the pride she strove in vain to quell.
Then mark him, him who could so long rebel,   5
The crime confessed, a kneeling Penitent
Before the Altar, where the Sacrament
Softens his heart, till from his eyes outwell
Tears of salvation. Welcome death! while Heaven
Does in this change exceedingly rejoice;   10
While yet the solemn heed the State hath given
Helps him to meet the last Tribunal's voice
In faith, which fresh offences, were he cast
On old temptations, might for ever blast.

XIII

CONCLUSION

YES, though He well may tremble at the sound
Of his own voice, who from the judgment-seat
Sends the pale Convict to his last retreat
In death; though Listeners shudder all around,
They know the dread requital's source profound;   5
Nor is, they feel, its wisdom obsolete—
(Would that it were!) the sacrifice unmeet
For Christian Faith. But hopeful signs abound;
The social rights of man breathe purer air;

XII. 1 alone within] recumbent in   MS.   2 And] Or   MS.   3 Hath
stung him, and, with more prevailing force   MS.   4 strove in vain] failed
at first   MS.
5–7 . . . kneeling when the Chapel-bell
    Hath called to prayer, submissive, penitent;
    Or at   MS.

Religion deepens her preventive care;   10
Then, moved by needless fear of past abuse,
Strike not from Law's firm hand that awful rod,
But leave it thence to drop for lack of use:
Oh, speed the blessed hour, Almighty God!

XIV

APOLOGY

THE formal World relaxes her cold chain
For One who speaks in numbers; ampler scope
His utterance finds; and, conscious of the gain,
Imagination works with bolder hope
The cause of grateful reason to sustain;   5
And, serving Truth, the heart more strongly beats
Against all barriers which his labour meets
In lofty place, or humble Life's domain.
Enough;—before us lay a painful road,
And guidance have I sought in duteous love   10
From Wisdom's heavenly Father. Hence hath flowed
Patience, with trust that, whatsoe'er the way
Each takes in this high matter, all may move
Cheered with the prospect of a brighter day.

XIV. 9 No more; a painful path before me lay MS.
11-12 From Him who governs, earthly thrones above;
    And with assured belief, whate'er MS.

MISCELLANEOUS POEMS

I

EPISTLE

TO SIR GEORGE HOWLAND BEAUMONT, BART.

From the South-west Coast of Cumberland.—1811.

[Composed August, 1811.—Published: vol. of 1842.]

FAR from our home by Grasmere's quiet Lake,
From the Vale's peace which all her fields partake,
Here on the bleakest point of Cumbria's shore
We sojourn stunned by Ocean's ceaseless roar;
While, day by day, grim neighbour! huge Black Comb   5
Frowns deepening visibly his native gloom,
Unless, perchance rejecting in despite
What on the Plain *we* have of warmth and light,
In his own storms he hides himself from sight.
Rough is the time; and thoughts, that would be free   10
From heaviness, oft fly, dear Friend, to thee;
Turn from a spot where neither sheltered road
Nor hedge-row screen invites my steps abroad;
Where one poor Plane-tree, having as it might
Attained a stature twice a tall man's height,   15
Hopeless of further growth, and brown and sere
Through half the summer, stands with top cut sheer,
Like an unshifting weathercock which proves
How cold the quarter that the wind best loves,
Or like a Centinel that, evermore   20
Darkening the window, ill defends the door

I. 1–5 Far from the stillness of our Grasmere lake,
   Our nest as *cozy* as a Bird could make,
   (Far from our home by Grasmere's lake serene
   Her Vale profound and mountains ever green)
   My time is spent, where thoughts that would be free
   From heaviness, turn oft, dear Friend, to Thee,
   In constant hearing of loud Ocean's roar,
   Where daily on a bleak and lonesome shore
   Even at this summer season huge Black Comb MSS.
10–13 Here are we, fixed, where neither sheltered road Nor MS. 1   20
like a 1845: stedfast MS., 1842   21 Darkening . . . ill] Darkens . . .
not MSS.

Of this unfinished house—a Fortress bare,
Where strength has been the Builder's only care;
Whose rugged walls may still for years demand
The final polish of the Plasterer's hand.   25
—This Dwelling's Inmate more than three weeks' space
And oft a Prisoner in the cheerless place,
I—of whose touch the fiddle would complain,
Whose breath would labour at the flute in vain,
In music all unversed, nor blessed with skill   30
A bridge to copy, or to paint a mill,
Tired of my books, a scanty company!
And tired of listening to the boisterous sea—
Pace between door and window muttering rhyme,
An old resource to cheat a froward time!   35
Though these dull hours (mine is it, or their shame?)
Would tempt me to renounce that humble aim.
—But if there be a Muse who, free to take
Her seat upon Olympus, doth forsake
Those heights (like Phœbus when his golden locks   40
He veiled, attendant on Thessalian flocks)
And, in disguise, a Milkmaid with her pail
Trips down the pathways of some winding dale;
Or, like a Mermaid, warbles on the shores
To fishers mending nets beside their doors;   45
Or, Pilgrim-like, on forest moss reclined,
Gives plaintive ditties to the heedless wind,
Or listens to its play among the boughs
Above her head and so forgets her vows—
If such a Visitant of Earth there be   50
And she would deign this day to smile on me
And aid my verse, content with local bounds
Of natural beauty and life's daily rounds,
Thoughts, chances, sights, or doings, which we tell
Without reserve to those whom we love well—   55

28 fiddle] viol MS.   30 nor blessed with] and void of   MS.   34
muttering] murmuring MS.
36–7 And it would well content me to disclaim
     In these dull hours a more ambitious aim MS. 1
39 on heights Olympian MS.
46–7 Or like a tired Way-farer faint in mind Gives plaintive Ballads MS. 1
47 ditties] Ave Marias MS. 2.   52–3 with narrow bounds, Life's beaten
road and Nature's MSS.

Then haply, Beaumont! words in current clear
Will flow, and on a welcome page appear
Duly before thy sight, unless they perish here.

What shall I treat of ? News from Mona's Isle ?
Such have we, but unvaried in its style ;   60
No tales of Runagates fresh landed, whence
And wherefore fugitive or on what pretence ;
Of feasts, or scandal, eddying like the wind
Most restlessly alive when most confined.
Ask not of me, whose tongue can best appease   65
The mighty tumults of the HOUSE OF KEYS ;
The last year's cup whose Ram or Heifer gained,
What slopes are planted, or what mosses drained :
An eye of fancy only can I cast
On that proud pageant now at hand or past,   70
When full five hundred boats in trim array,
With nets and sails outspread and streamers gay,
And chanted hymns and stiller voice of prayer,
For the old Manx-harvest to the Deep repair,
Soon as the herring-shoals at distance shine   75
Like beds of moonlight shifting on the brine.

Mona from our Abode is daily seen,
But with a wilderness of waves between ;
And by conjecture only can we speak
Of aught transacted there in bay or creek ;   80
No tidings reach us thence from town or field,
Only faint news her mountain-sunbeams yield,
And some we gather from the misty air,
And some the hovering clouds, our telegraph, declare.
But these poetic mysteries I withhold ;   85
For Fancy hath her fits both hot and cold,
And should the colder fit with You be on.
When You might read, my credit would be gone.

56–8 Then haply Beaumont, for my pen is near,
      The unlaboured lines to your indulgent ear
      May be transmitted, else will perish here.   MS. 1
57–8 May flow, unlaboured lines that from thy ear
      Audience will crave unless they   MS. 2
77–9 our . . . we] my . . . I *and so in* 81, 83, 84 MSS.

Let more substantial themes the pen engage,
And nearer interests culled from the opening stage　　90
Of our migration.—Ere the welcome dawn
Had from the east her silver star withdrawn,
The Wain stood ready, at our Cottage-door,
Thoughtfully freighted with a various store;
And long or ere the uprising of the Sun　　95
O'er dew-damped dust our journey was begun,
A needful journey, under favouring skies,
Through peopled Vales; yet something in the guise
Of those old Patriarchs when from well to well
They roamed through Wastes where now the tented Arabs dwell.

Say first, to whom did we the charge confide,　　101
Who promptly undertook the Wain to guide
Up many a sharply-twining road and down,
And over many a wide hill's craggy crown,
Through the quick turns of many a hollow nook,　　105
And the rough bed of many an unbridged brook?
A blooming Lass—who in her better hand
Bore a light switch, her sceptre of command
When, yet a slender Girl, she often led,
Skilful and bold, the horse and burthened *sled*[1]　　110
From the peat-yielding Moss on Gowdar's head.
What could go wrong with such a Charioteer
For goods and chattels, or those Infants dear,
A Pair who smilingly sat side by side,
Our hope confirming that the salt-sea tide,　　115
Whose free embraces we were bound to seek,
Would their lost strength restore and freshen the pale cheek?
Such hope did either Parent entertain
Pacing behind along the silent lane.

Blithe hopes and happy musings soon took flight,　　120
For lo! an uncouth melancholy sight—
On a green bank a creature stood forlorn

　　　　　　[1] A local word for sledge.

---

89 the pen] our care MSS.
90–1 And humbler business occupy the stage.
　　First for our journey hither. Ere the dawn MS. 1
95 or ere] before MSS.　　96 journey] travel MSS.　　97 favouring]
summer MS. 1
113/14 Escaped not long from malady severe, MSS.　　122 What see
we there? A creature stood forlorn MS. 2

Just half protruded to the light of morn,
Its hinder part concealed by hedge-row thorn.
The Figure called to mind a beast of prey   125
Stript of its frightful powers by slow decay,
And, though no longer upon rapine bent,
Dim memory keeping of its old intent.
We started, looked again with anxious eyes,
And in that griesly object recognise   130
The Curate's Dog—his long-tried friend, for they,
As well we knew, together had grown grey.
The Master died, his drooping servant's grief
Found at the Widow's feet some sad relief;
Yet still he lived in pining discontent,   135
Sadness which no indulgence could prevent;
Hence whole day wanderings, broken nightly sleeps
And lonesome watch that out of doors he keeps;
Not oftentimes, I trust, as we, poor brute!
Espied him on his legs sustained, blank, mute,   140
And of all visible motion destitute,
So that the very heaving of his breath
Seemed stopt, though by some other power than death.
Long as we gazed upon the form and face,
A mild domestic pity kept its place,   145
Unscared by thronging fancies of strange hue
That haunted us in spite of what we knew.
Even now I sometimes think of him as lost

129 anxious eyes] blank surprize MS.
133–5 *so* 1845.
     [The Master died, such comfort as remained
     To the poor brute he from the Widow gained MS: 1842 *as text*]
     Until the Vale she quitted, [Now she had left the valley MS.] and
          their door
     Was closed; to which she will return no more;
     But first old Faithful [Trusty MS.] to a neighbour's care
     Was given in charge; [Had been transferred MS.] nor lacked he
          dainty fare,
     And in the chimney nook was free to lie
     And doze, or, if his hour were come, to die
     Yet [And MS.] still he lived MS. 1842
142–3 So that . . . Seemed] As if . . . Were MS.
145–50 Our first unquiet pity held its place,
          Strange images we saw, and fancy drew
          As strange to haunt us, spite of what we knew.
          Imbecile seemed he, or by madness crossed
          Or stiffened and benumbed by ruthless frost,
          (He seemed by inoffensive madness crossed

In second-sight appearances, or crost
By spectral shapes of guilt, or to the ground,   150
On which he stood, by spells unnatural bound,
Like a gaunt shaggy Porter forced to wait
In days of old romance at Archimago's gate.

Advancing Summer, Nature's law fulfilled,
The choristers in every grove had stilled;   155
But we, we lacked not music of our own,
For lightsome Fanny had thus early thrown,
Mid the gay prattle of those infant tongues,
Some notes prelusive, from the round of songs
With which, more zealous than the liveliest bird   160
That in wild Arden's brakes was ever heard,
Her work and her work's partners she can cheer,
The whole day long, and all days of the year.
Thus gladdened from our own dear Vale we pass
And soon approach Diana's Looking-glass!   165
To Loughrigg-tarn, round clear and bright as heaven,
Such name Italian fancy would have given,
Ere on its banks the few grey cabins rose
That yet disturb not its concealed repose
More than the feeblest wind that idly blows.   170

Ah, Beaumont! when an opening in the road
Stopped me at once by charm of what it showed,
The encircling region vividly exprest
Within the mirror's depth, a world at rest—
Sky streaked with purple, grove and craggy *bield*,[1]   175
And the smooth green of many a pendent field,
And, quieted and soothed, a torrent small,
A little daring would-be waterfall.

---

[1] A word common in the country, signifying shelter, as in Scotland.

Or in some second-sight appearance, lost)
By helpless hunger crazed, or to the ground MS. 1
155 every] copse and MS. 1   158 infant] busy MSS.   161 wild]
wide MSS.
164–5 Thus gladdened soon we saw, and could not pass
        Without a pause MSS.
166 To Loughrigg's pool MS. 1   169 disturb] molest MS. 1
170 feeblest] ruffling MSS.
173–5 And I beheld, within its glassy breast
        The encircling landscape, lodged in perfect rest,
        Woods intermingling with a rocky *bield* MSS.
177 And hurrying down the cleft a streamlet small MS.

One chimney smoking and its azure wreath,
Associate all in the calm Pool beneath,   180
With here and there a faint imperfect gleam
Of water-lilies veiled in misty steam—
What wonder at this hour of stillness deep,
A shadowy link 'tween wakefulness and sleep,
When Nature's self, amid such blending, seems   185
To render visible her own soft dreams,
If, mixed with what appeared of rock, lawn, wood,
Fondly embosomed in the tranquil flood,
A glimpse I caught of that Abode, by Thee
Designed to rise in humble privacy,   190
A lowly Dwelling, here to be outspread,
Like a small Hamlet, with its bashful head
Half hid in native trees. Alas 'tis not,
Nor ever was; I sighed, and left the spot
Unconscious of its own untoward lot,   195
And thought in silence, with regret too keen,
Of unexperienced joys that might have been;
Of neighbourhood and intermingling arts,
And golden summer days uniting cheerful hearts.
But time, irrevocable time, is flown,   200
And let us utter thanks for blessings sown
And reaped—what hath been, and what is, our own.

     Not far we travelled ere a shout of glee,
Startling us all, dispersed my reverie;
Such shout as many a sportive echo meeting   205
Oft-times from Alpine *chalets* sends a greeting.
Whence the blithe hail? behold a Peasant stand
On high, a kerchief waving in her hand!
Not unexpectant that by early day
Our little Band would thrid this mountain way,   210
Before her cottage on the bright hill side
She hath advanced with hope to be descried.
Right gladly answering signals we displayed,
Moving along a tract of morning shade,
And vocal wishes sent of like good will   215
To our kind Friend high on the sunny hill—

180 Together imaged in the pool beneath MS 1.   185-6 ... these watery
gleams Is rendering visible MS.   188 Fondly embosomed] Truly
repeated MS. 1   195 Unconscious of] Repining at MS.   199 cheerful]
peaceful *corr. to* tender MS. 1

Luminous region, fair as if the prime
Were tempting all astir to look aloft or climb;
Only the centre of the shining cot
With door left open makes a gloomy spot,   220
Emblem of those dark corners sometimes found
Within the happiest breast on earthly ground.

Rich prospect left behind of stream and vale,
And mountain-tops, a barren ridge we scale;
Descend and reach, in Yewdale's depths, a plain   225
With haycocks studded, striped with yellowing grain—
An area level as a Lake and spread
Under a rock too steep for man to tread,
Where sheltered from the north and bleak north-west
Aloft the Raven hangs a visible nest,   230
Fearless of all assaults that would her brood molest.
Hot sunbeams fill the steaming vale; but hark,
At our approach, a jealous watch-dog's bark,
Noise that brings forth no liveried Page of state,
But the whole household, that our coming wait.   235
With Young and Old warm greetings we exchange,
And jocund smiles, and toward the lowly Grange
Press forward by the teasing dogs unscared.
Entering, we find the morning meal prepared:
So down we sit, though not till each had cast   240
Pleased looks around the delicate repast—
Rich cream, and snow-white eggs fresh from the nest,
With amber honey from the mountain's breast;
Strawberries from lane or woodland, offering wild
Of children's industry, in hillocks piled,   245
Cakes for the nonce, and butter fit to lie
Upon a lordly dish; frank hospitality

217 Clear, luminous as if the conscious prime   MS.   218 look aloft]
gaze MS.
223–4 Two vallies crossed that from a spacious vale
       Branch off, a rough and heathy ridge *etc.* MS. 1
225 Descend and soon have reached a fertile plain MS. 1   228 Under a
huge black steep that knows not human tread MS. 1
235–9 But hearty friends that on our coming wait
        With jocund smiles, warm greetings we exchange
        And soon the threshold of a lonely grange
        We enter *etc.*
        And on the table find the morning meal prepared. MS. 1
246 *for the nonce*   1842

Where simple art with bounteous nature vied,
And cottage comfort shunned not seemly pride.

Kind Hostess! Handmaid also of the feast,   250
If thou be lovelier than the kindling East,
Words by thy presence unrestrained may speak
Of a perpetual dawn from brow and cheek
Instinct with light whose sweetest promise lies,
Never retiring, in thy large dark eyes,   255
Dark but to every gentle feeling true,
As if their lustre flowed from ether's purest blue.

Let me not ask what tears may have been wept
By those bright eyes, what weary vigils kept,
Beside that hearth what sighs may have been heaved   260
For wounds inflicted, nor what toil relieved
By fortitude and patience, and the grace
Of heaven in pity visiting the place.
Not unadvisedly those secret springs
I leave unsearched: enough that memory clings,   265
Here as elsewhere, to notices that make
Their own significance for hearts awake,
To rural incidents, whose genial powers
Filled with delight three summer morning hours.

More could my pen report of grave or gay   270
That through our gipsy travel cheered the way;
But, bursting forth above the waves, the Sun
Laughs at my pains, and seems to say, "Be done."
Yet, Beaumont, thou wilt not, I trust, reprove
This humble offering made by Truth to Love,   275
Nor chide the Muse that stooped to break a spell
Which might have else been on me yet:—

FAREWELL.

252–4 The admiring poet without blame may speak
        Of thy perpetual dawn—of brow and cheek
        Blest with a light (And that fair light) that in contentment lies MS.
257 ether's purest] heaven's etherial MS.   270 More] Much MS. 1
272 bursting] breaking MS. 1   273 Chides me with smiles that seem
etc. MS. 1
274–7 . . . I trust wilt ne'er refuse
        Kindly to take this offering from a Muse
        Who stooped to aid me, studious of an end
        My spirits else had missed; farewell, dear Friend! MS. 1

UPON PERUSING THE FOREGOING EPISTLE
THIRTY YEARS AFTER ITS COMPOSITION

[Composed 1841.—Published: vol. of 1842.]

Soon did the Almighty Giver of all rest
Take those dear young Ones to a fearless nest;
And in Death's arms has long reposed the Friend
For whom this simple Register was penned.
Thanks to the moth that spared it for our eyes;   5
And Strangers even the slighted Scroll may prize,
Moved by the touch of kindred sympathies.
For—save the calm, repentance sheds o'er strife
Raised by remembrances of misused life,
The light from past endeavours purely willed   10
And by Heaven's favour happily fulfilled;
Save hope that we, yet bound to Earth, may share
The joys of the Departed—what so fair
As blameless pleasure, not without some tears,
Reviewed through Love's transparent veil of years?   15

Note.—Loughrigg Tarn, alluded to in the foregoing Epistle, resembles, though much smaller in compass, the Lake Nemi, or *Speculum Dianæ* as it is often called, not only in its clear waters and circular form, and the beauty immediately surrounding it, but also as being overlooked by the eminence of Langdale Pikes as Lake Nemi is by that of Monte Calvo. Since this Epistle was written Loughrigg Tarn has lost much of its beauty by the felling of many natural clumps of wood, relics of the old forest, particularly upon the farm called "The Oaks", from the abundance of that tree which grew there.

It is to be regretted, upon public grounds, that Sir George Beaumont did not carry into effect his intention of constructing here a Summer Retreat in the style I have described; as his taste would have set an example how buildings, with all the accommodations modern society requires, might be introduced even into the most secluded parts of this country without injuring their native character. The design was not abandoned from failure of inclination on his part, but in consequence of local untowardness which need not be particularised.

II
GOLD AND SILVER FISHES IN A VASE

[Composed November, 1829.—Published 1835.]

The soaring lark is blest as proud
  When at heaven's gate she sings;
The roving bee proclaims aloud
  Her flight by vocal wings;

7 For its own sake, and MS.

While Ye, in lasting durance pent,   5
    Your silent lives employ
For something more than dull content,
    Though haply less than joy.

Yet might your glassy prison seem
    A place where joy is known,   10
Where golden flash and silver gleam
    Have meanings of their own;
While, high and low, and all about,
    Your motions, glittering Elves!
Ye weave—no danger from without,   15
    And peace among yourselves.

Type of a sunny human breast
    Is your transparent cell;
Where Fear is but a transient guest,
    No sullen Humours dwell;   20
Where, sensitive of every ray
    That smites this tiny sea,
Your scaly panoplies repay
    The loan with usury.

How beautiful!—Yet none knows why   25
    This ever-graceful change,
Renewed—renewed incessantly—
    Within your quiet range.
Is it that ye with conscious skill
    For mutual pleasure glide;   30
And sometimes, not without your will,
    Are dwarfed, or magnified?

Fays, Genii of gigantic size!
    And now, in twilight dim,
Clustering like constellated eyes   35
    In wings of Cherubim,
When the fierce orbs abate their glare;—
    Whate'er your forms express,
Whate'er ye seem, whate'er ye are—
    All leads to gentleness.   40

II. 19 transient] lingering MS.   22 this] your MS.   26 ever-
varying MS.   34 in twilight] when air is MS.   35 Lustrous as
regal gems, or eyes MS.   37 *so* 1837: When they abate their fiery
glare; MS., 1835

Cold though your nature be, 'tis pure;
  Your birthright is a fence
From all that haughtier kinds endure
  Through tyranny of sense.
Ah! not alone by colours bright   45
  Are Ye to heaven allied,
When, like essential Forms of light,
  Ye mingle, or divide.

For day-dreams soft as e'er beguiled
  Day-thoughts while limbs repose;   50
For moonlight fascinations mild,
  Your gift, ere shutters close—
Accept, mute Captives! thanks and praise;
  And may this tribute prove
That gentle admirations raise   55
  Delight resembling love.

III
LIBERTY
SEQUEL TO THE PRECEDING

Addressed to a friend; the gold and silver fishes having been removed to
a pool in the pleasure-ground of Rydal Mount.

"The liberty of a people consists in being governed by laws which they have
made for themselves, under whatever form it be of government. The
liberty of a private man, in being master of his own time and actions,
as far as may consist with the laws of God and of his country. Of this
latter we are here to discourse."—COWLEY.

[Composed 1829.—Published 1835.]

THOSE breathing Tokens of your kind regard,
(Suspect not, Anna, that their fate is hard;
Not soon does aught to which mild fancies cling
In lonely spots, become a slighted thing;)
Those silent Inmates now no longer share,   5
Nor do they need, our hospitable care,
Removed in kindness from their glassy Cell
To the fresh waters of a living Well—

41-8 *not in* MS.   53 Accept] Receive MS.   mute] meek MS.

An elfin pool so sheltered that its rest
No winds disturb ; the mirror of whose breast   10
Is smooth as clear, save where with dimples small
A fly may settle, or a blossom fall.
—*There* swims, of blazing sun and beating shower
Fearless (but how obscured!) the golden Power,
That from his bauble prison used to cast   15
Gleams by the richest jewel unsurpast ;
And near him, darkling like a sullen Gnome,
The silver Tenant of the crystal dome ;
Dissevered both from all the mysteries
Of hue and altering shape that charmed all eyes.   20
Alas! they pined, they languished while they shone ;
And, if not so, what matters beauty gone
And admiration lost, by change of place
That brings to the inward creature no disgrace ?
But if the change restore his birthright, then,   25
Whate'er the difference, boundless is the gain.
Who can divine what impulses from God
Reach the caged lark, within a town-abode,
From his poor inch or two of daisied sod ?
O yield him back his privilege!—No sea   30
Swells like the bosom of a man set free ;
A wilderness is rich with liberty.
Roll on, ye spouting whales, who die or keep
Your independence in the fathomless Deep!
Spread, tiny nautilus, the living sail ;   35
Dive, at thy choice, or brave the freshening gale!
If unreproved the ambitious eagle mount
Sunward to seek the daylight in its fount,
Bays, gulfs, and ocean's Indian width, shall be,
Till the world perishes, a field for thee!   40

III. 9–12 *so* 1845:
    That spreads into an elfin pool opaque
    Of which close boughs a glimmering mirror make,
    On whose smooth breast with dimples light and small
    The fly may settle, leaf or blossom fall. MS., 1835–7, *but* 1837
settle, or the blossom
13–14 Hailstones and big drops of the thunder shower
        There swims (but how obscured) *etc.* MS.
17–18 And there, a darkling Gnome, in sullen robe . . . globe MS.   21
so 1845: They pined, perhaps, MS., 1835–43   40/41 *Here follows in the*
MS. "Humanity" (*v. p.* 102)

While musing here I sit in shadow cool,
And watch these mute Companions, in the pool,
(Among reflected boughs of leafy trees)
By glimpses caught—disporting at their ease,
Enlivened, braced, by hardy luxuries,   45
I ask what warrant fixed them (like a spell
Of witchcraft fixed them) in the crystal cell;
To wheel with languid motion round and round,
Beautiful, yet in mournful durance bound.
Their peace, perhaps, our lightest footfall marred;   50
On their quick sense our sweetest music jarred;
And whither could they dart, if seized with fear?
No sheltering stone, no tangled root was near.
When fire or taper ceased to cheer the room,
They wore away the night in starless gloom;   55
And, when the sun first dawned upon the streams,
How faint their portion of his vital beams!
Thus, and unable to complain, they fared,
While not one joy of ours by them was shared.

    Is there a cherished bird (I venture now   60
To snatch a sprig from Chaucer's reverend brow)—
Is there a brilliant fondling of the cage,
Though sure of plaudits on his costly stage,
Though fed with dainties from the snow-white hand
Of a kind mistress, fairest of the land,   65
But gladly would escape; and, if need were,
Scatter the colours from the plumes that bear
The emancipated captive through blithe air
Into strange woods, where he at large may live
On best or worst which they and Nature give?   70
The beetle loves his unpretending track,
The snail the house he carries on his back;
The far-fetched worm with pleasure would disown
The bed we give him, though of softest down;
A noble instinct; in all kinds the same,   75
All ranks! What Sovereign, worthy of the name,
If doomed to breathe against his lawful will
An element that flatters him—to kill,

42 And watch (by glimpses caught) in this calm pool MS.   44 Those
mute Companions, as they sport at ease MS.   47 crystal] glassy MS.
49 mournful 1837: a mournful 1835: piteous MS.

But would rejoice to barter outward show
For the least boon that freedom can bestow ?   80

 But most the Bard is true to inborn right,
Lark of the dawn, and Philomel of night,
Exults in freedom, can with rapture vouch
For the dear blessings of a lowly couch,
A natural meal—days, months, from Nature's hand ;   85
Time, place, and business, all at his command !—
Who bends to happier duties, who more wise
Than the industrious Poet, taught to prize,
Above all grandeur, a pure life uncrossed
By cares in which simplicity is lost ?   90
That life—the flowery path that winds by stealth—
Which Horace needed for his spirit's health ;
Sighed for, in heart and genius, overcome
By noise and strife, and questions wearisome,
And the vain splendours of Imperial Rome ?—   95
Let easy mirth his social hours inspire,
And fiction animate his sportive lyre,
Attuned to verse that, crowning light Distress
With garlands, cheats her into happiness ;
Give *me* the humblest note of those sad strains   100
Drawn forth by pressure of his gilded chains,
As a chance-sunbeam from his memory fell
Upon the Sabine farm he loved so well ;
Or when the prattle of Blandusia's spring
Haunted his ear—he only listening—   105
He proud to please, above all rivals, fit
To win the palm of gaiety and wit ;
He, doubt not, with involuntary dread,
Shrinking from each new favour to be shed,
By the world's Ruler, on his honoured head !   110

 In a deep vision's intellectual scene,
Such earnest longings and regrets as keen
Depressed the melancholy Cowley, laid
Under a fancied yew-tree's luckless shade ;
A doleful bower for penitential song,   115
Where Man and Muse complained of mutual wrong ;
While Cam's ideal current glided by,

104 Blandusia 1837: Bandusia 1835   110 honoured] laurel'd MS.

And antique towers nodded their foreheads high,
Citadels dear to studious privacy.
But Fortune, who had long been used to sport   120
With this tried Servant of a thankless Court,
Relenting met his wishes; and to you
The remnant of his days at least was true;
You, whom, though long deserted, he loved best;
You, Muses, books, fields, liberty, and rest!   125

Far happier they who, fixing hope and aim
On the humanities of peaceful fame,
Enter betimes with more than martial fire
The generous course, aspire, and still aspire;
Upheld by warnings heeded not too late   130
Stifle the contradictions of their fate,
And to one purpose cleave, their Being's godlike mate!

Thus, gifted Friend, but with the placid brow
That woman ne'er should forfeit, keep *thy* vow;
With modest scorn reject whate'er would blind   135
The ethereal eyesight, cramp the wingèd mind!
Then, with a blessing granted from above
To every act, word, thought, and look of love,
Life's book for Thee may lie unclosed, till age
Shall with a thankful tear bedrop its latest page.[1]   140

[1] There is now, alas! no possibility of the anticipation, with which the
above Epistle concludes, being realised: nor were the verses ever seen by
the Individual for whom they were intended. She accompanied her husband, the Rev. Wm. Fletcher, to India, and died of cholera, at the age of
thirty-two or thirty-three years, on her way from Shalapore to Bombay,
deeply lamented by all who knew her.

Her enthusiasm was ardent, her piety steadfast; and her great talents
would have enabled her to be eminently useful in the difficult path of life
to which she had been called. The opinion she entertained of her own performances, given to the world under her maiden name, Jewsbury, was
modest and humble, and, indeed, far below their merits, as is often the case
with those who are making trial of their powers, with a hope to discover
what they are best fitted for. In one quality, viz. quickness in the motions
of her mind, she had, within the range of the Author's acquaintance, no
equal.

125/6 Whose was that voice that like a Trumpet spake
          From lawn and woodland, from the gleaming lake,
          From heaven's blue depth above the mountain's head
          And from my heart not dulled by age? It said
          "Thrice happy they *etc.* MS. *deleted*
126 Far   1837: But   1835   127 humanities] humanity MS.

IV
POOR ROBIN[1]

[Composed March, 1840.—Published: vol. of 1842.]

Now when the primrose makes a splendid show,
And lilies face the March-winds in full blow,
And humbler growths as moved with one desire
Put on, to welcome spring, their best attire,
Poor Robin is yet flowerless; but how gay   5
With his red stalks upon this sunny day!
And, as his tufts of leaves he spreads, content
With a hard bed and scanty nourishment,
Mixed with the green, some shine not lacking power
To rival summer's brightest scarlet flower;   10
And flowers they well might seem to passers-by
If looked at only with a careless eye;
Flowers—or a richer produce (did it suit
The season) sprinklings of ripe strawberry fruit.

But while a thousand pleasures come unsought,   15
Why fix upon his wealth or want a thought?
Is the string touched in prelude to a lay
Of pretty fancies that would round him play
When all the world acknowledged elfin sway?
Or does it suit our humour to commend   20
Poor Robin as a sure and crafty friend,
Whose practice teaches, spite of names to show
Bright colours whether they deceive or no?—
Nay, we would simply praise the free good-will
With which, though slighted, he, on naked hill   25
Or in warm valley, seeks his part to fill;
Cheerful alike if bare of flowers as now,
Or when his tiny gems shall deck his brow:
Yet more, we wish that men by men despised,
And such as lift their foreheads overprized,   30
Should sometimes think, where'er they chance to spy

---

[1] The small wild Geranium known by that name.

IV. 5 Flowerless is ragged Robin! MS.   7 tufts 1845: tuft 1842
16 Upon his want or wealth why fix a thought? MS.   20 Or would the
humour of our verse commend MS.   24 free] pure MS.   25–6 With
which, though scorned, he seeks his part to fill MS.   28 gems shall deck]
wreaths adorn MS.
31–4 . . . when they this Plant espy
        Even though a sleety blast be whirling by MS.

This child of Nature's own humility,
What recompense is kept in store or left
For all that seem neglected or bereft;
With what nice care equivalents are given,   35
How just, how bountiful, the hand of Heaven.

V

THE GLEANER

SUGGESTED BY A PICTURE

[Composed March, 1828.—Published, as "The Country Girl", 1829 (*The Keepsake*); ed. 1832.]

THAT happy gleam of vernal eyes,
Those locks from summer's golden skies,
 That o'er thy brow are shed;
That cheek—a kindling of the morn,
That lip—a rose-bud from the thorn,   5
 I saw; and Fancy sped
To scenes Arcadian, whispering, through soft air,
Of bliss that grows without a care,
And happiness that never flies—
(How can it where love never dies?)   10
Whispering of promise, where no blight
Can reach the innocent delight;
Where pity, to the mind conveyed
In pleasure, is the darkest shade
That Time, unwrinkled grandsire, flings   15
From his smoothly gliding wings.

 What mortal form, what earthly face
Inspired the pencil, lines to trace,
And mingle colours, that should breed
Such rapture, nor want power to feed;   20
For had thy charge been idle flowers,
Fair Damsel! o'er my captive mind,
To truth and sober reason blind,
'Mid that soft air, those long-lost bowers,
The sweet illusion might have hung, for hours.   25

V. 1 gleam] smile MS. 9 And happiness 1837: Of loveliness MS.
Of happiness 1829, 1832 11 *so* 1837: Of promise whispering, MS.,
1829, 1832 20 power] skill MS.

Thanks to this tell-tale sheaf of corn,
That touchingly bespeaks thee born
Life's daily tasks with them to share
Who, whether from their lowly bed
They rise, or rest the weary head,   30
Ponder the blessing they entreat
From Heaven, and *feel* what they repeat,
While they give utterance to the prayer
That asks for daily bread.

VI

TO A REDBREAST

(IN SICKNESS)

[Composed ?.—Published: vol. of 1842.]

STAY, little cheerful Robin! stay,
    And at my casement sing,
Though it should prove a farewell lay
    And this our parting spring.

Though I, alas! may ne'er enjoy   5
    The promise in thy song;
A charm, *that* thought can not destroy,
    Doth to thy strain belong.

Methinks that in my dying hour
    Thy song would still be dear,   10
And with a more than earthly power
    My passing Spirit cheer.

Then, little Bird, this boon confer,
    Come, and my requiem sing,
Nor fail to be the harbinger   15
    Of everlasting Spring.

           S. H.

VII

[Composed January, 1846.—Published 1850.]

I KNOW an aged Man constrained to dwell
In a large house of public charity,
Where he abides, as in a Prisoner's cell,
With numbers near, alas! no company.

31 Ponder   1832: Do *weigh* MS., 1829

When he could creep about, at will, though poor   5
And forced to live on alms, this old Man fed
A Redbreast, one that to his cottage door
Came not, but in a lane partook his bread.

There, at the root of one particular tree,
An easy seat this worn-out Labourer found   10
While Robin pecked the crumbs upon his knee
Laid one by one, or scattered on the ground.

Dear intercourse was theirs, day after day;
What signs of mutual gladness when they met!
Think of their common peace, their simple play,   15
The parting moment and its fond regret.

Months passed in love that failed not to fulfil,
In spite of season's change, its own demand,
By fluttering pinions here and busy bill;
There by caresses from a tremulous hand.   20

Thus in the chosen spot a tie so strong
Was formed between the solitary pair,
That when his fate had housed him 'mid a throng
The Captive shunned all converse proffered there.

Wife, children, kindred, they were dead and gone;   25
But, if no evil hap his wishes crossed,
One living Stay was left, and in that one
Some recompense for all that he had lost.

O that the good old Man had power to prove,
By message sent through air or visible token,   30
That still he loves the Bird, and still must love;
That friendship lasts though fellowship is broken!

VII. 5 When he was free to move about MS. 1   6 this old Man] he duly
MS. 1   8 lane] grove MSS.   13 Thither alone he crept MSS.
15 The common meal, the pastime grave or gay MSS.
17–18 . . . and love failed never to fulfil
         With the returning light, its fresh demand MSS.
21 the chosen spot] that shady grove MSS.   23–4 That when compelled to house . . . The old Man shunned MSS.; That when the aged Pauper
. . . Was housed, he shunned MS. 2   24 proffered] that was MS.   25
Wife, child and kindred all MS.   27 in MS.; on 1850

VIII

SONNET

TO AN OCTOGENARIAN

[Composed 1846.—Published 1850.]

AFFECTIONS lose their object; Time brings forth
No successors; and, lodged in memory,
If love exist no longer, it must die,—
Wanting accustomed food, must pass from earth,
Or never hope to reach a second birth.   5
This sad belief, the happiest that is left
To thousands, share not Thou; howe'er bereft,
Scorned, or neglected, fear not such a dearth.
Though poor and destitute of friends thou art,
Perhaps the sole survivor of thy race,   10
One to whom Heaven assigns that mournful part
The utmost solitude of age to face,
Still shall be left some corner of the heart
Where Love for living Thing can find a place.

IX

FLOATING ISLAND

These lines are by the Author of the Address to the Wind, &c., published
heretofore along with my poems. Those to a Redbreast are by a deceased female Relative.

[Composed ?.—Published: vol. of 1842.]

HARMONIOUS Powers with Nature work
On sky, earth, river, lake and sea;
Sunshine and cloud, whirlwind and breeze,
All in one duteous task agree.

Once did I see a slip of earth   5
(By throbbing waves long undermined)
Loosed from its hold; how, no one knew,
But all might see it float, obedient to the wind;

VIII. 1 When Man's affections perish, Time *etc.* MS.   2 lodged in]
in the MS.   3 . . exist not, it must droop and die MS.   5 To gain
another world, a second birth MS.   6 Wanderer, this sad belief the
happiest left MS. 2   8 fear] dread MS.   13 shall be] is there MS.

Might see it, from the mossy shore
Dissevered, float upon the Lake,   10
Float with its crest of trees adorned
On which the warbling birds their pastime take.

Food, shelter, safety, there they find;
There berries ripen, flowerets bloom;
There insects live their lives, and die;   15
A peopled world it is; in size a tiny room.

And thus through many seasons' space
This little Island may survive;
But Nature, though we mark her not,
Will take away, may cease to give.   20

Perchance when you are wandering forth
Upon some vacant sunny day,
Without an object, hope, or fear,
Thither your eyes may turn—the Isle is passed away;

Buried beneath the glittering Lake,   25
Its place no longer to be found;
Yet the lost fragments shall remain
To fertilise some other ground.

                               D. W.

X
[Composed ?.—Published 1850.]

How beautiful the Queen of Night, on high
Her way pursuing among scattered clouds,
Where, ever and anon, her head she shrouds
Hidden from view in dense obscurity.
But look, and to the watchful eye   5
A brightening edge will indicate that soon
We shall behold the struggling Moon
Break forth,—again to walk the clear blue sky.

XI

"Late, late yestreen I saw the new moone
Wi' the auld moone in hir arme."
               Ballad of Sir Patrick Spence,
                    Percy's Reliques.
[Composed 1826.—Published 1827.]

ONCE I could hail (howe'er serene the sky)
The Moon re-entering her monthly round,
No faculty yet given me to espy

The dusky Shape within her arms imbound,
That thin memento of effulgence lost   5
Which some have named her Predecessor's ghost.

Young, like the Crescent that above me shone,
Nought I perceived within it dull or dim;
All that appeared was suitable to One
Whose fancy had a thousand fields to skim;   10
To expectations spreading with wild growth,
And hope that kept with me her plighted troth.

I saw (ambition quickening at the view)
A silver boat launched on a boundless flood;
A pearly crest, like Dian's when it threw   15
Its brightest splendour round a leafy wood;
But not a hint from under-ground, no sign
Fit for the glimmering brow of Proserpine.

Or was it Dian's self that seemed to move
Before me?—nothing blemished the fair sight;   20
On her I looked whom jocund Fairies love,
Cynthia, who puts the *little* stars to flight,
And by that thinning magnifies the great,
For exaltation of her sovereign state.

And when I learned to mark the spectral Shape   25
As each new Moon obeyed the call of Time,
If gloom fell on me, swift was my escape;
Such happy privilege hath life's gay Prime,
To see or not to see, as best may please
A buoyant Spirit, and a heart at ease.   30

Now, dazzling Stranger! when thou meet'st my glance,
Thy dark Associate ever I discern;
Emblem of thoughts too eager to advance
While I salute my joys, thoughts sad or stern;
Shades of past bliss, or phantoms that, to gain   35
Their fill of promised lustre, wait in vain.

So changes mortal Life with fleeting years;
A mournful change, should Reason fail to bring
The timely insight that can temper fears,
And from vicissitude remove its sting;   40
While Faith aspires to seats in that domain
Where joys are perfect—neither wax nor wane.

XII

TO THE LADY FLEMING

ON SEEING THE FOUNDATION PREPARING FOR THE ERECTION
OF RYDAL CHAPEL, WESTMORELAND
[Composed January, 1823.—Published 1827.]

I

BLEST is this Isle—our native Land;
Where battlement and moated gate
Are objects only for the hand
Of hoary Time to decorate;
Where shady hamlet, town that breathes   5
Its busy smoke in social wreaths,
No rampart's stern defence require,
Nought but the heaven-directed spire,
And steeple tower (with pealing bells
Far-heard)—our only citadels.   10

II

O Lady! from a noble line
Of chieftains sprung, who stoutly bore
The spear, yet gave to works divine
A bounteous help in days of yore,
(As records mouldering in the Dell   15
Of Nightshade[1] haply yet may tell;)
Thee kindred aspirations moved
To build, within a vale beloved,
For Him upon whose high behests
All peace depends, all safety rests.   20

III

How fondly will the woods embrace
This daughter of thy pious care,
Lifting her front with modest grace
To make a fair recess more fair;
And to exalt the passing hour;   25

[1] Bekangs Ghyll—or the dell of the Nightshade—in which stands St. Mary's Abbey in Low Furness.

XII. 6 busy . . . social] tranquil . . . silver MS. 1
21-3 *so* MS. 1, 1832:
        Even Strangers, slackening here their pace,
        Shall bless this work of pious care,
        Lifting its   1827
21-30, 31-40 *in reverse order* 1827

Or soothe it with a healing power
Drawn from the Sacrifice fulfilled,
Before this rugged soil was tilled,
Or human habitation rose
To interrupt the deep repose!   30

IV

Well may the villagers rejoice!
Nor heat, nor cold, nor weary ways,
Will be a hindrance to the voice
That would unite in prayer and praise;
More duly shall wild wandering Youth   35
Receive the curb of sacred truth,
Shall tottering Age, bent earthward, hear
The Promise, with uplifted ear;
And all shall welcome the new ray
Imparted to their sabbath-day.   40

V

Nor deem the Poet's hope misplaced,
His fancy cheated—that can see
A shade upon the future cast,
Of time's pathetic sanctity;
Can hear the monitory clock   45
Sound o'er the lake with gentle shock
At evening, when the ground beneath
Is ruffled o'er with cells of death;
Where happy generations lie,
Here tutored for eternity.   50

VI

Lives there a man whose sole delights
Are trivial pomp and city noise,
Hardening a heart that loathes or slights
What every natural heart enjoys?

26–8 With saintly thoughts on Him whose power
    The circuit of these mountains filled
    Ere the primaeval MS. 1
31–50 *not in* MS. 1   **32** Nor storms henceforth MS.   **37** The aged
38 caught with steadfast ear; MS.
shall be free to hear MS.   **41–50** *not in* MS. 2
41–6 *so* 1832: Not yet the corner stone is laid
        With solemn rite; but Fancy sees
        The tower time-stricken, and in shade
        Embosomed of coeval trees;
        Hears, o'er the lake, the warning clock
        As it shall sound with gentle shock 1827

Who never caught a noon-tide dream   55
From murmur of a running stream;
Could strip, for aught the prospect yields
To him, their verdure from the fields;
And take the radiance from the clouds
In which the sun his setting shrouds.   60

VII

A soul so pitiably forlorn,
If such do on this earth abide,
May season apathy with scorn,
May turn indifference to pride;
And still be not unblest—compared   65
With him who grovels, self-debarred
From all that lies within the scope
Of holy faith and christian hope;
Or, shipwreck'd, kindles on the coast
False fires, that others may be lost.   70

VIII

Alas! that such perverted zeal
Should spread on Britain's favoured ground!
That public order, private weal,
Should e'er have felt or feared a wound
From champions of the desperate law   75
Which from their own blind hearts they draw;
Who tempt their reason to deny
God, whom their passions dare defy,
And boast that they alone are free
Who reach this dire extremity!   80

55 noon-tide] soothing MS. 1
61–7 Fields—sunset clouds—and sky of morn
        Opening in splendor deep and wide——
        That Worldling may renounce with scorn,
        And in his chosen seat abide;
        A Spirit not unblest—compared
        With One who fosters disregard
        For *etc.* MS. 1
69–70 *so* 1827, 1845:
        Yea, strives for others to bedim
        The glorious Light too pure for him MS. 2, 1832–43; strives that
lustre ... For others, which has failed for him MS. 1
71 perverted] distempered MS. 1   72 favoured] happy MS. 1
75–6 From Scoffers leagued in desperate plot
        To make their own the general lot; MS. 2
From reckless (lawless) Men who *etc. corr. to* From impious Anarchists MS. 1
78 dare] do MS. 1

IX

But turn we from these "bold bad" men;
The way, mild Lady! that hath led
Down to their "dark opprobrious den,"
Is all too rough for Thee to tread.
Softly as morning vapours glide   85
Down Rydal-cove from Fairfield's side,
Should move the tenor of *his* song
Who means to charity no wrong;
Whose offering gladly would accord
With this day's work, in thought and word.   90

X

Heaven prosper it! may peace, and love,
And hope, and consolation, fall,
Through its meek influence, from above,
And penetrate the hearts of all;
All who, around the hallowed Fane,   95
Shall sojourn in this fair domain;
Grateful to Thee, while service pure,
And ancient ordinance, shall endure,
For opportunity bestowed
To kneel together, and adore their God!   100

XIII
ON THE SAME OCCASION

Oh! gather whencesoe'er ye safely may
The help which slackening Piety requires;
Nor deem that he perforce must go astray
Who treads upon the footmarks of his sires.

Our churches, invariably perhaps, stand east and west, but *why* is by few
persons *exactly* known; nor that the degree of deviation from *due* east
often noticeable in the ancient ones was determined, in each particular
case, by the point in the horizon at which the sun rose upon the day of
the saint to whom the church was dedicated. These observances of our
ancestors, and the causes of them, are the subject of the following stanzas.

[Composed 1823.—Published 1827.]

WHEN in the antique age of bow and spear
And feudal rapine clothed with iron mail,
Came ministers of peace, intent to rear
The Mother Church in yon sequestered vale;

85–6 Soft as the morning mists that glide Through MS. 1   86 *so* 1832:
Through Mosedale-cove from Carrock's side 1827   87 tenor] motion
MS. 1
XIII. 4 The Church that hallows yon MS. 1

Then, to her Patron Saint a previous rite   5
Resounded with deep swell and solemn close,
Through unremitting vigils of the night,
Till from his couch the wished-for Sun uprose.

He rose, and straight—as by divine command,
They, who had waited for that sign to trace   10
Their work's foundation, gave with careful hand
To the high altar its determined place;

Mindful of Him who in the Orient born
There lived, and on the cross his life resigned,
And who, from out the regions of the morn,   15
Issuing in pomp, shall come to judge mankind.

So taught *their* creed;—nor failed the eastern sky,
'Mid these more awful feelings, to infuse
The sweet and natural hopes that shall not die,
Long as the sun his gladsome course renews.   20

For us hath such prelusive vigil ceased;
Yet still we plant, like men of elder days,
Our christian altar faithful to the east,
Whence the tall window drinks the morning rays;

That obvious emblem giving to the eye   25
Of meek devotion, which erewhile it gave,
That symbol of the day-spring from on high,
Triumphant o'er the darkness of the grave.

XIV
THE HORN OF EGREMONT CASTLE
[Composed 1806.—Published 1807.]

ERE the Brothers through the gateway
Issued forth with old and young,
To the Horn Sir Eustace pointed
Which for ages there had hung.

9 Straight, as if urged by a MSS.   14 and there a bitter death did find
MS. 1   20 gladsome] vital MS. 1
25–8   That emblem yielding as it fronts the source
          Of light restored which heretofore it gave
          Of dust enkindled—and thy mouldered corse
          O Man! resurgent from the gloomy grave. MS.
XIV. 1–4 *so* 1845:
          When the Brothers reach'd the gateway,
          Eustace pointed with his lance
          To the Horn which there was hanging;
          Horn of the inheritance. 1807–43

Horn it was which none could sound,   5
No one upon living ground,
Save He who came as rightful Heir
To Egremont's Domains and Castle fair.

Heirs from times of earliest record
Had the House of Lucie born,   10
Who of right had held the Lordship
Claimed by proof upon the Horn:
Each at the appointed hour
Tried the Horn,—it owned his power;
He was acknowledged: and the blast,   15
Which good Sir Eustace sounded, was the last.

With his lance Sir Eustace pointed,
And to Hubert thus said he,
"What I speak this Horn shall witness
For thy better memory.   20
Hear, then, and neglect me not!
At this time, and on this spot,
The words are uttered from my heart,
As my last earnest prayer ere we depart.

"On good service we are going   25
Life to risk by sea and land,
In which course if Christ our Saviour
Do my sinful soul demand,
Hither come thou back straightway,
Hubert, if alive that day;   30
Return, and sound the Horn, that we
May have a living House still left in thee!"

"Fear not," quickly answered Hubert;
"As I am thy Father's son,
What thou askest, noble Brother,   35
With God's favour shall be done."
So were both right well content:
Forth they from the Castle went,
And at the head of their Array
To Palestine the Brothers took their way.   40

9 *so* 1845: Heirs from ages without record   1807–43   **11 held** **1845:**
claim'd   1807–43   12 Claimed by 1845: By the   1807–43   **38** *so*
1845: From the Castle forth they went,   1807–43

Side by side they fought (the Lucies
Were a line for valour famed)
And where'er their strokes alighted,
There the Saracens were tamed.
Whence, then, could it come—the thought—   45
By what evil spirit brought?
Oh! can a brave Man wish to take
His Brother's life, for Lands' and Castle's sake?

"Sir!" the Ruffians said to Hubert,
"Deep he lies in Jordan flood."   50
Stricken by this ill assurance,
Pale and trembling Hubert stood.
"Take your earnings."—Oh! that I
Could have *seen* my Brother die!
It was a pang that vexed him then;   55
And oft returned, again, and yet again.

Months passed on, and no Sir Eustace!
Nor of him were tidings heard;
Wherefore, bold as day, the Murderer
Back again to England steered.   60
To his Castle Hubert sped;
Nothing has he now to dread.
But silent and by stealth he came,
And at an hour which nobody could name.

None could tell if it were night-time,   65
Night or day, at even or morn;
No one's eye had seen him enter,
No one's ear had heard the Horn.
But bold Hubert lives in glee:
Months and years went smilingly;   70
With plenty was his table spread;
And bright the Lady is who shares his bed.

Likewise he had sons and daughters;
And, as good men do, he sate
At his board by these surrounded,   75
Flourishing in fair estate.

62 *so* 1845: He has nothing   1807–43
67–8 *so* 1845: For the sound was heard by no one
           Of the proclamation-horn. 1807–43

And while thus in open day
Once he sate, as old books say,
A blast was uttered from the Horn,
Where by the Castle-gate it hung forlorn.   80

'Tis the breath of good Sir Eustace!
He is come to claim his right:
Ancient castle, woods, and mountains
Hear the challenge with delight.
Hubert! though the blast be blown   85
He is helpless and alone:
Thou hast a dungeon, speak the word!
And there he may be lodged, and thou be Lord.

Speak!—astounded Hubert cannot;
And, if power to speak he had,   90
All are daunted, all the household
Smitten to the heart, and sad.
'Tis Sir Eustace; if it be
Living man, it must be he!
Thus Hubert thought in his dismay,   95
And by a postern-gate he slunk away.

Long, and long was he unheard of:
To his Brother then he came,
Made confession, asked forgiveness,
Asked it by a brother's name,   100
And by all the saints in heaven;
And of Eustace was forgiven:
Then in a convent went to hide
His melancholy head, and there he died.

But Sir Eustace, whom good angels   105
Had preserved from murderers' hands,
And from Pagan chains had rescued,
Lived with honour on his lands.
Sons he had, saw sons of theirs:
And through ages, heirs of heirs,   110
A long posterity renowned,
Sounded the Horn which they alone could sound.

XV
GOODY BLAKE AND HARRY GILL
A TRUE STORY
[Composed 1798.—Published 1798.]

OH! what 's the matter? what 's the matter?
What is 't that ails young Harry Gill?
That evermore his teeth they chatter,
Chatter, chatter, chatter still!
Of waistcoats Harry has no lack,   5
Good duffle grey, and flannel fine;
He has a blanket on his back,
And coats enough to smother nine.

In March, December, and in July,
'Tis all the same with Harry Gill;   10
The neighbours tell, and tell you truly,
His teeth they chatter, chatter still.
At night, at morning, and at noon,
'Tis all the same with Harry Gill;
Beneath the sun, beneath the moon,   15
His teeth they chatter, chatter still!

Young Harry was a lusty drover,
And who so stout of limb as he?
His cheeks were red as ruddy clover;
His voice was like the voice of three.   20
Old Goody Blake was old and poor;
Ill fed she was, and thinly clad;
And any man who passed her door
Might see how poor a hut she had.

All day she spun in her poor dwelling: 25
And then her three hours' work at night,
Alas! 'twas hardly worth the telling,
It would not pay for candle-light.
Remote from sheltered village-green,
On a hill's northern side she dwelt,   30
Where from sea-blasts the hawthorns lean,
And hoary dews are slow to melt.

XV. 21 Old 1802: Auld 1798–1800
29–32 *so* 1837: This woman dwelt in Dorsetshire,
          Her hut was on a cold hill-side,
          And in that country coals are dear,
          For they come far by wind and tide. 1798–1815; 1820–32
as text but sheltering (29) *and in* 1820 *only* Upon a bleak hill-side (30)

By the same fire to boil their pottage,
Two poor old Dames, as I have known,
Will often live in one small cottage;   35
But she, poor Woman! housed alone.
'Twas well enough, when summer came,
The long, warm, lightsome summer-day,
Then at her door the *canty* Dame
Would sit, as any linnet, gay.   40

But when the ice our streams did fetter,
Oh then how her old bones would shake!
You would have said, if you had met her,
'Twas a hard time for Goody Blake.
Her evenings then were dull and dead: 45
Sad case it was, as you may think,
For very cold to go to bed;
And then for cold not sleep a wink.

O joy for her! whene'er in winter
The winds at night had made a rout;   50
And scattered many a lusty splinter
And many a rotten bough about.
Yet never had she, well or sick,
As every man who knew her says,
A pile beforehand, turf or stick,   55
Enough to warm her for three days.

Now, when the frost was past enduring,
And made her poor old bones to ache,
Could any thing be more alluring
Than an old hedge to Goody Blake?   60
And, now and then, it must be said,
When her old bones were cold and chill,
She left her fire, or left her bed,
To seek the hedge of Harry Gill.

Now Harry he had long suspected   65
This trespass of old Goody Blake;
And vowed that she should be detected—
That he on her would vengeance take.
And oft from his warm fire he'd go,
And to the fields his road would take;   70
And there, at night, in frost and snow,
He watched to seize old Goody Blake.

36 housed   1820: dwelt 1798–1815   55 turf 1827: wood 1798–1820

And once, behind a rick of barley,
Thus looking out did Harry stand:
The moon was full and shining clearly, 75
And crisp with frost the stubble land.
—He hears a noise—he's all awake—
Again?—on tip-toe down the hill
He softly creeps—'tis Goody Blake;
She's at the hedge of Harry Gill! 80

Right glad was he when he beheld her:
Stick after stick did Goody pull:
He stood behind a bush of elder,
Till she had filled her apron full.
When with her load she turned about, 85
The by-way back again to take;
He started forward, with a shout,
And sprang upon poor Goody Blake.

And fiercely by the arm he took her,
And by the arm he held her fast, 90
And fiercely by the arm he shook her,
And cried, "I've caught you then at last!"
Then Goody, who had nothing said,
Her bundle from her lap let fall;
And, kneeling on the sticks, she prayed 95
To God that is the judge of all.

She prayed, her withered hand uprearing,
While Harry held her by the arm—
"God! who art never out of hearing,
O may he never more be warm!" 100
The cold, cold moon above her head,
Thus on her knees did Goody pray;
Young Harry heard what she had said:
And icy cold he turned away.

He went complaining all the morrow 105
That he was cold and very chill:
His face was gloom, his heart was sorrow,
Alas! that day for Harry Gill!
That day he wore a riding-coat,
But not a whit the warmer he: 110
Another was on Thursday brought,
And ere the Sabbath he had three.

86 by-way 1827: by-road 1798–1820

'Twas all in vain, a useless matter,
And blankets were about him pinned;
Yet still his jaws and teeth they clatter,　　115
Like a loose casement in the wind.
And Harry's flesh it fell away;
And all who see him say, 'tis plain,
That, live as long as live he may,
He never will be warm again.　　120

No word to any man he utters,
A-bed or up, to young or old;
But ever to himself he mutters,
"Poor Harry Gill is very cold."
A-bed or up, by night or day;　　125
His teeth they chatter, chatter still.
Now think, ye farmers all, I pray,
Of Goody Blake and Harry Gill!

XVI
PRELUDE

PREFIXED TO THE VOLUME ENTITLED "POEMS CHIEFLY OF
EARLY AND LATE YEARS"

[Composed March, 1842.—Published: vol. of 1842.]

In desultory walk through orchard grounds,
Or some deep chestnut grove, oft have I paused
The while a Thrush, urged rather than restrained
By gusts of vernal storm, attuned his song
To his own genial instincts; and was heard　　5
(Though not without some plaintive tones between)
To utter, above showers of blossom swept
From tossing boughs, the promise of a calm,
Which the unsheltered traveller might receive
With thankful spirit. The descant, and the wind　　10
That seemed to play with it in love or scorn,
Encouraged and endeared the strain of words
That haply flowed from me, by fits of silence
Impelled to livelier pace. But now, my Book!
Charged with those lays, and others of like mood,　　15
Or loftier pitch if higher rose the theme,

Go, single—yet aspiring to be joined
With thy Forerunners that through many a year
Have faithfully prepared each other's way—
Go forth upon a mission best fulfilled   20
When and wherever, in this changeful world,
Power hath been given to please for higher ends
Than pleasure only; gladdening to prepare
For wholesome sadness, troubling to refine,
Calming to raise; and, by a sapient Art   25
Diffused through all the mysteries of our Being,
Softening the toils and pains that have not ceased
To cast their shadows on our mother Earth
Since the primeval doom. Such is the grace
Which, though unsued for, fails not to descend   30
With heavenly inspiration; such the aim
That Reason dictates; and, as even the wish
Has virtue in it, why should hope to me
Be wanting that sometimes, where fancied ills
Harass the mind and strip from off the bowers   35
Of private life their natural pleasantness,
A Voice—devoted to the love whose seeds
Are sown in every human breast, to beauty
Lodged within compass of the humblest sight,
To cheerful intercourse with wood and field,   40
And sympathy with man's substantial griefs—
Will not be heard in vain? And in those days
When unforeseen distress spreads far and wide
Among a People mournfully cast down,
Or into anger roused by venal words   45
In recklessness flung out to overturn
The judgment, and divert the general heart
From mutual good—some strain of thine, my Book!
Caught at propitious intervals, may win
Listeners who not unwillingly admit   50
Kindly emotion tending to console
And reconcile; and both with young and old
Exalt the sense of thoughtful gratitude
For benefits that still survive, by faith
In progress, under laws divine, maintained.   55
    RYDAL MOUNT, *March* 26, 1842.

XVII

TO A CHILD

WRITTEN IN HER ALBUM

[Composed 1834.—Published 1835.]

SMALL service is true service while it lasts:
Of humblest Friends, bright Creature! scorn not one:
The Daisy, by the shadow that it casts,
Protects the lingering dew-drop from the Sun.

XVIII

LINES

WRITTEN IN THE ALBUM OF THE COUNTESS OF LONSDALE

[Composed November 5, 1834.—Published 1835.]

LADY! a Pen (perhaps with thy regard,
Among the Favoured, favoured not the least)
Left, 'mid the Records of this Book inscribed,
Deliberate traces, registers of thought
And feeling, suited to the place and time   5
That gave them birth:—months passed, and still this hand,
That had not been too timid to imprint
Words which the virtues of thy Lord inspired,
Was yet not bold enough to write of Thee.
And why that scrupulous reserve? In sooth   10
The blameless cause lay in the Theme itself.
Flowers are there many that delight to strive
With the sharp wind, and seem to court the shower,
Yet are by nature careless of the sun
Whether he shine on them or not; and some,   15
Where'er he moves along the unclouded sky,
Turn a broad front full on his flattering beams:
Others do rather from their notice shrink,
Loving the dewy shade,—a humble band,
Modest and sweet, a progeny of earth,   20
Congenial with thy mind and character,
High-born Augusta!

Witness, Towers and Groves!
And Thou, wild Stream, that giv'st the honoured name

XVII. *In* 1835 *entitled* "Written in an Album"; *in* 1837–43 "Written in
the Album of a Child"   2 *so* 1845: Of Friends, however humble. 1835–43
XVIII. COUNTESS OF LONSDALE   1837: COUNTESS OF —— 1835 1 Lady,
erewhile a willing Pen by thee MS.

Of Lowther to this ancient Line, bear witness
From thy most secret haunts; and ye Parterres,   25
Which She is pleased and proud to call her own,
Witness how oft upon my noble Friend
Mute offerings, tribute from an inward sense
Of admiration and respectful love,
Have waited—till the affections could no more   30
Endure that silence, and broke out in song,
Snatches of music taken up and dropt
Like those self-solacing, those under, notes
Trilled by the redbreast, when autumnal leaves
Are thin upon the bough. Mine, only mine,   35
The pleasure was, and no one heard the praise,
Checked, in the moment of its issue, checked
And reprehended, by a fancied blush
From the pure qualities that called it forth.

Thus Virtue lives debarred from Virtue's meed;   40
Thus, Lady, is retiredness a veil
That, while it only spreads a softening charm
O'er features looked at by discerning eyes,
Hides half their beauty from the common gaze;
And thus, even on the exposed and breezy hill   45
Of lofty station, female goodness walks,
When side by side with lunar gentleness,
As in a cloister. Yet the grateful Poor
(Such the immunities of low estate,
Plain Nature's enviable privilege,   50
Her sacred recompence for many wants)
Open their hearts before Thee, pouring out
All that they think and feel, with tears of joy;
And benedictions not unheard in heaven:
And friend in the ear of friend, where speech is free   55
To follow truth, is eloquent as they.

Then let the Book receive in these prompt lines
A just memorial; and thine eyes consent
To read that they, who mark thy course, behold
A life declining with the golden light   60
Of summer, in the season of sere leaves;

22-4 *so* 1837:   . . . Towers, and stately Groves
          Bear witness for me; thou, too, Mountain-stream! 1835
40 lives debarred] is self-robbed MS.

See cheerfulness undamped by stealing Time;
See studied kindness flow with easy stream,
Illustrated with inborn courtesy;
And an habitual disregard of self   65
Balanced by vigilance for others' weal.

   And shall the Verse not tell of lighter gifts
With these ennobling attributes conjoined
And blended, in peculiar harmony,
By Youth's surviving spirit? What agile grace!   70
A nymph-like liberty, in nymph-like form,
Beheld with wonder; whether floor or path
Thou tread; or sweep—borne on the managed steed—
Fleet as the shadows, over down or field,
Driven by strong winds at play among the clouds.   75

Yet one word more—one farewell word—a wish
Which came, but it has passed into a prayer—
That, as thy sun in brightness is declining,
So—at an hour yet distant for *their* sakes
Whose tender love, here faltering on the way   80
Of a diviner love, will be forgiven—
So may it set in peace, to rise again
For everlasting glory won by faith.

XIX

GRACE DARLING

[Composed 1843.—Privately printed 1843, published 1845.]

AMONG the dwellers in the silent fields
The natural heart is touched, and public way
And crowded street resound with ballad strains,
Inspired by ONE whose very name bespeaks
Favour divine, exalting human love;   5
Whom, since her birth on bleak Northumbria's coast,
Known unto few but prized as far as known,

63–5   . . . feelingly allied
        With inborn courtesy; in every act
        And habit utter disregard of Self MS.
   73 *so* 1837: or on the managed steed art borne MS., 1835
   79–83 God's favour still vouchsafed, so may it set—
        And be the hour yet distant for our sakes—
        To rise again in glory won by Faith MS.

A single Act endears to high and low
Through the whole land—to Manhood, moved in spite
Of the world's freezing cares—to generous Youth—   10
To Infancy, that lisps her praise—to Age
Whose eye reflects it, glistening through a tear
Of tremulous admiration. Such true fame
Awaits her *now;* but, verily, good deeds
Do no imperishable record find   15
Save in the rolls of heaven, where hers may live
A theme for angels, when they celebrate
The high-souled virtues which forgetful earth
Has witness'd. Oh! that winds and waves could speak
Of things which their united power called forth   20
From the pure depths of her humanity!
A Maiden gentle, yet, at duty's call,
Firm and unflinching, as the Lighthouse reared
On the Island-rock, her lonely dwelling-place;
Or like the invincible Rock itself that braves,   25
Age after age, the hostile elements,
As when it guarded holy Cuthbert's cell.

All night the storm had raged, nor ceased, nor paused,
When, as day broke, the Maid, through misty air,
Espies far off a Wreck, amid the surf,   30
Beating on one of those disastrous isles—
Half of a Vessel, half—no more; the rest
Had vanished, swallowed up with all that there
Had for the common safety striven in vain,
Or thither thronged for refuge. With quick glance   35
Daughter and Sire through optic-glass discern,
Clinging about the remnant of this Ship,
Creatures—how precious in the Maiden's sight!
For whom, belike, the old Man grieves still more
Than for their fellow-sufferers engulfed   40
Where every parting agony is hushed,
And hope and fear mix not in further strife.
"But courage, Father! let us out to sea—
A few may yet be saved." The Daughter's words,
Her earnest tone, and look beaming with faith,   45
Dispel the Father's doubts: nor do they lack
The noble-minded Mother's helping hand

XIX 11 to] and   1843

To launch the boat; and with her blessing cheered,
And inwardly sustained by silent prayer,
Together they put forth, Father and Child!   50
Each grasps an oar, and struggling on they go—
Rivals in effort; and, alike intent
Here to elude and there surmount, they watch
The billows lengthening, mutually crossed
And shattered, and re-gathering their might;   55
As if the tumult, by the Almighty's will
Were, in the conscious sea, roused and prolonged
That woman's fortitude—so tried, so proved—
May brighten more and more!

                                     True to the mark,
They stem the current of that perilous gorge,   60
Their arms still strengthening with the strengthening heart,
Though danger, as the Wreck is near'd, becomes
More imminent. Not unseen do they approach;
And rapture, with varieties of fear
Incessantly conflicting, thrills the frames   65
Of those who, in that dauntless energy,
Foretaste deliverance; but the least perturbed
Can scarcely trust his eyes, when he perceives
That of the pair—tossed on the waves to bring
Hope to the hopeless, to the dying, life—   70
One is a Woman, a poor earthly sister,
Or, be the Visitant other than she seems,
A guardian Spirit sent from pitying Heaven,
In woman's shape. But why prolong the tale,
Casting weak words amid a host of thoughts   75
Armed to repel them? Every hazard faced
And difficulty mastered, with resolve
That no one breathing should be left to perish,
This last remainder of the crew are all
Placed in the little boat, then o'er the deep   80
Are safely borne, landed upon the beach,
And, in fulfilment of God's mercy, lodged
Within the sheltering Lighthouse.—Shout, ye Waves!
Send forth a song of triumph. Waves and Winds,

56–7 As if the wrath and trouble of the sea
        Were by the Almighty's sufferance prolonged,   1843
84 Pipe a glad song of triumph, ye fierce Winds!   1843

Exult in this deliverance wrought through faith   85
In Him whose Providence your rage hath served!
Ye screaming Sea-mews, in the concert join!
And would that some immortal Voice—a Voice
Fitly attuned to all that gratitude
Breathes out from floor or couch, through pallid lips   90
Of the survivors—to the clouds might bear—
Blended with praise of that parental love,
Beneath whose watchful eye the Maiden grew
Pious and pure, modest and yet so brave,
Though young so wise, though meek so resolute—   95
Might carry to the clouds and to the stars,
Yea, to celestial Choirs, GRACE DARLING'S name!

XX
THE RUSSIAN FUGITIVE
PART I

[Composed 1828.—Published 1835.]

ENOUGH of rose-bud lips, and eyes
   Like harebells bathed in dew,
Of cheek that with carnation vies,
   And veins of violet hue;
Earth wants not beauty that may scorn   5
   A likening to frail flowers;
Yea, to the stars, if they were born
   For seasons and for hours.

Through Moscow's gates, with gold unbarred,
   Stepped One at dead of night,   10
Whom such high beauty could not guard
   From meditated blight;
By stealth she passed, and fled as fast
   As doth the hunted fawn,
Nor stopped, till in the dappling east   15
   Appeared unwelcome dawn.

85–6 *not in priv. printed ed.* 1843
XX. THE RUSSIAN FUGITIVE: Ina, or The Lodge in the Forest, A
Russian Tale MS.
5–8 Earth lacks not beauty that will bear
   No *etc.*
  More lofty is its character
   More lasting are its powers. MS.

Seven days she lurked in brake and field,
   Seven nights her course renewed,
Sustained by what her scrip might yield,
   Or berries of the wood;   20
At length, in darkness travelling on,
   When lowly doors were shut,
The haven of her hope she won,
   Her Foster-mother's hut.

"To put your love to dangerous proof   25
   I come," said she, "from far;
For I have left my Father's roof,
   In terror of the Czar."
No answer did the Matron give,
   No second look she cast,   30
But hung upon the Fugitive,
   Embracing and embraced.

She led the Lady to a seat
   Beside the glimmering fire,
Bathed duteously her wayworn feet,   35
   Prevented each desire:—
The cricket chirped, the house-dog dozed,
   And on that simple bed,
Where she in childhood had reposed,
   Now rests her weary head.   40

When she, whose couch had been the sod,
   Whose curtain pine or thorn,
Had breathed a sigh of thanks to God,
   Who comforts the forlorn;
While over her the Matron bent   45
   Sleep sealed her eyes, and stole
Feeling from limbs with travel spent,
   And trouble from the soul.

Refreshed, the Wanderer rose at morn,
   And soon again was dight   50
In those unworthy vestments worn
   Through long and perilous flight;

30 cast; 1835   31 But] 1837: She 1835   33 the] 1837: her 1835
45–8 Upon her lids with travel spent
    Sleep dropped, and gently stole
   (While o'er her head the Matron bent)
   Into her dreamless soul. MS.

And "O beloved Nurse," she said,
　"My thanks with silent tears
Have unto Heaven and You been paid:　　55
　Now listen to my fears!

"Have you forgot"—and here she smiled—
　"The babbling flatteries
You lavished on me when a child
　Disporting round your knees?　　60
I was your lambkin, and your bird,
　Your star, your gem, your flower;
Light words, that were more lightly heard
　In many a cloudless hour!

"The blossom you so fondly praised　　65
　Is come to bitter fruit;
A mighty One upon me gazed;
　I spurned his lawless suit,
And must be hidden from his wrath:
　You, Foster-father dear,　　70
Will guide me in my forward path;
　I may not tarry here!

"I cannot bring to utter woe
　Your proved fidelity."—
"Dear child, sweet Mistress, say not so!　　75
　For you we both would die."
"Nay, nay, I come with semblance feigned
　And cheek embrowned by art;
Yet, being inwardly unstained,
　With courage will depart."　　80

"But whither would you, could you, flee?
　A poor Man's counsel take;
The Holy Virgin gives to me
　A thought for your dear sake;
Rest, shielded by our Lady's grace,　　85
　And soon shall you be led
Forth to a safe abiding-place,
　Where never foot doth tread."

73–88 *not in* MS.

PART II

T<small>HE</small> dwelling of this faithful pair
   In a straggling village stood,   90
For One who breathed unquiet air
   A dangerous neighbourhood;
But wide around lay forest ground
   With thickets rough and blind;
And pine-trees made a heavy shade   95
   Impervious to the wind.

And there, sequestered from the sight,
   Was spread a treacherous swamp,
On which the noonday sun shed light
   As from a lonely lamp;   100
And midway in the unsafe morass,
   A single Island rose
Of firm dry ground, with healthful grass
   Adorned, and shady boughs.

The Woodman knew, for such the craft   105
   This Russian vassal plied,
That never fowler's gun, nor shaft
   Of archer, there was tried;
A sanctuary seemed the spot
   From all intrusion free;   110
And there he planned an artful Cot
   For perfect secrecy.

With earnest pains unchecked by dread
   Of Power's far-stretching hand,
The bold good Man his labour sped   115
   At Nature's pure command;
Heart-soothed, and busy as a wren,
   While, in a hollow nook,
She moulds her sight-eluding den
   Above a murmuring brook.   120

---

93 lay] was MS.   101 And out of one a broad morass,   109–10 That
no one ventured to the spot   Belike from age to age MS.   111 an
artful] a sylvan MS.   112 A lurking Hermitage. MS.   113 With
tender care MS.

His task accomplished to his mind,
   The twain ere break of day
Creep forth, and through the forest wind
   Their solitary way;
Few words they speak, nor dare to slack   125
   Their pace from mile to mile,
Till they have crossed the quaking marsh,
   And reached the lonely Isle.

The sun above the pine-trees showed
   A bright and cheerful face;   130
And Ina looked for her abode,
   The promised hiding-place;
She sought in vain, the Woodman smiled;
   No threshold could be seen,
Nor roof, nor window;—all seemed wild   135
   As it had ever been.

Advancing, you might guess an hour,
   The front with such nice care
Is masked, "if house it be or bower,"
   But in they entered are;   140
As shaggy as were wall and roof
   With branches intertwined,
So smooth was all within, air-proof,
   And delicately lined:

And hearth was there, and maple dish,   145
   And cups in seemly rows,
And couch—all ready to a wish
   For nurture or repose;
And Heaven doth to her virtue grant
   That there she may abide   150
In solitude, with every want
   By cautious love supplied.

No queen before a shouting crowd
   Led on in bridal state,
E'er struggled with a heart so proud,   155
   Entering her palace gate;

121 When all was finished MS.   122 The twain] Abroad MS.   123
They thro' the houseless MS.
137-9 Approaching etc.
    So nice the builder's care
  Whether it were a house or bower MS.
150 there 1850: here 1835-45   154 bridal] pride and MS.

Rejoiced to bid the world farewell,
   No saintly anchoress
E'er took possession of her cell
   With deeper thankfulness.   160

"Father of all, upon thy care
   And mercy am I thrown;
Be thou my safeguard!"—such her prayer
   When she was left alone,
Kneeling amid the wilderness   165
   When joy had passed away,
And smiles, fond efforts of distress
   To hide what they betray!

The prayer is heard, the Saints have seen,
   Diffused through form and face,   170
Resolves devotedly serene;
   That monumental grace
Of Faith, which doth all passions tame
   That Reason *should* control;
And shows in the untrembling frame   175
   A statue of the soul.

PART III

'TIS sung in ancient minstrelsy
   That Phœbus wont to wear
The leaves of any pleasant tree
   Around his golden hair;   180
Till Daphne, desperate with pursuit
   Of his imperious love,
At her own prayer transformed, took root,
   A laurel in the grove.

Then did the Penitent adorn   185
   His brow with laurel green;
And 'mid his bright locks never shorn
   No meaner leaf was seen;
And poets sage, through every age,
   About their temples wound   190
The bay; and conquerors thanked the Gods,
   With laurel chaplets crowned.

167–8 . . the sunshine of distress,
     That hide, yet more betray MS.
172–3 Exalting lowly grace, A Faith MS.   181 flying from the suit
MS.

Into the mists of fabling Time
　So far runs back the praise
Of Beauty, that disdains to climb　　　　　195
　Along forbidden ways;
That scorns temptation; power defies
　Where mutual love is not;
And to the tomb for rescue flies
　When life would be a blot.　　　　　　200

To this fair Votaress a fate
　More mild doth Heaven ordain
Upon her Island desolate;
　And words, not breathed in vain,
Might tell what intercourse she found,　　205
　Her silence to endear;
What birds she tamed, what flowers the ground
　Sent forth her peace to cheer.

To one mute Presence, above all,
　Her soothed affections clung,　　　　　210
A picture on the cabin wall
　By Russian usage hung—
The Mother-maid, whose countenance bright
　With love abridged the day;
And, communed with by taper light,　　　215
　Chased spectral fears away.

And oft, as either Guardian came,
　The joy in that retreat
Might any common friendship shame,
　So high their hearts would beat;　　　　220
And to the lone Recluse, whate'er
　They brought, each visiting
Was like the crowding of the year
　With a new burst of spring.

But, when she of her Parents thought,　　225
　The pang was hard to bear;
And, if with all things not enwrought,
　That trouble still is near.

204–5　Nor were it labor vain
　　　To tell what company MS.
209–16 *not in* MS.

Before her flight she had not dared
   Their constancy to prove,   ,   230
Too much the heroic Daughter feared
   The weakness of their love.

Dark is the past to them, and dark
   The future still must be,
Till pitying Saints conduct her bark   235
   Into a safer sea—
Or gentle Nature close her eyes,
   And set her Spirit free
From the altar of this sacrifice,
   In vestal purity.   240

Yet, when above the forest-glooms
   The white swans southward passed,
High as the pitch of their swift plumes
   Her fancy rode the blast;
And bore her toward the fields of France,   245
   Her Father's native land,
To mingle in the rustic dance,
   The happiest of the band!

Of those belovèd fields she oft
   Had heard her Father tell   250
In phrase that now with echoes soft
   Haunted her lonely cell;
She saw the hereditary bowers,
   She heard the ancestral stream;
The Kremlin and its haughty towers   255
   Forgotten like a dream!

PART IV

THE ever-changing Moon had traced
   Twelve times her monthly round,
When through the unfrequented Waste
   Was heard a startling sound;   260
A shout thrice sent from one who chased
   At speed a wounded deer,
Bounding through branches interlaced,
   And where the wood was clear.

245 tow'rd 1835   fields] groves MS.

The fainting creature took the marsh,   265
   And toward the Island fled,
While plovers screamed with tumult harsh
   Above his antlered head;
This, Ina saw; and, pale with fear,
   Shrunk to her citadel;   270
The desperate deer rushed on, and near
   The tangled covert fell.

Across the marsh, the game in view,
   The Hunter followed fast,
Nor paused, till o'er the stag he blew   275
   A death-proclaiming blast;
Then, resting on her upright mind,
   Came forth the Maid—"In me
Behold," she said, "a stricken Hind
   Pursued by destiny!   280

"From your deportment, Sir! I deem
   That you have worn a sword,
And will not hold in light esteem
   A suffering woman's word;
There is my covert, there perchance   285
   I might have lain concealed,
My fortunes hid, my countenance
   Not even to you revealed.

"Tears might be shed, and I might pray,
   Crouching and terrified,   290
That what has been unveiled to-day,
   You would in mystery hide;
But I will not defile with dust
   The knee that bends to adore
The God in heaven;—attend, be just;   295
   This ask I, and no more!

"I speak not of the winter's cold
   For summer's heat exchanged,
While I have lodged in this rough hold,
   From social life estranged;   300

269–70 Affrighted Ina saw and heard
        And shrank into her cell: MS.
272 To her dark threshold fell MS.   280 by evil destiny MS.   282
worn] borne MS.

Nor yet of trouble and alarms:
  High Heaven is my defence;
And every season has soft arms
  For injured Innocence.

"From Moscow to the Wilderness   305
  It was my choice to come,
Lest virtue should be harbourless,
  And honour want a home;
And happy were I, if the Czar
  Retain his lawless will,   310
To end life here like this poor deer,
  Or a lamb on a green hill."

"Are you the Maid," the Stranger cried,
  "From Gallic parents sprung,
Whose vanishing was rumoured wide,   315
  Sad theme for every tongue;
Who foiled an Emperor's eager quest?
  You, Lady, forced to wear
These rude habiliments, and rest
  Your head in this dark lair!"   320

But wonder, pity, soon were quelled;
  And in her face and mien
The soul's pure brightness he beheld
  Without a veil between:
He loved, he hoped,—a holy flame   325
  Kindled 'mid rapturous tears;
The passion of a moment came
  As on the wings of years.

"Such bounty is no gift of chance,"
  Exclaimed he: "righteous Heaven,   330
Preparing your deliverance,
  To me the charge hath given.
The Czar full oft in words and deeds
  Is stormy and self-willed;
But, when the Lady Catherine pleads,   335
  His violence is stilled.

317–20 You, Lady, in those humble weeds
    Disguised, and here so long
Hovel'd under heath and reeds
    The barren trees among?" MS.

"Leave open to my wish the course,
  And I to her will go;
From that humane and heavenly source
  Good, only good, can flow."   340
Faint sanction given, the Cavalier
  Was eager to depart,
Though question followed question, dear
  To the Maiden's filial heart.

Light was his step,—his hopes, more light,   345
  Kept pace with his desires;
And the fifth morning gave him sight
  Of Moscow's glittering spires.
He sued:—heart-smitten by the wrong,
  To the lorn Fugitive   350
The Emperor sent a pledge as strong
  As sovereign power could give.

O more than mighty change! If e'er
  Amazement rose to pain,
And joy's excess produced a fear   355
  Of something void and vain;
'Twas when the Parents, who had mourned
  So long the lost as dead,
Beheld their only Child returned
  The household floor to tread.   360

Soon gratitude gave way to love
  Within the Maiden's breast;
Delivered and Deliverer move
  In bridal garments drest;
Meek Catherine had her own reward;   365
  The Czar bestowed a dower;
And universal Moscow shared
  The triumph of that hour.

337–8 Her will I seek—along my course
         In confidence I go MS.
341–4 This said, the gallant Cavalier
         Withdrew, ere full reply
       Was made to crowding questions, dear
         To filial piety. MS.
347 fifth] third MS. *and* 1835   348 glittering] golden MS.   355 joy's
excess] overjoy MS. *and* 1835

Flowers strewed the ground ; the nuptial feast
   Was held with costly state ;   370
And there, 'mid many a noble guest,
   The Foster-parents sate ;
Encouraged by the imperial eye,
   They shrank not into shade ;
Great was their bliss, the honour high   375
   To them and nature paid !

369–72 Faith rules the song, nor deem it care
        Too humble to relate
     That at the Spousal feast the Pair
      Of rustic Guardians sate. MS.

INSCRIPTIONS

I

IN THE GROUNDS OF COLEORTON, THE SEAT OF SIR GEORGE
BEAUMONT, BART., LEICESTERSHIRE

[Composed 1811.—Published 1815.]

THE embowering rose, the acacia, and the pine,
Will not unwillingly their place resign;
If but the Cedar thrive that near them stands,
Planted by Beaumont's and by Wordsworth's hands.
One wooed the silent Art with studious pains: 5
These groves have heard the Other's pensive strains;
Devoted thus, their spirits did unite
By interchange of knowledge and delight.
May Nature's kindliest powers sustain the Tree,
And Love protect it from all injury!   10
And when its potent branches, wide out-thrown,
Darken the brow of this memorial Stone,
Here may some Painter sit in future days,
Some future Poet meditate his lays;
Not mindless of that distant age renowned   15
When Inspiration hovered o'er this ground,
The haunt of him who sang how spear and shield
In civil conflict met on Bosworth-field;
And of that famous Youth, full soon removed
From earth, perhaps by Shakespeare's self approved,   20
Fletcher's Associate, Jonson's Friend beloved.

II

IN A GARDEN OF THE SAME

[Composed 1811.—Published 1815.]

OFT is the medal faithful to its trust
When temples, columns, towers, are laid in dust;
And 'tis a common ordinance of fate
That things obscure and small outlive the great:
Hence, when yon mansion and the flowery trim   5
Of this fair garden, and its alleys dim,

I. 12/13 And to a favorite Resting-place invite,
         For coolness grateful and a sober light; MS., 1815–20
    20 perhaps by] by mighty MS.

And all its stately trees, are passed away,
This little Niche, unconscious of decay,
Perchance may still survive. And be it known
That it was scooped within the living stone,— 10
Not by the sluggish and ungrateful pains
Of labourer plodding for his daily gains,
But by an industry that wrought in love;
With help from female hands, that proudly strove
To aid the work, what time these walks and bowers 15
Were shaped to cheer dark winter's lonely hours.

III

WRITTEN AT THE REQUEST OF SIR GEORGE BEAUMONT, BART., AND
IN HIS NAME, FOR AN URN, PLACED BY HIM AT THE TERMINATION
OF A NEWLY-PLANTED AVENUE, IN THE SAME GROUNDS

[Composed November, 1811.—Published 1815.]

YE Lime-trees, ranged before this hallowed Urn,
Shoot forth with lively power at Spring's return;
And be not slow a stately growth to rear
Of pillars, branching off from year to year,
Till they have learned to frame a darksome aisle;— 5
That may recal to mind that awful Pile
Where Reynolds, 'mid our country's noblest dead,
In the last sanctity of fame is laid.
—There, though by right the excelling Painter sleep
Where Death and Glory a joint sabbath keep, 10
Yet not the less his Spirit would hold dear
Self-hidden praise, and Friendship's private tear:
Hence, on my patrimonial grounds, have I

II. 10 scooped within] fashioned in MS.
13–14 But by prompt hands of Pleasure and of Love
　　　Female and Male, that emulously strove MS.
15–16 aid . . . shaped 1827: shape . . . framed MS., 1815–20
III. 1 before] around MS.
4–7 Bending your docile boughs from year to year
　　　Till in a solemn concave they unite,
　　　Like that Cathedral Dome beneath whose height
　　　Reynolds among our Country's noble Dead MS.
5 Till they at length have framed 1815
5–6 Till ye have framed at length . . .
　　　Like a Recess within that sacred Pile MS.
13–14 my native grounds, unblamed, may I
　　　Raise MS.
13–15 Hence an obscure Memorial, without blame
　　　In these domestic grounds, may bear his Name;

Raised this frail tribute to his memory;
From youth a zealous follower of the Art   15
That he professed; attached to him in heart;
Admiring, loving, and with grief and pride
Feeling what England lost when Reynolds died.

IV

FOR A SEAT IN THE GROVES OF COLEORTON

[Composed November 19, 1811.—Published 1815.]

BENEATH yon eastern ridge, the craggy bound,
Rugged and high, of Charnwood's forest ground,
Stand yet, but, Stranger! hidden from thy view,
The ivied Ruins of forlorn GRACE DIEU;
Erst a religious House, which day and night   5
With hymns resounded, and the chanted rite:
And when those rites had ceased, the Spot gave birth
To honourable Men of various worth:
There, on the margin of a streamlet wild,
Did Francis Beaumont sport, an eager child;   10
There, under shadow of the neighbouring rocks,
Sang youthful tales of shepherds and their flocks;
Unconscious prelude to heroic themes,
Heart-breaking tears, and melancholy dreams
Of slighted love, and scorn, and jealous rage,   15
With which his genius shook the buskined stage.
Communities are lost, and Empires die,
And things of holy use unhallowed lie;
They perish;—but the Intellect can raise,
From airy words alone, a Pile that ne'er decays.   20

Unblamed this votive Urn may oft renew
Some mild sensations to his Genius due
From One, a humble follower of the Art MS.
IV. 7-8 But when the formal Mass had long been stilled
And wise and mighty changes were fulfilled,
That Ground gave birth to Men of various Parts
For knightly services and liberal Arts; MS.
16 genius shook] skill inspired MS.   19 But Truth and Intellectual
Power MS.

V

WRITTEN WITH A PENCIL UPON A STONE IN THE WALL OF THE
HOUSE (AN OUT-HOUSE), ON THE ISLAND AT GRASMERE

[Composed 1800.—Published 1800.]

RUDE is this Edifice, and Thou hast seen
Buildings, albeit rude, that have maintained
Proportions more harmonious, and approached
To closer fellowship with ideal grace.
But take it in good part:—alas! the poor   5
Vitruvius of our village had no help
From the great City; never, upon leaves
Of red Morocco folio saw displayed,
In long succession, pre-existing ghosts
Of Beauties yet unborn—the rustic Lodge   10
Antique, and Cottage with verandah graced,
Nor lacking, for fit company, alcove,
Green-house, shell-grot, and moss-lined hermitage.
Thou see'st a homely Pile, yet to these walls
The heifer comes in the snow-storm, and here   15
The new-dropped lamb finds shelter from the wind.
And hither does one Poet sometimes row
His pinnace, a small vagrant barge, up-piled
With plenteous store of heath and withered fern,
(A lading which he with his sickle cuts,   20
Among the mountains) and beneath this roof
He makes his summer couch, and here at noon
Spreads out his limbs, while, yet unshorn, the Sheep,
Panting beneath the burthen of their wool,
Lie round him, even as if they were a part   25
Of his own Household: nor, while from his bed
He looks, through the open door-place, toward the lake
And to the stirring breezes, does he want
Creations lovely as the work of sleep—
Fair sights, and visions of romantic joy!   30

V. WRITTEN *ETC.* 1815: INSCRIPTION FOR THE HOUSE *ETC.* 1800: LINES
WRITTEN *ETC.* 1802–5
4–5 *so* 1837: To somewhat of a closer fellowship
        With the ideal grace. Yet as it is
        Do take it in good part, for he [alas! 1815–32] the poor   1800–32
7 upon 1837: on the 1800–32   9 *so* 1837: The skeletons and 1800–32
10–13 *so* 1837: ...the rustic Box,
        Snug cot, with Coach-house, Shed and Hermitage. 1800–32
14 Thou seest 1815: It is 1800–5   27 *so* 1837: He through that door-
place looks   1800–32

VI

WRITTEN WITH A SLATE PENCIL ON A STONE, ON THE SIDE OF THE MOUNTAIN OF BLACK COMB

[Composed 1813.—Published 1815.]

STAY, bold Adventurer; rest awhile thy limbs
On this commodious Seat! for much remains
Of hard ascent before thou reach the top
Of this huge Eminence,—from blackness named,
And, to far-travelled storms of sea and land,   5
A favourite spot of tournament and war!
But thee may no such boisterous visitants
Molest; may gentle breezes fan thy brow;
And neither cloud conceal, nor misty air
Bedim, the grand terraqueous spectacle,   10
From centre to circumference, unveiled!
Know, if thou grudge not to prolong thy rest,
That on the summit whither thou art bound,
A geographic Labourer pitched his tent,
With books supplied and instruments of art,   15
To measure height and distance; lonely task,
Week after week pursued!—To him was given
Full many a glimpse (but sparingly bestowed
On timid man) of Nature's processes
Upon the exalted hills. He made report   20
That once, while there he plied his studious work
Within that canvass Dwelling, colours, lines,
And the whole surface of the out-spread map,
Became invisible: for all around
Had darkness fallen—unthreatened, unproclaimed—   25
As if the golden day itself had been
Extinguished in a moment; total gloom,
In which he sate alone, with unclosed eyes,
Upon the blinded mountain's silent top!

VI. 1–4 Glad welcome bold Adventurer! who at length
    By patient or impatient toil hast clomb
    This speculative Mount; MS.
7–13 But thee may no such visitants disturb
    May calm transpicuous air reward thy [   ]
    And cloud and haze and vapour be removed
    From the terrestrial Vision. On the crown
    Of this bare Eminence where now thou standst MS. 1
12–13 Know that upon the Summit where thou stand'st MS.   22–3
so 1837: suddenly The many coloured Map before his eyes   1815–32. *so*
MS., *but* sight *for* eyes   29 mountain's] region's MS.

VII

WRÍTTEN WITH A SLATE PENCIL UPON A STONE, THE LARGEST OF A HEAP LYING NEAR A DESERTED QUARRY, UPON ONE OF THE ISLANDS AT RYDAL

[Composed 1800.—Published 1800.]

STRANGER! this hillock of mis-shapen stones
Is not a Ruin spared or made by time,
Nor, as perchance thou rashly deem'st, the Cairn
Of some old British Chief: 'tis nothing more
Than the rude embryo of a little Dome   5
Or Pleasure-house, once destined to be built
Among the birch-trees of this rocky isle.
But, as it chanced, Sir William having learned
That from the shore a full-grown man might wade,
And make himself a freeman of this spot   10
At any hour he chose, the prudent Knight
Desisted and the quarry and the mound
Are monuments of his unfinished task.
The block on which these lines are traced, perhaps,
Was once selected as the corner-stone   15
Of that intended Pile, which would have been
Some quaint odd plaything of elaborate skill,
So that, I guess, the linnet and the thrush,
And other little builders who dwell here,
Had wondered at the work. But blame him not,   20
For old Sir William was a gentle Knight,
Bred in this vale, to which he appertained
With all his ancestry. Then peace to him,
And for the outrage which he had devised
Entire forgiveness!—But if thou art one   25
On fire with thy impatience to become
An inmate of these mountains,—if, disturbed
By beautiful conceptions, thou has hewn
Out of the quiet rock the elements
Of thy trim Mansion destined soon to blaze   30

VII. 2 spared or made by 1837: of the ancient [antique MS.] 1800–32
4–7   . . . British warrior, no, to speak
   An honest truth 'tis neither more nor less
   Than the rude germs of what was to have been
   A pleasure-house MS.
6 *so* 1802: which was to have been built 1800   10 spot] rock MS.
11 prudent Knight 1837: Knight forthwith 1800–32

In snow-white splendour,—think again; and, taught
By old Sir William and his quarry, leave
Thy fragments to the bramble and the rose;
There let the vernal slow-worm sun himself,
And let the redbreast hop from stone to stone.   35

VIII

[Composed June 26, 1830.—Published 1835.]

In these fair vales hath many a Tree
    At Wordsworth's suit been spared;
And from the builder's hand this Stone,
For some rude beauty of its own,
    Was rescued by the Bard: 5
So let it rest; and time will come
    When here the tender-hearted
May heave a gentle sigh for him,
    As one of the departed.

IX

[Composed 1826.—Published 1835.]

The massy Ways, carried across these heights
By Roman perseverance, are destroyed,
Or hidden under ground, like sleeping worms.
How venture then to hope that Time will spare
This humble Walk? Yet on the mountain's side   5

31 splendour   1800, 1815: glory   1802–5
VIII. INSCRIPTION INTENDED FOR A STONE IN THE GROUNDS OF RYDAL
MOUNT. 1835
    1 this fair Vale MS. 1
3–5 The builder touched this old grey Stone
    'Twas rescued by the Bard; MS. 1
    He sav'd this old grey stone that pleas'd
    The grove-frequenting Bard MS. 3
6–7 Long may it last! and here, perchance,
    The good and tender-hearted MS.
    To let it rest in peace; and here
    (Heaven knows how soon) the tender-hearted 1835, *corr. to text in*
errata
6–8 Long may it rest in peace—and here
    Perchance the . . .
    Will MS. 2
IX. INSCRIPTION. 1835. Intended to be placed on the door of the further
Gravel Terrace if we had quitted Rydal Mount. MS.   1 once carried
o'er these hills MS.   4 Time will spare] private claims Will from the
injuries of time protect MS.

A Poet's hand first shaped it; and the steps
Of that same Bard—repeated to and fro
At morn, at noon, and under moonlight skies
Through the vicissitudes of many a year—
Forbade the weeds to creep o'er its grey line.　　　　　10
No longer, scattering to the heedless winds
The vocal raptures of fresh poesy,
Shall he frequent these precincts; locked no more
In earnest converse with belovèd Friends,
Here will he gather stores of ready bliss,　　　　　15
As from the beds and borders of a garden
Choice flowers are gathered! But, if Power may spring
Out of a farewell yearning—favoured more
Than kindred wishes mated suitably
With vain regrets—the Exile would consign　　　　　20
This Walk, his loved possession, to the care
Of those pure Minds that reverence the Muse.

X

INSCRIPTIONS SUPPOSED TO BE FOUND IN AND NEAR
A HERMIT'S CELL

[This group (X–XIV) was composed 1818.—Published 1820.]

I

Hopes what are they?—Beads of morning
Strung on slender blades of grass;
Or a spider's web adorning
In a strait and treacherous pass.

What are fears but voices airy?　　　　　5
Whispering harm where harm is not;
And deluding the unwary
Till the fatal bolt is shot!

IX. 6–8 steps . . . repeated . . . at noon] foot . . . by pacing . . . and noon
11–20 Murmuring his unambitious verse alone
　　　Or in sweet converse with beloved Friends,
　　　No more must he frequent it. Yet might power
　　　Follow the yearnings of the spirit, he
　　　Reluctantly departing, would consign MS.
21 loved] heart's MS.
X. *Before l.* 1 Methought that traversing a moorland waste
　　　　　I reached a shaggy deeply-cloven dell
　　　　　And found these melancholy fragments traced
　　　　　On the stone threshold of a Hermit's cell. MSS.
4 Some strait and dangerous MS. 1　　6 Whispering] Threatening MS. 2:
Haunting Man where MS. 1

What is glory ?—in the socket
See how dying tapers fare!   10
What is pride ?—a whizzing rocket
That would emulate a star.

What is friendship ?—do not trust her,
Nor the vows which she has made ;
Diamonds dart their brightest lustre   15
From a palsy-shaken head.

What is truth ?—a staff rejected ;
Duty ?—an unwelcome clog ;
Joy ?—a moon by fits reflected
In a swamp or watery bog ;   20

Bright, as if through ether steering,
To the Traveller's eye it shone:
He hath hailed it re-appearing—
And as quickly it is gone ;

Such is Joy—as quickly hidden,   25
Or mis-shapen to the sight,
And by sullen weeds forbidden
To resume its native light.

What is youth ?—a dancing billow,
(Winds behind, and rocks before!)   30
Age ?—a drooping, tottering willow
On a flat and lazy shore.

What is peace ?—when pain is over,
And love ceases to rebel,
Let the last faint sigh discover   35
That precedes the passing-knell!

17 staff] pearl MSS.   19 *so* 1827: a dazzling moon 1820   20 watery]
plashy MS. 1   22 Traveller's] Shepherd's MS. 2
23–4 Can we trust its reappearing,
        No, 'tis dim, misshapen, gone MSS.
25 *so* 1827: Gone, as if for ever hidden   1820: Bright, and in a moment
hidden C   28 native] dazzling C   29 dancing] sparkling MS. 1
30 Shaped, and instantly no more MS. 2   32 flat and lazy] melancholy MS. 1   33–6 *not in* MSS.: *in their place is* No. XII, *infra, but*
l. 5 See yon undulating meadow MS. 1

XI

INSCRIBED UPON A ROCK

II

PAUSE, Traveller! whosoe'er thou be
Whom chance may lead to this retreat,
Where silence yields reluctantly
Even to the fleecy straggler's bleat;

Give voice to what my hand shall trace,   5
And fear not lest an idle sound
Of words unsuited to the place
Disturb its solitude profound.

I saw this Rock, while vernal air
Blew softly o'er the russet heath,   10
Uphold a Monument as fair
As church or abbey furnisheth.

Unsullied did it meet the day,
Like marble, white, like ether, pure;
As if, beneath, some hero lay,   15
Honoured with costliest sepulture.

My fancy kindled as I gazed;
And, ever as the sun shone forth,
The flattered structure glistened, blazed,
And seemed the proudest thing on earth.   20

But frost had reared the gorgeous Pile
Unsound as those which Fortune builds—
To undermine with secret guile,
Sapped by the very beam that gilds.

And, while I gazed, with sudden shock   25
Fell the whole Fabric to the ground;
And naked left this dripping Rock,
With shapeless ruin spread around!

XI. 5–8 Read thou what I shall here engrave
        And dread not that an idle sound
        Will break the peace which nature gave
        To this her MS.
    9 vernal] April MS.

XII

III

HAST thou seen, with flash incessant,
Bubbles gliding under ice,
Bodied forth and evanescent,
No one knows by what device?

Such are thoughts!—A wind-swept meadow   5
Mimicking a troubled sea,
Such is life; and death a shadow
From the rock eternity!

XIII

NEAR THE SPRING OF THE HERMITAGE

IV

TROUBLED long with warring notions
Long impatient of Thy rod,
I resign my soul's emotions
Unto Thee, mysterious God!

What avails the kindly shelter   5
Yielded by this craggy rent,
If my spirit toss and welter
On the waves of discontent?

Parching Summer hath no warrant
To consume this crystal Well;   10
Rains, that make each rill a torrent,
Neither sully it nor swell.

Thus, dishonouring not her station,
Would my Life present to Thee,
Gracious God, the pure oblation   15
Of divine tranquillity!

XII. (*v. app. crit. to* X. 33–6). 1 flash 1820 (*Misc. Poems*): train 1820
(*Duddon vol.*)
XIII. 8/9 Be my purpose one and single
        Give me the repose to feel
        Of this spring whose waters mingle
        With thy Servant's daily meal. MS.
13 protected in her station MS.

XIV

V

NOT seldom, clad in radiant vest,
Deceitfully goes forth the Morn;
Not seldom Evening in the west
Sinks smilingly forsworn.

The smoothest seas will sometimes prove,   5
To the confiding Bark, untrue;
And, if she trust the stars above
They can be treacherous too.

The umbrageous Oak, in pomp outspread,
Full oft, when storms the welkin rend,   10
Draws lightning down upon the head
It promised to defend.

But Thou art true, incarnate Lord,
Who didst vouchsafe for man to die;
Thy smile is sure, Thy plighted word   15
No change can falsify!

I bent before Thy gracious throne,
And asked for peace on suppliant knee;
And peace was given,—nor peace alone,
But faith sublimed to ecstasy!   20

XV

FOR THE SPOT WHERE THE HERMITAGE STOOD ON ST. HERBERT'S ISLAND, DERWENT-WATER

[Composed 1800.—Published 1800.]

IF thou in the dear love of some one Friend
Hast been so happy that thou know'st what thoughts
Will sometimes in the happiness of love
Make the heart sink, then wilt thou reverence
This quiet spot; and, Stranger! not unmoved   5

XIV. 1–4 Not seldom they repent who rest
          Their hopes upon the flattering morn;
          Oft lover-like the ruddy west
          Is etc. MS.
9–12 not in MS.   18 on   1827: with   MS., 1820   20 so 1827: faith
and hope and MS., 1820
XV. 1–14 so 1832: 1800–5 as text 1–4, but sick for sink   1802–5; and for
ll. 5–14:

Wilt thou behold this shapeless heap of stones,
The desolate ruins of St. Herbert's Cell.
Here stood his threshold; here was spread the roof
That sheltered him, a self-secluded Man,
After long exercise in social cares   10
And offices humane, intent to adore
The Deity, with undistracted mind,
And meditate on everlasting things,
In utter solitude.—But he had left
A Fellow-labourer, whom the good Man loved   15
As his own soul. And, when with eye upraised
To heaven he knelt before the crucifix,
While o'er the lake the cataract of Lodore
Pealed to his orisons, and when he paced

> This quiet spot—St. Herbert hither came,
> And here, for many seasons, from the world
> Removed, and the affections of the world
> He dwelt in solitude.   1800–5

> This Island, guarded from profane approach
> By mountains high and waters widely spread,
> Is that recess to which St. Herbert came
> In life's decline; a self-secluded Man,
> After long exercise *etc. as text* . . . *things.*
> —Stranger! this shapeless heap of stones and earth
> (Long be its mossy covering undisturbed!)
> Is reverenced as a vestige of the Abode
> In which, through many seasons *etc. as* 1800, 1815–20

> Stranger! this shapeless heap of stones and earth
> Is the last relic of St. Herbert's Cell.
> Here stood his threshold; here was spread the roof
> That sheltered him, a self-secluded Man *etc. as text* 1827

MS. 1 *as* 1815, *but* Seclusion which . . . chose *for* recess to which . . . came, *and*
> Hither he came in life's austere decline,
> And, Stranger! this black heap *etc. for* Stranger! this shapeless
> heap *etc.*

MS 2, *for* Is that recess *etc. has*
> Gave to St. Herbert a benign retreat,
> Upon a Staff supported, and his Brow
> White with the peaceful diadem of age,
> Hither he came—a self-secluded Man *etc. to* things
> Behold that shapeless heap *etc.*
> 'Tis reverenced *etc.*

14–15 But . . . labourer] He living here
> This Island's sole inhabitant! had left
> A Fellow-labourer   MS. *and* 1800 *only*

16–17 *so* 1815: And when within his cave
> Alone he *etc.* 1800–5

Along the beach of this small isle and thought   20
Of his Companion, he would pray that both
(Now that their earthly duties were fulfilled)
Might die in the same moment. Nor in vain
So prayed he:—as our chronicles report,
Though here the Hermit numbered his last day   25
Far from St. Cuthbert his belovèd Friend,
Those holy Men both died in the same hour.

XVI

ON THE BANKS OF A ROCKY STREAM

[Composed ?.—Published 1850.]

BEHOLD an emblem of our human mind
Crowded with thoughts that need a settled home,
Yet, like to eddying balls of foam
Within this whirlpool, they each other chase
Round and round, and neither find   5
An outlet nor a resting-place!
Stranger, if such disquietude be thine,
Fall on thy knees and sue for help divine.

21 would pray   1802; had pray'd   1800   22 *not in* 1800–5   25 day
1815: days   1800–5
XVI.   1–4 Grant me, O blessed Lord, a mind
            In which my thoughts may have a quiet home
            Thoughts which now fret like balls of foam
            That in a whirlpool each the other chase MS.

SELECTIONS FROM CHAUCER

MODERNISED

I

THE PRIORESS' TALE

"Call up him who left half told
The story of Cambuscan bold."

In the following Poem no further deviation from the original has been made
than was necessary for the fluent reading and instant understanding of
the Author: so much, however, is the language altered since Chaucer's
time, especially in pronunciation, that much was to be removed, and its
place supplied with as little incongruity as possible. The ancient accent
has been retained in a few conjunctions, as *also* and *alway*, from a conviction that such sprinklings of antiquity would be admitted, by persons
of taste, to have a graceful accordance with the subject. [1820] The
fierce bigotry of the Prioress forms a fine back-ground for her tender-
hearted sympathies with the Mother and Child; and the mode in which
the story is told amply atones for the extravagance of the miracle. [1827]

[Written December 4–5, 1801.—Published 1820.]

I

"O LORD, our Lord! how wondrously," (quoth she)
"Thy name in this large world is spread abroad!
For not alone by men of dignity
Thy worship is performed and precious laud;
But by the mouths of children, gracious God!   5
Thy goodness is set forth; they when they lie
Upon the breast Thy name do glorify.

II

"Wherefore in praise, the worthiest that I may,
Jesu! of Thee, and the white Lily-flower
Which did Thee bear, and is a Maid for aye,   10
To tell a story I will use my power;
Not that I may increase her honour's dower,
For she herself is honour, and the root
Of goodness, next her Son, our soul's best boot.

I. 1–2 wondrously . . . large] marvellous . . . huge MS.   6 Thy bounty
is performed MS.   7 glorify] magnify MS.   10 for aye] alway
MS.   11 use] do MS.

III

"O Mother Maid! O Maid and Mother free!　　15
O bush unburnt! burning in Moses' sight!
That down didst ravish from the Deity,
Through humbleness, the spirit that did alight
Upon thy heart, whence, through that glory's might,
Conceivèd was the Father's sapience,　　20
Help me to tell it in thy reverence!

IV

"Lady! thy goodness, thy magnificence,
Thy virtue, and thy great humility,
Surpass all science and all utterance;
For sometimes, Lady! ere men pray to thee　　25
Thou goest before in thy benignity,
The light to us vouchsafing of thy prayer,
To be our guide unto thy Son so dear.

V

"My knowledge is so weak, O blissful Queen!
To tell abroad thy mighty worthiness,　　30
That I the weight of it may not sustain;
But as a child of twelvemonths old or less,
That laboureth his language to express,
Even so fare I; and therefore, I thee pray,
Guide thou my song which I of thee shall say.　　35

VI

"There was in Asia, in a mighty town,
'Mong Christian folk, a street where Jews might be,
Assigned to them and given them for their own
By a great Lord, for gain and usury,
Hateful to Christ and to His company;　　40
And through this street who list might ride and wend;
Free was it, and unbarred at either end.

VII

"A little school of Christian people stood
Down at the farther end, in which there were
A nest of children come of Christian blood,　　45

24 Surpass] Passeth MS.
27-8 And givest us the guidance of thy prayer
　　To be a light unto *etc.* MS.
42 For it was free and open MS.　　43 Christian folk there stood MS.

That learnèd in that school from year to year
Such sort of doctrine as men usèd there,
That is to say, to sing and read alsò,
As little children in their childhood do.

VIII

"Among these children was a Widow's son,   50
A little scholar, scarcely seven years old,
Who day by day unto this school hath gone,
And eke, when he the image did behold
Of Jesu's Mother, as he had been told,
This Child was wont to kneel adown and say   55
Ave Marie, as he goeth by the way.

IX

"This Widow thus her little Son hath taught
Our blissful Lady, Jesu's Mother dear,
To worship aye, and he forgat it not;
For simple infant hath a ready ear.   60
Sweet is the holiness of youth: and hence,
Calling to mind this matter when I may,
Saint Nicholas in my presence standeth aye,
For he so young to Christ did reverence.

X

"This little Child, while in the school he sate   65
His Primer conning with an earnest cheer,
The whilst the rest their anthem-book repeat
The *Alma Redemptoris* did he hear;
And as he durst he drew him near and near,
And hearkened to the words and to the note,   70
Till the first verse he learned it all by rote.

XI

"This Latin knew he nothing what it said,
For he too tender was of age to know;

51 scarcely] that was MS.
65–7 . . . learning his little book
     As he sate at his primer in the school
     Where children learn the anthem-book by rule MS.
71 And . . . he knew it . . . MS.
72–6 This Latin wist he nought what it did say,
     For he so young and tender was of age;

But to his comrade he repaired, and prayed
That he the meaning of this song would show,   75
And unto him declare why men sing so;
This oftentimes, that he might be at ease,
This child did him beseech on' his bare knees.

XII

"His Schoolfellow, who elder was than he,
Answered him thus:—'This song, I have heard say,   80
Was fashioned for our blissful Lady free;
Her to salute, and also her to pray
To be our help upon our dying day:
If there is more in this, I know it not;
Song do I learn,—small grammar I have got.'   85

XIII

" 'And is this song fashioned in reverence
Of Jesu's Mother?' said this Innocent;
'Now, certès, I will use my diligence
To con it all ere Christmas-tide be spent;
Although I for my Primer shall be shent,   90
And shall be beaten three times in an hour,
Our Lady I will praise with all my power.'

XIV

"His Schoolfellow, whom he had so besought,
As they went homeward taught him privily
And then he sang it well and fearlessly,   95
From word to word according to the note:
Twice in a day it passèd through his throat;
Homeward and schoolward whensoe'er he went,
On Jesu's Mother fixed was his intent.

XV

"Through all the Jewry (this before said I)   100
This little Child, as he came to and fro,
Full merrily then would he sing and cry,
O *Alma Redemptoris!* high and low:

But on a day his fellow he gan pray
To expound to him the song that he might know
Its proper meaning and why *etc.* MS.
77 have his ease MS.   78 Prayed this child to him *etc.* MS.   85 Song
do] The song MS.

The sweetness of Christ's Mother piercèd so
His heart, that her to praise, to her to pray,   105
He cannot stop his singing by the way.

XVI

"The Serpent, Satan, our first foe, that hath
His wasp's nest in Jew's heart, upswelled—'O woe,
O Hebrew people!' said he in his wrath,
'Is it an honest thing? Shall this be so?   110
That such a Boy where'er he lists shall go
In your despite, and sing his hymns and saws,
Which is against the reverence of our laws!'

XVII

"From that day forward have the Jews conspired
Out of the world this Innocent to chase;   115
And to this end a Homicide they hired,
That in an alley had a privy place,
And, as the Child 'gan to the school to pace,
This cruel Jew him seized, and held him fast
And cut his throat, and in a pit him cast.   120

XVIII

"I say that him into a pit they threw,
A loathsome pit, whence noisome scents exhale;
O cursèd folk! away, ye Herods new!
What may your ill intentions you avail?
Murder will out; certès it will not fail;   125
Know, that the honour of high God may spread,
The blood cries out on your accursèd deed.

XIX

"O Martyr 'stablished in virginity!
Now may'st thou sing for aye before the throne,
Following the Lamb celestial," quoth she,   130
"Of which the great Evangelist, Saint John,
In Patmos wrote, who saith of them that go
Before the Lamb singing continually,
That never fleshly woman they did know.

111 list 1820   119 cruel] cursed MS.   122 Where[to] these Jews
their things unclean did trail MS.   123 ... O Herods old and new MS.

XX

"Now this poor Widow waiteth all that night　　135
After her little Child, and he came not;
For which, by earliest glimpse of morning light,
With face all pale with dread and busy thought,
She at the School and elsewhere him hath sought,
Until thus far she learned, that he had been　　140
In the Jews' street, and there he last was seen.

XXI

"With Mother's pity in her breast enclosed
She goeth, as she were half out of her mind,
To every place wherein she hath supposed
By likelihood her little Son to find;　　145
And ever on Christ's Mother meek and kind
She cried, till to the Jewry she was brought,
And him among the accursèd Jews she sought.

XXII

"She asketh, and she piteously doth pray
To every Jew that dwelleth in that place　　150
To tell her if her child had passed that way;
They all said—Nay; but Jesu of His grace
Gave to her thought, that in a little space
She for her Son in that same spot did cry
Where he was cast into a pit hard by.　　155

XXIII

"O Thou great God that dost perform Thy laud
By mouths of Innocents, lo! here Thy might;
This gem of chastity, this emerald,
And eke of martyrdom this ruby bright,
There, where with mangled throat he lay upright,　　160
The *Alma Redemptoris* 'gan to sing
So loud, that with his voice the place did ring.

137 at daybreak, soon as it was light MS.　　144 To all and every place
where she MS.
153-4 Gave it to her in thought that in that place
　　　　She for her little Son anon did cry MS.
162 . . . all the place therewith did ring. MS.

XXIV

"The Christian folk that through the Jewry went
Come to the spot in wonder at the thing;
And hastily they for the Provost sent;   165
Immediately he came, not tarrying,
And praiseth Christ that is our heavenly King,
And eke His Mother, honour of Mankind:
Which done, he bade that they the Jews should bind.

XXV

"This Child with piteous lamentation then   170
Was taken up, singing his song alwày;
And with procession great and pomp of men
To the next Abbey him they bare away;
His Mother swooning by the body lay:
And scarcely could the people that were near   175
Remove this second Rachel from the bier.

XXVI

"Torment and shameful death to every one
This Provost doth for those bad Jews prepare
That of this murder wist, and that anon:
Such wickedness his judgments cannot spare;   180
Who will do evil, evil shall he bear;
Them therefore with wild horses did he draw.
And after that he hung them by the law.

XXVII

"Upon his bier this Innocent doth lie
Before the altar while the Mass doth last: 185
The Abbot with his convent's company
Then sped themselves to bury him full fast;
And, when they holy water on him cast,
Yet spake this Child when sprinkled was the water;
And sang, O *Alma Redemptoris Mater!*   190

XXVIII

"This Abbot, for he was a holy man,
As all Monks are, or surely ought to be,
In supplication to the Child began

174 body 1845: bier MS., 1820–43, 1850
191–2 This Abbot who had been a holy man   .
         And was, as all monks are, or ought to be. MS.

Thus saying, 'O dear Child! I summon thee
In virtue of the holy Trinity   195
Tell me the cause why thou dost sing this hymn,
Since that thy throat is cut, as it doth seem.'

XXIX

" 'My throat is cut unto the bone, I trow,'
Said this young Child, 'and by the law of kind
I should have died, yea many hours ago;   200
But Jesus Christ, as in the books ye find,
Will that His glory last, and be in mind;
And, for the worship of His Mother dear,
Yet may I sing, O *Alma!* loud and clear.

XXX

" 'This well of mercy, Jesu's Mother sweet,   205
After my knowledge I have loved alwày;
And in the hour when I my death did meet
To me she came, and thus to me did say,
'Thou in thy dying sing this holy lay,'
As ye have heard; and soon as I had sung   210
Methought she laid a grain upon my tongue.

XXXI

" 'Wherefore I sing, nor can from song refrain,
In honour of that blissful Maiden free,
Till from my tongue off-taken is the grain;
And after that thus said she unto me;   215
'My little Child, then will I come for thee
Soon as the grain from off thy tongue they take:
Be not dismayed, I will not thee forsake!'

XXXII

"This holy Monk, this Abbot—him mean I,
Touched then his tongue, and took away the grain;   220
And he gave up the ghost full peacefully;
And, when the Abbot had this wonder seen,
His salt tears trickled down like showers of rain;
And on his face he droppęd upon the ground,
And still he lay as if he had been bound.   225

199 in my natural kind MS.

XXXIII

"Eke the whole Convent on the pavement lay,
Weeping and praising Jesu's Mother dear;
And after that they rose, and took their way,
And lifted up this Martyr from the bier,
And in a tomb of precious marble clear 230
Enclosed his uncorrupted body sweet.—
Where'er he be, God grant us him to meet!

XXXIV

"Young Hew of Lincoln! in like sort laid low
By cursèd Jews—thing well and widely known,
For it was done a little while ago— 235
Pray also thou for us, while here we tarry
Weak sinful folk, that God, with pitying eye,
In mercy would his mercy multiply
On us, for reverence of his Mother Mary!"

II

THE CUCKOO AND THE NIGHTINGALE

[Written December 7–9, 1801.—Published 1841 (R. H. Horne's *The Poems of Geoffrey Chaucer, Modernised*); vol. of 1842.]

I

THE God of Love—*ah, benedicite!*
How mighty and how great a Lord is he!
For he of low hearts can make high, of high
He can make low, and unto death bring nigh;
And hard hearts he can make them kind and free. 5

II

Within a little time, as hath been found,
He can make sick folk whole and fresh and sound:
Them who are whole in body and in mind,
He can make sick,—bind can he and unbind
All that he will have bound, or have unbound. 10

231 They did enclose his little body sweet MS.   232 There he is now *etc.* MS.
235 *so* 1837:
         For it was done but little while ago MS.
         For not long since was dealt the cruel blow 1820–32
II.   3–4 High can he make the heart that's low and poor
         The high heart low, and bring it to death's door MSS.
(And high hearts low, through pains which [that] they endure MSS. *alt.*)

III

To tell his might my wit may not suffice;
Foolish men he can make them out of wise;—
For he may do all that he will devise;
Loose livers he can make abate their vice,
And proud hearts can make tremble in a trice.   15

IV

In brief, the whole of what he will, he may;
Against him dare not any wight say nay;
To humble or afflict whome'er he will,
To gladden or to grieve, he hath like skill;
But most his might he sheds on the eve of May.   20

V

For every true heart, gentle heart and free,
That with him is, or thinketh so to be,
Now against May shall have some stirring—whether
To joy, or be it to some mourning; never
At other time, methinks, in like degree.   25

VI

For now when they may hear the small birds' song,
And see the budding leaves the branches throng,
This unto their rememberance doth bring
All kinds of pleasure mix'd with sorrowing;
And longing of sweet thoughts that ever long.   30

VII

And of that longing heaviness doth come,
Whence oft great sickness grows of heart and home;
Sick are they all for lack of their desire;
And thus in May their hearts are set on fire,
So that they burn forth in great martyrdom.   35

VIII

In sooth, I speak from feeling, what though now
Old am I, and to genial pleasure slow;
Yet have I felt of sickness through the May,

25 In no time else (*corr. to* At other time) so much, as thinketh me. MS.
27 And see the leaves spring green and plentiful MS.   28 rememberance MS., 1842: remembrance 1850   30 And lusty thoughts of mighty
longing full. MS.
36–7 And this of feeling truly have I spoken
     What though that I be old and now down broken MS.

Both hot and cold, and heart-aches every day,—
How hard, alas! to bear, I only know.   40

IX

Such shaking doth the fever in me keep
Through all this May that I have little sleep;
And also 'tis not likely unto me,
That any living heart should sleepy be
In which Love's dart its fiery point doth steep.   45

X

But tossing lately on a sleepless bed,
I of a token thought which Lovers heed;
How among them it was a common tale,
That it was good to hear the Nightingale,
Ere the vile Cuckoo's note be utterèd.   50

XI

And then I thought anon as it was day,
I gladly would go somewhere to essay
If I perchance a Nightingale might hear,
For yet had I heard none, of all that year,
And it was then the third night of the May.   55

XII

And soon as I a glimpse of day espied,
No longer would I in my bed abide,
But straightway to a wood that was hard by,
Forth did I go, alone and fearlessly,
And held the pathway down by a brook-side;   60

XIII

Till to a lawn I came all white and green,
I in so fair a one had never been.
The ground was green, with daisy powdered over;
Tall were the flowers, the grove a lofty cover,
All green and white; and nothing else was seen.   65

XIV

There sate I down among the fair fresh flowers,
And saw the birds come tripping from their bowers,

40 hard] sore MS. I only] no wight can MS.   45 In whom his
fiery arrow love MS.   46–7 But on the other night as I lay waking
. . . of Lovers making MS.   50 Before the sorry Cuckoo silence
breaking. MS.

Where they had rested them all night; and they,
Who were so joyful at the light of day,
Began to honour May with all their powers.   70

XV

Well did they know that service all by rote,
And there was many and many a lovely note,
Some, singing loud, as if they had complained;
Some with their notes another manner feigned;
And some did sing all out with the full throat.   75

XVI

They pruned themselves, and made themselves right gay,
Dancing and leaping light upon the spray;
And ever two and two together were,
The same as they had chosen for the year,
Upon Saint Valentine's returning day.   80

XVII

Meanwhile the stream, whose bank I sate upon,
Was making such a noise as it ran on
Accordant to the sweet Birds' harmony;
Methought that it was the best melody
Which ever to man's ear a passage won.   85

XVIII

And for delight, but how I never wot,
I in a slumber and a swoon was caught,
Not all asleep and yet not waking wholly;
And as I lay, the Cuckoo, bird unholy,
Broke silence, or I heard him in my thought.   90

XIX

And that was right upon a tree fast by,
And who was then ill satisfied but I?
Now, God, quoth I, that died upon the rood,
From thee and thy base throat, keep all that's good,
Full little joy have I now of thy cry.   95

70 Began to do the honours of the May. MS.   86–7 . . . know not
well Into a . . . I fell MS.   92 But who had then an evil game but
I ? MS.

XX

And, as I with the Cuckoo thus 'gan chide,
In the next bush that was me fast beside,
I heard the lusty Nightingale so sing,
That her clear voice made a loud rioting,
Echoing thorough all the green wood wide.   100

XXI

Ah! good sweet Nightingale! for my heart's cheer,
Hence hast thou stayed a little while too long;
For we have had the sorry Cuckoo here,
And she hath been before thee with her song;
Evil light on her! she hath done me wrong.   105

XXII

But hear you now a wondrous thing, I pray;
As long as in that swooning-fit I lay,
Methought I wist right well what these birds meant,
And had good knowing both of their intent,
And of their speech, and all that they would say.   110

XXIII

The Nightingale thus in my hearing spake:—
Good Cuckoo, seek some other bush or brake,
And, prithee, let us that can sing dwell here;
For every wight eschews thy song to hear,
Such uncouth singing verily dost thou make.   115

XXIV

What! quoth she then, what is't that ails thee now?
It seems to me I sing as well as thou;
For mine's a song that is both true and plain,—
Although I cannot quaver so in vain
As thou dost in thy throat, I wot not how.   120

XXV

All men may understanding have of me,
But, Nightingale, so may they not of thee;

98 ... a Nightingale so gladly sing MS.   103 had   1842: heard MS., 1841
111–13   ... saith
     Now honest Cuckoo, go away somewhere,
     And let us that can sing inhabit here; MS.
115 ... is it in good faith. MS.

For thou hast many a foolish and quaint cry:—
Thou say'st OSEE, OSEE, then how may I
Have knowledge, I thee pray, what this may be ?   125

XXVI

Ah, fool! quoth she, wist thou not what it is ?
Oft as I say OSEE, OSEE, I wis,
Then mean I, that I should be wonderous fain
That shamefully they one and all were slain,
Whoever against Love mean aught amiss.   130

XXVII

And also would I that they all were dead,
Who do not think in love their life to lead ;
For who is loth the God of Love to obey,
Is only fit to die, I dare well say,
And for that cause OSEE I cry ; take heed!   135

XXVIII

Ay, quoth the Cuckoo, that is a quaint law,
That all must love or die ; but I withdraw,
And take my leave of all such company,
For mine intent it neither is to die,
Nor ever while I live Love's yoke to draw.   140

XXIX

For lovers, of all folk that be alive,
The most disquiet have and least do thrive ;
Most feeling have of sorrow, woe and care,
And the least welfare cometh to their share ;
What need is there against the truth to strive ?   145

XXX

What! quoth she, thou art all out of thy mind,
That in thy churlishness a cause canst find
To speak of Love's true Servants in this mood ;
For in this world no service is so good
To every wight that gentle is of kind.   150

123 nice and curious cry MS.   124 I've heard thee say Jug jug MS.
127 As often as I say Jug jug MS.   135 OSEE] Jug jug MS.
137–8 That all must love and perish shamefully,
          But I take leave MS.

XXXI

For thereof comes all goodness and all worth;
All gentiless and honour thence come forth;
Thence worship comes, content and true heart's pleasure,
And full-assured trust, joy without measure,
And jollity, fresh cheerfulness, and mirth;   155

XXXII

And bounty, lowliness, and courtesy,
And seemliness, and faithful company,
And dread of shame that will not do amiss;
For he that faithfully Love's servant is,
Rather than be disgraced, would chuse to die.   160

XXXIII

And that the very truth it is which I
Now say—in such belief I'll live and die;
And Cuckoo, do thou so, by my advice.
Then, quoth she, let me never hope for bliss,
If with that counsel I do e'er comply.   165

XXXIV

Good Nightingale! thou speakest wondrous fair,
Yet for all that, the truth is found elsewhere;
For Love in young folk is but rage, I wis;
And Love in old folk a great dotage is;
Who most it useth, him 'twill most impair.   170

XXXV

For thereof come all contraries to gladness;
Thence sickness comes, and overwhelming sadness,
Mistrust and jealousy, despite, debate,
Dishonour, shame, envy importunate,
Pride, anger, mischief, poverty, and madness.   175

151–3   . . . verily
   Thereof all honour and all gentleness,
   Thereof comes worship, hope, and all heart's pleasure, MS.
152 gentiless 1842: gentleness 1841   155 And freshness, and delight,
and jollity, MS.   160 had liefer die MS.
161–5 And that then is the truth which now I say,
   In that belief I will both live and die,
   And, Cuckoo, eke do thou my counsel try.
   Then, quoth she, may no pleasure with me stay,
   If I that counsel ever do obey. MS.
167 And yet the truth is contrary to this; MS.

XXXVI

Loving is aye an office of despair,
And one thing is therein which is not fair;
For whoso gets of love a little bliss,
Unless it alway stay with him, I wis
He may full soon go with an old man's hair.　　180

XXXVII

And, therefore, Nightingale! do thou keep nigh,
For trust me well, in spite of thy quaint cry,
If long time from thy mate thou be, or far,
Thou'lt be as others that forsaken are;
Then shalt thou raise a clamour as do I.　　185

XXXVIII

Fie, quoth she, on thy name, Bird ill beseen!
The God of Love afflict thee with all teen,
For thou art worse than mad a thousand fold;
For many a one hath virtues manifold,
Who had been nought, if Love had never been.　　190

XXXIX

For evermore his servants Love amendeth,
And he from every blemish them defendeth;
And maketh them to burn, as in a fire,
In loyalty, and worshipful desire,
And, when it likes him, joy enough them sendeth.　　195

XL

Thou Nightingale! the Cuckoo said, be still,
For Love no reason hath but his own will;—
For to th' untrue he oft gives ease and joy;
True lovers doth so bitterly annoy,
He lets them perish through that grievous ill.　　200

XLI

With such a master would I never be;[1]
For he, in sooth, is blind, and may not see,
And knows not when he hurts and when he heals;
Within this court full seldom Truth avails,
So diverse in his wilfulness is he.　　205

[1] From a manuscript in the Bodleian, as are also stanzas 44 and 45
[1841], which are necessary to complete the sense. [1842]

192 And from all evil stains he MS.　　200 That for distress of mind
themselves they kill. MS.

XLII

Then of the Nightingale did I take note,
How from her inmost heart a sigh she brought,
And said, Alas! that ever I was born,
Not one word have I now, I am so forlorn,—
And with that word, she into tears burst out. 210

XLIII

Alas, alas! my very heart will break,
Quoth she, to hear this churlish bird thus speak
Of Love, and of his holy services;
Now, God of Love! thou help me in some wise,
That vengeance on this Cuckoo I may wreak. 215

XLIV

And so methought I started up anon,
And to the brook I ran and got a stone,
Which at the Cuckoo hardily I cast,
And he for dread did fly away full fast;
And glad, in sooth, was I when he was gone. 220

XLV

And as he flew, the Cuckoo, ever and aye,
Kept crying, "Farewell!—farewell, Popinjay!"
As if in scornful mockery of me;
And on I hunted him from tree to tree,
Till he was far, all out of sight, away. 225

XLVI

Then straightway came the Nightingale to me,
And said, Forsooth, my friend, do I thank thee,
That thou wert near to rescue me; and now,
Unto the God of Love I make a vow,
That all this May I will thy songstress be. 230

207 How that she cast a sigh from out her throat, MS.
216–25 Methought that he did then start up anon,
      And glad was I, in truth, that he was gone,
      And ever as the Cuckoo flew away
      He cried out farewell, farewell Popinjay
      As though he had been scorning me alone. MS.
227–8 And "Friend" she said, "I thank thee gratefully
      That thou hast been my rescue, and I now MS.
229 I] do MS.

XLVII

Well satisfied, I thanked her, and she said,
By this mishap no longer be dismayed,
Though thou the Cuckoo heard, ere thou heard'st me;
Yet if I live it shall amended be,
When next May comes, if I am not afraid. 235

XLVIII

And one thing will I counsel thee alsó,
The Cuckoo trust not thou, nor his Love's saw;
All that she said is an outrageous lie.
Nay, nothing shall me bring thereto, quoth I,
For Love, and it hath done me mighty woe. 240

XLIX

Yea, hath it? use, quoth she, this medicine;
This May-time, every day before thou dine,
Go look on the fresh daisy; then say I,
Although for pain thou may'st be like to die,
Thou wilt be eased, and less wilt droop and pine. 245

L

And mind always that thou be good and true,
And I will sing one song, of many new,
For love of thee, as loud as I may cry;
And then did she begin this song full high,
"Beshrew all them that are in love untrue." 250

LI

And soon as she had sung it to the end,
Now farewell, quoth she, for I hence must wend;
And, God of Love, that can right well and may,
Send unto thee as mickle joy this day,
As ever he to Lover yet did send. 255

LII

Thus takes the Nightingale her leave of me;
I pray to God with her always to be,
And joy of love to send her evermore;

231–2 I gave her [?] thanks and was well paid
     Yea, said she then, and be thou not dismayed MS.
237–8 Believe thou not the Cuckoo, no, no, no!
     For he hath spoken *etc.* MS.
243–5 On the fresh daisy go and cast thine eye
     And though for woe at point of death thou lie
     'Twill greatly ease thee, and thou less wilt pine. MS.
246 mind] look MS.

And shield us from the Cuckoo and her lore,
For there is not so false a bird as she.   260

LIII

Forth then she flew, the gentle Nightingale,
To all the Birds that lodged within that dale,
And gathered each and all into one place;
And them besought to hear her doleful case,
And thus it was that she began her tale.   265

LIV

The Cuckoo—'tis not well that I should hide
How she and I did each the other chide,
And without ceasing, since it was daylight;
And now I pray you all to do me right
Of that false Bird whom Love can not abide.   270

LV

Then spake one Bird, and full assent all gave;
This matter asketh counsel good as grave,
For birds we are—all here together brought;
And, in good sooth, the Cuckoo here is not;
And therefore we a Parliament will have.   275

LVI

And thereat shall the Eagle be our Lord,
And other Peers whose names are on record;
A summons to the Cuckoo shall be sent,
And judgment there be given; or that intent
Failing, we finally shall make accord.   280

LVII

And all this shall be done, without a nay,
The morrow after Saint Valentine's day,
Under a maple that is well beseen,
Before the chamber-window of the Queen,
At Woodstock, on the meadow green and gay.   285

LVIII

She thankèd them; and then her leave she took,
And flew into a hawthorn by that brook;
And there she sate and sung—upon that tree—
"For term of life Love shall have hold of me"—
So loudly, that I with that song awoke.   290

260 MS. *ends here and* Finis *is written.*

Unlearned Book and rude, as well I know,
For beauty thou hast none, nor eloquence,
Who did on thee the hardiness bestow
To appear before my Lady? but a sense
Thou surely hast of her benevolence,   295
Whereof her hourly bearing proof doth give;
For of all good she is the best alive.

Alas, poor Book! for thy unworthiness,
To show to her some pleasant meanings writ
In winning words, since through her gentiless,   300
Thee she accepts as for her service fit!
Oh! it repents me I have neither wit
Nor leisure unto thee more worth to give;
For of all good she is the best alive.

Beseech her meekly with all lowliness,   305
Though I be far from her I reverence,
To think upon my truth and stedfastness,
And to abridge my sorrow's violence,
Caused by the wish, as knows your sapience,
She of her liking proof to me would give;   310
For of all good she is the best alive.

L'ENVOY

Pleasure's Aurora, Day of gladsomeness!
Luna by night, with heavenly influence
Illumined! root of beauty and goodnesse,
Write, and allay, by your beneficence,   315
My sighs breathed forth in silence,—comfort give!
Since of all good you are the best alive.

EXPLICIT

III

TROILUS AND CRESIDA

[Written 1801.—Same dates of publication as II.]

NEXT morning Troilus began to clear
His eyes from sleep, at the first break of day,
And unto Pandarus, his own Brother dear,
For love of God, full piteously did say,
We must the Palace see of Cresida;   5

300 gentiless 1842: gentleness 1841
III. TROILUS AND CRESIDA. EXTRACT FROM CHAUCER, 1842.

For since we yet may have no other feast,
Let us behold her Palace at the least!

And therewithal to cover his intent
A cause he found into the Town to go,
And they right forth to Cresid's Palace went;   10
But, Lord, this simple Troilus was woe,
Him thought his sorrowful heart would break in two;
For when he saw her doors fast bolted all,
Well nigh for sorrow down he 'gan to fall.

Therewith when this true Lover 'gan behold,   15
How shut was every window of the place,
Like frost he thought his heart was icy cold;
For which, with changèd, pale, and deadly face,
Without word uttered, forth he 'gan to pace;
And on his purpose bent so fast to ride,   20
That no wight his continuance espied.

Then said he thus,—O Palace desolate!
O house of houses, once so richly dight!
O Palace empty and disconsolate!
Thou lamp of which extinguished is the light;   25
O Palace whilom day that now art night,
Thou ought'st to fall and I to die; since she
Is gone who held us both in sovereignty.

O, of all houses once the crownèd boast!
Palace illumined with the sun of bliss;   30
O ring of which the ruby now is lost,
O cause of woe, that cause has been of bliss:
Yet, since I may no better, would I kiss
Thy cold doors; but I dare not for this rout;
Farewell, thou shrine of which the Saint is out!   35

Therewith he cast on Pandarus an eye,
With changèd face, and piteous to behold;
And when he might his time aright espy,
Aye as he rode, to Pandarus he told
Both his new sorrow and his joys of old,   40
So piteously, and with so dead a hue,
That every wight might on his sorrow rue.

12 break   1842: burst   1841   32 has   1842: hast   1841   36 an
1842: his   1841

Forth from the spot he rideth up and down,
And everything to his rememberànce
Came as he rode by places of the town   45
Where he had felt such perfect pleasure once.
Lo, yonder saw I mine own Lady dance,
And in that Temple she with her bright eyes,
My Lady dear, first bound me captive-wise.

And yonder with joy-smitten heart have I   50
Heard my own Cresid's laugh; and once at play
I yonder saw her eke full blissfully;
And yonder once she unto me 'gan say—
Now, my sweet Troilus, love me well, I pray!
And there so graciously did me behold,   55
That hers unto the death my heart I hold.

And at the corner of that self-same house
Heard I my most beloved Lady dear,
So womanly, with voice melodious
Singing so well, so goodly, and so clear,   60
That in my soul methinks I yet do hear
The blissful sound; and in that very place
My Lady first me took unto her grace.

O blissful God of Love! then thus he cried,
When I the process have in memory,   65
How thou hast wearied me on every side,
Men thence a book might make, a history;
What need to seek a conquest over me,
Since I am wholly at thy will? what joy
Hast thou thy own liege subjects to destroy?   70

Dread Lord! so fearful when provoked, thine ire
Well hast thou wreaked on me by pain and grief;
Now mercy, Lord! thou know'st well I desire

49 First caught me captive my true Lady dear. MS.
50-2 And yonder have I heard full lustily
        My dear heart Cresseid laugh; and yonder play
        I saw her also once *etc.* MS.
55 And here so goodly did she me behold MS.
57 corner there of yonder house MS. *corr. to text*   58 most] own MS.
62 Yonder in that same place   MS.   68 on me to seek a victory MS.
71-2 Well hast thou Lord! on me avenged thine ire,
        Thou mighty God, Sovereign of joy and grief; MS.

Thy grace above all pleasures first and chief;
And live and die I will in thy belief;   75
For which I ask for guerdon but one boon,
That Cresida again thou send me soon.

Constrain her heart as quickly to return,
As thou dost mine with longing her to see,
Then know I well that she would not sojourn.   80
Now, blissful Lord, so cruel do not be
Unto the blood of Troy, I pray of thee,
As Juno was unto the Theban blood,
From whence to Thebes came griefs in multitude.

And after this he to the gate did go   85
Whence Cresid rode, as if in haste she was;
And up and down there went, and to and fro,
And to himself full oft he said, alas!
From hence my hope and solace forth did pass.
O would the blissful God now for his joy,   90
I might her see again coming to Troy!

And up to yonder hill was I her guide;
Alas, and there I took of her my leave;
Yonder I saw her to her Father ride,
For very grief of which my heart shall cleave;—   95
And hither home I came when it was eve;
And here I dwell an outcast from all joy,
And shall, unless I see her soon in Troy.

And of himself did he imagine oft,
That he was blighted, pale, and waxen less   100
Than he was wont; and that in whispers soft
Men said, what may it be, can no one guess
Why Troilus hath all this heaviness?
All which he of himself conceited wholly
Out of his weakness and his melancholy.   105

Another time he took into his head,
That every wight, who in the way passed by,
Had of him ruth, and fancied that they said,
I am right sorry Troilus will die:
And thus a day or two drove wearily;   110

As ye have heard; such life 'gan he to lead
As one that standeth betwixt hope and dread.

For which it pleased him in his songs to show
The occasion of his woe, as best he might;
And made a fitting song, of words but few,   115
Somewhat his woeful heart to make more light;
And when he was removed from all men's sight,
With a soft voice, he of his Lady dear,
That absent was, 'gan sing as ye may hear.

O star, of which I lost have all the light,   120
With a sore heart well ought I to bewail,
That ever dark in torment, night by night,
Toward my death with wind I steer and sail;
For which upon the tenth night if thou fail
With thy bright beams to guide me but one hour,   125
My ship and me Charybdis will devour.

As soon as he this song had thus sung through,
He fell again into his sorrows old;
And every night, as was his wont to do,
Troilus stood the bright moon to behold;   130
And all his trouble to the moon he told,
And said: I wis, when thou art horn'd anew,
I shall be glad if all the world be true.

Thy horns were old as now upon that morrow,
When hence did journey my bright Lady dear,   135
That cause is of my torment and my sorrow;
For which, oh, gentle Luna, bright and clear,
For love of God, run fast about thy sphere;
For when thy horns begin once more to spring,
Then shall she come, that with her bliss may bring.   140

The day is more, and longer every night
Than they were wont to be—for he thought so;
And that the sun did take his course not right,
By longer way than he was wont to go;
And said, I am in constant dread I trow,   145
That Phäeton his son is yet alive,
His too fond father's car amiss to drive.

118 soft voice   1841: soft night voice   1842–50
138 about] above 1841–50

Upon the walls fast also would he walk,
To the end that he the Grecian host might see;
And ever thus he to himself would talk:—   150
Lo! yonder is my own bright Lady free;
Or yonder is it that the tents must be;
And thence does come this air which is so sweet,
That in my soul I feel the joy of it.

And certainly this wind, that more and more   155
By moments thus increaseth in my face,
Is of my Lady's sighs heavy and sore;
I prove it thus; for in no other space
Of all this town, save only in this place,
Feel I a wind, that soundeth so like pain;   160
It saith, Alas, why severed are we twain?

A weary while in pain he tosseth thus,
Till fully past and gone was the ninth night;
And ever at his side stood Pandarus,
Who busily made use of all his might   165
To comfort him, and make his heart more light;
Giving him always hope, that she the morrow
Of the tenth day will come, and end his sorrow.

151 my   1842: mine   1841
163 past   1845: passed   1850

POEMS REFERRING TO THE PERIOD OF OLD AGE

I

THE OLD CUMBERLAND BEGGAR

The class of Beggars, to which the Old Man here described belongs, will probably soon be extinct. It consisted of poor, and, mostly, old and infirm persons, who confined themselves to a stated round in their neighbourhood, and had certain fixed days, on which, at different houses, they regularly received alms, sometimes in money, but mostly in provisions.

[Composed 1797.—Published 1800.]

I saw an aged Beggar in my walk;
And he was seated, by the highway side,
On a low structure of rude masonry
Built at the foot of a huge hill, that they
Who lead their horses down the steep rough road   5
May thence remount at ease. The aged Man
Had placed his staff across the broad smooth stone
That overlays the pile; and, from a bag
All white with flour, the dole of village dames,
He drew his scraps and fragments, one by one;   10
And scanned them with a fixed and serious look
Of idle computation. In the sun,
Upon the second step of that small pile,
Surrounded by those wild unpeopled hills,
He sat, and ate his food in solitude: 15
And ever, scattered from his palsied hand,
That, still attempting to prevent the waste,
Was baffled still, the crumbs in little showers
Fell on the ground; and the small mountain birds,
Not venturing yet to peck their destined meal,   20
Approached within the length of half his staff.

Him from my childhood have I known; and then
He was so old, he seems not older now;
He travels on, a solitary Man,
So helpless in appearance, that for him   25

I. THE BEGGAR MS. *The words* A Description *added to title* 1800–20.
4 Built] Placed MS.   15 sat, and ate   1805: sate, and eat 1800–2

The sauntering Horseman throws not with a slack
And careless hand his alms upon the ground,
But stops,—that he may safely lodge the coin
Within the old Man's hat; nor quits him so,
But still, when he has given his horse the rein,   30
Watches the aged Beggar with a look
Sidelong, and half-reverted. She who tends
The toll-gate, when in summer at her door
She turns her wheel, if on the road she sees
The aged Beggar coming, quits her work,   35
And lifts the latch for him that he may pass.
The post-boy, when his rattling wheels o'ertake
The aged Beggar in the woody lane,
Shouts to him from behind; and, if thus warned
The old man does not change his course, the boy   40
Turns with less noisy wheels to the roadside,
And passes gently by, without a curse
Upon his lips or anger at his heart.

He travels on, a solitary Man;
His age has no companion. On the ground   45
His eyes are turned, and, as he moves along,
They move along the ground; and, evermore,
Instead of common and habitual sight
Of fields with rural works, of hill and dale,
And the blue sky, one little span of earth   50
Is all his prospect. Thus, from day to day.
Bow-bent, his eyes for ever on the ground,
He plies his weary journey; seeing still,
And seldom knowing that he sees, some straw,
Some scattered leaf, or marks which, in one track,   55
The nails of cart or chariot-wheel have left

26–7 *so* 1837: The sauntering horseman-traveller does not throw With
MS., 1800–32   28–9 safely . . . Within] lodge the copper coin Safe in
MS.   31 *so* 1827: Towards the aged Beggar turns a look, MS., 1800–
20   39 thus warned   1827: perchance   MS., 1800–20
48–50 Instead of Nature's fair variety
        Her ample scope of hill and dale, of clouds
        And the blue sky, the same short span of earth MS.
51 Is all his prospect. When the little birds
    Flit over him, if their quick shadows strike
    Across his path he does not lift his head
    Like one whose thoughts have been unsettled. So MS.
54 seldom   1827: never   MS., 1800–20

Impressed on the white road,—in the same line,
At distance still the same. Poor Traveller!
His staff trails with him ; scarcely do his feet
Disturb the summer dust ; he is so still   60
In look and motion, that the cottage curs,
Ere he has passed the door, will turn away,
Weary of barking at him. Boys and girls,
The vacant and the busy, maids and youths,
The urchins newly breeched—all pass him by: 65
Him even the slow-paced waggon leaves behind.

But deem not this Man useless—Statesmen! ye
Who are so restless in your wisdom, ye
Who have a broom still ready in your hands
To rid the world of nuisances ; ye proud,   70
Heart-swoln, while in your pride ye contemplate
Your talents, power, or wisdom, deem him not
A burthen of the earth! 'Tis Nature's law
That none, the meanest of created things,
Of forms created the most vile and brute,   75
The dullest or most noxious, should exist
Divorced from good—a spirit and pulse of good,
A life and soul, to every mode of being
Inseparably linked. Then be assured
That least of all can aught—that ever owned   80
The heaven-regarding eye and front sublime
Which man is born to—sink, howe'er depressed,
So low as to be scorned without a sin ;

59 his slow footsteps scarce   MS.
61–3   . . . that the miller's dog
    Is tired of barking at him   MS.
62 has   1837: have   MS., 1800–32
67–70   . . . useless. Not perhaps
    Less useful than the smooth (red) and portly squire
    Who with his steady coachman, steady steeds
    All slick and bright with comfortable gloss
    Doth in his broad glass'd chariot drive along
    (Who (Heaven forbid that he should want his praise)
    Lives by his [?] and spreads his name abroad.)   Alf. MS.
72 or   1837: and   1800–32
79–88 so 1837:   . . . linked. While thus he creeps
    From door to door, the villagers in him   MS., 1800–32
80–9 Dismantled as he is of limbs to act
    Almost of sense to feel, by Nature's self
    Long banish'd from the cares and the concerns

Without offence to God cast out of view;
Like the dry remnant of a garden-flower   85
Whose seeds are shed, or as an implement
Worn out and worthless. While from door to door,
This old Man creeps, the villagers in him
Behold a record which together binds
Past deeds and offices of charity,   90
Else unremembered, and so keeps alive
The kindly mood in hearts which lapse of years,
And that half-wisdom half-experience gives,
Make slow to feel, and by sure steps resign
To selfishness and cold oblivious cares.   95
Among the farms and solitary huts,
Hamlets and thinly-scattered villages,
Where'er the aged Beggar takes his rounds,
The mild necessity of use compels
To acts of love; and habit does the work   100
Of reason; yet prepares that after-joy
Which reason cherishes. And thus the soul,
By that sweet taste of pleasure unpursued,
Doth find herself insensibly disposed
To virtue and true goodness. Some there are,   105
By their good works exalted, lofty minds,
And meditative, authors of delight
And happiness, which to the end of time
Will live, and spread, and kindle: even such minds
In childhood, from this solitary Being,   110
Or from like wanderer, haply have received
(A thing more precious far than all that books

Business and reciprocities of life
His very name forgotten among those
By whom he lives, while thus from house to house
He creeps, the villagers behold in him
A living record that together ties *Alf.* MS.
104 herself 1832: itself MS., 1800–27
107–10 And meditative, in which reason falls
        Like a strong radiance of the setting sun
        On each minutest feeling of the heart,
        Illuminates, and to their view brings forth
        In one harmonious prospect, minds like these
        In childhood *Alf.* MS.
109 *so* 1827: . . . minds like these 1800–20: Will spread and grow and
kindle; minds like these MS.   111 *so* 1827: This helpless Wanderer,
have perchance received 1800–20; . . . did . . . receive MS.

Or the solicitudes of love can do!)
That first mild touch of sympathy and thought,
In which they found their kindred with a world   115
Where want and sorrow were. The easy man
Who sits at his own door,—and, like the pear
That overhangs his head from the green wall,
Feeds in the sunshine ; the robust and young,
The prosperous and unthinking, they who live   120
Sheltered, and flourish in a little grove
Of their own kindred ;—all behold in him
A silent monitor, which on their minds
Must needs impress a transitory thought
Of self-congratulation, to the heart   125
Of each recalling his peculiar boons,
His charters and exemptions ; and, perchance,
Though he to no one give the fortitude
And circumspection needful to preserve
His present blessings, and to husband up   130
The respite of the season, he, at least,
And 'tis no vulgar service, makes them felt.

Yet further.————Many, I believe, there are
Who live a life of virtuous decency,
Men who can hear the Decalogue and feel   135
No self-reproach ; who of the moral law
Established in the land where they abide
Are strict observers ; and not negligent
In acts of love to those with whom they dwell,
Their kindred, and the children of their blood.   140
Praise be to such, and to their slumbers peace!
—But of the poor man ask, the abject poor ;
Go, and demand of him, if there be here
In this cold abstinence from evil deeds,
And these inevitable charities,   145
Wherewith to satisfy the human soul ?

128 Although to each he may not give the strength MS.
133–5 Not small the number, I believe, of those
        Who hear the decalogue of God, and feel MS.
139 *so* 1827: Meanwhile, in any tenderness of heart
            Or act of love . . . live, [dwell 1800–20] MS., 1800–20
143–55 If such there be whose virtues have attained
        This point, demand of him if there be here
        Wherewith to satisfy the human soul.

No—man is dear to man; the poorest poor
Long for some moments in a weary life
When they can know and feel that they have been,
Themselves, the fathers and the dealers-out   150
Of some small blessings; have been kind to such
As needed kindness, for this single cause,
That we have all of us one human heart.
—Such pleasure is to one kind Being known,
My neighbour, when with punctual care, each week,   155
Duly as Friday comes, though pressed herself
By her own wants, she from her store of meal
Takes one unsparing handful for the scrip
Of this old Mendicant, and, from her door
Returning with exhilarated heart,   160
Sits by her fire, and builds her hope in heaven.

Then let him pass, a blessing on his head!
And while in that vast solitude to which
The tide of things has borne him, he appears
To breathe and live but for himself alone,   165
Unblamed, uninjured, let him bear about
The good which the benignant law of Heaven
Has hung around him: and, while life is his,
Still let him prompt the unlettered villagers
To tender offices and pensive thoughts.   170
—Then let him pass, a blessing on his head!
And, long as he can wander, let him breathe
The freshness of the valleys; let his blood
Struggle with frosty air and winter snows;
And let the chartered wind that sweeps the heath   175
Beat his grey locks against his withered face.
Reverence the hope whose vital anxiousness
Gives the last human interest to his heart.
May never HOUSE, misnamed of INDUSTRY,
Make him a captive!—for that pent-up din,   180

Oh by the joy which one good human knows
My neighbour, when MS.
156-7   . . . albeit poor
      And scantly fed she from her chest of meal MS.
157 store   1827: chest   1800-20.   161/2 Oh, by that widow's hope I
answer No! MS.   164 borne   1827: led MS., 1800-20   174/5
Waste not on him your busy tenderness *Alf.* MS.

Those life-consuming sounds that clog the air,
Be his the natural silence of old age!
Let him be free of mountain solitudes;
And have around him, whether heard or not,
The pleasant melody of woodland birds.   185
Few are his pleasures: if his eyes have now
Been doomed so long to settle upon earth
That not without some effort they behold
The countenance of the horizontal sun,
Rising or setting, let the light at least   190
Find a free entrance to their languid orbs,
And let him, *where* and *when* he will, sit down
Beneath the trees, or on a grassy bank
Of highway side, and with the little birds
Share his chance-gathered meal; and, finally,   195
As in the eye of Nature he has lived,
So in the eye of Nature let him die!

II

THE FARMER OF TILSBURY VALE

[Composed 1800.—Published July 21, 1800 (*Morning Post*); ed. 1815.]

'TIS not for the unfeeling, the falsely refined,
The squeamish in taste, and the narrow of mind,
And the small critic wielding his delicate pen,
That I sing of old Adam, the pride of old men.

He dwells in the centre of London's wide Town;   5
His staff is a sceptre—his grey hairs a crown;

186-9 *so* 1837:   . . . if his eyes so long
　　　　　　Familiar with the earth almost have looked
　　　　　　Their farewell on the horizontal sun MS.
　　　　　　　　　　　. . . if his eyes, which now
　　　　　　Have been so long familiar with the earth,
　　　　　　No more behold *etc.*   1800-5
　　　　　　　　　　　. . . if his eyes have now
　　　　　　Been doomed so long to settle on the earth
　　　　　　That not without some effort they behold
　　　　　　The countenance *etc. as text*   1815-32
193 on a 1837: by the   1800-32
II. 1-12 There's an old man in London, the prime of old men,
　　　　　You may hunt for his match through ten thousand and ten;
　　　　　Of prop or of staff, does he walk, does he run,
　　　　　No more need has he than a flow'r of the sun. 1800

And his bright eyes look brighter, set off by the streak
Of the unfaded rose that still blooms on his cheek.

'Mid the dews, in the sunshine of morn,—'mid the joy
Of the fields, he collected that bloom, when a boy;   10
That countenance there fashioned, which, spite of a stain
That his life hath received, to the last will remain.

A Farmer he was; and his house far and near
Was the boast of the country for excellent cheer;
How oft have I heard in sweet Tilsbury Vale   15
Of the silver-rimmed horn whence he dealt his mild ale!

Yet Adam was far as the farthest from ruin,
His fields seemed to know what their Master was doing;
And turnips, and corn-land, and meadow, and lea,
All caught the infection—as generous as he.   20

Yet Adam prized little the feast and the bowl,—
The fields better suited the ease of his soul:
He strayed through the fields like an indolent wight,
The quiet of nature was Adam's delight.

For Adam was simple in thought; and the poor,   25
Familiar with him, made an inn of his door:
He gave them the best that he had; or, to say
What less may mislead you, they took it away.

Thus thirty smooth years did he thrive on his farm:
The Genius of plenty preserved him from harm: 30
At length, what to most is a season of sorrow,
His means are run out,—he must beg, or must borrow.

7–8 *so* 1837: Erect as a sunflower he stands, and the streak
        Of the unfaded rose is expressed on his cheek. 1815–20;
so 1827–32, *but* still enlivens his cheek.
11 *so* 1840: There fashion'd that countenance, which, in spite of a stain
1815–37   13 house 1815: name 1800   14 boast 1815: Top 1800
15–16 *so* 1827: *so* 1815–20 *but* good *for* mild
        Not less than the skill of an Exchequer Teller
        Could count the shoes worn on the steps of his cellar.   1800
19 corn-land 1815: plough'd land 1800   21 feast and 1815: noise of
1800
28/9 On the works of the world, on the bustle and sound,
        Seated still in his boat, he look'd leisurely round;
        And if now and then he his hands did employ,
        'Twas with vanity, wonder, and infantine joy.   1800
32 are 1815: were 1800

To the neighbours he went,—all were free with their money;
For his hive had so long been replenished with honey,
That they dreamt not of dearth;—He continued his rounds,   35
Knocked here—and knocked there, pounds still adding to pounds.

He paid what he could with his ill-gotten pelf,
And something, it might be, reserved for himself:
Then (what is too true) without hinting a word,
Turned his back on the country—and off like a bird.   40

You lift up your eyes!—but I guess that you frame
A judgment too harsh of the sin and the shame;
In him it was scarcely a business of art,
For this he did all in the *ease* of his heart.

To London—a sad emigration I ween—   45
With his grey hairs he went from the brook and the green;
And there, with small wealth but his legs and his hands,
As lonely he stood as a crow on the sands.

All trades, as need was, did old Adam assume,—
Served as stable-boy, errand-boy, porter, and groom;   50
But nature is gracious, necessity kind,
And, in spite of the shame that may lurk in his mind,

He seems ten birthdays younger, is green and is stout;
Twice as fast as before does his blood run about;
You would say that each hair of his beard was alive,   55
And his fingers as busy as bees in a hive.

For he's not like an Old Man that leisurely goes
About work that he knows, in a track that he knows;
But often his mind is compelled to demur,
And you guess that the more then his body must stir.   ₔ   60

34–5 *so* 1815: For they all still imagin'd his hive full of honey;
          Like a Church-warden, Adam continu'd his rounds, 1800
37 his 1837: this 1815–32   38 reserved for 1815: he kept to 1800
41–2 *so* 1820: *so* 1815 *but* and (41) *for* but
          You lift up your eyes, "O the merciless Jew!"
          But in truth he was never more cruel than you; 1800
43 scarcely 1815: scarce e'en 1800   44 *ease* 1815: ease 1800   46
brook 1815: lawn 1800   48 *so* 1815: He stood all alone like 1800
49 need 1800, 1827: needs 1815–20   50 Served as 1815: Both 1800
51–3 *so* 1815: You'd think it the life of a Devil in H—l,
          But nature was kind, and with Adam 'twas well.
          He's ten birthdays younger, he's green, and he's stout, 1800
58 work that he knows 1815: ... does 1800

In the throng of the town like a stranger is he,
Like one whose own country's far over the sea;
And Nature, while through the great city he hies,
Full ten times a day takes his heart by surprise.

This gives him the fancy of one that is young.   65
More of soul in his face than of words on his tongue;
Like a maiden of twenty he trembles and sighs,
And tears of fifteen will come into his eyes.

What's a tempest to him, or the dry parching heats?
Yet he watches the clouds that pass over the streets;   70
With a look of such earnestness often will stand,
You might think he'd twelve reapers at work in the Strand.

Where proud Covent-garden, in desolate hours
Of snow and hoar-frost, spreads her fruits and her flowers,
Old Adam will smile at the pains that have made   75
Poor winter look fine in such strange masquerade.

'Mid coaches and chariots, a waggon of straw,
Like a magnet, the heart of old Adam can draw;
With a thousand soft pictures his memory will teem,
And his hearing is touched with the sounds of a dream.   80

Up the Haymarket hill he oft whistles his way,
Thrusts his hands in a waggon, and smells at the hay;
He thinks of the fields he so often hath mown,
And is happy as if the rich freight were his own.

68 will   1800, 1820: have   1815   71 will   1815: he'll   1800
73–6 *so* 1837: *so* 1815–32, *but* fruit *for* fruits
       Where proud Covent Garden, in frost and in snow,
       Spreads her fruit and her flow'rs, built up row after row;
       Old Adam will point with his finger and say,
       To them that stand by, "I've seen better than they."   1800
76/7 Where the apples are heap'd on the barrows in piles,
       You see him stop short, he looks long, and he smiles;
       He looks, and he smiles, and a Poet might spy
       The image of fifty green fields in his eye. 1800
82 *so* 1837: in the waggons, and smells to 1800; in the Waggon, and smells
at   1815–32   83 hath 1815: has   1800   84 *so* 1815: And
sometimes he dreams that the hay is   1800

But chiefly to Smithfield he loves to repair,—   85
If you pass by at morning, you'll meet with him there.
The breath of the cows you may see him inhale,
And his heart all the while is in Tilsbury Vale.

Now farewell, old Adam! when low thou art laid,
May one blade of grass spring up over thy head;   90
And I hope that thy grave, wheresoever it be,
Will hear the wind sigh through the leaves of a tree.

III

THE SMALL CELANDINE

[Composed 1804.—Published 1807.]

THERE is a Flower, the lesser Celandine,
That shrinks, like many more, from cold and rain;
And, the first moment that the sun may shine,
Bright as the sun himself, 'tis out again!

When hailstones have been falling, swarm on swarm,   5
Or blasts the green field and the trees distrest,
Oft have I seen it muffled up from harm,
In close self-shelter, like a Thing at rest.

But lately, one rough day, this Flower I passed
And recognised it, though an altered form,   10
Now standing forth an offering to the blast,
And buffeted at will by rain and storm.

I stopped, and said with inly-muttered voice,
"It doth not love the shower, nor seek the cold:
This neither is its courage nor its choice,   15
But its necessity in being old.

"The sunshine may not cheer it, nor the dew;
It cannot help itself in its decay;
Stiff in its members, withered, changed of hue."
And, in my spleen, I smiled that it was grey.   20

III.   2–4 wet and cold . . . sun it doth itself unfold MS.   4 himself
1837: itself   1807–32   5–7 coming down in swarms . . . harms. MS.
17 cheer] bless MS.

To be a Prodigal's Favourite—then, worse truth,
A miser's Pensioner—behold our lot!
O Man, that from thy fair and shining youth
Age might but take the things Youth needed not!

IV

THE TWO THIEVES

OR,

THE LAST STAGE OF AVARICE

[Composed 1800.—Published 1800.]

O now that the genius of Bewick were mine,
And the skill which he learned on the banks of the Tyne,
Then the Muses might deal with me just as they chose,
For I'd take my last leave both of verse and of prose.

What feats would I work with my magical hand!   5
Book-learning and books should be banished the land:
And, for hunger and thirst and such troublesome calls,
Every ale-house should then have a feast on its walls.

The traveller would hang his wet clothes on a chair;
Let them smoke, let them burn, not a straw would he care! 10
For the Prodigal Son, Joseph's Dream and his sheaves,
Oh, what would they be to my tale of two Thieves?

The One, yet unbreeched, is not three birthdays old,
His Grandsire that age more than thirty times told;
There are ninety good seasons of fair and foul weather   15
Between them, and both go a-pilfering together.

With chips is the carpenter strewing his floor?
Is a cart-load of turf at an old woman's door?
Old Daniel his hand to the treasure will slide!
And his Grandson's as busy at work by his side.   20

IV. 1–6 Oh! now that the boxwood and graver were mine,
         Of the Poet who lives on the banks of the Tyne!
         Who has plied his rude tools with more fortunate toil
         Than Reynolds e'er brought to his canvas and oil.

         Then Books, and Book-learning, I'd ring out your knell,
         The Vicar should scarce know an A from an L, MS.

13 *so* 1820: Little Dan is unbreech'd—he is 1800–15   15 There **are**
1802: There's MS., 1800   16 a-pilfering 1837: a-stealing MS., 1800–32
18 turf 1827: peats MS., 1800–20

Old Daniel begins; he stops short—and his eye,
Through the lost look of dotage, is cunning and sly:
'Tis a look which at this time is hardly his own,
But tells a plain tale of the days that are flown.

He once had a heart which was moved by the wires   25
Of manifold pleasures and many desires:
And what if he cherished his purse? 'Twas no more
Than treading a path trod by thousands before.

'Twas a path trod by thousands; but Daniel is one
Who went something farther than others have gone,   30
And now with old Daniel you see how it fares;
You see to what end he has brought his grey hairs.

The pair sally forth hand in hand: ere the sun
Has peered o'er the beeches, their work is begun:
And yet, into whatever sin they may fall,   35
This child but half knows it, and that not at all.

They hunt through the streets with deliberate tread,
And each, in his turn, becomes leader or led;
And, wherever they carry their plots and their wiles,
Every face in the village is dimpled with smiles.   40

Neither checked by the rich nor the needy they roam;
For the grey-headed Sire has a daughter at home,
Who will gladly repair all the damage that's done;
And three, were it asked, would be rendered for one.

Old Man! whom so oft I with pity have eyed,   45
I love thee, and love the sweet Boy at thy side:
Long yet may'st thou live! for a teacher we see
That lifts up the veil of our nature in thee.

22 lost] last 1805 *only*   25 He 1820: Dan MS., 1800–15
29–30 'Twas a smooth pleasant pathway, a gentle descent,
       And leisurely down it, and down it, he went. MS.
30 farther 1800, 1802, 1827–50: further 1805–20   38 becomes leader
or 1837: is both leader and MS., 1800–32   42 *so* 1837: For gray-
headed Dan MS., 1800–15: The gray-headed Sire 1820–32

V

ANIMAL TRANQUILLITY AND DECAY

[Composed 1797.—Published 1798.]

THE little hedgerow birds,
That peck along the road, regard him not.
He travels on, and in his face, his step,
His gait, is one expression: every limb,
His look and bending figure, all bespeak   5
A man who does not move with pain, but moves
With thought.—He is insensibly subdued
To settled quiet: he is one by whom
All effort seems forgotten; one to whom
Long patience hath such mild composure given,   10
That patience now doth seem a thing of which
He hath no need. He is by nature led
To peace so perfect that the young behold
With envy, what the Old Man hardly feels.

V.   "Old Man Travelling; Animal Tranquillity and Decay, *A Sketch*" 1798;
1800–43 *omit first three words*, 1845 *omits also last two*.
3–5 . . . his face and every limb
      His look and bending figure all alike
      Have one expression, all the same it is. MS.
7–8 resigned to quietness MS., *margin*   10 hath 1805: has 1798–
1802
After 14 —I asked him whither he was bound, and what
        The object of his journey; he replied
        "Sir! I am going many miles to take
        A last leave of my son, a mariner,
        Who from a sea-fight has been brought to Falmouth,
        And there is dying in an hospital.—"   1798: That he was going
        . . . his son . . . had . . . was dying . . . MS.
1800–5, *but* lying *for* dying in 1800. *Not in* 1815 *etc.*

EPITAPHS AND ELEGIAC PIECES

EPITAPHS

TRANSLATED FROM CHIABRERA

I

[Composed ?—Published 1837.]

WEEP not, belovèd Friends! nor let the air
For me with sighs be troubled. Not from life
Have I been taken; this is genuine life
And this alone—the life which now I live
In peace eternal; where desire and joy   5
Together move in fellowship without end.—
Francesco Ceni willed that, after death,
His tombstone thus should speak for him. And surely
Small cause there is for that fond wish of ours
Long to continue in this world; a world   10
That keeps not faith, nor yet can point a hope
To good, whereof itself is destitute.

II

[Composed 1809 or 1810.—Published February 22, 1810 (*The Friend*);
ed. 1815.]

PERHAPS some needful service of the State
Drew TITUS from the depth of studious bowers,
And doomed him to contend in faithless courts,
Where gold determines between right and wrong.
Yet did at length his loyalty of heart,   5
And his pure native genius, lead him back
To wait upon the bright and gracious Muses,
Whom he had early loved. And not in vain˙
Such course he held! Bologna's learned schools
Were gladdened by the Sage's voice, and hung   10
With fondness on those sweet Nestorian strains.
There pleasure crowned his days; and all his thoughts

EPITAPHS AND ELEGIAC PIECES 1837–50
EPITAPHS - - - POEMS 1815–32
I. 7–8 *so* 1850: . . . after death enjoined That thus his tomb 1837–45
II. 11 Nestrian 1810   12–13 *so* 1815 There did he live content . . .
Were blithe as vernal flowers 1810

A roseate fragrance breathed.[1]—O human life,
That never art secure from dolorous change!
Behold a high injunction suddenly   15
To Arno's side hath brought him, and he charmed
· A Tuscan audience: but full soon was called
To the perpetual silence of the grave.
Mourn, Italy, the loss of him who stood
A Champion stedfast and invincible,   20
To quell the rage of literary War!

III

[Composed 1809 or 1810.—Published February 22, 1810 (*The Friend*);
ed. 1815.]

O THOU who movest onward with a mind
Intent upon thy way, pause, though in haste!
'Twill be no fruitless moment. I was born
Within Savona's walls, of gentle blood.
On Tiber's banks my youth was dedicate   5
To sacred studies; and the Roman Shepherd
Gave to my charge Urbino's numerous flock.
Well did I watch, much laboured, nor had power
To escape from many and strange indignities;
Was smitten by the great ones of the world,   10
But did not fall; for Virtue braves all shocks,
Upon herself resting immoveably.
Me did a kindlier fortune then invite
To serve the glorious Henry, King of France,
And in his hands I saw a high reward   15
Stretched out for my acceptance,—but Death came.
Now, Reader, learn from this my fate, how false,
How treacherous to her promise, is the world;
And trust in God—to whose eternal doom
Must bend the sceptred Potentates of earth.   20

[1] Ivi vivea giocondo e i suoi pensieri
Erano tutti rose.
The Translator had not skill to come nearer to his original.

---

16 hath brought 1837: conducts 1810–32
III. 8 Well 1837: Much 1810–32

IV

[Composed 1809.—Published December 28, 1809 (*The Friend*); ed. 1815.]

THERE never breathed a man who, when his life
Was closing, might not of that life relate
Toils long and hard.—The warrior will report
Of wounds, and bright swords flashing in the field,
And blast of trumpets. He who hath been doomed   5
To bow his forehead in the courts of kings,
Will tell of fraud and never-ceasing hate,
Envy and heart-inquietude, derived
From intricate cabals of treacherous friends.
I, who on shipboard lived from earliest youth,   10
Could represent the countenance horrible
Of the vexed waters, and the indignant rage
Of Auster and Boötes. Fifty years
Over the well-steered galleys did I rule:—
From huge Pelorus to the Atlantic pillars,   15
Rises no mountain to mine eyes unknown;
And the broad gulfs I traversed oft and oft.
Of every cloud which in the heavens might stir
I knew the force; and hence the rough sea's pride
Availed not to my Vessel's overthrow.   20
What noble pomp and frequent have not I
On regal decks beheld! yet in the end
I learned that one poor moment can suffice
To equalise the lofty and the low.
We sail the sea of life—a *Calm* One finds,   25
And One a *Tempest*—and, the voyage o'er,
Death is the quiet haven of us all.
If more of my condition ye would know,
Savona was my birthplace, and I sprang
Of noble parents: seventy years and three   30
Lived I—then yielded to a slow disease.

V

[Composed ?—Published 1837.]

TRUE is it that Ambrosio Salinero
With an untoward fate was long involved
In odious litigation; and full long,
Fate harder still! had he to endure assaults

IV. 13 Fifty 1837: Forty 1809–32   23 learned 1837: learnt 1832:
learn 1809–27   30 seventy 1837: sixty 1809–32

Of racking malady. And true it is   5
That not the less a frank courageous heart
And buoyant spirit triumphed over pain ;
And he was strong to follow in the steps
Of the fair Muses. Not a covert path
Leads to the dear Parnassian forest's shade,   10
That might from him be hidden ; not a track
Mounts to pellucid Hippocrene, but he
Had traced its windings.—This Savona knows,
Yet no sepulchral honors to her Son
She paid, for in our age the heart is ruled   15
Only by gold. And now a simple stone
Inscribed with this memorial here is raised
By his bereft, his lonely, Chiabrera.
Think not, O Passenger! who read'st the lines
That an exceeding love hath dazzled me ;   20
No—he was One whose memory ought to spread
Where'er Permessus bears an honoured name,
And live as long as its pure stream shall flow.

VI

[Composed 1809.—Published December 28, 1809 (*The Friend*); ed. 1815.]

DESTINED to war from very infancy
Was I, Roberto Dati, and I took
In Malta the white symbol of the Cross:
Nor in life's vigorous season did I shun
Hazard or toil ; among the sands was seen   5
Of Lybia ; and not seldom, on the banks
Of wide Hungarian Danube, 'twas my lot
To hear the sanguinary trumpet sounded.
So lived I, and repined not at such fate:
This only grieves me, for it seems a wrong   10
That stripped of arms I to my end am brought
On the soft down of my paternal home.
Yet haply Arno shall be spared all cause
To blush for me. Thou, loiter not nor halt
In thy appointed way, and bear in mind   15
How fleeting and how frail is human life!

VII

[Composed ?—Published 1837.]

O FLOWER of all that springs from gentle blood,
And all that generous nurture breeds to make
Youth amiable; O friend so true of soul
To fair Aglaia; by what envy moved,
Lelius! has death cut short thy brilliant day   5
In its sweet opening? and what dire mishap
Has from Savona torn her best delight?
For thee she mourns, nor e'er will cease to mourn;
And, should the out-pourings of her eyes suffice not
For her heart's grief, she will entreat Sebeto   10
Not to withhold his bounteous aid, Sebeto
Who saw thee, on his margin, yield to death,
In the chaste arms of thy belovèd Love!
What profit riches? what does youth avail?
Dust are our hopes;—I, weeping bitterly,   15
Penned these sad lines, nor can forbear to pray
That every gentle Spirit hither led
May read them not without some bitter tears.

VIII

[Composed 1809.—Published January 4, 1810 (*The Friend*); ed. 1815.]

NOT without heavy grief of heart did He
On whom the duty fell (for at that time
The father sojourned in a distant land)
Deposit in the hollow of this tomb
A brother's Child, most tenderly beloved!   5
FRANCESCO was the name the Youth had borne,
POZZOBONNELLI his illustrious house;
And, when beneath this stone the Corse was laid,
The eyes of all Savona streamed with tears.
Alas! the twentieth April of his life   10
Had scarcely flowered: and at this early time,
By genuine virtue he inspired a hope
That greatly cheered his country: to his kin
He promised comfort; and the flattering thoughts

VII.   *For earlier version v. notes p.* 449

His friends had in their fondness entertained,[1]   15
He suffered not to languish or decay.
Now is there not good reason to break forth
Into a passionate lament?—O Soul!
Short while a Pilgrim in our nether world,
Do thou enjoy the calm empyreal air;   20
And round this earthly tomb let roses rise,
An everlasting spring! in memory
Of that delightful fragrance which was once
From thy mild manners quietly exhaled.

IX

[Composed 1809.—Published January 4, 1810 (*The Friend*); ed. 1815.]

PAUSE, courteous Spirit!—Baldi supplicates
That Thou, with no reluctant voice, for him
Here laid in mortal darkness, wouldst prefer
A prayer to the Redeemer of the world.
This to the dead by sacred right belongs;   5
All else is nothing.—Did occasion suit
To tell his worth, the marble of this tomb
Would ill suffice: for Plato's lore sublime,
And all the wisdom of the Stagyrite,
Enriched and beautified his studious mind: 10
With Archimedes also he conversed
As with a chosen friend; nor did he leave
Those laureat wreaths ungathered which the Nymphs
Twine near their loved Permessus.—Finally,
Himself above each lower thought uplifting,   15
His ears he closed to listen to the songs
Which Sion's Kings did consecrate of old;
And his Permessus found on Lebanon.
A blessèd Man! who of protracted days
Made not, as thousands do, a vulgar sleep;   20
But truly did *He* live his life. Urbino,
Take pride in him!—O Passenger, farewell!

[1] In justice to the Author, I subjoin the original:
——————— e degli amici
Non lasciava languire i bei pensieri.

IX. 1 Balbi 1815–50   8 lore 1815: love 1810   14 *so* 1837: Twine
on the top of Pindus 1810–32   16 songs 1837: Song 1810–32
18 *so* 1837: And fixed his Pindus upon 1810–32   21 *He*] he 1810

I

[Composed ?—Published 1835.]

By a blest Husband guided, Mary came
From nearest kindred, Vernon her new name ;
She came, though meek of soul, in seemly pride
Of happiness and hope, a youthful Bride.
O dread reverse! if aught *be* so, which proves   5
That God will chasten whom he dearly loves.
Faith bore her up through pains in mercy given,
And troubles that were each a step to Heaven:
Two Babes were laid in earth before she died ;
A third now slumbers at the Mother's side ;   10
Its Sister-twin survives, whose smiles afford
A trembling solace to her widowed Lord.

Reader! if to thy bosom cling the pain
Of recent sorrow combated in vain ;
Or if thy cherished grief have failed to thwart   15
Time still intent on his insidious part,
Lulling the mourner's best good thoughts asleep,
Pilfering regrets we would, but cannot, keep ;
Bear with Him—judge *Him* gently who makes known
His bitter loss by this memorial Stone ;   20
And pray that in his faithful breast the grace
Of resignation find a hallowed place.

II

[Composed after 1812.—Published 1837.]

Six months to six years added he remained
Upon this sinful earth, by sin unstained:
O blessèd Lord! whose mercy then removed
A Child whom every eye that looked on loved ;
Support us, teach us calmly to resign   5
What we possessed, and now is wholly thine!

I. 2 Vernon   1837: * * * * * *   1835

III
CENOTAPH

In affectionate remembrance of Frances Fermor, whose remains are deposited in the church of Claines, near Worcester, this stone is erected by her sister, Dame Margaret, wife of Sir George Beaumont, Bart., who, feeling not less than the love of a brother for the deceased, commends this memorial to the care of his heirs and successors in the possession of this place.

[Composed 1824.—Published 1842.]

By vain affections unenthralled,
Though resolute when duty called
To meet the world's broad eye,
Pure as the holiest cloistered nun
That ever feared the tempting sun,   5
Did Fermor live and die.

This Tablet, hallowed by her name,
One heart-relieving tear may claim;
But if the pensive gloom
Of fond regret be still thy choice,   10
Exalt thy spirit, hear the voice
Of Jesus from her tomb!
"I AM THE WAY, THE TRUTH, AND THE LIFE."

IV
EPITAPH

IN THE CHAPEL-YARD OF LANGDALE, WESTMORELAND

[Composed 1841.—Published: vol. of 1842.]

By playful smiles, (alas! too oft
A sad heart's sunshine) by a soft
And gentle nature, and a free
Yet modest hand of charity,
Through life was OWEN LLOYD endeared   5
To young and old; and how revered
Had been that pious spirit, a tide
Of humble mourners testified,
When, after pains dispensed to prove
The measure of God's chastening love,   10
Here, brought from far, his corse found rest,—
Fulfilment of his own request;—

III. 7 This cenotaph (This sacred stone) that bears her name MS.

Urged less for this Yew's shade, though he
Planted with such fond hope the tree;
Less for the love of stream and rock,   15
Dear as they were, than that his Flock,
When they no more their Pastor's voice
Could hear to guide them in their choice
Through good and evil, help might have,
Admonished, from his silent grave,   20
Of righteousness, of sins forgiven,
For peace on earth and bliss in heaven.

V

ADDRESS TO THE SCHOLARS OF THE VILLAGE
SCHOOL OF ——
1798

[Composed 1798.—Published: vol. of 1842.]

I COME, ye little noisy Crew,
Not long your pastime to prevent;
I heard the blessing which to you
Our common Friend and Father sent.
I kissed his cheek before he died;   5
And when his breath was fled,
I raised, while kneeling by his side,
His hand:—it dropped like lead.
Your hands, dear Little-ones, do all
That can be done, will never fall   10
Like his till they are dead.
By night or day, blow foul or fair,
Ne'er will the best of all your train
Play with the locks of his white hair,
Or stand between his knees again.   15

    Here did he sit confined for hours;
But he could see the woods and plains,
Could hear the wind and mark the showers
Come streaming down the streaming panes.
Now stretched beneath his grass-green mound   20
He rests a prisoner of the ground.

V. 1 I bring MS.   2–3 Fulfilling a most kind intent The pious MS.
12 Oh never more . . . MS. 14 Have Matthew's hand upon his hair MS.
16 *v. note to* 48/9 *app. crit.*

He loved the breathing air,
He loved the sun, but if it rise
Or set, to him where now he lies,
Brings not a moment's care.   25
Alas! what idle words; but take
The Dirge which for our Master's sake
And yours, love prompted me to make.
The rhymes so homely in attire
With learnèd ears may ill agree,   30
But chanted by your Orphan Quire
Will make a touching melody.

DIRGE

Mourn, Shepherd, near thy old grey stone;
Thou Angler, by the silent flood;
And mourn when thou art all alone,   35
Thou Woodman, in the distant wood!

Thou one blind Sailor, rich in joy
Though blind, thy tunes in sadness hum;
And mourn, thou poor half-witted Boy!
Born deaf, and living deaf and dumb.   40

Thou drooping sick Man, bless the Guide
Who checked or turned thy headstrong youth,
As he before had sanctified
Thy infancy with heavenly truth.

Ye Striplings, light of heart and gay,   45
Bold settlers on some foreign shore,
Give, when your thoughts are turned this way,
A sigh to him whom we deplore.

For us who here in funeral strain
With one accord our voices raise,   50
Let sorrow overcharged with pain
Be lost in thankfulness and praise.

48/9 Yet why lament? in humble state
       He shewed the good a Man of worth,
       A single Mortal, can create
       Upon a single spot of earth. MSS., *followed in one* MS. *by*
       May Heaven forgive if aught amiss
       With wilful mind he did or said,
       And both in sorrow and in bliss
       Let us remember his grey head. *v. note, p.* 451.
49–52 Weep, weep no more . . . But while we here . . . May Sorrow . . .
Give place to MS.

And when our hearts shall feel a sting
From ill we meet or good we miss,
May touches of his memory bring   55
Fond healing, like a mother's kiss.

BY THE SIDE OF THE GRAVE SOME YEARS AFTER

LONG time his pulse hath ceased to beat;
But benefits, his gift, we trace—
Expressed in every eye we meet
Round this dear Vale, his native place.   60

To stately Hall and Cottage rude
Flowed from his life what still they hold,
Light pleasures, every day renewed;
And blessings half a century old.

Oh true of heart, of spirit gay,   65
Thy faults, where not already gone
From memory, prolong their stay
For charity's sweet sake alone.

Such solace find we for our loss;
And what beyond this thought we crave   70
Comes in the promise from the Cross,
Shining upon thy happy grave.[1]

VI
ELEGIAC STANZAS

SUGGESTED BY A PICTURE OF PEELE CASTLE, IN A STORM,
PAINTED BY SIR GEORGE BEAUMONT

[Composed 1805.—Published 1807.]

I WAS thy neighbour once, thou rugged Pile!
Four summer weeks I dwelt in sight of thee:
I saw thee every day; and all the while
Thy Form was sleeping on a glassy sea.

[1] See upon the subject of the three foregoing pieces *The Fountain*, &c.,
[pp. 68–73].

56/7 Prompted by the sight of his Grave a few years afterwards MS.
57 Long, long thy pulse . . . MS.   58 But benefits of thine MS.
62 From thee did flow MS.
65–8 Oh good of heart, and gay in mind,
        If ought of ill by thee were done
        May human frailty pardon find
        At Mercy's everlasting Throne. MS.

So pure the sky, so quiet was the air! 5
So like, so very like, was day to day!
Whene'er I looked, thy Image still was there;
It trembled, but it never passed away.

How perfect was the calm! it seemed no sleep;
No mood, which season takes away, or brings: 10
I could have fancied that the mighty Deep
Was even the gentlest of all gentle Things.

Ah! THEN, if mine had been the Painter's hand,
To express what then I saw; and add the gleam,
The light that never was, on sea or land, 15
The consecration, and the Poet's dream;

I would have planted thee, thou hoary Pile
Amid a world how different from this!
Beside a sea that could not cease to smile;
On tranquil land, beneath a sky of bliss. 20

Thou shouldst have seemed a treasure-house divine
Of peaceful years; a chronicle of heaven;—
Of all the sunbeams that did ever shine
The very sweetest had to thee been given.

A Picture had it been of lasting ease, 25
Elysian quiet, without toil or strife;
No motion but the moving tide, a breeze,
Or merely silent Nature's breathing life.

Such, in the fond illusion of my heart,
Such Picture would I at that time have made: 30
And seen the soul of truth in every part,
A stedfast peace that might not be betrayed.

So once it would have been,—'tis so no more;
I have submitted to a new control:
A power is gone, which nothing can restore; 35
A deep distress hath humanised my Soul.

VI. 14–16 *so* 1807–15, 1832–50: . . . and add a gleam,
    Of lustre, known to neither sea nor land
    But borrowed from the youthful Poet's dream; 1820; *so* 1827, *but*
the gleam, The lustre *as in* Errata 1820
21 *so* 1845: a treasure house, a mine 1807–15   21–4 *not in* 1820–43
27 morning tide L   29 illusion 1815: delusion 1807   32 *so*
1837: A faith, a trust, that could not 1807–32

Not for a moment could I now behold
A smiling sea, and be what I have been:
The feeling of my loss will ne'er be old;
This, which I know, I speak with mind serene.   40

Then, Beaumont, Friend! who would have been the Friend,
If he had lived, of Him whom I deplore,
This work of thine I blame not, but commend;
This sea in anger, and that dismal shore.

O 'tis a passionate Work!—yet wise and well,   45
Well chosen is the spirit that is here;
That Hulk which labours in the deadly swell,
This rueful sky, this pageantry of fear!

And this huge Castle, standing here sublime,
I love to see the look with which it braves,   50
Cased in the unfeeling armour of old time,
The lightning, the fierce wind, and trampling waves.

Farewell, farewell the heart that lives alone,
Housed in a dream, at distance from the Kind!
Such happiness, wherever it be known,   55
Is to be pitied; for 'tis surely blind.

But welcome fortitude, and patient cheer,
And frequent sights of what is to be borne!
Such sights, or worse, as are before me here.—
Not without hope we suffer and we mourn.   60

VII

TO THE DAISY

[Composed 1805.—Published 1815.]

Sweet Flower! belike one day to have
A place upon thy Poet's grave,
I welcome thee once more:
But He, who was on land, at sea,
My Brother, too, in loving thee,   5
Although he loved more silently,
Sleeps by his native shore.

Ah! hopeful, hopeful was the day
When to that Ship he bent his way,
To govern and to guide: 10
His wish was gained: a little time
Would bring him back in manhood's prime
And free for life, these hills to climb;
With all his wants supplied.

And full of hope day followed day   15
While that stout Ship at anchor lay
Beside the shores of Wight;
The May had then made all things green;
And, floating there, in pomp serene,
That Ship was goodly to be seen,   20
His pride and his delight!

Yet then, when called ashore, he sought
The tender peace of rural thought:
In more than happy mood
To your abodes, bright daisy Flowers!   25
He then would steal at leisure hours,
And loved you glittering in your bowers,
A starry multitude.

But hark the word!—the ship is gone;—
Returns from her long course:—anon   30
Sets sail:—in season due,
Once more on English earth they stand:
But, when a third time from the land
They parted, sorrow was at hand
For Him and for his crew.   35

Ill-fated Vessel!—ghastly shock!
—At length delivered from the rock,
The deep she hath regained;
And through the stormy night they steer;

VII. 9 bent] went MS.   15 And hopeful, hopeful was the day MS.
18–20 And goodly, also, to be seen
       Was that proud Ship, of Ships the Queen,
       His hope *etc.* MS.
22–3 he sought . . . thought] I know
       The truth of this (From his own pen) he told me so MS. *corr. to text*
26 He then would steal] He sometimes stole *corr. to* He oft would steal MS.
30 *so* MS., 1837: From her long course returns   1815–32   36–49 *not*
in MS.

Labouring for life, in hope and fear,   40
To reach a safer shore—how near,
Yet not to be attained!

"Silence!" the brave Commander cried;
To that calm word a shriek replied,
It was the last death-shriek.   45
—A few (my soul oft sees that sight)
Survive upon the tall mast's height;
But one dear remnant of the night—
For Him in vain I seek.

Six weeks beneath the moving sea   50
He lay in slumber quietly;
Unforced by wind or wave
To quit the Ship for which he died,
(All claims of duty satisfied);
And there they found him at her side;   55
And bore him to the grave.

Vain service! yet not vainly done
For this, if other end were none,
That He, who had been cast
Upon a way of life unmeet   60
For such a gentle Soul and sweet,
Should find an undisturbed retreat
Near what he loved, at last—

That neighbourhood of grove and field
To Him a resting-place should yield,   65
A meek man and a brave!
The birds shall sing and ocean make
A mournful murmur for *his* sake;
And Thou, sweet Flower, shalt sleep and wake
Upon his senseless grave.   70

41 To reach   1837: Towards   1815–32
46–8 *so* 1837: —A few appear by morning light
                 Preserved upon the tall mast's height
                 Oft in my Soul I see that sight;   1815–32
64 grove] wood MS.

VIII
ELEGIAC VERSES

IN MEMORY OF MY BROTHER, JOHN WORDSWORTH

Commander of the E. I. Company's ship, the Earl of Abergavenny, in which
he perished by calamitous shipwreck, Feb. 6th, 1805. Composed near
the Mountain track, that leads from Grasmere through Grisdale Hawes,
where it descends towards Patterdale.

[Composed 1805.—Published: vol. of 1842.]

I

THE Sheep-boy whistled loud, and lo!
That instant, startled by the shock,
The Buzzard mounted from the rock
Deliberate and slow:
Lord of the air, he took his flight;   5
Oh! could he on that woeful night
Have lent his wing, my Brother dear,
For one poor moment's space to Thee,
And all who struggled with the Sea,
When safety was so near.   10

II

Thus in the weakness of my heart
I spoke (but let that pang be still)
When rising from the rock at will,
I saw the Bird depart.

VIII.   *Before l.* 1 I only look'd for pain and grief
                    And trembled as I drew more near,
                    But God's unbounded love is here
                    And I have found relief.
                    The precious Spot is all my own
                    Save only that this Plant unknown,
                    A little one and lowly sweet,
                    Not surely now without Heav'n's grace
                    First seen, and seen too in this place,
                    Is flowering at my feet.

                    The Shepherd Boy hath disappear'd,
                    The Buzzard too, hath soar'd away,
                    And undisturb'd I now may pay
                    My debt to what I fear'd,
                    Sad register! but this is sure,
                    Peace built on suffering will endure;
                    But such the peace that will be ours
                    Though many suns alas! must shine
                    Ere tears shall cease from me and mine
                    To fall in bitter show'rs. MS.

And let me calmly bless the Power   15
That meets me in this unknown Flower,
Affecting type of him I mourn!
With calmness suffer and believe,
And grieve, and know that I must grieve,
Not cheerless, though forlorn.   20

III

Here did we stop; and here looked round
While each into himself descends,
For that last thought of parting Friends
That is not to be found.
Hidden was Grasmere Vale from sight,   25
Our home and his, his heart's delight,
His quiet heart's selected home.
But time before him melts away,
And he hath feeling of a day
Of blessedness to come.   30

IV

Full soon in sorrow did I weep,
Taught that the mutual hope was dust,
In sorrow, but for higher trust,
How miserably deep!
All vanished in a single word,   35
A breath, a sound, and scarcely heard.
Sea—Ship—drowned—Shipwreck—so it came,
The meek, the brave, the good, was gone;
He who had been our living John
Was nothing but a name.   40

25 Our Grasmere vale was out of sight MS.   27 His gentle heart's
delicious home. MS.
30/1 Here did we part, and seated here
     With One he lov'd, I saw him bound
     Downwards along the rocky ground
     As if with eager chear.
     A lovely sight as on he went,
     For he was bold and innocent,
     Had liv'd a life of self-command,
     Heaven, did it seem to me and her
     Had laid on such a Mariner
     A consecrating hand. MS.
31–2 Then let not those be blamed who weep
     Now taught that such a faith was dust MS.

V

That was indeed a parting! oh,
Glad am I, glad that it is past;
For there were some on whom it cast
Unutterable woe.
But they as well as I have gains;—   45
From many a humble source, to pains
Like these, there comes a mild release;
Even here I feel it, even this Plant
Is in its beauty ministrant
To comfort and to peace.   50

VI

He would have loved thy modest grace,
Meek Flower! To Him I would have said,
"It grows upon its native bed
Beside our Parting-place;
There, cleaving to the ground, it lies   55
With multitude of purple eyes,
Spangling a cushion green like moss;
But we will see it, joyful tide!
Some day, to see it in its pride,
The mountain will we cross."   60

VII

—Brother and friend, if verse of mine
Have power to make thy virtues known,
Here let a monumental Stone
Stand—sacred as a Shrine;
And to the few who pass this way,   65
Traveller or Shepherd, let it say,
Long as these mighty rocks endure,—
Oh do not Thou too fondly brood,
Although deserving of all good,
On any earthly hope, however pure![1]   70

---

[1] The plant alluded to is the Moss Campion (Silene acaulis, of Linnæus).
See Note, p. 456. See among the Poems on the "Naming of Places", No. VI.

---

55 ⎧ Close to the ground like dew it lies
   ⎨ As loth to leave the ground it lies
   ⎩ It climbs not from the ground but lies MS.
61 Well, well, if ever verse of mine MS.   62 thy virtues] his merits
MS.

IX
SONNET

[Composed January, 1846.—Published 1850.]

WHY should we weep or mourn, Angelic boy,
For such thou wert ere from our sight removed,
Holy, and ever dutiful—beloved
From day to day with never-ceasing joy,
And hopes as dear as could the heart employ   5
In aught to earth pertaining ? Death has proved
His might, nor less his mercy, as behoved—
Death conscious that he only could destroy
The bodily frame. That beauty is laid low
To moulder in a far-off field of Rome ;   10
But Heaven is now, blest Child, thy Spirit's home:
When such divine communion, which we know,
Is felt, thy Roman burial-place will be
Surely a sweet remembrancer of Thee.

X
LINES

Composed at Grasmere, during a walk one Evening, after a stormy day,
the Author having just read in a Newspaper that the dissolution of Mr.
Fox was hourly expected.

[Composed September, 1806.—Published 1807.]

LOUD is the Vale! the Voice is up
With which she speaks when storms are gone,
A mighty unison of streams!
Of all her Voices, One!

Loud is the Vale ;—this inland Depth   5
In peace is roaring like the Sea ;
Yon star upon the mountain-top
Is listening quietly.

Sad was I, even to pain deprest,
Importunate and heavy load!¹   10
The Comforter hath found me here,
Upon this lonely road ;

¹ Importuna e grave salma.
MICHAEL ANGELO.

IX. 12 such] this MS.

And many thousands now are sad—
Wait the fulfilment of their fear;
For he must die who is their stay,   15
Their glory disappear.

A Power is passing from the earth
To breathless Nature's dark abyss;
But when the great and good depart
What is it more than this—   20

That Man, who is from God sent forth,
Doth yet again to God return?—
Such ebb and flow must ever be,
Then wherefore should we mourn?

XI

INVOCATION TO THE EARTH

FEBRUARY, 1816

[Composed February, 1816.—Published 1816.]

I

"REST, rest, perturbèd Earth!
    O rest, thou doleful Mother of Mankind!"
A Spirit sang in tones more plaintive than the wind:
"From regions where no evil thing has birth
I come—thy stains to wash away,   5
Thy cherished fetters to unbind,
And open thy sad eyes upon a milder day.
The Heavens are thronged with martyrs that have risen
        From out thy noisome prison;
        The penal caverns groan   10
With tens of thousands rent from off the tree
Of hopeful life,—by battle's whirlwind blown
Into the deserts of Eternity.
Unpitied havoc! Victims unlamented!
But not on high, where madness is resented,   15
And murder causes some sad tears to flow,
Though, from the widely-sweeping blow,
The choirs of Angels spread, triumphantly augmented.

X. 19 *so* 1837: But when the Mighty pass away   1807-32

II

"False Parent of Mankind!
   Obdurate, proud, and blind,   20
I sprinkle thee with soft celestial dews,
Thy lost, maternal heart to re-infuse!
Scattering this far-fetched moisture from my wings,
Upon the act a blessing I implore,
Of which the rivers in their secret springs,   25
The rivers stained so oft with human gore,
Are conscious;—may the like return no more!
May Discord—for a Seraph's care
Shall be attended with a bolder prayer—
May she, who once disturbed the seats of bliss   30
   These mortal spheres above,
Be chained for ever to the black abyss!
And thou, O rescued Earth, by peace and love,
And merciful desires, thy sanctity approve!"
   The Spirit ended his mysterious rite,   35
And the pure vision closed in darkness infinite.

XII

LINES

WRITTEN ON A BLANK LEAF IN A COPY OF THE AUTHOR'S POEM
"THE EXCURSION", UPON HEARING OF THE DEATH OF THE LATE
VICAR OF KENDAL

[Composed November 13, 1814.—Published 1815.]

To public notice, with reluctance strong,
Did I deliver this unfinished Song;
Yet for one happy issue;—and I look
With self-congratulation on the Book
Which pious, learned, MURFITT saw and read;—   5
Upon my thoughts his saintly Spirit fed;
He conned the new-born Lay with grateful heart—
Foreboding not how soon he must depart;
Unweeting that to him the joy was given
Which good men take with them from earth to heaven. 10

XIII

ELEGIAC STANZAS

(ADDRESSED TO SIR G. H. B. UPON THE DEATH
OF HIS SISTER-IN-LAW)

[Composed probably December, 1824.—Published 1827.]

O FOR a dirge! But why complain?
Ask rather a triumphal strain
When FERMOR'S race is run;
A garland of immortal boughs
To twine around the Christian's brows,   5
Whose glorious work is done.

We pay a high and holy debt;
No tears of passionate regret
Shall stain this votive lay;
Ill-worthy, Beaumont! were the grief   10
That flings itself on wild relief
When Saints have passed away.

Sad doom, at Sorrow's shrine to kneel,
For ever covetous to feel,
And impotent to bear!   15
Such once was hers—to think and think
On severed love, and only sink
From anguish to despair!

But nature to its inmost part
Faith had refined; and to her heart   20
A peaceful cradle given:
Calm as the dew-drop's, free to rest
Within a breeze-fanned rose's breast
Till it exhales to Heaven.

Was ever Spirit that could bend   25
So graciously?—that could descend,
Another's need to suit,
So promptly from her lofty throne?—
In works of love, in these alone,
How restless, how minute!   30

XIII. Title *so* 1837: ELEGIAC STANZAS 1824   1827–32.   5 twine
1845: bind   1827–43   20 Faith had   1837: Had Faith   1827–32   26
graciously] courteously   MS.

Pale was her hue; yet mortal cheek
Ne'er kindled with a livelier streak
When aught had suffered wrong,—
When aught that breathes had felt a wound;
Such look the Oppressor might confound, 35
However proud and strong.

But hushed be every thought that springs
From out the bitterness of things;
Her quiet is secure;
No thorns can piece her tender feet, 40
Whose life was, like the violet, sweet,
As climbing jasmine, pure—

As snowdrop on an infant's grave,
Or lily heaving with the wave
That feeds it and defends; 45
As Vesper, ere the star hath kissed
The mountain top, or breathed the mist
That from the vale ascends.

Thou takest not away, O Death!
Thou strikest—absence perisheth, 50
Indifference is no more;
The future brightens on our sight;
For on the past hath fallen a light
That tempts us to adore.

XIV
ELEGIAC MUSINGS

IN THE GROUNDS OF COLEORTON HALL, THE SEAT OF THE
LATE SIR G. H. BEAUMONT, BART.

In these grounds stands the Parish Church, wherein is a mural monument
bearing an inscription which, in deference to the earnest request of the
deceased, is confined to name, dates, and these words:—"Enter not into
judgment with thy servant, O Lord!"

[Composed November, 1830.—Published 1835.]

WITH copious eulogy in prose or rhyme
Graven on the tomb we struggle against Time,
Alas, how feebly! but our feelings rise
And still we struggle when a good man dies.

50 *so* 1843: Thou strik'st—and 1827–37
XIV. 1 or 1837, MSS.: and 1835

Such offering BEAUMONT dreaded and forbade,   5
A spirit meek in self-abasement clad.
Yet *here* at least, though few have numbered days
That shunned so modestly the light of praise,
His graceful manners, and the temperate ray
Of that arch fancy which would round him play,   10
Brightening a converse never known to swerve
From courtesy and delicate reserve;
That sense, the bland philosophy of life,
Which checked discussion ere it warmed to strife;
Those rare accomplishments, and varied powers,   15
Might have their record among sylvan bowers.
Oh, fled for ever! vanished like a blast
That shook the leaves in myriads as it passed;—
Gone from this world of earth, air, sea, and sky,
From all its spirit-moving imagery,   20
Intensely studied with a painter's eye,
A poet's heart; and, for congenial view,
Portrayed with happiest pencil, not untrue
To common recognitions while the line
Flowed in a course of sympathy divine;—   25
Oh! severed, too abruptly, from delights
That all the seasons shared with equal rights;—
Rapt in the grace of undismantled age,
From soul-felt music, and the treasured page
Lit by that evening lamp which loved to shed   30
Its mellow lustre round thy honoured head;
While Friends beheld thee give with eye, voice, mien,
More than theatric force to Shakspeare's scene;—
If thou hast heard me—if thy Spirit know
Aught of these bowers and whence their pleasures flow;   35
If things in our remembrance held so dear,
And thoughts and projects fondly cherished here,
To thy exalted nature only seem
Time's vanities, light fragments of earth's dream—
Rebuke us not!—The mandate is obeyed   40
That said, "Let praise be mute where I am laid;"
The holier deprecation, given in trust
To the cold marble, waits upon thy dust;
Yet have we found how slowly genuine grief

15 rare   1837: fine   MSS., 1835   34–9 *not in* MSS., 1835

From *silent* admiration wins relief. 45
Too long abashed thy Name is like a rose
That doth "within itself its sweetness close;"
A drooping daisy changed into a cup
In which her bright-eyed beauty is shut up.
Within these groves, where still are flitting by 50
Shades of the Past, oft noticed with a sigh,
Shall stand a votive Tablet, haply free,
When towers and temples fall, to speak of Thee!
If sculptured emblems of our mortal doom
Recal not there the wisdom of the Tomb, 55
Green ivy risen from out the cheerful earth
Will fringe the lettered stone; and herbs spring forth,
Whose fragrance, by soft dews and rain unbound,
Shall penetrate the heart without a wound;
While truth and love their purposes fulfil, 60
Commemorating genius, talent, skill,
That could not lie concealed where Thou wert known;
Thy virtues *He* must judge, and He alone,
The God upon whose mercy they are thrown.

XV
WRITTEN AFTER THE DEATH OF CHARLES LAMB

[Ll. 1–38 composed November 19, 1835, and privately printed with title
Epitaph, 1835; ll. 39–131 composed December, 1835, and privately printed
1836.—Published 1837.]

To a good Man of most dear memory
This Stone is sacred. Here he lies apart
From the great city where he first drew breath,
Was reared and taught; and humbly earned his bread,
To the strict labours of the merchant's desk 5
By duty chained. Not seldom did those tasks
Tease, and the thought of time so spent depress,
His spirit, but the recompence was high;
Firm Independence, Bounty's rightful sire;
Affections, warm as sunshine, free as air; 10
And when the precious hours of leisure came,
Knowledge and wisdom, gained from converse sweet

57 Will 1837: Shall MS., 1835
XV. Title added in 1845   1 To the dear memory of a frail good
Man 1835–6

With books, or while he ranged the crowded streets
With a keen eye, and overflowing heart:
So genius triumphed over seeming wrong,   15
And poured out truth in works by thoughtful love
Inspired—works potent over smiles and tears.
And as round mountain-tops the lightning plays,
Thus innocently sported, breaking forth
As from a cloud of some grave sympathy,   20
Humour and wild instinctive wit, and all
The vivid flashes of his spoken words.
From the most gentle creature nursed in fields
Had been derived the name he bore—a name,
Wherever Christian altars have been raised,   25
Hallowed to meekness and to innocence;
And if in him meekness at times gave way,
Provoked out of herself by troubles strange,
Many and strange, that hung about his life;
Still, at the centre of his being, lodged   30
A soul by resignation sanctified:
And if too often, self-reproached, he felt
That innocence belongs not to our kind,
A power that never ceased to abide in him,
Charity, 'mid the multitude of sins   35
That she can cover, left not his exposed
To an unforgiving judgment from just Heaven.
O, he was good, if e'er a good Man lived!

     .   .   .   .

From a reflecting mind and sorrowing heart
Those simple lines flowed with an earnest wish,   40

15–17 *These lines were not in the original draft*
20/1 Or suddenly dislodged by strong rebound
    Of animal spirits that had sunk too low   *original draft*
34–5 He had a constant friend in Charity;
    Her who, among a multitude of sins 1835–6; (1835 *italicizes* Charity,
his *in* l. 36 *and* if e'er *in* l. 38)
40–9 This tribute flow'd, with hope that it might guard
    The dust of him whose virtues called it forth;
    But 'tis a little space of earth that man,
    Stretch'd out in death, is doom'd to occupy;
    Still smaller space doth modest custom yield
    On sculptured tomb or tablet, to the claims
    Of the deceased, or rights of the bereft.
    'Tis well; and, tho' the record overstepped
    Those narrow bounds, yet on the printed page

Though but a doubting hope, that they might serve
Fitly to guard the precious dust of him
Whose virtues called them forth. That aim is missed;
For much that truth most urgently required
Had from a faltering pen been asked in vain: 45
Yet, haply, on the printed page received,
The imperfect record, there, may stand unblamed
As long as verse of mine shall breathe the air
Of memory, or see the light of love.

    Thou wert a scorner of the fields, my Friend,   50
But more in show than truth; and from the fields,
And from the mountains, to thy rural grave
Transported, my soothed spirit hovers o'er
Its green untrodden turf, and blowing flowers;
And taking up a voice shall speak (tho' still   55
Awed by the theme's peculiar sanctity
Which words less free presumed not even to touch)
Of that fraternal love, whose heaven-lit lamp
From infancy, through manhood, to the last
Of threescore years, and to thy latest hour,   60
Burned on with ever-strengthening light, enshrined
Within thy bosom.   "Wonderful" hath been
The love established between man and man,
"Passing the love of women;" and between
Man and his help-mate in fast wedlock joined   65
Through God, is raised a spirit and soul of love
Without whose blissful influence Paradise
Had been no Paradise; and earth were now

Received, there may it stand, I trust, unblamed
(Aptly received, there it may stand unblamed *Proof copy*)
As long as verse of mine shall steal from tears
Their bitterness, or live to shed a gleam
Of solace over one dejected thought   1836[1]

'Tis well; and tho' the appropriate bounds have here
Been overstepped, yet may the imprinted page
Receive the record, there to stand, unblamed,
As long as verse of mine etc. *as text*   1836[2]

'Tis well, and if the Record in the strength
And earnestness of feeling, overpass'd
Those narrow limits and so miss'd its aim
Yet will I trust that on the printed page
Received, it there may keep a place unblamed MS. *quoted by Dowden*

61 Burned on] Burned, and   1836   66 Through] By   1836

A waste where creatures bearing human form,
Direst of savage beasts, would roam in fear,   70
Joyless and comfortless. Our days glide on;
And let him grieve who cannot choose but grieve
That he hath been an Elm without his Vine,
And her bright dower of clustering charities,
That, round his trunk and branches, might have clung   75
Enriching and adorning. Unto thee,
Not so enriched, not so adorned, to thee
Was given (say rather thou of later birth
Wert given to her) a Sister—'tis a word
Timidly uttered, for she *lives*, the meek,   80
The self-restraining, and the ever-kind;
In whom thy reason and intelligent heart
Found—for all interests, hopes, and tender cares,
All softening, humanising, hallowing powers,
Whether withheld, or for her sake unsought—   85
More than sufficient recompence!
                                    Her love
(What weakness prompts the voice to tell it here?)
Was as the love of mothers; and when years,
Lifting the boy to man's estate, had called
The long-protected to assume the part   90
Of a protector, the first filial tie
Was undissolved; and, in or out of sight,
Remained imperishably interwoven
With life itself. Thus, 'mid a shifting world,
Did they together testify of time   95
And season's difference—a double tree
With two collateral stems sprung from one root;
Such were they—such thro' life they *might* have been
In union, in partition only such;
Otherwise wrought the will of the Most High;   100
Yet, thro' all visitations and all trials,
Still they were faithful; like two vessels launched
From the same beach one ocean to explore

71 glide] pass 1836   94 Thus] Yet 1836
94–5 Together stood they (witnessing of time
    And season's difference) as a double tree 1836¹
95 Fix'd—they together testified of time   1836²   100 *added to Proof*
copy   101–2 Yet thro' . . . and . . . they were] And in . . . through . . .
were they, *Proof copy*   102–3 like two goodly ships Launched from
the beach   1836

With mutual help, and sailing—to their league
True, as inexorable winds, or bars   105
Floating or fixed of polar ice, allow.

But turn we rather, let my spirit turn
With thine, O silent and invisible Friend!
To those dear intervals, nor rare nor brief,
When reunited, and by choice withdrawn   110
From miscellaneous converse, ye were taught
That the remembrance of foregone distress,
And the worse fear of future ill (which oft
Doth hang around it, as a sickly child
Upon its mother) may be both alike   115
Disarmed of power to unsettle present good
So prized, and things inward and outward held
In such an even balance, that the heart
Acknowledges God's grace, his mercy feels,
And in its depth of gratitude is still.   120

O gift divine of quiet sequestration!
The hermit, exercised in prayer and praise,
And feeding daily on the hope of heaven,
Is happy in his vow, and fondly cleaves
To life-long singleness; but happier far   125
Was to your souls, and, to the thoughts of others,
A thousand times more beautiful appeared,
Your *dual* loneliness. The sacred tie
Is broken; yet why grieve? for Time but holds
His moiety in trust, till Joy shall lead   130
To the blest world where parting is unknown.

XVI

EXTEMPORE EFFUSION UPON THE DEATH OF
JAMES HOGG

[Composed November, 1835.—Published December 12, 1835 (*The Athe-
næum*); ed. 1837.]

WHEN first, descending from the moorlands,
I saw the Stream of Yarrow glide
Along a bare and open valley,
The Ettrick Shepherd was my guide.

128–31 . . . The sacred tie
        Is broken, to become more sacred still. 1836

When last along its banks I wandered,   5
Through groves that had begun to shed
Their golden leaves upon the pathways,
My steps the Border-minstrel led.

The mighty Minstrel breathes no longer,
'Mid mouldering ruins low he lies;   10
And death upon the braes of Yarrow,
Has closed the Shepherd-poet's eyes:

Nor has the rolling year twice measured,
From sign to sign, its stedfast course,
Since every mortal power of Coleridge   15
Was frozen at its marvellous source;

The rapt One, of the godlike forehead,
The heaven-eyed creature sleeps in earth:
And Lamb, the frolic and the gentle,
Has vanished from his lonely hearth.   20

Like clouds that rake the mountain-summits,
Or waves that own no curbing hand,
How fast has brother followed brother,
From sunshine to the sunless land!

Yet I, whose lids from infant slumber   25
Were earlier raised, remain to hear
A timid voice, that asks in whispers,
"Who next will drop and disappear?"

Our haughty life is crowned with darkness,
Like London with its own black wreath,   30
On which with thee, O Crabbe! forth-looking.
I gazed from Hampstead's breezy heath.

As if but yesterday departed,
Thou too art gone before; but why,
O'er ripe fruit, seasonably gathered,   35
Should frail survivors heave a sigh?

Mourn rather for that holy Spirit,
Sweet as the spring, as ocean deep;

XVI. 25 slumber   1845: slumbers   1835–43
37–9 She too, a Muse whose holy Spirit
      Was sweet as *etc.*
      She, ere her Summer yet was faded **MS.**
      Grieve rather for that holy Spirit
      Pure as the sky *etc.* C

For Her who, ere her summer faded,
Has sunk into a breathless sleep.   40

No more of old romantic sorrows,
For slaughtered Youth or love-lorn Maid!
With sharper grief is Yarrow smitten,
And Ettrick mourns with her their Poet dead.[1]

XVII
INSCRIPTION

FOR A MONUMENT IN CROSTHWAITE CHURCH, IN THE VALE
OF KESWICK

[Composed December, 1843.—Published 1845.]

YE vales and hills whose beauty hither drew
The poet's steps, and fixed him here, on you
His eyes have closed! And ye, lov'd books, no more
Shall Southey feed upon your precious lore,
To works that ne'er shall forfeit their renown,   5
Adding immortal labours of his own—
Whether he traced historic truth, with zeal
For the State's guidance, or the Church's weal,
Or Fancy, disciplined by studious art,
Inform'd his pen, or wisdom of the heart,   10
Or judgments sanctioned in the Patriot's mind
‘ By reverence for the rights of all mankind.
Wide were his aims, yet in no human breast
Could private feelings meet for holier rest.
His joys, his griefs, have vanished like a cloud   15
From Skiddaw's top; but he to heaven was vowed
Through his industrious life, and Christian faith
Calmed in his soul the fear of change and death.

¹ See Note.

---

44 And Ettrick mourns her Shepherd poet dead C
XVII. *Before* l. 1 Ye torrents, foaming down the rocky steeps,
            Ye lakes, wherein the spirit of water sleeps, MS.
7–8 *not in* MS. 1   9 Or] As MS. 1   11 sanctioned] rooted MS. 1
12 Taught to revere the rights MS. 1
13–14 Friends, Family—ah wherefore touch that string.
       To them so fondly did the good man cling MS. 1 *corr. to*
       Friends, Family—within no human breast
       Could private feelings need (find) a holier nest.
13 Wide] Large MS.
17–18 Through a long life; and calmed by Christian faith
       In his pure soul MS. 1 *corr. to*
       Through a life long and pure; and Christian [steadfast] faith
       Calmed *etc. as text. v. note* p. 463.

ODE

INTIMATIONS OF IMMORTALITY FROM RECOLLECTIONS OF EARLY CHILDHOOD

The Child is father of the Man;
And I could wish my days to be
Bound each to each by natural piety.

[Composed 1802–1804.—Published 1807.]

I

THERE was a time when meadow, grove, and stream,
The earth, and every common sight,
  To me did seem
  Apparelled in celestial light,
The glory and the freshness of a dream.   5
It is not now as it hath been of yore;—
  Turn wheresoe'er I may,
  By night or day,
The things which I have seen I now can see no more.

II

  The Rainbow comes and goes,   10
  And lovely is the Rose,
  The Moon doth with delight
Look round her when the heavens are bare;
  Waters on a starry night
  Are beautiful and fair;   15
 The sunshine is a glorious birth;
 But yet I know, where'er I go,
That there hath past away a glory from the earth.

III

Now, while the birds thus sing a joyous song,
 And while the young lambs bound   **20**
  As to the tabor's sound,
To me alone there came a thought of grief:
A timely utterance gave that thought relief,
  And I again am strong:

Title INTIMATIONS *etc. not in* 1807 Paulo majora canamus 1807
The Child . . . piety 1815: **6** hath 1820: has MSS.–1815 **9**
I now can see] I see them now MS. M 13 bare; MSS.–1837: bare,
1845–50

The cataracts blow their trumpets from the steep;   25
No more shall grief of mine the season wrong;
I hear the Echoes through the mountains throng,
The Winds come to me from the fields of sleep,
      And all the earth is gay;
         Land and sea   30
    Give themselves up to jollity,
      And with the heart of May
    Doth every Beast keep holiday;—
      Thou Child of Joy,
Shout round me, let me hear thy shouts, thou happy Shep-
    herd-boy!   35

IV

Ye blessèd Creatures, I have heard the call
    Ye to each other make; I see
The heavens laugh with you in your jubilee;
    My heart is at your festival,
      My head hath its coronal,   40
The fulness of your bliss, I feel—I feel it all.
      Oh evil day! if I were sullen
      While Earth herself is adorning,
        This sweet May-morning,
      And the Children are culling   45
        On every side,
    In a thousand valleys far and wide,
    Fresh flowers; while the sun shines warm,
And the Babe leaps up on his Mother's arm:—
      I hear, I hear, with joy I hear!   50
      —But there's a Tree, of many, one,
A single Field which I have looked upon,
Both of them speak of something that is gone:
      The Pansy at my feet
      Doth the same tale repeat: 55
Whither is fled the visionary gleam?
Where is it now, the glory and the dream?

36–57 *not in* MS. B
41 Even yet more gladness—I can hold it all MS. M *deleted in* L   43
Earth 1837: the Earth MSS.—1832   45 culling 1837: pulling MSS.—
1832   49 on] in MS. M   57 now] gone MS. M, *corr. to* now
MS. L

V

Our birth is but a sleep and a forgetting:
The Soul that rises with us, our life's Star,
    Hath had elsewhere its setting,   60
      And cometh from afar:
    Not in entire forgetfulness,
    And not in utter nakedness,
But trailing clouds of glory do we come
    From God, who is our home: 65
Heaven lies about us in our infancy!
Shades of the prison-house begin to close
    Upon the growing Boy,
      But He
Beholds the light, and whence it flows,   70
    He sees it in his joy;
The Youth, who daily farther from the east
    Must travel, still is Nature's Priest,
    And by the vision splendid
    Is on his way attended;   75
At length the Man perceives it die away,
And fade into the light of common day.

VI

Earth fills her lap with pleasures of her own;
Yearnings she hath in her own natural kind,
And, even with something of a Mother's mind,   80
    And no unworthy aim,
    The homely Nurse doth all she can
To make her Foster-child, her Inmate Man,
    Forget the glories he hath known,
And that imperial palace whence he came.   85

VII

Behold the Child among his new-born blisses,
A six years' Darling of a pigmy size!
See, where 'mid work of his own hand he lies,
Frettied by sallies of his mother's kisses,

69 But He
    Beholds the light *etc.*   MS. L *corr. from text in W.W.'s hand:* But He
beholds *etc. as one line.* MS. M, 1807–50
76 perceives] beholds MSS.   78 pleasures] pleasure MS. M and MS.
L *corr. to text*   87 six 1815: four MSS., 1807 ·

With light upon him from his father's eyes!   90
See, at his feet, some little plan or chart,
Some fragment from his dream of human life,
Shaped by himself with newly-learned art;
          A wedding or a festival,
          A mourning or a funeral;   95
               And this hath now his heart,
               And unto this he frames his song:
               Then will he fit his tongue
To dialogues of business, love, or strife;
          But it will not be long   100
          Ere this be thrown aside,
          And with new joy and pride
The little Actor cons another part;
Filling from time to time his "humorous stage"
With all the Persons, down to palsied Age,   105
That Life brings with her in her equipage;
          As if his whole vocation
          Were endless imitation.

VIII

Thou, whose exterior semblance doth belie
          Thy Soul's immensity;   110
Thou best Philosopher, who yet dost keep
Thy heritage, thou Eye among the blind,
That, deaf and silent, read'st the eternal deep,
Haunted for ever by the eternal mind,—
          Mighty Prophet! Seer blest!   115
          On whom those truths do rest,
Which we are toiling all our lives to find,
In darkness lost, the darkness of the grave;
Thou, over whom thy Immortality
Broods like the Day, a Master o'er a Slave,   120
A Presence which is not to be put by;

109 O Thou whose outward seeming   MS. M: exterior presence   MS. L,
corr. to text   115 Thou mighty   MS. M
118 *so* 1820: *not in* MSS.–1815   119 O Thou on whom MS. M
121/2 To whom the grave
          Is but a lonely bed without the sense or sight
          Of day or the warm light,
          A place of thought where we in waiting lie;   1807–15: *so* MS. M, *but*
Thou unto whom . . . *and* living place *for* place of thought

Thou little Child, yet glorious in the might
Of heaven-born freedom on thy being's height,
Why with such earnest pains dost thou provoke
The years to bring the inevitable yoke, 125
· Thus blindly with thy blessedness at strife ?
Full soon thy Soul shall have her earthly freight,
And custom lie upon thee with a weight,
Heavy as frost, and deep almost as life!

IX

O joy! that in our embers 130
Is something that doth live,
That nature yet remembers
What was so fugitive!
The thought of our past years in me doth breed
Perpetual benediction: not indeed 135
For that which is most worthy to be blest;
Delight and liberty, the simple creed
Of Childhood, whether busy or at rest,
With new-fledged hope still fluttering in his breast:—
Not for these I raise 140
The song of thanks and praise;
But for those obstinate questionings
Of sense and outward things,
Fallings from us, vanishings;
Blank misgivings of a Creature 145
Moving about in worlds not realised,
High instincts before which our mortal Nature
Did tremble like a guilty Thing surprised:
But for those first affections,
Those shadowy recollections, 150
Which, be they what they may,
Are yet the fountain light of all our day,
Are yet a master light of all our seeing;

122–3 *not in* MSS. L, M   123 *so* 1815: Of untam'd pleasures, on thy
Being's height 1807: *so* MS. L *but* nature *corr. to* being.   127/8 The world
upon thy noble nature seize, With all its vanities MSS.L, B   135 benediction 1827: benedictions MSS.—1820   138–9 busy . . . new-fledged hopes
still fluttering 1815: fluttering . . . new-born hope for ever MSS., 1807
142–5 But for those blank misgivings of a Creature MS. M   153 a] the
MS. M
153/4 Throw off from us, or mitigate, the spell
        Of that strong frame of sense in which we dwell; MS. L

Uphold us, cherish, and have power to make
Our noisy years seem moments in the being   155
Of the eternal Silence: truths that wake,
          To perish never;
Which neither listlessness, nor mad endeavour,
          Nor Man nor Boy,
Nor all that is at enmity with joy,   160
Can utterly abolish or destroy!
          Hence in a season of calm weather
          Though inland far we be,
Our Souls have sight of that immortal sea
          Which brought us hither,   165
          Can in a moment travel thither,
And see the Children sport upon the shore,
And hear the mighty waters rolling evermore.

X

Then sing, ye Birds, sing, sing a joyous song!
          And let the young Lambs bound   170
          As to the tabor's sound!
We in thought will join your throng,
          Ye that pipe and ye that play,
          Ye that through your hearts to-day
          Feel the gladness of the May!   175
What though the radiance which was once so bright
Be now for ever taken from my sight,
          Though nothing can bring back the hour
Of splendour in the grass, of glory in the flower;
          We will grieve not, rather find   180
          Strength in what remains behind;
          In the primal sympathy
          Which having been must ever be;
          In the soothing thoughts that spring
          Out of human suffering;   185
          In the faith that looks through death,
In years that bring the philosophic mind.

154 *so* 1815: . . . cherish us, and make MSS., 1807
176–9 What though it be past the hour
          Of splendour *etc.* MS. M
182–3 *not in* MSS. (*but added to* MS. L)

XI

And O, ye Fountains, Meadows, Hills, and Groves,
Forebode not any severing of our loves!
Yet in my heart of hearts I feel your might;   190
I only have relinquished one delight
To live beneath your more habitual sway.
I love the Brooks which down their channels fret,
Even more than when I tripped lightly as they;
The innocent brightness of a new-born Day   195
        Is lovely yet;
The Clouds that gather round the setting sun
Do take a sober colouring from an eye
That hath kept watch o'er man's mortality;
Another race hath been, and other palms are won.   200
Thanks to the human heart by which we live,
Thanks to its tenderness, its joys, and fears,
To me the meanest flower that blows can give
Thoughts that do often lie too deep for tears.

188 Hills] fields MS. M.
189 Forbode not   1837: Think not of   MSS.—1832
191/2 Divine indeed of sense
      A blessed influence MS. B.: MS. L. (*but deleted*)
192 To acknowledge under you a higher sway MSS. L., B.   193–4 Dear
are the Brooks which . . . More dear than   MSS. L., B.
196/7 Nor (Not) unaccompanied with blithe desire
      Though many a serious pleasure it inspire MS. L. (*deleted*)
198 a sober] an awful MS. L., *corr. to text*

APPENDIX A

Translations of Virgil's Æneid I, II, and III, and other passages

TRANSLATION OF VIRGIL'S ÆNEID

[Translated 1819–23; I 901–1043 (Virgil 657–756) printed in *The Philological Museum*, 1832]

ADVERTISEMENT

It is proper to premise that the first Couplet of this Translation is adopted from Pitt;—as are likewise two Couplets in the second Book; and three or four lines, in different parts, are taken from Dryden. A few expressions will also be found, which, following the Original closely, are the same as the preceding Translators have unavoidably employed.

FIRST BOOK

ARMS, and the Man I sing, the first who bore
His course to Latium from the Trojan shore,
A Fugitive of Fate:—long time was He
By Powers celestial toss'd on land and sea,
Through wrathful Juno's far-famed enmity;   5
Much, too, from war endured; till new abodes
He planted, and in Latium fix'd his Gods;
Whence flowed the Latin People; whence have come
The Alban Sires, and Walls of lofty Rome.

    Say, Muse, what Powers were wrong'd, what grievance drove   10
To such extremity the Spouse of Jove,
Labouring to wrap in perils, to astound
With woes, a Man for piety renown'd!
In heavenly breasts is such resentment found?

    Right opposite the Italian Coast there stood   15
An ancient City, far from Tiber's flood,
Carthage its name; a Colony of Tyre,
Rich, strong, and bent on war with fierce desire.
No region, not even Samos, was so graced
By Juno's favour; here her Arms were placed,   20
Here lodged her Chariot; and unbounded scope,
Even then, the Goddess gave to partial hope;
Her aim (if Fate such triumph will allow)
That to this Nation all the world shall bow.
But Fame had told her that a Race, from Troy   25
Derived, the Tyrian ramparts would destroy;

5 Through Juno's unrelenting MS.

That from this stock a People, proud in war,
And train'd to spread dominion wide and far,
Should come, and through her favorite Lybian State
Spread utter ruin ;—such the doom of Fate.   30
In fear of this, while busy thought recalls
The war she raised against the Trojan Walls
For her lov'd Argos (and, with these combined,
Work'd other causes rankling in her mind,
The judgement given by Paris, and the slight   35
Her beauty had receiv'd on Ida's height,
Th' undying hatred which the Race had bred,
And honours given to ravish'd Ganymed),
Saturnian Juno far from Latium chaced
The Trojans, tossed upon the watery waste ;   40
Unhappy relics of the Grecian spear
And of the dire Achilles! Many a year
They roam'd ere Fate's decision was fulfill'd,
Such arduous toil it was the Roman State to build.

   Sicilian headlands scarcely out of sight,   45
They spread the canvas with a fresh delight ;
Then Juno, brooding o'er the eternal wound,
Thus inly ;—"Must I vanquish'd quit the ground
Of my attempt ? Or impotently toil
To bar the Trojans from the Italian soil ?   50
For the Fates thwart me ;—yet could Pallas raise
'Mid Argive vessels a destructive blaze,
And in the Deep plunge all, for fault of one,
The desperate frenzy of Oïleus' Son ;
She from the clouds the bolt of Jove might cast,   55
And ships and sea deliver to the blast!
Him, flames ejecting from a bosom fraught
With sulphurous fire, she in a whirlwind caught,
And on a sharp rock fix'd ;—but I who move
Heaven's Queen, the Sister and the Wife of Jove,   60
Wage with one Race the war I waged of yore! ⎫
Who then, henceforth, will Juno's name adore ? ⎬
Her altars grace with gifts, her aid implore ?" ⎭

   These things revolved in fiery discontent,
Her course the Goddess to Æolia bent,   65
Country of lowering clouds, where South-winds rave ;
There Æolus, within a spacious cave
With sovereign power controuls the struggling Winds,
And the sonorous Storms in durance binds.
Loud, loud the mountain murmurs as they wreak   70
Their scorn upon the barriers. On a peak

High-seated, Æolus his sceptre sways,
Soothes their fierce temper, and their wrath allays.
This did he not,—sea, earth, and heaven's vast deep
Would follow them, entangled in the sweep;   75
But in black caves the Sire Omnipotent
The winds sequester'd, fearing such event;
Heap'd over them vast mountains, and assign'd
A Monarch, that should rule the blustering kind;
By stedfast laws their violence restrain,   80
And give, on due command, a loosen'd rein.
As she approached, thus spake the suppliant Queen:
"Æolus! (for the Sire of Gods and men
On thee confers the power to tranquillise
The troubl'd waves, or summon them to rise)   85
A Race, my Foes, bears o'er the troubled Sea
Troy and her conquer'd Gods to Italy.
Throw power into the winds; the ships submerge,
Or part,—and give their bodies to the surge.
Twice seven fair Nymphs await on my command,   90
All beautiful;—the fairest of the Band,
Deïopeia, such desert to crown,
Will I, by stedfast wedlock, make thine own;
In everlasting fellowship with thee
To dwell, and yield a beauteous progeny."   95

    To this the God: "O Queen, declare thy will
And be it mine the mandate to fulfill.
To thee I owe my sceptre, and the place
Jove's favour hath assign'd me; through thy grace
I at the banquets of the Gods recline;   100
And my whole empire is a gift of thine."

    When Æolus had ceased, his spear he bent
Full on the quarter where the winds were pent,
And smote the mountain.—Forth, where way was made,
Rush his wild Ministers; the land pervade,   105
And fasten on the Deep. There Eurus, there
Notus, and Africus unused to spare
His tempests, work with congregated power,
To upturn the abyss, and roll the unwieldy waves ashore.
Clamour of Men ensues, and crash of shrouds,   110
Heaven and the day by the instantaneous clouds
Are ravish'd from the Trojans; on the floods
Black night descends, and, palpably, there broods.
The thundering Poles incessantly unsheath
Their fires, and all things threaten instant death.   115

Appall'd, and with slack limbs Æneas stands;
He groans, and heavenward lifting his clasp'd hands,
Exclaims: "Thrice happy they who chanc'd to fall
In front of lofty Ilium's sacred Wall,
Their parents witnessing their end;—Oh why,   120
Bravest of Greeks, Tydides, could not I
Pour out my willing spirit through a wound
From thy right hand received, on Trojan ground?
Where Hector lies, subjected to the spear
Of the invincible Achilles; where   125
The great Sarpedon sleeps; and o'er the plain   ⎫
Soft Simois whirls helmet, and shield, and men, ⎬
Throngs of the Brave in fearless combat slain!" ⎭

While thus he spake, the Aquilonian gale
Smote from the front upon his driving Sail,   130
And heaved the thwarted billows to the sky,
Round the Ship labouring in extremity.
Help from her shatter'd oars in vain she craves;
Then veers the prow, exposing to the waves
Her side; and lo! a surge, to mountain height   135
Gathering, prepares to burst with its whole weight.
Those hang aloft, as if in air: to these
Earth is disclosed between the boiling seas
Whirl'd on by Notus, three encounter shocks
In the main sea, received from latent rocks;   140
Rocks stretched in dorsal ridge of rugged frame
On the Deep's surface; ALTARS is the name
By which the Italians mark them. Three the force
Of Eurus hurries from an open course
On straits and Shallows, dashes on the strand,   145
And girds the wreck about with heaps of sand.
Another, on which Lyeus and his Mate,
Faithful Orontes, share a common fate,
As his own eyes full plainly can discern,
By a huge wave is swept from prow to stern;   150
Headlong the Pilot falls; thrice whirl'd around,
The Ship is buried in the gulph profound.
Amid the boundless eddy a lost Few,   ⎫
Drowning, or drown'd, emerge to casual view;   ⎬
On waves which planks, and arms, and Trojan wealth bestrew. ⎭ 155
Over the strong-ribb'd pinnace, in which sails
Ilioneus, the Hurricane prevails;
Now conquers Abas, then the Ships that hold
Valiant Achates, and Alethes old;
The joints all loosening in their sides, they drink   160
The hostile brine through many a greedy chink.

Meanwhile, what strife disturb'd the roaring sea,
And for what outrages the storm was free,
Troubling the Ocean to its inmost caves,
Neptune perceiv'd incensed; and o'er the waves   165
Forth-looking with a stedfast brow and eye
Raised from the Deep in placid majesty,
He saw the Trojan Gallies scatter'd wide,
The men they bore oppress'd and terrified;
Waters and ruinous Heaven against their peace allied.   170
Nor from the Brother was conceal'd the heat
Of Juno's anger, and each dark deceit.
Eurus he call'd, and Zephyrus,—and the Pair,
Who at his bidding quit the fields of air,
He thus address'd; "Upon your Birth and Kind   175
Have ye presumed with confidence so blind
As, heedless of my Godhead, to perplex
The Land with uproar, and the Sea to vex;
Which by your act, O winds! thus fiercely heaves
Whom I—but better calm the troubled waves.   180
Henceforth, atonement shall not prove so slight
For such a trespass; to your King take flight,
And say that not to *Him*, but unto *Me*,
Fate hath assigned this watery sovereignty;
Mine is the Trident—his a rocky Hold,   185
Thy mansion, Eurus!—vaunting uncontroll'd,
Let Æolus there occupy his hall,
And in that prison-house the winds enthrall!"

He spake; and, quicker than the word, his will
Felt through the sea abates each tumid hill,   190
Quiets the deep, and silences the shores,
And to a cloudless heaven the sun restores.
Cymothoe shoves, with leaning Triton's aid,
The stranded ships—or Neptune from their bed
With his own Trident lifts them;—then divides   195
The sluggish heaps of sand—and gently glides,
Skimming, on light smooth wheels, the level tides.
Thus oft, when a sedition hath ensued,
Arousing all the ignoble multitude,
Straight through the air do stones and torches fly,   200
With every missile frenzy can supply;
Then, if a venerable Man step forth,
Strong through acknowledged piety and worth,
Hush'd at the sight into mute peace, all stand
Listening, with eyes and ears at his command;   205
Their minds to him are subject; and the rage

That burns within their breasts his lenient words assuage.
So fell the Sea's whole tumult, overawed
Then, when the Sire, casting his eyes abroad,
Turns under open Heaven his docile Steeds,   210
And with his flowing Chariot smoothly speeds.

  The worn-out Trojans, seeking land where'er
The nearest coast invites, for Lybia steer.
There is a Bay whose deep retirement hides   ⎫
The place where Nature's self a Port provides, ⎬   215
Framed by a friendly island's jutting sides,   ⎭
Bulwark from which the billows of the Main
Recoil upon themselves, spending their force in vain.
Vast rocks are here; and, safe beneath the brows
Of two heaven-threatening Cliffs, the Floods repose.   220
Glancing aloft in bright theatric show
Woods wave, and gloomily impend below;
Right opposite this pomp of sylvan shade,
Wild crags and lowering rocks a cave have made;
Within, sweet waters gush; and all bestrown   225
Is the cool floor with seats of living stone;
Cell of the Nymphs, no chains, no anchors, here
Bind the tired vessels, floating without fear;
Led by Æneas, in this shelter meet
Seven ships, the scanty relics of his Fleet;   230
The Crews, athirst with longings for the land,
Here disembark, and range the wish'd-for strand;
Or on the sunny shore their limbs recline,
Heavy with dropping ooze, and drench'd with brine.
Achates, from a smitten flint, receives   235
The spark upon a bed of fostering leaves;
Dry fuel on the natural hearth he lays,
And speedily provokes a mounting blaze.
Then forth they bring, not utterly forlorn,
The needful implements, and injured corn,   240
Bruise it with stones, and by the aid of fire
Prepare the nutriment their frames require.

  Meanwhile Æneas mounts a cliff, to gain
An unobstructed prospect of the Main;
Happy if thence his wistful eyes may mark   245
The harass'd Antheus, or some Phrygian Bark,
Or Capys, or the guardian Sign descry
Which, at the stern, Caïcus bears on high.
No Sail appears in sight, nor toiling oar;
Only he spies three Stags upon the shore;   250

Behind, whole herds are following where these lead,
And in long order through the vallies feed.
He stops—and, with the bow, he seiz'd the store
Of swift-wing'd arrows which Achates bore;
And first the Leaders to his shafts have bow'd   255
Their heads elate with branching horns; the Crowd
Are stricken next; and all the affrighted Drove
Fly in confusion to the leafy grove.
Nor from the weapons doth his hand refrain, ⎫
Till Seven, a Stag for every Ship, are slain, ⎬   260
And with their bulky bodies press the plain. ⎭
Thence to the port he hies, divides the spoil;
And deals out wine, which on Trinacria's soil,
Acestes stored for his departing Guest;
Then with these words he soothes each sorrowing breast.   265

"O Friends, not unacquainted with your share
Of misery, ere doom'd these ills to bear!
O ye, whom worse afflictions could not bend!
Jove also hath for *these* prepared an end.
The voices of dread Scylla ye have heard,   270
Her belt of rabid mouths your prows have near'd;
Ye shunn'd with peril the Cyclopian den,
Cast off your fears, resume the hearts of men!
Hereafter, this our present lot may be
A cherish'd object for pleased memory.   275
Through strange mishaps, through hazards manifold
And various, we our course to Latium hold;
There, Fate a settled habitation shows;—
There, Trojan empire (this, too, Fate allows)
Shall be revived. Endure; with patience wait;   280
Yourselves reserving for a happier state!"

Æneas thus, though sick with weight of care,
Strives, by apt words their spirits to repair;
The hope he does not feel his countenance feigns,
And deep within he smothers his own pains.   285
They seize the Quarry; for the feast prepare;
Part use their skill the carcase to lay bare,
Stripping from off the limbs the dappled hide;
And Part the palpitating flesh divide;
The portions some expose to naked fire,   290
Some steep in cauldrons where the flames aspire.
Not wanting utensils, they spread the board;
And soon their wasted vigour is restored;
While o'er green turf diffused, in genial mood
They quaff the mellow wine, nor spare the forest food.   295

All hunger thus appeased, they ask in thought
For friends, with long discourses, vainly sought:
Hope, fear, and doubt contend if yet they live, ⎫
Or have endured the last; nor can receive   ⎬
The obsequies a duteous voice might give. ⎭   300
Apart, for Lycas mourns the pious Chief;
For Amycus is touch'd with silent grief;
For Gyas, for Cloanthes; and the Crew
That with Orontes perish'd in his view.

So finish'd their repast, while on the crown   305
Of Heaven stood Jupiter; whence looking down,
He traced the sea where winged vessels glide,
Saw Lands, and shores, the Nations scatter'd wide;
And, lastly, from that all-commanding Height,
He view'd the Lybian realms with stedfast sight.   310
To him, revolving mortal hopes and fears,
Venus (her shining eyes suffused with tears)
Thus, sorrowing, spake: "O Sire! who rul'st the way
Of Men and Gods with thy eternal sway,
And aw'st with thunder, what offence, unfit   315
For pardon, could my much-lov'd Son commit—
The Trojans what—thine anger to awake ?
That, after such dire loss, they for the sake
Of Italy see all the world denied
To their tired hopes, and nowhere may abide!   320
For, that the Romans hence should draw their birth
As years roll round, even hence, and govern earth
With power supreme, from Teucer's Line restor'd
Such was (O Father, why this change ?) thy word.
From this, when Troy had perish'd, for my grief   325
(Fates balancing with fates) I found relief;
Like fortune follows:—when shall thy decree
Close, mighty King, this long adversity ?
—Antenor, from amid the Grecian hosts
Escaped, could thrid Illyria's sinuous coasts;   330
Pierce the Lyburnian realms; o'erclimb the Fountain
Of loud Timarus, whence the murmuring Mountain
A nine-mouth'd channel to the torrent yields,
That rolls its headlong sea, a terror to the fields.
Yet to his Paduan seats he safely came;   335
A City built, whose People bear his name;
There hung his Trojan Arms, where now he knows
The consummation of entire repose.
But *we*, thy progeny, allow'd to boast   ⎫
Of future Heaven—betray'd,—our Navy lost— ⎬ 340
Through wrath of One, are driven far from the Italian coast. ⎭

Is piety thus honour'd ? Doth thy grace
Thus in our hands the allotted sceptre place ?"

On whom the Sire of Gods and human Kind
Half-smiling, turn'd the look that stills the wind   345
And clears the heavens ; then, touching with light kiss
His Daughter's lip, he speaks:
                        "Thy griefs dismiss:
And, Cytherea, these forebodings spare ;
No wavering fates deceive the objects of thy care,
Lavinian Walls full surely wilt thou see,   350
The promised City ; and, upborne by thee,
Magnanimous Æneas yet shall range
The starry heavens ; nor doth my purpose change.
He (since thy soul is troubled I will raise
Things from their depths, and open Fate's dark ways)   355
Shall wage dread wars in Italy, abate
Fierce Nations, build a Town and rear a State ;
Till three revolving summers have beheld
His Latian kingdom, the Rutulians quell'd.
But young Ascanius (Ilus heretofore,   360
Name which he held till Ilium was no more,
Now called Iülus) while the months repeat
Their course, and thirty annual orbs complete,
Shall reign, and quit Lavinium to preside
O'er Alba-longa, sternly fortified.   365
Here, under Chiefs of this Hectorian Race,
Three hundred years shall empire hold her place,
Ere Ilia, royal Priestess, gives to earth
From the embrace of Mars, a double birth.
Then Romulus, the elder, proudly drest   370
In tawny wolf-skin, his memorial vest,
Mavortian Walls, his Father's Seat, shall frame,
And from himself, the People Romans name.
To these I give dominion that shall climb
Uncheck'd by space, uncircumscrib'd by time ;   375
An empire without end. Even Juno, driven
To agitate with fear earth, sea and heaven,
With better mind shall for the past atone:
Prepar'd with me to cherish as her own
The Romans, lords o'er earth, The Nation of the Gown.   380
So 'tis decreed: As circling times roll on
Phthia shall fall, Mycenae shall be won ;
Descendants of Assaracus shall reign
O'er Argos subject to the Victor's chain.
From a fair Stem shall Trojan Caesar rise ;   385

Ocean may terminate his power;—the skies
Can be the only limit of his fame;
A Julius he, inheriting the name
From great Iulus. Fearless shalt thou greet
The Ruler, when to his celestial Seat   390
He shall ascend, spoil-laden from the East;
He, too, a God to be with vows address'd.
Then shall a rugged Age, full long defil'd
With cruel wars, grow placable and mild;
Then hoary Faith, and Vesta, shall delight⎫   395
To speak their laws, Quirinus shall unite ⎬
With his twin Brother to uphold the right.⎭
Fast shall be closed the iron-bolted Gates
Upon whose dreadful issues Janus waits
Within, on high-piled Arms, and from behind   400
With countless links of brazen chains confin'd
Shall Fury sit, breathing unholy threats
From his ensanguin'd mouth that impotently frets."

   This utter'd, Maia's Son he sends from high
To embolden Tyrian hospitality;   405
Lest haply Dido, ignorant of fate,
Should chase the Wanderers from her rising State.
He through the azure region works the oars
Of his swift wings, and lights on Lybian Shores.
Prompt is he there his mission to fulfil;   410
The Tyrians soften, yielding to Jove's will;—
And, above all, their Queen receives a mind
Fearless of harm, and to the Trojans kind.

   Æneas, much revolving through the night,
Rose with the earliest break of friendly light;   415
Resolv'd to certify by instant quest
Who rul'd the uncultur'd region—man or beast.
Forthwith he hides, beneath a rocky cove,
His Fleet, o'ershadow'd by the pendent grove;
And, brandishing two javelins, quits the Bay,   420
Achates sole companion of his way.
While they were journeying thus, before him stood
His Mother, met within a shady wood.
The habit of a virgin did she wear;
Her aspect suitable, her gait, and air;—   425
Arm'd like a Spartan Virgin, or of mien
Such as in Thrace Harpalyce is seen,
Urging to weariness the fiery horse,
Outstripping Hebrus in his headlong course.

Light o'er her shoulders had she given the bow 430
To hang; her tresses on the wind to flow;
—A Huntress with bare knee;—a knot upbound
The folds of that loose vest, which else had swept the ground.
"Ho!" she exclaim'd, their words preventing, "say
Have you not seen some Huntress here astray, 435
One of my Sisters, with a quiver graced;
Clothed by the spotted lynx, and o'er the waste
Pressing the foaming boar, with outcry chased?"

 Thus Venus;—thus her Son forthwith replied,
"None of thy Sisters have we here espied, 440
None have we heard:—O Virgin! in pure grace
Teach me to name Thee; for no mortal face
Is thine, nor bears thy voice a human sound;—
A Goddess surely, worthy to be own'd
By Phoebus as a Sister—or thy Line 445
Is haply of the Nymphs; O Power divine
Be thou propitious! and, whoe'er thou art,
Lighten our labour; tell us in what part
Of earth we roam, who these wild precincts trace,
Ignorant alike of person and of place! 450
Not as intruders come we: but were tost
By winds and waters on this savage coast.
Vouchsafe thy answer; victims oft shall fall
By this right hand, while on thy name we call."

 Then Venus;—"Offerings these which I disclaim 455
The Tyrian Maids who chase the sylvan game
Bear thus a quiver slung their necks behind,
With purple buskins thus their ancles bind;
Learn, Wanderers, that a Punic Realm you see.
Tyrians the men, Agenor's progeny; 460
But Lybian deem the soil; the natives are
Haughty and fierce, intractable in war.
Here Dido reigns; from Tyre compell'd to flee
By an unnatural Brother's perfidy;
Deep was the wrong; nor would it aught avail 465
Should we do more than skim the doleful tale.
Sichæus lov'd her as his wedded Mate,
The richest Lord of the Phoenician State;
A Virgin She, when from her Father's hands
By love induced, she pass'd to nuptial bands; 470
Unhappy Union! for to evil prone,
Worst of bad men, her Brother held the throne;
Dire fury came among them, and, made bold
By that blind appetite, the thirst of gold,

He, feeling not, or scorning what was due   475
To a Wife's tender love, Sichæus slew;
Rush'd on him unawares, and laid him low
Before the Altar, with an impious blow.
His arts conceal'd the crime, and gave vain scope
In Dido's bosom to a trembling hope.   480
But in a dream appear'd the unburied Man,
Lifting a visage wondrous pale and wan;
Urged her to instant flight, and shew'd the Ground
Where hoards of ancient treasure might be found,
Needful assistance. By the Vision sway'd,   485
Dido looks out for fellowship and aid.
They meet, who loathe the Tyrant, or who fear;
And, as some well-trimm'd Ships were lying near,
This help they seiz'd; and o'er the water fled
With all Pygmalion's wealth;—a Woman at their head.   490
The Exiles reach'd the Spot, where soon your eyes
Shall see the Turrets of New Carthage rise;
There purchas'd BARCA; so they nam'd the Ground
From the bull's hide whose thongs had girt it round.
Now say—who are Ye? Whence and whither bound?"   495

He answer'd, deeply sighing, "To their springs
Should I trace back the principles of things
For you, at leisure listening to our woes,   ⎫
Vesper, mid gathering shadows to repose   ⎬
Might lead the day, before the Tale would close.   ⎭   500
—From ancient Troy, if haply ye have heard
The name of Troy, through various seas we steer'd,
Until on Lybian Shores an adverse blast
By chance not rare our shatter'd vessels cast.
Æneas am I, wheresoe'er I go   505
Carrying the Gods I rescued from the Foe,
When Troy was overthrown. A Man you see
Fam'd above Earth for acts of piety;
Italy is my wish'd-for resting place;
There doth my Country lie, among a Race   510
Sprung from high Jove. The Phrygian Sea I tried
With thrice ten Ships which Ida's Grove supplied,
My Goddess Mother pointing out the way,
Nor did unwilling Fates oppose their sway.
Seven, scarcely, of that number now are left   515
By tempests torn;—myself unknown, bereft,
And destitute, explore the Lybian Waste,

497 those melancholy things MS.

Alike from Europe and from Asia chas'd."
He spake; nor haply at this point had clos'd
His mournful words: but Venus interpos'd.   520

"Whoe'er thou art, I trust, the heavenly Powers
Disown thee not, so near the Punic Towers;
But hasten to the Queen's imperial Court;
Thy Friends survive; their Ships are safe in port,
Indebted for the shelter which they find   525
To alter'd courses of the rough North-wind;
Unless fond Parents taught my simple youth
Deceitful auguries, I announce the truth.
Behold yon twelve fair Swans, a joyous troop!
Them did the Bird of Jove, with threatening swoop   530
Rout, in mid Heaven dispers'd; but now again
Have they assembled, and in order'd train
These touch, while those look down upon, the plain,
Hovering, and wheeling round with tuneful voice.
—As in recover'd union all rejoice;   535
So, with their Crews, thy Ships in harbour lie,
Or to some haven's mouth are drawing nigh
With every Sail full-spread; but Thou proceed;
And fear no hindrance where thy path shall lead."

She spake; and, as she turn'd away, all bright   540
Appear'd her neck, imbued with roseate light;
And from the exalted region of her head
Ambrosial hair a sudden fragrance shed,
Odours divinely breathing;—her Vest flow'd
Down to her feet;—and gait and motion shew'd   545
The unquestionable Goddess. Whom his eyes ⎫
Had seen and whom his soul could recognise, ⎬
His filial voice pursueth as she flies.   ⎭

"Why dost Thou, cruel as the rest, delude
Thy Son with Phantoms evermore renew'd?   550
Why not allow me hand with hand to join,
To hear thy genuine voice, and to reply with mine?"
This chiding utter'd from a troubl'd breast,
He to the appointed walls his steps address'd.
But Venus round him threw, as on they fare,   555
Impenetrable veil of misty air;
That none might see, or touch them with rude hand,
Obstruct their journey, or its cause demand.
She, borne aloft, resumes the joyful road
That leads to Paphos—her belov'd abode: 560

534 And wheel on whizzing wings with tuneful voice MS., S. H. *corr.*

There stands her Temple; garlands fresh and fair ⎫
Breathe round a hundred Altars hung, which there ⎬
Burn with Sabean incense, scenting all the air. ⎭

They who had measur'd a swift course were now
Climbing, as swift, a hill of lofty brow, 565
That overhangs wide compass of the Town,
And on the turrets, which it fronts, looks down.
Æneas views the City—pile on pile
Rising—a place of sordid Huts erewhile;
And, as he looks, the gates, the stretching ways, 570
The stir, the din, encreasing wonder raise.
The Tyrians work—one spirit in the whole;
These stretch the walls; these labour to uproll
Stones for the Citadel, with all their might;
These, for new Structures having mark'd a site, 575
Intrench the circuit. Some on laws debate,
Or chuse a Senate for the infant State;
Some dig the haven out; some toil to place
A Theatre, on deep and solid base;
Some from the rock hew columns, to compose 580
A goodly ornament for future Shows.
—Fresh summer calls the Bees such tasks to ply
Through flowery grounds, beneath a summer sky;
When first they lead their progeny abroad,
Each fit to undertake his several load; 585
Or in a mass the liquid produce blend,
And with pure nectar every cell distend;
Or, fast as homeward Labourers arrive, ⎫
Receive the freight they bring; or mustering, drive ⎬
The Drones, a sluggard people, from the hive. ⎭ 590
Glows the vast work; while thyme-clad hills and plains
Scent the pure honey that rewards their pains.
"Oh fortunate!" the Chief, Æneas, cries ⎫
As on the aspiring Town he casts his eyes, ⎬
"Fortunate Ye, whose walls are free to rise!" ⎭ 595
Then, strange to tell! with mist around him thrown,
In crowds he mingles, yet is seen by none.

Within the Town, a central Grove display'd
Its ample texture of delightful shade.
The storm-vex'd Tyrians, newly-landed, found 600
A hopeful sign while digging there the ground;
The head of a fierce horse from earth they drew,
By Juno's self presented to their view;
Presage of martial fame, and hardy toil

Bestow'd through ages on a generous soil.   605
Sidonian Dido here a Structure high
Rais'd to the tutelary Deity,
Rich with the Offerings through the Temple pour'd,
And bright with Juno's Image, there ador'd.
High rose, with steps, the brazen Porch; the Beams   610
With brass were fasten'd; and metallic gleams
Flashed from the valves of brazen doors, forth-sent
While on resounding hinges to and fro they went.
Within this Grove Æneas first beheld
A novel sight, by which his fears were quell'd;   615
Here first gave way to hope, so long withstood,
And look'd through present ill to future good.
For while, expectant of the Queen, the stores
Of that far-spreading Temple he explores;
Admires the strife of labour; nor forbears ⎫   620
To ponder o'er the lot of noble cares   ⎬
Which the young City for herself prepares; ⎭
He meets the Wars of Ilium; every Fight,
In due succession, offer'd to his sight.
There he beholds Atrides, Priam here,   625
And that stern Chief who was to both severe.
He stopp'd; and, not without a sigh, exclaim'd:
"By whom, Achates! hath not Troy been nam'd?
What region of the earth but overflows
With us, and the memorials of our woes?   630
Lo Priamus! Here also do they raise
To virtuous deeds fit monument of praise;
Tears for the frail estate of human kind
Are shed; and mortal changes touch the mind."
He spake (nor might the gushing tears controul);   635
And with an empty Picture feeds his soul.

He saw the Greeks fast flying o'er the plain,
The Trojan Youth—how in pursuit they strain!
There, o'er the Phrygians routed in the war,
Crested Achilles hanging from his Car.   640
Next, to near view the painted wall presents
The fate of Rhesus, and his snow-white tents,
In the first sleep of silent night, betray'd ⎫
To the wide-wasting sword of Diomed,   ⎬
Who to the camp the fiery horses led,   ⎭   645
Ere they from Trojan stalls had tasted food,
Or stoop'd their heads to drink Scamander's flood.
—The Stripling Troilus he next espied,
Flying, his arms now lost, or flung aside;

Ill-match'd with fierce Achilles! From the fight   650
He, by his horses borne in desperate flight,
Cleaves to his empty Chariot, on the plain
Supinely stretch'd, yet grasping still the rein;
Along the earth are dragg'd his neck and hair;
The dust is mark'd by his inverted spear.   655
Meanwhile, with tresses long and loose, a train
Of Trojan Matrons seek Minerva's Fane
As on they bear the dedicated Veil,
They beat their own sad breasts with suppliant wail.
The Goddess heeds not offerings, prayers, nor cries,   660
And on the ground are fix'd her sullen eyes.
— Thrice had incens'd Achilles whirl'd amain
About Troy Wall, the Corse of Hector slain,
And barters now that corse for proffer'd gold.
What grief, the Spoils and Chariot to behold!   665
And, suppliant, near his Friend's dead body, stands
Old Priam, stretching forth his unarm'd hands!
Himself, mid Grecian Chiefs, he can espy;
And saw the oriental blazonry
Of swarthy Memnon, and the Host he leads;   670
Her lunar shields Penthesilea leads;
A zone her mutilated breast hath bound;
And She, exulting on the embattled ground
A Virgin Warrior, with a Virgin Train,
Dares in the peril to conflict with Men.   675

    While on these animated pictures gaz'd
The Dardan Chief, enwrapt, disturb'd, amaz'd;
With a long retinue of Youth, the Queen
Ascends the Temple;—lovely was her mien;
And her form beautiful as Earth has seen;   680
Thus, where Eurotas flows, or on the heights
Of Cynthus, where Diana oft delights
To train her Nymphs, and lead the Choirs along,
Oreads, in thousands gathering, round her throng;
Where'er she moves, where'er the Goddess bears   685
Her pendant sheaf of arrows, she appears
Far, far above the immortal Company;
Latona's breast is thrill'd with silent ecstasy.
Even with such lofty bearing Dido pass'd
Among the busy crowd;—such looks she cast   690
Urging the various works, with mind intent
On future empire. Through the Porch she went,
And compass'd round with arm'd Attendants, sate
Beneath the Temple's dome, upon a Throne of State.

There, laws she gave; divided justly there   695
The labour; or by lot assigned to each his share.
When, turning from the Throne a casual glance,
Æneas saw an eager Crowd advance
With various Leaders, whom the storms of Heaven
Had scatter'd, and to other shores had driven.   700
With Antheus and Sergestus there appear'd
The brave Cloanthes,—followers long endear'd.
Joy smote his heart, joy temper'd with strange awe;
Achates, in like sort, by what he saw
Was smitten; and the hands of both were bent   705
On instant greeting; but they fear'd the event.
Stifling their wish, within that cloud involv'd,
They wait until the mystery shall be solv'd—
What has befallen their Friends; upon what shore
The Fleet is left, and what they would implore;   710
For Delegates from every Ship they were,
And sought the Temple with a clamorous prayer.

    All entered,—and, leave given, with tranquil breast
Ilioneus preferr'd their joint request:
"O Queen! empower'd by Jupiter to found   715
A hopeful City on this desart ground;
To whom he gives the curb, and guiding rein
Of Justice, a proud People to restrain,
We, wretched Trojans, rescued from a Fleet
Long toss'd through every Sea, thy aid entreat;   720
Let, at thy voice, the unhallow'd fire forbear ⎫
To touch our ships; a righteous People spare; ⎬
And on our fortunes look with nearer care! ⎭
We neither seek as plunderers your abodes,
Nor would our swords molest your household Gods;   725
Our spirit tempts us not such course to try;
Nor do the Vanquish'd lift their heads so high.
There is a Country call'd by Men of Greece
Hesperia, strong in arms, the soil of large increase,
Œnotrians held it; Men of later fame   730
Call it Italia, from their Leader's name.
That Land we sought; when, wrapt in mist, arose
Orion, help'd by every wind that blows;
Dispers'd us utterly—on shallows cast;
And we, we only, gain'd your shores at last.   735
What race of man is here? Was ever yet
The unnatural treatment known which we have met?
What country bears with customs that deny,
To shipwreck'd men, such hospitality

As the sands offer on the naked beach, 740
And the first quiet of the Land they reach ?
—Arms were *our* greeting; yet, if ye despise
Man and *his* power, look onward, and be wise;
The Gods for right and wrong have awful memories.
A man to no one second in the care 745
Of justice, nor in piety and war,
Ruled over us; if yet Æneas treads
On earth, nor has been summon'd to the shades,
Fear no repentance if, in acts of grace
Striving with him, thou gain the foremost place. 750
Nor want we, in Trinacria, towns and plains,
Where, sprung from Trojan blood, Acestes reigns.
Grant leave to draw our Ships upon your Shores,
Thence to refit their shatter'd hulks and oars.
Were Friends and Chief restor'd, whom now we mourn, 755
We to the Italian Coast with joy would turn,
Should Italy lie open to our aim;
But if our welfare be an empty name,
And Thou, best Father of the Family
Of Troy, hast perish'd in the Lybian Sea, 760
And young Iulus sank, engulph'd with thee,—
Then be it ours, at least, to cross the foam
Of the Sicilian Deep, and seek the home
Prepar'd by good Acestes, whence we come."

Thus spake Ilioneus: his Friends around 765
Declar'd their sanction by a murmuring sound.

With downcast looks, brief answer Dido made;
"Trojans, be griefs dismiss'd, anxieties allay'd.
The pressure of occasion, and a reign
Yet new, exact these rigours, and constrain 770
The jealous vigilance my coasts maintain.
The Ænean Race, with that heroic Town—
And widely-blazing war—to whom are they unknown ?
Not so obtuse the Punic breasts we bear;
Nor does the Giver of the Day so far 775
From this our Tyrian City yoke his Car.
But if Hesperia be your wish'd-for bourne,
Or to Trinacrian shores your prows would turn,
Then, with all aids that may promote your weal,
Ye shall depart;—but if desire ye feel, 780
Fix'd, in this growing Realm, to share my fate,
Yours are the walls which now I elevate.
Haste, and withdraw your Gallies from the sea,
—Trojans and Tyrians shall be one to me.

Would, too, that storm-compelled as ye have been,   785
The Person of your Chief might here be seen!
By trusty servants shall my shores be traced
To the last confines of the Lybian Waste,
For He, the Castaway of stormy floods,
May roam through cities, or in savage woods."   790

    Thus did the Queen administer relief
For their dejected hearts; and to the Chief,
While both were burning with desire to break
From out the darksome cloud, Achates spake.
"Son of a Goddess, what resolves ensue   795
From this deliverance whose effects we view?
All things are safe—thy Fleet and Friends restor'd ⎫
Save one, whom in our sight the Sea devour'd;   ⎬
All else respondent to thy Mother's word."   ⎭
He spake; the circumambient cloud anon   800
Melts and dissolves, the murky veil is gone;
And left Æneas, as it pass'd away,
With godlike mien and shoulders, standing in full day.
For that same Parent of celestial race
Had shed upon his hair surpassing grace;   805
And, breathing o'er her Son the purple light ⎫
Of youth, had glorified his eyes, made bright, ⎬
Like those of Heaven, with joyance infinite. ⎭
So stood he forth, an unexpected Guest,
And, while all wonder'd, thus the Queen address'd.   810

    "He whom ye seek am I, Æneas—flung
By storms the Lybian solitudes among.
O Sole, who for the unutterable state
Of Troy art humanly compassionate;
Who not alone a shelter dost afford   815
To the thin relics of the Grecian sword,
Perpetually exhausted by pursuit
Of dire mischance, of all things destitute,
But in thy purposes with them hast shar'd
City and home;—not we, who thus have far'd,   820
Not we, not all the Dardan Race that live,
Scatter'd through Earth, sufficient thanks can give.
The Gods (if they the Pious watch with love,
If Justice dwell about us, or above)
And a mind conscious to itself of right,   825
Shall, in fit measure thy deserts requite!
What happy Age gave being to such worth?
What blessed Parents, Dido! brought thee forth?

While down their channels Rivers seaward flow,
While shadowy Groves sweep round the mountain's brow, 830
While ether feeds the stars, where'er be cast ⎫
My lot, whatever Land by me be traced, ⎬
Thy name, thy honour, and thy praise, shall last." ⎭
He spake; and turning tow'rds the Trojan Band,
Salutes Ilioneus with the better hand, 835
And grasps Serestus with the left—then gave
Like greeting to the rest, to Gyas brave
And brave Cloanthes.
             Inwardly amaz'd, ⎫
Sidonian Dido on the Chief had gaz'd ⎬
When first he met her view;—his words like wonder rais'd. ⎭ 840
"What Force", said She, "pursues thee—hath impell'd
To these wild shores? In Thee have I beheld
That Trojan whom bright Venus, on the shore
Of Phrygian Simois, to Anchises bore?
And well do I recall to mind the day 845
When to our Sidon Teucer found his way,
An Outcast from his native Borders driven,
With hope to win new Realms by aid from Belus given,
Belus, my Father, then the conquering Lord
Of Cyprus newly-ravaged by his sword. 850
Thenceforth I knew the fate of Troy that rings
Earth round,—thy Name, and the Pelasgian kings.
Teucer himself, with liberal tongue, would raise
His Adversaries to just heights of praise,
And vaunt a Trojan lineage with fair proof; 855
Then welcome, noble Strangers, to our Roof!
—Me, too, like Fortune, after devious strife
Stay'd in this Land, to breathe a calmer life;
From no light ills which on myself have press'd,
Pitying I learn to succour the distress'd." 860
These words pronounced, and mindful to ordain ⎫
Fit sacrifice, she issues from the Fane, ⎬
And tow'rds the Palace leads Æneas and his Train. ⎭
Nor less regardful of his distant Friends,
To the sea coast she hospitably sends 865
Twice ten selected steers, a hundred lambs
Swept from the plenteous herbage with their dams;
A hundred bristly ridges of huge swine,
And what the God bestows in sparkling wine.
But the interior Palace doth display 870
Its whole magnificence in set array;
And in the centre of a spacious Hall
Are preparations for high festival;

There, gorgeous vestments—skilfully enwrought
With Eastern purple; and huge tables—fraught   875
With massive argentry; there, carv'd in gold,
Through long, long series, the atchievements bold
Of Forefathers, each imaged in his place,
From the beginning of the ancient Race.

Æneas, whose parental thoughts obey   880
Their natural impulse, brooking no delay,
Despatch'd the prompt Achates, to report
The new events, and lead Ascanius to the Court.
Ascanius, for on him the Father's mind
Now rests, as if to that sole care confin'd;   885
And bids him bring, attendant on the Boy,
The richest Presents, snatch'd from burning Troy;
A Robe of tissue stiff with shapes exprest
In threads of gleaming gold; an upper Vest
Round which acanthus twines its yellow flowers;   890
By Argive Helen worn in festal hours;
Her Mother Leda's wonderous gift—and brought
To Ilium from Mycenae when she sought
Those unpermitted nuptials;—thickly set
With golden gems, a twofold coronet;   895
And Sceptre which Ilione of yore,
Eldest of Priam's royal Daughters wore,
And orient Pearls, which on her neck she bore.
This to perform, Achates speeds his way
To the Ships anchor'd in that peaceful Bay.   900

But Cytherea, studious to invent
Arts yet untried, upon new counsels bent,
Resolves that Cupid, changed in form and face
To young Ascanius, should assume his place;
Present the maddening gifts, and kindle heat   905
Of passion at the bosom's inmost seat.
She dreads the treacherous House, the double tongue;
She burns, she frets—by Juno's rancour stung;
The calm of night is powerless to remove
These cares, and thus she speaks to winged Love: 910

"O Son, my strength, my power! who dost despise
(What, save thyself, none dares through earth and skies)
The giant-quelling bolts of Jove, I flee,
O Son, a suppliant to thy Deity!
What perils meet Æneas in his course,   915
How Juno's hate with unrelenting force

907 the double] and Punic MS.
908 By Juno's rancour is her quiet stung MS.

Pursues thy Brother—this to thee is known ;
And oft-times hast thou made my griefs thine own.
Him now the generous Dido by soft chains
Of bland entreaty at her court detains ;   920
Junonian hospitalities prepare
Such apt occasion that I dread a snare.
Hence, ere some hostile God can intervene,
Would I, by previous wiles, inflame the Queen
With passion for Æneas, such strong love   925
That at my beck, mine only, she shall move.
Hear, and assist ;—the Father's mandate calls
His young Ascanius to the Tyrian Walls ;
He comes, my dear delight,—and costliest things
Preserv'd from fire and flood for presents brings.   930
Him will I take, and in close covert keep, ⎫
'Mid Groves Idalian, lull'd to gentle sleep, ⎬
Or on Cythera's far-sequestered Steep,   ⎭
That he may neither know what hope is mine,
Nor by his presence traverse the design.   935
Do Thou, but for a single night's brief space,
Dissemble ; be that Boy in form and face :
And when enraptur'd Dido shall receive
Thee to her arms, and kisses interweave
With many a fond embrace, while joy runs high,   940
And goblets crown the proud festivity,
Instil thy subtle poison, and inspire,
At every touch, an unsuspected fire."

Love, at the word, before his Mother's sight
Puts off his wings, and walks, with proud delight,   945
Like young Iulus ; but the gentlest dews
Of slumber Venus sheds, to circumfuse
The true Ascanius steep'd in placid rest ;
Then wafts him, cherish'd on her careful breast,
Through upper air to an Idalian glade,   ⎫   950
Where he on soft *amaracus* is laid,   ⎬
With breathing flowers embraced, and fragrant shade.⎭
But Cupid, following cheerily his Guide
Achates, with the Gifts to Carthage hied ;
And, as the hall he entered, there, between⎫   955
The sharers of her golden couch, was seen ⎬
Reclin'd in festal pomp the Tyrian queen.   ⎭

919–20 . . . Phoenician Dido in soft chains
          Of a seductive blandishment detains MS.
955–7   He reach'd the Hall where now the Queen repos'd
          Amid a golden couch, with awnings half enclos'd MS.

The Trojans too (Æneas at their head), ⎫
On couches lie, with purple overspread: ⎬
Meantime in canisters is heap'd the bread, ⎭   960
Pellucid water for the hands is borne,
And napkins of smooth texture, finely shorn.
Within are fifty Handmaids, who prepare,
As they in order stand, the dainty fare;
And fume the household Deities with store   965
Of odorous incense; while a hundred more
Match'd with an equal number of like age,
But each of manly sex, a docile Page,
Marshal the banquet, giving with due grace
To cup or viand its appointed place.   970
The Tyrians rushing in, an eager Band,
Their painted couches seek, obedient to command.
They look with wonder on the Gifts—they gaze
Upon Iulus, dazzled with the rays
That from his ardent countenance are flung,   975
And charm'd to hear his simulating tongue;
Nor pass unprais'd the robe and veil divine,
Round which the yellow flowers and wandering foliage twine.

But chiefly Dido, to the coming ill
Devoted, strives in vain her vast desires to fill;   980
She views the Gifts; upon the child then turns
Insatiable looks, and gazing burns.
To ease a Father's cheated love he hung
Upon Æneas, and around him clung;
Then seeks the Queen; with her his arts he tries;   985
She fastens on the boy enamour'd eyes,
Clasps in her arms, nor weens (O lot unblest!)
How great a God, incumbent o'er her breast,
Would fill it with his spirit. He, to please
His Acidalian mother, by degrees   990
Blots out Sichæus, studious to remove
The dead, by influx of a living love,
By stealthy entrance of a perilous guest,
Troubling a heart that had been long at rest.

981 child] Boy MS.   982 looks] eyes MS.
985-9 Then sought the Queen, who fix'd on him the whole
       That she possess'd of look, mind, life, and soul;
       And sometimes doth unhappy Dido plant
       The Fondling in her bosom, ignorant
       How great a God deceives her. MS.
991   Would sap Sichæus, studious to remove MS.
993-4 Through a subsided spirit dispossess'd
       Of amorous passion, through a torpid breast MS.

Now when the viands were withdrawn, and ceas'd   995
The first division of the splendid Feast,
While round a vacant board the Chiefs recline,
Huge goblets are brought forth; they crown the wine;
Voices of gladness roll the walls around;
Those gladsome voices from the courts rebound;   1000
From gilded rafters many a blazing light
Depends, and torches overcome the night.
The minutes fly—till, at the Queen's commands,
A bowl of state is offered to her hands:
Then She, as Belus wont, and all the Line   1005
From Belus, filled it to the brim with wine;
Silence ensued. "O Jupiter, whose care
Is hospitable Dealing, grant my prayer!
Productive day be this of lasting joy
To Tyrians, and these Exiles driven from Troy;   1010
A day to future generations dear!
Let Bacchus, donor of soul-quick'ning cheer, }
Be present; kindly Juno, be thou near!
And, Tyrians, may your choicest favours wait
Upon this hour, the bond to celebrate!"   1015
She spake and shed an Offering on the board;
Then sipp'd the bowl whence she the wine had pour'd
And gave to Bitias, urging the prompt lord;
He rais'd the bowl, and took a long deep draught;
Then every Chief in turn the beverage quaff'd.   1020

Graced with redundant hair, Iopas sings
The lore of Atlas, to resounding strings, }
The labours of the Sun, the lunar wanderings;
Whence human kind, and brute; what natural powers
Engender lightning, whence are falling showers.   1025
He chaunts Arcturus,—that fraternal twain
The glittering Bears,—the Pleiads fraught with rain;
—Why suns in winter, shunning Heaven's steep heights
Post seaward,—what impedes the tardy nights.
The learned song from Tyrian hearers draws   1030
Loud shouts,—the Trojans echo the applause.
—But, lengthening out the night with converse new,
Large draughts of love unhappy Dido drew;

1003 as the Queen commands MS.
1018 . . . bidding him take heart;
    He rais'd—and not unequal to the part,
    Drank deep self-drench'd from out the brimming gold
    Thereafter a like course the encircling Nobles hold. MS.
1026 that fraternal] and that social MS.   1027 fraught] charged MS.

Of Priam ask'd, of Hector,—o'er and o'er—
What arms the son of bright Aurora wore;—   1035
What steeds the car of Diomed could boast;
Among the Leaders of the Grecian host
How looked Achilles—their dread Paramount—
"But nay—the fatal wiles, O guest, recount,
Retrace the Grecian cunning from its source,   1040
Your own grief and your Friends'—your wandering course;
For now, till this seventh summer have ye ranged
The sea, or trod the earth, to peace estranged."

SECOND BOOK

ALL breathed in silence, and intensely gaz'd,
When from the lofty couch his voice Æneas rais'd,
And thus began: "The task which you impose
O Queen, revives unutterable woes;
How by the Grecians Troy was overturn'd,   5
And her power fell—to be for ever mourn'd;
Calamities which with a pitying heart
I saw, of which I form'd no common part.
Oh! 'twas a miserable end! What One
Of all our Foes, Dolopian, Myrmidon,   10
Or Soldier bred in stern Ulysses' train
Such things could utter, and from tears refrain?
And hastens now from Heaven the dewy night,
And the declining stars to sleep invite.
But since such strong desire prevails to know   15
Our wretched fate, and Troy's last overthrow
I will attempt the theme though in my breast
Memory recoils and shudders at the test.

  The Grecian Chiefs, exhausted of their strength
By war protracted to such irksome length,   20
And, from the siege repuls'd, new schemes devise;
A wooden horse they build of mountain size.
Assisted by Minerva's art divine,
They frame the work, and sheathe its ribs with pine,
An offering to the Gods—that they may gain   25
Their home in safety; this they boldly feign,

1036–9 What coursers those of Diomed; how great,
          Achilles—but O Guest! the whole relate; MS.
1041   griefs MS.
17–18 I will begin with spirit resolute
          To stifle pangs which well might keep me mute C. W.

And spread the Tale abroad;—meanwhile they hide
Selected Warriors in its gloomy side;
Throng the huge concave to its utmost den,
And fill that mighty Womb with armed Men.   30

   In sight of Troy, an Island lies, by Fame
Amply distinguish'd, Tenedos its name;
Potent and rich while Priam's sway endured,
Now a bare hold for keels, unsafely moor'd.
Here did the Greeks, when for their native land   35
We thought them sail'd, lurk on the desart strand.
From her long grief at once the Realm of Troy
Broke loose;—the gates are opened, and with joy
We seek the Dorian Camp, and wander o'er
The spots forsaken, the abandon'd shore.   40
Here, the Dolopian ground its line presents;
And here the dread Achilles pitch'd his tents;
There lay the Ships drawn up along the coast,
And here we oft encounter'd host with host.
Meanwhile, the rest an eye of wonder lift,   45
Unwedded Pallas! on the fatal Gift
To thee devoted. First Thymœtes calls
For its free ingress through disparted walls
To lodge within the Citadel—thus He
Treacherous, or such the course of destiny.   50
Capys, with some of wiser mind, would sweep
The insidious Grecian offering to the Deep,
Or to the flames subject it; or advise
To perforate and search the cavities;
Into conflicting judgments break and split   55
The crowd, as random thoughts the fancy hit.

   Down from the Citadel a numerous throng
Hastes with Laocoon; they sweep along,
And He, the foremost, crying from afar,
What would ye? wretched Maniacs, as ye are!   60
Think ye the Foe departed? Or that e'er
A boon from Grecian hands can prove sincere?
Thus do ye read Ulysses? Foes unseen
Lurk in these chambers; or the huge Machine
Against the ramparts brought, by pouring down   65
Force from aloft, will seize upon the Town.

28 By stealth, choice warriors *etc.* C. W.
33–4 Potent and rich, in time of Priam's sway,
    A faithless Shiproad now, a lonely bay C. W.
55–6 This way and that the multitude divide
    And still unsettled veer from side to side. C. W.

Let not a fair pretence your minds enthrall;
For me, I fear the Greeks and most of all
When they are offering gifts." With mighty force
This said, he hurl'd a spear against the Horse;   70
It smote the curved ribs, and quivering stood
While groans made answer through the hollow wood.
We too, upon this impulse, had not Fate ⎫
Been adverse, and our minds infatuate,   ⎬
We too, had rush'd the den to penetrate,   ⎭   75
Streams of Argolic blood our swords had stained,
Troy, thou might'st yet have stood, and Priam's Towers remained.

But lo! an unknown youth with hand to hand
Bound fast behind him, whom a boisterous Band
Of Dardan Swains with clamour hurrying   80
Force to the shore and place before the King.
Such his device when he those chains had sought
A voluntary captive, fix'd in thought
Either the City to betray, or meet
Death, the sure penalty of foil'd deceit.   85
The curious Trojans, pouring in, deride
And taunt the Prisoner, with an emulous pride.
Now see the cunning of the Greeks exprest
By guilt of One, true image of the rest!
For, while with helpless looks, from side to side   90
Anxiously cast, the Phrygian throng he ey'd,
"Alas! what Land," he cries, "can now, what Sea,
Can offer refuge? what resource for me?
Who mid the Greeks no breathing-place can find,
And whom ye, Trojans, have to death consign'd!"   95
Thus were we wrought upon; and now, with sense
Of pity touch'd, that check'd all violence,
We cheer'd and urged him boldly to declare
His origin, what tidings he may bear,
And on what claims he ventures to confide;   100
Then, somewhat eas'd of fear, he thus replied:

"O King, a plain confession shall ensue
On these commands, in all things plain and true.
And first, the tongue that speaks shall not deny
My origin; a Greek by birth am I.   105

67–70 Trojans! mistrust the Horse: whate'er it be,
        Though offering gifts, the Greeks are Greeks to me."
        This said, Laocoon hurl'd with mighty force
        A ponderous spear against the monster horse C. W.
73–82 *Pasted over the MS., in* D. W.'*s hand, corrected by* C. W.
99 His birth, his fortunes, what his tidings are C. W.

Fortune made Sinon wretched ;—to do more,
And make him false,—*that* lies not in her power.
In converse, haply, ye have heard the name
Of Palamedes, and his glorious fame ;
A Chief with treason falsely charg'd, and whom ⎫
The Achaians crush'd by a nefarious doom,   ⎬
And now lament when cover'd with the tomb. ⎭
His kinsman I ; and hither by his side
Me my poor Father sent, when first these fields were tried.
While yet his voice the Grecian Chieftains sway'd
And due respect was to his counsel paid,
Ere that high influence was with life cut short,
I did not walk ungraced by fair report.
Ulysses, envy rankling in his breast,
(And these are things which thousands can attest)
Thereafter turn'd his subtlety to give
That fatal injury, and he ceas'd to live.
I dragg'd my days in sorrow and in gloom,
And mourn'd my guiltless Friend, indignant at his doom ;
This inwardly ; and yet not always mute,
Rashly I vow'd revenge—my sure pursuit,
If e'er the shores of Argos I again
Should see, victorious with my Countrymen.
Sharp hatred did these open threats excite ;
Hence the first breathings of a deadly blight ;
Hence, to appal me, accusations came,
Which still Ulysses was at work to frame ;
Hence would he scatter daily 'mid the crowd
Loose hints, at will sustain'd or disavow'd,
Beyond himself for instruments he look'd,
And in this search for means no respite brook'd
Till Calchas his accomplice—but the chain
Of foul devices why untwist in vain ?
Why should I linger ? if ye Trojans place
On the same level all of Argive race,
And 'tis enough to know that I am one,
Punish me ; would Ulysses might look on !
And let the Atridae hear, rejoiced with what is done !"

110 A guiltless Chief, for this condemn'd to die,
     That he dissuaded war—could that be treachery ? C. W.
119–22 But when Ulysses (thousands can attest
          This truth) with envy rankling in his breast ;
          Had compassed what he blushed not to contrive
          And hapless Palamedes ceas'd to live. C. W.
129 Nor fail'd these threats sharp hatred to excite C. W.
142-3 Punish me promptly ! Ithacus, that done,
          Would be rejoic'd, the brother Kings to buy
          That service, would esteem no price too high. C. W.

110

115

120

125

130

135

140

This stirr'd us more, whose judgments were asleep
To all suspicion of a crime so deep   145
And craft so fine. Our questions we renew'd ;
And, trembling, thus the fiction he pursued.

"Oft did the Grecian Host the means prepare
To flee from Troy, tired with so long a war ;
Would they had fled ! but winds as often stopp'd   150
Their going, and the twisted sails were dropp'd ;
And when this pine-ribb'd Horse of monstrous size ⎫
Stood forth, a finish'd Work, before their eyes,   ⎬
Then chiefly peal'd the storm through blacken'd skies. ⎭
So that the Oracle its aid might lend   155
To quell our doubts, Eurypylus we send,
Who brought the answer of the voice divine
In these sad words given from the Delphic shrine.
—'Blood flow'd, a Virgin perish'd to appease
The winds, when first for Troy ye pass'd the seas ;   160
O Grecians ! for return across the Flood,
Life must be paid, a sacrifice of blood.'
—With this response an universal dread
Among the shuddering multitude was spread ;
All quak'd to think at whom the Fates had aim'd   165
This sentence, who the Victim Phoebus claim'd.
Then doth the Ithacan with tumult loud
Bring forth the Prophet Calchas to the crowd ;
Asks what the Gods would have ; and some, meanwhile,
Discern what end the Mover of the guile   170
Is compassing ; and do not hide from me
The crime which they in mute reserve foresee.
Ten days refus'd he still with guarded breath
To designate the Man, to fix the death ;
The Ithacan still urgent for the deed ;   175
At last the unwilling voice announc'd that *I* must bleed.
All gave assent, each happy to be clear'd,
By one Man's fall, of what himself had fear'd.
Now came the accursed day ; the salted cates
Are spread,—the Altar for the Victim waits ;   180
The fillets bind my temples—I took flight
Bursting my chains, I own, and through the night

156 To fix our wavering minds, C. W.
165 to think] in doubt C. W.   170–1 what crime . . . Is bent upon C. W.
172 crime which] issue, C. W.   176 the accomplice Seer C. W.
177–8 Assenting all with joyful transfer laid
        What each himself had fear'd upon one wretched head. C. W.

Lurk'd among oozy swamps, and there lay hid
Till winds might cease their voyage to forbid.
And now was I compell'd at once to part   185
With all the dear old longings of the heart,
Never to see my Country, Children, Sire,
Whom they, perchance, will for this flight require
For this offence of mine of them will make
An expiation, punish'd for my sake.   190
But Thee, by all the Powers who hold their seat
In Heaven, and know the truth, do I entreat
O King! and by whate'er may yet remain
Among mankind of faith without a stain,
Have pity on my woes; commiserate   195
A mind that ne'er deserved this wretched fate."

His tears prevail, we spare the Suppliant's life
Pitying the man we spare, without a strife;
Even Priam's self, He first of all commands
To loose the fetters and unbind his hands,   200
Then adds these friendly words;—"Whoe'er thou be
Henceforth forget the Grecians, lost to thee;
We claim thee now, and let me truly hear
Who mov'd them first this monstrous Horse to rear?
And why? Was some religious vow the aim?   205
Or for what use in war the Engine might they frame?
Straight were these artful words in answer given
While he uprais'd his hands, now free, to Heaven.

"Eternal Fires, on you I call; O Ye!
And your inviolable Deity!   210
Altars, and ruthless swords from which I fled!
Ye fillets, worn round my devoted head!
Be it no crime if Argive sanctions cease
To awe me,—none to hate the men of Greece!
The law of Country forfeiting its hold,   215
Mine be the voice their secrets to unfold!
And ye, O Trojans! keep the word ye gave;
Save me, if truth I speak, and Ilium save!

The Grecian Host on Pallas still relied;
Nor hope had they but what her aid supplied;   220

197–8 We grant to tears, thus seconding his pray'r,
       His life, and freely pity whom we spare C. W.
204–6 Why, and by whom instructed did they rear
       This huge unwieldy fabric? was the aim
       Religion, or for war some engine did they frame? C. W.

But all things droop'd since that ill-omen'd time
In which Ulysses, Author of the crime,
Was leagued with impious Diomed, to seize
That Image pregnant with your destinies;
Tore the Palladium from the Holy Fane,   225
The Guards who watch'd the Citadel first slain.
And, fearing not the Goddess, touch'd the Bands
Wreathed round her virgin brow, with gory hands.
Hope ebb'd, strength fail'd the Grecians since that day,
From them the Goddess turn'd her mind away.   230
This by no doubtful signs Tritonia shew'd,
The uplifted eyes with flames coruscant glow'd,
Soon as they plac'd her Image in the Camp;
And trickl'd o'er its limbs a briny damp;
And from the ground, the Goddess (strange to hear!)   235
Leapt thrice, with buckler grasp'd, and quivering spear.
—Then Calchas bade to stretch the homeward sail,
And prophesied that Grecian Arms would fail,
Unless we for new omens should repair
To Argos, thither the Palladium bear;   240
And thence to Phrygian Shores recross the Sea,
Fraught with a more propitious Deity.
They went; but only to return in power
With favouring Gods, at some unlook'd-for hour.
—So Calchas read those signs; the Horse was built   245
To soothe Minerva, and atone for guilt.
Compact in strength you see the Fabric rise,
A pile stupendous, towering to the skies!
This was ordain'd by Calchas, with intent
That the vast bulk its ingress might prevent,   250
And Ilium ne'er within her Walls enfold
Another Safeguard reverenced like the old.
For if, unaw'd by Pallas, ye should lift
A sacrilegious hand against the Gift,
The Phrygian Realm shall perish (May the Gods   255
Turn on himself the mischief he forebodes!)
But if your Town it enter—by your aid
Ascending—Asia, then, in arms array'd
Shall storm the walls of Pelops, and a fate
As dire on our posterity await."   260

    Even so the arts of perjur'd Sinon gain'd
Belief for this, and all that he had feign'd;
Thus were they won by wiles, by tears compell'd

225–6 They, when the warders of the fort were slain, Tore *etc.* C. W.
230 Incens'd the Goddess turn'd her face away C. W.

Whom not Tydides, not Achilles quell'd;
Who fronted ten years' war with safe disdain,   265
'Gainst whom a thousand Ships had tried their strength in vain.

To speed our fate, a thing did now appear
Yet more momentous, and of instant fear.
Laocoon, Priest by lot to Neptune, stood
Where to his hand a Bull pour'd forth its blood,   270
Before the Altar, in high offering slain;—
But lo! two Serpents, o'er the tranquil Main
Incumbent, roll from Tenedos, and seek
Our Coast together (shuddering do I speak);
Between the waves, their elevated breasts,   275
Upheav'd in circling spires, and sanguine crests,
Tower o'er the flood; the parts that follow, sweep
In folds voluminous and vast, the Deep.
The agitated brine, with noisy roar
Attends their coming, till they touch the shore;   280
Sparkle their eyes suffus'd with blood, and quick
The tongues shot forth their hissing mouths to lick.
Dispers'd with fear we fly; in close array   ⎫
These move, and tow'rds Laocoon point their way, ⎬
But first assault his Sons, their youthful prey.   ⎭   285
—A several Snake in tortuous wreaths engrasps
Each slender frame; and fanging what it clasps
Feeds on the limbs; the Father rushes on,
Arms in his hand, for rescue; but anon
Himself they seize; and, coiling round his waist   290
Their scaly backs, they bind him, twice embrac'd
With monstrous spires, as with a double zone;   ⎫
And, twice around his neck in tangles thrown,   ⎬
High o'er the Father's head each Serpent lifts its own. ⎭
His priestly fillets then are sprinkled o'er   295
With sable venom and distain'd with gore;
And while his labouring hands the knots would rend
The cries he utters to the Heavens ascend;
Loud as a Bull—that, wounded by the axe
Shook off the uncertain steel, and from the altar breaks,   300
To fill with bellowing voice the depths of air!
—But tow'rds the Temple slid the Hydra Pair,
Their work accomplish'd, and there lie conceal'd,
Couched at Minerva's feet, beneath her orbed Shield.
Nor was there *One* who trembled not with fear,   305
Or deem'd the expiation too severe,

295 Lo! while his priestly wreaths are C. W.
297–8 He strives with . . . to rend
     And utters cries that . . . C. W.

For him whose lance had pierc'd the votive Steed,
Which to the Temple they resolve to lead;
There to be lodg'd with pomp of service high
And supplication, such the general cry.   310

   Shattering the Walls, a spacious breach we make,
We cleave the bulwarks—toil which all partake,
Some to the feet the rolling wheels apply,
Some round the lofty neck the cables tye;
The Engine, pregnant with our deadly foes,   315
Mounts to the breach; and ever, as it goes,
Boys, mix'd with Maidens, chaunt a holy song
And press to touch the cords, a happy throng.
The Town it enters thus, and threatening moves along.

   My Country, glorious Ilium! and ye Towers,   320
Lov'd habitation of celestial Powers!
Four times it halted mid the gates,—a din
Of armour four times warn'd us from within;
Yet tow'rds the sacred Dome with reckless mind
We still press on, and in the place assign'd   325
Lodge the portentous Gift, through frenzy blind.

   Nor fail'd Cassandra now to scatter wide
Words that of instant ruin prophesied.
—But Phoebus will'd that none should heed her voice,
And we, we miserable men, rejoice,   330
And hang our Temples round with festal boughs,
Upon that day, the last that Fate allows.

   Meanwhile had Heaven revolv'd with rapid flight,
And fast from Ocean climbs the punctual Night,
With boundless shade involving earth and sky   335
And Myrmidonian frauds;—the Trojans lie
Scatter'd throughout the weary Town, and keep
Unbroken quiet in the embrace of sleep.

   This was the time when, furnish'd and array'd,
Nor wanting silent moonlight's friendly aid,   340
From Tenedos the Grecian Navy came,
Led by the royal Galley's signal flame,
And Sinon now, our hostile fates his guard,
By stealth the dungeon of the Greeks unbarr'd.
Straight, by a pendant rope adown the side   345
Of the steep Horse, the armed Warriors glide.
The Chiefs Thersander, Sthenelus are there,
With joy deliver'd to the open air;

Ulysses, Thoas, Achamas the cord
Lets down to earth and Helen's injur'd Lord,   350
—Pyrrhus, who from Pelides drew his birth,
And bold Machaon, first to issue forth,
Nor him forget whose skill had fram'd the Pile
Epeus, glorying in his prosperous wile.
They rush upon the City that lay still,   355
Buried in sleep and wine; the Warders kill;
And at the wide-spread Gates in triumph greet
Expectant Comrades crowding from the Fleet.

It was the earliest hour of slumbrous rest,
Gift of the Gods to Man with toil opprest,   360
When, present to my dream, did Hector rise
And stood before me with fast-streaming eyes;
Such as he was when horse had striven with horse,
Whirling along the plain his lifeless Corse,
The thongs that bound him to the Chariot thrust   365
Through his swoln feet, and black with gory dust,—
A spectacle how pitiably sad!
How chang'd from that returning Hector, clad
In glorious spoils, Achilles' own attire!
From Hector hurling shipward the red Phrygian fire!   370
—A squalid beard, hair clotted thick with gore,
And that same throng of patriot wounds he bore,
In front of Troy receiv'd; and now, methought,   ⎫
That I myself was to a passion wrought   ⎬
Of tears, which to my voice this greeting brought. ⎭   375
"O Light of Dardan Realms! most faithful Stay
To Trojan courage, why these lingerings of delay?
Where hast thou tarried, Hector? From what coast
Com'st thou, long wish'd-for? That so many lost
Thy kinsmen or thy friends,—such travail borne   380
By this afflicted City—we outworn
Behold thee. Why this undeserv'd disgrace?
Who thus defil'd with wounds that honour'd face?"
He nought to this—unwilling to detain

359–61 It was the earliest hour when sweet repose,
        Gift of the Gods, creeps softly on, to close
        The eyes of weary mortals. Then arose
        Hector, or to my dream appear'd to rise C. W.
379 Com'st thou, long-look'd for. After thousands lost C. W.
381–3 By desolated Troy, how tired and worn
        Are we who thus behold thee! how forlorn!
        These gashes whence? this undeserv'd disgrace?
        Who thus defiled that calm majestic face? C. W.

One, who had ask'd vain things, with answer vain;   385
But, groaning deep, "Flee, Goddess-born," he said,
"Snatch thyself from these flames around thee spread;
Our Enemy is master of the Walls;
Down from her elevation Ilium falls.
Enough for Priam; the long strife is o'er,   390
Nor doth our Country ask one effort more.
Could Pergamus have been defended—hence,
Even from this hand, had issued her defence;
Troy her Penates doth to thee commend,
Her sacred stores,—let these thy fates attend!   395
Sail under their protection for the Land
Where mighty Realms shall grow at thy command!"
—No more was utter'd, but his hand he stretch'd,
And from the inmost Sanctuary fetch'd
The consecrated wreaths, the potency   400
Of Vesta, and the fires that may not die.

   Meantime, wild tumult through the streets is pour'd,
And though apart, and mid thick trees embower'd,
My Father's mansion stood, the loud alarms
Came pressing thither, and the clash of Arms.   405
Sleep fled; I climb the roof and where it rears
Its loftiest summit, stand with quicken'd ears.
So, when a fire by raging south winds borne
Lights on a billowy sea of ripen'd corn,
Or rapid torrent sweeps with mountain flood   410
The fields, the harvest prostrates, headlong bears the wood;
High on a rock, the unweeting Shepherd, bound,
In blank amazement, listens to the sound.
Then was apparent to *whom* faith was due,
And Grecian plots lie bare to open view.   415
Above the spacious palace where abode
Deiphobus, the flames in triumph rode;
Ucalegon burns next; through lurid air
Sigean Friths reflect a widening glare.
Clamor and clangor to the heavens arise,   420
The blast of trumpets mix'd with vocal cries;
Arms do I snatch—weak reason scarcely knows
What aid they promise, but my spirit glows;
I burn to gather Friends, whose firm array
On to the Citadel shall force its way.   425

395 stores] rites C. W.
396–7 Far sailing, seek for these the fated land
     Where mighty walls at length shall rise at thy command C. W.
402 Now wailings wild from street to street are pour'd C. W.

Precipitation works with desperate charms;
It seems a lovely thing to die in arms.

   Lo Pantheus! fugitive from Grecian spears,
Apollo's Priest;—his vanquish'd Gods he bears;
The other hand his little Grandson leads,   430
While from the Sovereign Fort, he tow'rd my threshold speeds.
"Pantheus, what hope? Which Fortress shall we try?
Where plant resistance?" He in prompt reply
Said, deeply mov'd,—" 'Tis come—the final hour;
The inevitable close of Dardan power   435
Hath come:—we have been Trojans, Ilium was,
And the great name of Troy; now all things pass
To Argos; so wills angry Jupiter:
Within the burning Town the Grecians domineer.
Forth from its central stand the enormous Horse   440
Pours in continual stream an armed Force;
Sinon, insulting victor, aggravates
The flames; and thousands hurry through the Gates,
Throng'd, as might seem, with press of all the Hosts
That e'er Mycenae sent to Phrygian Coasts.   445
Others with spears in serried files blockade
The passes;—hangs, with quivering point, the blade
Unsheath'd for slaughter,—scarcely to the foes
A blind and baffled fight the Warders can oppose."

   Urg'd by these words, and as the Gods inspire,   450
I rush into the battle and the fire,
Where sad Erinnys, where the shock of fight,
The roar, the tumult, and the groans invite;
Rypheus is with me, Epytus, the pride
Of battles, joins his aid, and to my side   455
Flock Dymas, Hypanis, the moon their guide;
With young Coroebus, who had lately sought
Our walls, by passion for Cassandra brought;
He led to Priam an auxiliar train,
His Son by wedlock, miserable Man   460
For whom a raving Spouse had prophesied in vain.

   When these I saw collected, and intent
To face the strife with deeds of hardiment,
I thus began: "O Champions, vainly brave
If, like myself, to dare extremes ye crave,   465

457-9 Nor last the young Coroebus, he who fed
      A senseless passion, whom desire to wed
      Cassandra, in those days to Troy had led,
      He fought, the hopes of Priam to sustain C. W.

You see our lost condition,—not a God,
Of all the Powers by whom this Empire stood,
But hath renounced his Altar—fled from his abode. ⎤
—Ye would uphold a City wrapp'd in fire;
Die rather;—let us rush, in battle to expire.   470
At least one safety shall the vanquish'd have
If they no safety seek but in the grave."
—Thus to their minds was fury added,—then,
Like wolves driven forth by hunger from the den,
To prowl amid blind vapours, whom the brood   475
Expect, their jaws all parch'd with thirst for blood,
Through flying darts, through pressure of the Foe,
To death, to not uncertain death, we go.
Right through the Town our midway course we bear,
Aided by hovering darkness, strengthen'd by despair.   480
Can words the havoc of that night express?
What power of tears may equal the distress?
An ancient City sinks to disappear;
She sinks who rul'd for ages,—Far and near
The Unresisting through the streets, the abodes   485
Of Men and hallow'd Temples of the Gods,
Are fell'd by massacre that takes no heed;
Nor are the Trojans only doom'd to bleed;
The Vanquish'd sometimes to their hearts recall
Old virtues, and the conquering Argives fall.   490
Sorrow is everywhere and fiery skaith, ⎤
Fear, Anguish struggling to be rid of breath, ⎬
And Death still crowding on the shape of Death. ⎦

Androgeus, whom a numerous Force attends,
Was the first Greek we met; he rashly deems us Friends.   495
"What sloth," he cries, "retards you? Warriors haste!
Troy blazes, sack'd by others, and laid waste;
And ye come lagging from your Ships the last!"
Thus he; and straight mistrusting our replies,
He felt himself begirt with enemies;   500
Voice fail'd—step faulter'd, at the dire mistake; ⎤
Like one who through a deeply tangl'd brake ⎬
Struggling, hath trod upon a lurking Snake, ⎦

471–2 For safety hoping not; the vanquish'd have
         The best of safety, in a noble grave. C. W.
         Could but the vanquished beat out of their mind
         All hope of safety, safety they might find MS. 101
485–7 Multitudes, passive creatures, through streets, roads,
         Houses of men, and thresholds of the Gods
         By ruthless massacre are prostrated C. W.
492–3 Fear . . . breath, Are everywhere: about, above, beneath, Is
Death etc. C.W.

And shrunk in terror from the unlook'd-for Pest
Lifting his blue-swoln neck and wrathful crest.   505
Even so Androgeus, smit with sudden dread,
Recoils from what he saw, and would have fled,
Forward we rush, with arms the Troop surround,
The Men, surpriz'd and ignorant of the ground,
Subdued by fear, become an easy prey;   510
So are we favor'd in our first essay.

 With exultation here Coroebus cries,
"Behold, O Friends, how bright our destinies!
Advance;—the road which they point out is plain;
Shields let us change, and bear the insignia of the Slain,   515
Grecians in semblance; wiles are lawful—who
To simple valour would restrict a foe?
Themselves shall give us Arms." When this was said
The Leader's helmet nods upon his head,
The emblazon'd buckler on his arm is tied,   520
He fits an Argive falchion to his side.
The like doth Ripheus, Dymas,—all put on,
With eager haste, the spoils which they had won.
Then in the combat mingling, Heaven averse,
Amid the gloom a multitude we pierce,   525
And to the shades dismiss them. Others flee,
Appall'd by this imagin'd treachery;
Some to the Ships—some in the Horse would hide. ⎫
Ah! what reap they but sorrow who confide   ⎬
In aught to which the Gods their sanction have denied? ⎭   530
Behold Cassandra, Priam's royal Child,
By sacrilegeous men, with hair all wild,
Dragg'd from Minerva's Temple! Tow'rd the skies
The Virgin lifts in vain her glowing eyes,
Her eyes, she could no more, for Grecian bands   535
Had rudely manacled her tender hands.
The intolerable sight to madness stung   ⎫
Coroebus; and his desperate self he flung   ⎬
For speedy death the ruthless Foe among!   ⎭
We follow, and with general shock assail   540
The hostile Throng:—here first our efforts fail:
While, from the summit of the lofty Fane
Darts, by the People flung, descend amain;
In miserable heaps their Friends are laid,
By shew of Grecian Arms and Crests betray'd.   545

510 fear, become] terror, fall C. W.

Wroth for the Virgin rescu'd, by defeat
Provok'd, the Grecians from all quarters meet.
With Ajax combat there the Brother Kings;
And the Dolopian Squadron thither brings
Its utmost rage. Thus Winds break forth and fly   550
To conflict from all regions of the sky;
Notus and Zephyrus, while Eurus feeds
The strife, exulting in his orient steeds;
Woods roar, and foaming Nereus stirs the waves
Rouz'd by his trident from their lowest caves.   555
They also whomsoe'er through shades of night
Our stratagem had driven to scatter'd flight
Now reappear—by them our Shields are known; ⎫
The simulating Javelins they disown,   ⎬
And mark our utterance of discordant tone. ⎭   560
Numbers on numbers bear us down; and first
Coroebus falls; him Peneleus hath pierc'd
Before Minerva's Altar; next, in dust
Sinks Rhypeus, one above all Trojans just,
And righteous above all; but heavenly Powers   565
Ordain by lights that ill agree with ours.
Then Dymas, Hypanis are slain by Friends;
—Nor thee abundant piety defends,
O Pantheus! falling with the garland wound,
As fits Apollo's Priest, thy brows around.   570

    Ashes of Ilium! and ye duteous fires,
Lit for my Friends upon their funeral pyres;
Amid your fall bear witness to my word!
I shunn'd no hazards of the Grecian sword,
No turns of war; with hand unsparing fought;   575
And earn'd, had Fate so will'd, the death I sought,
Thence am I hurried by the rolling tide,
With Iphitus and Pelias at my side;
One bow'd with years; and Pelias, from a wound
Given by Ulysses, halts along the ground.   580
New clamours rise; The Abode of Priam calls,
Besieged by thousands swarming round the walls;
Concourse how thick! as if, throughout the space
Of the whole City, war in other place

548–50 The brother Kings and Ajax that way bend
        Their efforts; the Dolopian squadron spend
        Their fury there. C. W.
563 Falls bold Coroebus by Peneleus pierc'd C. W.
566 Judge by a light that ill agrees C. W.

Were hush'd—no death elsewhere. The Assailants wield   585
Above their heads shield, shell-wise lock'd in shield;
Climb step by step the ladders, near the side
Of the strong portal daringly applied;
The weaker hand its guardian shield presents;
The right is stretch'd to grasp the battlements.   590
The Dardans tug at roof and turrets high,
Rend fragments off, and with these weapons try
Life to preserve in such extremity,
Roll down the massy rafters deck'd with gold,
Magnific splendours rais'd by Kings of old;   595
Others with naked weapons stand prepar'd
In thick array, the doors below to guard.

  A bolder hope inspirits me to lend
My utmost aid the Palace to defend,
And strengthen those afflicted. From behind,   600
A gateway open'd, whence, a passage blind
The various Mansions of the Palace join'd.
—Unblest Andromache, while Priam reign'd
Oft by this way the royal Palace gain'd,
A lonely Visitant; this way would tread   605
With young Astyanax, to his Grandsire led.
Entering the gate, I reach'd the roof, where stand
The Trojans, hurling darts with ineffectual hand.
A Tower there was; precipitous the site,
And the Pile rose to an unrivall'd height;   610
Frequented Station, whence, in circuit wide
Troy might be seen, the Argive Fleet descried,
And all the Achaian Camp. This sovereign Tower
With irons grappling where the loftiest floor
Press'd with its beams the wall we shake, we rend,   615
And, in a mass of thundering ruin, send
To crush the Greeks beneath. But numbers press
To new assault with reckless eagerness:
Weapons and missiles from the ruins grow,
And what their hasty hands can seize they throw!   620

  In front stands Pyrrhus, glorying in the might
Of his own weapons, while his armour bright
Casts from the portal gleams of brazen light,
So shines a Snake, when kindling, he hath crept
Forth from the winter bed in which he slept,   625
Swoln with a glut of poisonous herbs,—but now

600 And succour there the vanquish'd. C. W.
605 All unattended oft this way would tread C. W.

Fresh from the shedding of his annual slough,
Glittering in youth, warm with instinctive fires,
He, with rais'd breast, involves his back in gyres,
Darts with his forked tongue, and tow'rd the sun aspires.   630
Join'd with redoubted Periphas, comes on
To storm the Palace fierce Automedon,
Who drove the Achillean Car;—the Bands
Of Scyros follow hurling fiery brands.
Pyrrhus himself hath seiz'd an axe, would cleave   635
The ponderous doors, or from their hinges heave;
And now, reiterating stroke on stroke
Hath hewn, through plates of brass and solid oak,
A broad-mouth'd entrance;—to their inmost seats
The long-drawn courts lie open; the retreats   640
Of Priam and ancestral Kings are bar'd
To instantaneous view; and Lo! the Guard
Stands at the threshold, for defence prepar'd.

But tumult spreads through all the space within;
The vaulted roofs repeat the mournful din   645
Of female Ululation, a strange vent
Of agony, that strikes the starry firmament!
The Matrons range with wildering step the floors;
Embrace, and print their kisses on, the doors.
Pyrrhus, with all his father's might, dispels   650
Barriers and bolts, and living obstacles;
Force shapes her own clear way;—the doors are thrown
Off from their hinges; gates are batter'd down
By the onrushing Soldiery, who kill
Whom first they meet, and the broad area fill.   655
—Less irresistibly, o'er dams and mounds,
Burst by its rage, a foaming River bounds,
Herds sweeping with their stalls along the ravag'd grounds.
Pyrrhus I saw with slaughter desperate;
The two Atridae near the Palace gate   660
Did I behold; and by these eyes were seen
The hundred Daughters with the Mother Queen,
And hoary-headed Priam, where he stood
Beside the Altar, staining with his blood
Fires which himself had hallow'd. Hope had he   665
Erewhile, none equal hope, of large posterity.
There, fifty bridal chambers might be told—

635-6 . . . a halberd, cleaves . . . heaves C. W.
652-4 the doors have flown . . . overthrown
          By shock of horned engines batter'd down.
          In rush the Grecian soldiery; they kill C. W.

Superb with trophies and barbaric gold,
All, in their pomp, lie level with the ground,
And where the fire is not, are Grecian Masters found. 670

Ask ye the fate of Priam ? On that night
When captur'd Ilium blaz'd before his sight,
And the Foe, bursting through the Palace gate
Spread through the privacies of royal state,
In vain to tremulous shoulders he restor'd 675
Arms which had long forgot their ancient Lord,
And girt upon his side a useless sword ;
Then, thus accoutr'd, forward did he hie,
As if to meet the Enemy and die.
—Amid the Courts, an Altar stood in view 680
Of the wide heavens, near which a long-lived Laurel grew,
And, bending over this great Altar, made
For its Penates an embracing shade.
With all her Daughters, throng'd like Doves that lie
Cowering, when storms have driven them from the sky, 685
Hecuba shelters in that sacred place
Where they the Statues of the Gods embrace.
But when she saw in youthful Arms array'd
Priam himself; "What ominous thought," she said,
"Hangs, wretched Spouse, this weight on limbs decay'd ? 690
And whither would'st thou hasten ? If we were
More helpless still, this succour we might spare.
Not such Defenders doth the time demand ;
Profitless here would be even Hector's hand.
Retire ; this Altar can protect us all, 695
Or thou wilt not survive when we must fall."
This to herself: and tow'rd the sacred spot
She drew the aged Man, to wait their common lot.

But see Polites, one of Priam's Sons,
Charg'd with the death which he in terror shuns ! 700
The wounded Youth, escap'd from Pyrrhus, flies
Through showers of darts, through press of enemies,
Where the long Porticos invite ; the space
Of widely-vacant Courts his footsteps trace.
Him, Pyrrhus, following near and still more near, 705
Hath caught at with his hand, and presses with his spear ;

669–70 Pillar and portal to the dust are brought ;
     And the Greeks lord it, where the fire is not. C. W.
697–8 Then to herself she drew the aged Sire
     And to the laurel shade together they retire C. W.

But when at length this unremitting flight
Had brought him full before his Father's sight,
He fell—and scarcely prostrate on the ground,
Pour'd forth his life from many a streaming wound. 710
Here Priam, scorning death and self-regard,
His voice restrain'd not, nor his anger spar'd;
But "Shall the Gods," he cries, "if Gods there be
Who note such acts, and care for piety,
Requite this heinous crime with measure true, 715
Nor one reward withhold that is thy due;
Who thus a Father's presence hast defil'd,
And forc'd upon his sight the murder of a Child.
Not thus Achilles' self, from whom a tongue
Vers'd in vainglorious falsehood boasts thee sprung. 720
Dealt with an enemy; my prayer he heard;
A Suppliant's rights in Priam he rever'd,
Gave Hector back to rest within the tomb,
And me remitted to my royal home."
This said, the aged Man a javelin cast; 725
With weak arm—faltering to the shield it past;
The tinkling shield the harmless point repell'd,
Which, to the boss it hung from, barely held.
—Then Pyrrhus, "To my Sire, Pelides, bear ⎫
These feats of mine, ill relish'd as they are, ⎬ 730
Tidings of which I make thee messenger! ⎭
To him a faithful history relate
Of Neoptolemus degenerate.
Now die!" So saying, towards the Altar, through
A stream of filial blood, the tottering Sire he drew; 735
His left hand lock'd within the tangled hair
Rais'd, with the right, a brandish'd sword in air,
Then to the hilt impell'd it through his side;
Thus, mid a blazing City, Priam died.
Troy falling round him, thus he clos'd his fate, 740
And the proud Lord of many an Asian State!
Upon the shore lies stretch'd his mangled frame,
Head from the shoulders torn, a Body without name.

Then first it was, that Horror girt me round;
Chill'd my frail heart, and all my senses bound; 745
The image of my Father cross'd my mind;

714–15 acts . . . heinous crime] crimes . . . deed of thine C. W.
727–8 Straight by the brass impell'd that feebly rung
  Down from the boss the harmless weapon hung C. W.
742–3 The abandon'd corse lies stretch'd upon the shore
  Head from the shoulders torn, its very name no more. C. W.

Perchance in fate with slaughter'd Priam join'd;
Equal in age, thus may He breathe out life,
Creusa also, my deserted Wife!
The Child Iulus left without defence, 750
And the whole House laid bare to violence!
Backward I look'd, and cast my eyes before;
My Friends had fail'd, and courage was no more;
All, wearied out, had follow'd desperate aims,
Self-dash'd to earth, or stifled in the flames. 755

Thus was I left alone; such light my guide
As the conflagrant walls and roofs supplied;
When my far-wandering eyesight chanc'd to meet
Helen sequester'd on a lonely seat
Amid the Porch of Vesta; She, through dread 760
Of Trojan vengeance amply merited,
Of Grecian punishment, and what the ire
Of a deserted Husband might require,
Thither had flown—there sate, the common bane
Of Troy and of her Country—to obtain 765
Protection from the Altar, or to try
What hope might spring from trembling secresy.
Methought my falling Country cried aloud,
And the revenge it seem'd to ask, I vow'd;
"What! shall she visit Sparta once again? 770
In triumph enter with a loyal Train?
Consort, and Home, and Sires and Children view
By Trojan Females serv'd, a Phrygian retinue?
For this was Priam slain? Troy burnt? the shore
Of Dardan Seas so often drench'd in gore? 775
Not so; for though such victory can claim
In its own nature no renown of fame,
The punishment that ends the guilty days
Even of a Woman, shall find grateful praise;
My soul, at least, shall of her weight be eas'd, 780
The ashes of my Countrymen appeas'd."

Such words broke forth; and in my own despite ⎫
Onward I bore, when through the dreary night ⎬
Appear'd my gracious Mother, vested in pure light; ⎭
Never till now before me did she shine 785
So much herself, so thoroughly divine;
Goddess reveal'd in all her beauty, love, ⎫
And majesty, as she is wont to move, ⎬
A Shape familiar to the Courts of Jove! ⎭

763 deserted] forsaken C. W.   786 so thoroughly] of aspect so C. W.

The hand she seiz'd her touch suffic'd to stay,   790
Then through her roseate mouth these words found easy way.

    "O Son! what pain excites a wrath so blind ?
Or could all thought of me desert thy mind ?
Where now is left thy Parent worn with age ?
Wilt thou not rather in that search engage ?   795
Learn with thine eyes if yet Creusa live,
And if the Boy Ascanius still survive.
Them do the Greeks environ:—that they spare, ⎫
That swords so long abstain, and flames forbear, ⎬
Is through the intervention of my care.   ⎭   800
Not Spartan Helen's beauty, so abhorr'd
By thee, not Paris, her upbraided Lord—
The hostile Gods have laid this grandeur low,
Troy from the Gods receives her overthrow.
Look! for the impediment of misty shade   805
With which thy mortal sight is overlaid
I will disperse ; nor thou refuse to hear
Parental mandates, nor resist through fear!
There, where thou seest block rolling upon block,
Mass rent from mass, and dust condens'd with smoke   810
In billowy intermixture, Neptune smites
The walls, with labouring Trident disunites
From their foundation—tearing up, as suits
His anger, Ilium from her deepest roots.
Fiercest of all, before the Scaean Gate,   815
Arm'd Juno stands, beckoning to animate
The Bands she summons from the Argive Fleet,
Tritonian Pallas holds *her* chosen seat
High on the Citadel,—look back! see there
Her Ægis beaming forth a stormy glare!   820
The very Father, Jove himself, supplies
Strength to the Greeks, sends heaven-born enemies
Against the Dardan Arms. My Son, take flight,
And close the struggle of this dismal night!
I will not quit thy steps whate'er betide,   ⎫   825
But to thy Father's House will safely guide."   ⎬
She ceas'd, and did in shades her presence hide. ⎭

791 through . . . mouth] from . . . lips C. W.
811–14   Tower and wall
        Upheav'd by Neptune's mighty trident fall,
        To earth ; his wrath their deep foundation bares
        And the strong City by the roots uptears. MS.
827 did in gathering shades C. W.

Dire Faces still are seen and Deities
Adverse to Troy appear, her mighty Enemies.

Now was all Ilium, far as sight could trace,⎫   830
Settling and sinking in the Fire's embrace, ⎬
Neptunian Troy subverted from her base.   ⎭
Even so, a Mountain-Ash, long tried by shock
Of storms endur'd upon the native rock,
When he is doom'd from rustic arms to feel   835
The rival blows of persevering steel,
Nods high with threatening forehead, till at length
Wounds unremitting have subdued his strength;
With groans the ancient Tree foretells his end;⎫
He falls; and fragments of the mountain blend ⎬   840
With the precipitous ruin.—I descend   ⎭
And, as the Godhead leads, 'twixt foe and fire
Advance:—the darts withdraw, the flames retire.

But when beneath her guidance I had come
Far as the Gates of the paternal Dome,   845
My Sire, whom first I sought and wish'd to bear
For safety to the Hills, disdains that care;
Nor will he now, since Troy hath fall'n, consent
Life to prolong, or suffer banishment.
"Think *Ye*," he says, "the current of whose blood   850
Is unimpair'd, whose vigour unsubdued,
Think *Ye* of flight;—that I should live, the Gods
Wish not, or they had sav'd me these Abodes.
Not once, but twice, this City to survive,
What need against such destiny to strive?   855
While thus, even thus dispos'd the body lies,
Depart! pronounce my funeral obsequies!
Not long shall I have here to wait for death,
A pitying Foe will rid me of my breath,
Will seek my spoils; and should I lie forlorn   860
Of sepulture, the loss may well be borne.
Full long obnoxious to the Powers divine
Life lingers out these barren years of mine;
Even since the date when me the eternal Sire
Swept with the thunderbolt, and scath'd with fire."   865
Thus he persists;—Creusa and her Son
Second the counter-prayer by me begun;
The total House with weeping deprecate

828 still are seen and] are apparent C. W.   829 appear] the Gods
C. W.   856 dispos'd the] composed my C. W.   868 The
whole House weeping round him C. W.

This weight of wilful impulse given to Fate;
He, all unmov'd by pleadings and by tears,   870
Guards his resolve, and to the spot adheres.

   Arms once again attract me, hurried on
In misery, and craving death alone.
"And hast thou hop'd that I could move to find
A place of rest, thee, Father, left behind?   875
How could parental lips the guilty thought unbind?
If in so great a City Heaven ordain
Utter extinction; if thy soul retain
With stedfast longing that abrupt design
Which would to falling Troy add thee and thine;   880
That way to Death lies open;—soon will stand
Pyrrhus before thee with the reeking brand
That drank the blood of Priam; He whose hand
The Son in presence of the Father slays,
And at the Altar's base the slaughter'd Father lays.   885
For this, benignant Mother! didst thou lead
My steps along a way from danger freed,
That I might see remorseless Men invade
The holiest places that these roofs o'ershade?
See Father, Consort, Son, all tinged and dy'd   890
With mutual sprinklings, perish side by side?
Arms bring me, Friends; bring Arms! our last hour speaks,
It calls the Vanquish'd; cast me on the Greeks.
In rallying combat let us join;—not all,
This night, unsolac'd by revenge shall fall."   895

   The sword resumes its place; the shield I bear;
And hurry now to reach the open air;
When on the ground before the threshold cast
Lo! where Creusa hath my feet embrac'd
And holding up Iulus, there cleaves fast!   900
"If thou, departing, be resolv'd to die,
Take us through all that in thy road may lie;
But if on Arms, already tried, attend
A single hope, then first this House defend;
On whose protection Sire and Son are thrown,   905
And I, the Wife that once was call'd thine own."

   Such outcry fill'd the Mansion, when behold
A strange portent, and wonderous to be told!
All suddenly a luminous crest was seen;

891 Each in the other's life-blood C. W.   899 Creusa check'd my
course C. W.   902 Let us be partners of thy destiny C. W.

Which, where the Boy Iulus hung between   910
The arms of each sad Parent, rose and shed,
Tapering aloft, a lustre from his head;
Along the hair the lambent flame proceeds
With harmless touch, and round his temples feeds.
In fear we haste, the burning tresses shake,   915
And from the fount the holy fire would slake;
But joyfully his hands Anchises rais'd,
His voice not silent as on Heaven he gaz'd:

"Almighty Jupiter! if prayers have power
To bend thee, look on us; I seek no more;   920
If aught our piety deserve, Oh deign   ⎫
The hope this Omen proffers to sustain;   ⎬
Nor, Father, let us ask a second Sign in vain!"   ⎭

Thus spake the Sire, and scarcely ended, ere
A peal of sudden thunder, loud and clear,   925
Broke from the left; and shot through Heaven a star
Trailing its torch, that sparkled from afar;
Above the roof the star, conspicuous sight,   ⎫
Ran to be hid on Ida's sylvan height.   ⎬
The long way marking with a train of light.   ⎭   930
The furrowy track the distant sky illumes,
And far and wide are spread sulphureous fumes.
Uprisen from earth, my aged Sire implores
The Deities, the holy Star adores;
—"Now am I conquer'd—now is no delay;   935
Gods of my Country! where Ye lead the way
'Tis not in me to hesitate or swerve;
Preserve my House, Ye Powers, this Little One preserve!
Yours is this augury; and Troy hath still
Life in the signs that manifest your will!   940
I cannot chuse but yield; and now to Thee,
O Son, a firm Associate will I be!"

He spake; and nearer through the City came
Rolling more audibly, the sea of flame.
"Now give, dear Father, to this neck the freight   945
Of thy old age;—the burthen will be light
For which my shoulders bend; henceforth one fate,
Evil or good shall we participate.
The Boy shall journey, tripping at my side;
Our steps, at distance mark'd, will be Creusa's guide.   950
My Household! heed these words: upon a Mound
(To those who quit the City obvious ground)

928–9 . . . it ran, and in our sight,
Set on the brow of C. W.

A Temple, once by Ceres honour'd, shews
Its mouldering front ; hard by a Cypress grows,
Through ages guarded with religious care ;   955
Thither, by various roads, let all repair.
Thou, Father! take these relics ; let thy hand
Bear the Penates of our native land ;
I may not touch them, fresh from deeds of blood,
Till the stream cleanse me with its living flood."   960

Forthwith an ample vest my shoulders clad,
Above the vest a lion's skin was spread,
Next came the living Burthen ; fast in mine
His little hand Iulus doth entwine,
Following his Father with no equal pace ;   965
Creusa treads behind ; the darkest ways we trace.
And me, erewhile insensible to harms,   ⎫
Whom adverse Greeks agglomerate in Arms   ⎬
Mov'd not, now every breath of air alarms ; ⎭
All sounds have power to trouble me with fear,   970
Anxious for whom I lead, and whom I bear.

Thus, till the Gates were nigh, my course I shap'd,
And thought the hazards of the time escap'd,
When through the gloom a noise of feet we hear,
Quick sounds that seem'd to press upon the ear ;   975
"Fly," cries my Father, looking forth, "Oh fly!
They come—I see their shields and dazzling panoply!"
Here, in my trepidation was I left,
Through some unfriendly Power, of mind bereft,
For, while I journey'd devious and forlorn,   980
From me, me wretched, was Creusa torn ;
Whether stopp'd short by death, or from the road
She wander'd, or sank down beneath a load
Of weariness, no vestiges made plain :
She vanish'd, ne'er to meet these eyes again.   985
Nor did I seek her lost, nor backward turn
My mind, until we reach'd the sacred bourne
Of ancient Ceres. All, even all, save One
Were in the spot assembl'd ; She alone,
As if her melancholy fate disown'd   990
Companion, Son, and Husband, nowhere could be found.
Who, man or God, from my reproach was free ?
Had desolated Troy a heavier woe for me ?
'Mid careful friends my Sire and Son I place,

986–7 I sought her not, misgiving none had I
        Until I reached the sacred boundary C. W.

With the Penates of our Phrygian race,   995
Deep in a winding vale; my footsteps then retrace;
Resolv'd the whole wide City to explore
And face the perils of the night once more.

So, with refulgent Arms begirt, I haste
Tow'rd the dark gates through which my feet had pass'd,   1000
Remeasure, where I may, the beaten ground,
And turn at every step a searching eye around.
Horror prevails on all sides, while with dread
The very silence is impregnated.
Fast to my Father's Mansion I repair,   1005
If haply, haply, She had harbour'd there.
Seiz'd by the Grecians was the whole Abode:
And now, voracious fire its mastery shew'd,
Roll'd upward by the wind in flames that meet   ⎫
High o'er the roof,—air rages with the heat;   ⎬   1010
Thence to the Towers I pass, where Priam held his Seat. ⎭
Already Phoenix and Ulysses kept,
As chosen Guards, the spoils of Ilium, heap'd
In Juno's Temple, and the wealth that rose
Pil'd on the floors of vacant porticos,   1015
Prey torn through fire from many a secret Hold,
Vests, tables of the Gods, and cups of massy gold.
And, in long order, round these treasures stand
Matrons, and Boys, and Youths, a trembling Band!

Nor did I spare with fearless voice to raise   1020
Shouts in the gloom that fill'd the streets and ways,
And with reduplication sad and vain,
Creusa call'd, again and yet again.
While thus I prosecute an endless quest
A Shape was seen, unwelcome and unblest;   1025
Creusa's Shade appear'd before my eyes,
Her Image, but of more than mortal size;
Then I, as if the power of life had pass'd
Into my upright hair, stood speechless and aghast.
—She thus—to stop my troubles at their source: 1030
"Dear Consort, why this fondly-desperate course?
Supernal Powers, not doubtfully, prepare
These issues; going hence thou wilt not bear
Creusa with thee; know that Fate denies
This Fellowship, and this the Ruler of the skies.   1035
Long wanderings will be thine, no home allow'd;
Vast the extent of sea that must be plough'd

1035 and this] nor this permits C. W.

Ere, mid Hesperian fields where Tiber flows
With gentle current, thy tired keels repose.
Joy meets thee there, a Realm and royal Bride, ⎫   1040
—For lov'd Creusa let thy tears be dried;   ⎬
I go not where the Myrmidons abide.   ⎭
No proud Dolopian Mansion shall I see
Nor shall a Grecian Dame be serv'd by me,
Deriv'd from Jove, and rais'd by thee so high,   1045
Spouse to the Offspring of a Deity,—
Far otherwise; upon my native plains
Me the great Mother of the Gods detains.
Now, fare thee well! protect our Son, and prove
By tenderness for him, our common love."   1050

This having said—my trouble to subdue,
Into thin air she silently withdrew;
Left me while tears were gushing from their springs,
And on my tongue a thousand hasty things;
Thrice with my arms I strove her neck to clasp,   1055
Thrice had my hands succeeded in their grasp,
From which the Image slipp'd away, as light
As the swift winds, or sleep when taking flight.

Such was the close; and now the night thus spent,
Back to my Friends an eager course I bent,   1060
And here a crowd with wonder I behold
Of new Associates, concourse manifold!
Matrons, and Men, and Youths that hither hied, ⎫
For exile gathering; and from every side   ⎬
The wretched people throng'd and multiplied;   ⎭   1065
Prepar'd with mind and means their flight to speed
Across the seas, where I might chuse to lead.

Now on the ridge of Ida's summit grey
Rose Lucifer, prevenient to the day.
The Grecians held the Gates in close blockade,   1070
Hope was there none of giving further aid;
I yielded, took my Father up once more,
And sought the Mountain, with the Freight I bore.

THIRD BOOK

Now when the Gods had crush'd the Asian State
And Priam's race, by too severe a fate;
When they were pleas'd proud Ilium to destroy,
And smokes upon the ground Neptunian Troy;
The sad Survivors, from their country driven,   5

1047 This fate I dread not; on *etc.* C. W.

Seek distant shores, impell'd by signs from Heaven.
Beneath Antandros we prepare a Fleet—
There my Companions muster at the feet
Of Phrygian Ida, dubious in our quest,
And where the Fates may suffer us to rest.   10
Scarcely had breath'd the earliest summer gales
Before Anchises bid to spread the sails;
Weeping I quit the Port, my native coast,
And fields where Troy once was; and soon am lost
An Exile on the bosom of the seas,   15
With Friends, Son, household Gods and the great Deities.

   Right opposite is spread a peopled Land,
Where once the fierce Lycurgus held command;
The martial Thracians plough its champain wide, ⎫
To Troy by hospitable rites allied,   ⎬ 20
While Fortune favour'd to this coast we hied;   ⎭
Where entering with unfriendly Fates, I lay
My first foundations in a hollow bay;
And call the men Æneades,—to share
With the new Citoyens the name I bear.   25
To Dionaean Venus we present,
And to the Gods who aid a fresh intent,
The sacred offerings; and with honour due
Upon the shore a glossy Bull I slew
To the great King of Heaven. A Mount was near ⎫   30
Upon whose summit cornel trees uprear   ⎬
Their boughs, and myrtles rough with many a spear.⎭
Studious to deck the Altar with green shoots,
Thither I turn'd; and, tugging at the roots
Strove to despoil the thicket; when behold   35
A dire portent, and wondrous to be told!
No sooner was the shatter'd root laid bare
Of the first Tree I struggled to uptear,
Than from the fibres drops of blood distill'd,   ⎫
Whose blackness stain'd the ground:—me horror thrill'd: ⎬ 40
My frame all shudder'd, and my blood was chill'd. ⎭
Persisting in the attempt, I toil'd to free
The flexile body of another tree,
Anxious the latent causes to explore;
And from the bark blood trickled as before.   45
Revolving much in mind forthwith I paid
Vows to the sylvan Nymphs, and sought the aid
Of Father Mars, spear-shaking God who yields
His stern protection to the Thracian fields;
That to a prosperous issue they would guide   50

The accident, the omen turn aside.
But, for a third endeavour, when with hands
Eagerly strain'd, knees press'd against the sands,
I strive the myrtle lances to uproot
With my whole strength (speak shall I, or be mute ?)   55
From the deep tomb a mournful groan was sent
And a voice follow'd, uttering this lament:
"Torment me not, Æneas. Why this pain ⎫
Given to a buried Man ? O cease, refrain, ⎬
And spare thy pious hands this guilty stain! ⎭   60
Troy brought me forth, no alien to thy blood;
Nor yields a senseless trunk this sable flood.
Oh fly the cruel land; the greedy shore
Forsake with speed, for I am Polydore.
A flight of iron darts have pierced me through,   65
Took life, and into this sharp thicket grew."
Then truly did I stand aghast, cold fear
Strangling my voice, and lifting up my hair.
Erewhile from Troy had Priam sent by stealth
This Polydore, and with him stores of wealth;   70
Trusting the Thracian King his Son would rear:
For wretched Priam now gave way to fear,
Seeing the Town beleaguer'd. These alarms
Spread to the Thracian King, and when the Arms
Of Troy were quelled, to the victorious side   75
Of Agamemnon he his hopes allied;
Breaking through sacred laws without remorse,
Slew Polydore, and seized the gold by force.
What mischief to poor mortals has not thirst
Of gold created! appetite accurs'd!   80
Soon as a calmer mind I could recal
I seek the Chiefs, my Father above all;
Report the omen, and their thoughts demand.
One mind is theirs,—to quit the impious Land;
With the first breezes of the South to fly   85
Sick of polluted hospitality.
Forthwith on Polydore our hands bestow
A second burial, and fresh mould upthrow;
And to his Manes raise beside the mound ⎫
Altars, which, as they stood in mournful round, ⎬   90
Cerulean fillets and black cypress bound; ⎭
And with loose hair a customary Band
Of Trojan Women in the circle stand.
From cups warm milk and sacred blood we pour, ⎫
Thus to the tomb the Spirit we restore; ⎬   95
And with a farewell cry its future rest implore. ⎭

Then, when the sea grew calm, and gently creeps
The soft South-wind and calls us to the Deeps,
The Crew draw down our Ships; they crowd the Shore, ⎫
The Port we leave; with Cities sprinkl'd o'er,   ⎬   100
Slowly the Coast recedes, and then is seen no more. ⎭

In the 'mid Deep there lies a spot of earth,
Sacred to her who gave the Nereids birth;
And to Ægean Neptune. Long was toss'd
This then unfruitful ground, and driven from coast to coast;   105
But, as it floated on the wide-spread sea,
The Archer-God, in filial piety,
Between two Sister islands bound it fast
For Man's abode, and to defy the blast.
Thither we steer. At length the unruffled Place   110
Received our Vessels in her calm embrace.
We land—and, when the pleasant soil we trod,
Adored the City of the Delian God.
Anius, the King (whose brows were wreath'd around
With laurel garlands and with fillets bound,   115
His sacred symbols as Apollo's Priest)
Advanc'd to meet us, from our ships releas'd;
He recognized Anchises; and their hands
Gladly they join, renewing ancient Bands
Of Hospitality; nor longer waits   120
The King, but leads us to his friendly gates.

To seek the Temple was my early care;
To whose Divinity I bow'd in prayer
Within the reverend Pile of ancient stone: ⎫
"Thymbreus! painful wanderings have we known ⎬   125
Grant, to the weary, dwellings of their own! ⎭
A City yield, a Progeny ensure,
A habitation destined to endure!—
—To us, sad relics of the Grecian Sword,
(All that is left of Troy) another Troy accord!   130
What shall we seek? whom follow? where abide? ⎫
Vouchsafe an augury our course to guide;   ⎬
Father, descend, and thro' our Spirits glide!" ⎭
—Then shook, or seem'd to shake, the entire Abode;
A trembling seiz'd the Laurels of the God;   135
The mountain rock'd; and sounds with murmuring swell ⎫
Roll'd from the Shrine; upon the ground I fell,   ⎬
And heard the guiding voice our fates foretell. ⎭
"Ye patient Dardans! that same Land which bore
From the first Stock your Fathers heretofore;   140

That ancient Mother will unfold her breast
For your return,—seek Her with faithful quest;
So shall the Ænean Line command the earth
As long as future years to future years give birth."

Thus Phoebus answer'd, and forthwith the crowd   145
Burst into transport vehement and loud:
All ask what Phoebus wills; and where the bourne
To which Troy's wandering Race are destin'd to return.
Then spake my aged Father, turning o'er
Traditions handed down from days of yore;   150
"Give ear," he said, "O Chieftains, while my words
Unfold the hopes this Oracle affords!
On the mid sea the Cretan Island lies,
Dear to the sovereign Lord of earth and skies;
There is the Idean Mount, and there we trace   155
The fountain-head, the cradle of our race.
A hundred Cities, places of command,
Rise in the circle of that fruitful land;
Thence to Rhoetean shores (if things oft heard
I faithfully remember) Teucer steer'd,   160
Our first progenitor; and chose a spot
His Seat of government when Troy was not;
While yet the Natives housed in vallies deep,
Ere Pergamus had risen, to crown the lofty steep.
From Crete came Cybele; from Crete we gained   165
All that the Mother of the Gods ordain'd;
The Corybantian Cymbals thence we drew,
The Idaean Grove; and faithful Silence, due
To rites mysterious; and the Lion pair
Ruled by the Goddess from her awful Car.   170
Then haste—the Mandate of the Gods obey
And to the Gnossian Realms direct our way;
But first the winds propitiate, and if Jove
From his high Throne the enterprize approve,
The third day's light shall bring our happy Fleet   175
To a safe harbour on the shores of Crete."

He spake, appropriate Victims forth were led,
And by his hand upon the Altars bled;
A Bull to soothe the God who rules the Sea—
A Bull, O bright Apollo! fell to thee,   180
A sable sheep for Hyems doth he smite,
For the soft Zephyrs one of purest white.
Fame told that regions would in Crete be found
Bare of the foe, deserted tracts of ground;

Left by Idomeneus, to recent flight 185
Driven from those realms—his patrimonial right.
Chear'd by a hope those valiant seats to gain
We quit the Ortygian Shore, and scud along the Main.
Near ridgy Naxos, travers'd by a rout
Of madding Bacchanals with song and shout; 190
By green Donysa rising o'er the Deeps;
Olearos, and snow-white Parian steeps;
Flying with prosperous sail thro' sounds and seas
Starr'd with the thickly-clustering Cyclades.
Confused and various clamour rises high; ⎫ 195
"To Crete and to our Ancestors" we cry ⎬
While Ships and Sailors each with other vie. ⎭
Still freshening from the stern the breezes blow,
And speed the Barks they chase, where'er we go;
Till rest is giv'n upon the ancient Shores 200
Of the Curetes to their Sails and Oars.
So with keen hope I trace a circling Wall ⎫
And the new City, by a name which all ⎬
Repeat with gladness, Pergamus I call. ⎭
The thankful Citoyens I then exhort 205
To love their hearths, and raise a guardian Fort.
—The Fleet is drawn ashore; in eager Bands
The Settlers cultivate the allotted lands;
And some for Hymeneal rites prepare; ⎫
I plan our new Abodes, fit laws declare; ⎬ 210
But pestilence now came, and tainted the wide air. ⎭
To piteous wasting were our limbs betrayed;
On trees and plants the deadly season preyed.
The men relinquished their dear lives,—or life
Remaining, dragged their frames in feeble strife. 215
Thereafter, Sirius clomb the sultry sky, ⎫
Parch'd every herb to bare sterility; ⎬
And forc'd the sickly corn its nurture to deny. ⎭
My anxious Sire exhorts to seek once more
The Delian shrine, and pardon thence implore; 220
Ask of the God to what these sorrows tend,
Whence we must look for aid, our voyage whither bend.

'Twas night, and couch'd upon the dewy ground
The weary Animals in sleep were bound,
When those Penates which my hands had snatch'd 225
From burning Troy, while on my bed I watch'd,
Appeared, and stood before me, to my sight
Made manifest by copious streams of light
Pour'd from the body of the full-orbed Moon,

That thro' the loop-holes of my chamber shone.   230
Thus did they speak: "We come, the Delegates
Of Phoebus, to foretell thy future fates:
Things which his Delian tripod to thine ear
Would have announced, thro' us he utters here.
When Troy was burnt we crost the billowy sea ⎫   235
Faithful Attendants on thy arms, and *We*   ⎬
Shall raise to Heaven thy proud Posterity.   ⎭
But thou thy destined wanderings stoutly bear,
And for the Mighty, mighty seats prepare;
These thou must leave;—Apollo ne'er design'd   240
That thou in Crete a resting-place should'st find.
There is a Country styled by Men of Greece
Hesperia—strong in arms—the soil of large increase,
Ænotrians held it; men of later fame
Call it Italia, from their Leader's name;   245
Our home is there; there lies the native place
Of Dardanus, and Iasius—whence our race.
Rise then; and to thy aged Father speak
Indubitable tidings;—bid him seek
The Ausonian Land, and Corithus; Jove yields   250
No place to us among Dictean fields."

   Upon the sacred spectacle I gaz'd,
And heard the utterance of the Gods, amaz'd.
Sleep in this visitation had no share;
Each face I saw—the fillets round their hair!   255
Chilled with damp fear I started from the bed,
And raised my hands and voice to heav'n—then shed
On the recipient hearth untemper'd wine
In prompt libation to the powers divine.
This rite performed with joy, my Sire I sought   260
Charged with the message that the Gods had brought;
When I had open'd all in order due
The truth found easy entrance; for he knew
The double Ancestors, the ambiguous race,
And own'd his new mistake in person and in place.   265
Then he exclaim'd "O Son, severely tried
In all that Troy is fated to abide,
This course Cassandra's voice to me made known;
She prophesied of this, and she alone;
Italia oft she cried, and words outthrew   270
Of realms Hesperian, to our Nation due:
But how should Phrygians such a power erect?
Whom did Cassandra's sayings then affect?
Now, let us yield to Phoebus, and pursue

The happier lot he offers to our view."   275
All heard with transport what my Father spake.
This habitation also we forsake;
And strait, a scanty remnant left behind,
Once more in hollow Ships we court the helpful wind.

But when along the Deep our Gallies steer'd,   280
And the last speck of land had disappear'd,
And nought was visible, above, around,
Save the blank sky, and ocean without bound,
Then came a Tempest-laden Cloud that stood
Right over me, and rouz'd the blackening flood.   285
The fleet is scatter'd, while around us rise
Billows that every moment magnifies.
Day fled, and heaven, enveloped in a night
Of stormy rains, is taken from our sight;
By instincts of their own the clouds are riven   290
And prodigal of fire—while we are driven
Far from the points we aim'd at, every bark
Errant upon the waters rough and dark.
Even Palinurus owns that night and day,
Thus in each other lost, confound his way.   295
Three sunless days we struggle with the gales,
And for three starless nights all guidance fails;
The fourth day came, and to our wistful eyes
The far-off Land then first began to rise,
Lifting itself in hills that gently broke   300
Upon our view, and rolling clouds of smoke.
Sails drop; the Mariners, with spring and stoop ⎫
Timed to their oars, the eddying waters scoop, ⎬
The Vessels skim the waves, alive from prow to poop. ⎭

Saved from the perils of the stormy seas,   305
We disembark upon the Strophades;
Amid the Ionian Waters lie this pair
Of Islands, and that Grecian name they bear.
The brood of Harpies, when in fear they left
The doors of Phineus,—of that home bereft   310
And of their former tables—thither fled,
There dwelt with dire Celæno at their head.
No plague so hideous, for impure abuse
Of upper air, did ever Styx produce,
Stirr'd by the anger of the Gods, to fling   315
From out her waves some new-born monstrous Thing.
Birds they, with virgin faces, crooked claws; ⎫
Of filthy paunch and of insatiate maws, ⎬
And pallid mien—from hunger without pause. ⎭

Here safe in port we saw the fields o'erspread 320
With beeves and goats, untended as they fed.
Prompt slaughter follows; offerings there we pay,
And call on Jove himself to share the prey.
Then, couch by couch, along the bay we rear,
And feast well pleased upon that goodly chear. 325
But, clapping loud their wings, the Harpy brood
Rush from the mountain—pounce upon our food,
Pollute the morsels which they fail to seize—
And, screaming, load with noisome scents the breeze.
Again—but now within a long-drawn glade 330
O'erhung with rocks and boughs of roughest shade
We deck our tables, and replace the fire
Upon the Altars; but, with noises dire,
From different points of Heaven, from blind retreats,
They flock—and hovering o'er defile the meats. 335
"War let them have," I cried, and gave command
To stem the next foul onset, arms in hand.
Forthwith the men withdraw from sight their shields
And hide their swords where grass a covert yields,
But when the Harpies with loud clang once more 340
Gathered, and spread upon the curved shore,
From a tall eminence in open view
His trumpet sound of charge Misenus blew;
Then do our swords assault those Fowls obscene,
Of generation aqueous and terrene. 345
But what avails it? oft repeated blows
They with inviolable plumes oppose;
Baffle the steel, and, leaving stains behind
And spoil half eaten, mount upon the wind;
Celæno only on a summit high 350
Perched—and there vented this sad prophecy.

"By war, Descendants of Laomedon!
For our slain Steers, by war would ye atone?
Why seek the blameless Harpies to expel
From regions where by right of birth they dwell? 355
But learn, and fast within your memories hold,⎫
Things which to Phoebus Jupiter foretold, ⎬
Phoebus to me, and I to you unfold,   ⎭
I, greatest of the Furies. Ye, who strive
For Italy, in Italy shall arrive; 360
Havens within that wished-for land, by leave
Of favouring winds, your Navy shall receive;
But do not hope to raise those promised Walls
Ere on your head the curse of hunger falls;

And, for the slaughter of our herds, your doom   365
Hath been your very tables to consume,
Gnaw'd and devour'd thro' utter want of food!"
She spake, and, borne on wings, sought refuge in the wood.

   The haughty spirits of the Men were quail'd,
A shuddering fear thro' every heart prevail'd;   370
On force of arms no longer they rely
To daunt whom prayers and vows must pacify,
Whether to Goddesses the offence were given,
Or they with dire and obscene Birds had striven.
Due Rites ordain'd, as on the shore he stands,   375
My Sire Anchises, with uplifted hands,
Invokes the greater Gods; "Ye Powers, disarm
This threat, and from your Votaries turn the harm!"
Then bids to loose the Cables and unbind
The willing canvas, to the breeze resign'd.   380

   Where guides the Steersman and the south winds urge
Our rapid keels, we skim the foaming surge,
Before us opens midway in the flood
Zacynthus, shaded with luxuriant wood;
Dulichium now, and Same next appears;   385
And Neritos a craggy summit rears;
We shun the rocks of Ithaca, ill Nurse
Of stern Ulysses! and her soil we curse;
Then Mount Leucate shews its vapoury head;
Where, from his temple, Phoebus strikes with dread   390
The passing Mariner; but no mischance
Now fear'd, to that small City we advance;
Gladly we haul the sterns ashore, and throw
The biting Anchor out from every prow.

   Unlook'd-for land thus reach'd, to Jove we raise   395
The votive Altars which with incense blaze;
Our Youth, illustrating the Actian Strand
With Trojan games, as in their native land
Imbue their naked limbs with slippery oil,
And pant for mastery in athletic toil;   400
Well pleas'd so fair a voyage to have shap'd
'Mid Grecian Towns on every side escap'd.
Sol thro' his annual round meanwhile had pass'd,
And the Sea roughened in the wintry blast;
High on the Temple Gate a brazen shield   405
I fixed, which mighty Abbas used to wield;
Inscriptive verse declar'd, why this was done,

"Arms from the conquering Greeks and by Æneas won."
Then at my word the Ships their moorings leave,
And with contending oars the waters cleave;   410
Phæacian Peaks beheld in air and lost
As we proceed, Epirus now we coast;
And, a Chaonian harbour won, we greet
Buthrotas, perch'd upon her lofty seat.

  Helenus, Son of Priam, here was Chief,   415
(So ran the tale ill-fitted for belief),
Govern'd where Grecian Pyrrhus once had reign'd,
Whose sceptre wielding he, therewith, had gain'd
Andromache his Spouse,—to nuptials led
Once more by one whom Troy had borne and bred.   420
I long'd to greet him, wish'd to hear his fate
As his own voice the Story would relate.
So from the Port in which our gallies lay,
Right tow'rds the City I pursu'd my way.
A Grove there was, where by a streamlet's side   425
With the proud name of Simois dignified,
Andromache a solemn service paid,
(As chanc'd that day) invoking Hector's shade;
There did her hands the mournful gifts present
Before a tomb—his empty monument   430
Of living green-sward hallowed by her care; ⎫
And two funereal Altars, planted near,   ⎬
Quicken'd the motion of each falling tear,   ⎭
When my approach she witness'd, and could see
Our Phrygian Arms, she shrank as from a prodigy,   435
In blank astonishment and terror shook,
While the warm blood her tottering limbs forsook.
She swoon'd and long lay senseless on the ground,
Before these broken words a passage found;
"Was that a real Shape which met my view?   440
Son of a Goddess, is thy coming true?
Liv'st thou? or, if the light of life be fled,
Hector, where is he?" This she spake,—then spread
A voice of weeping thro' the Grove, and I
Utter'd these few faint accents in disturb'd reply.   445
"Fear not to trust thine eyes; I live indeed,
And fraught with trouble is the life I lead.
Fallen from the height, where with thy glorious Mate
Thou stood'st, Andromache, what change had Fate
To offer worthy of thy former state?   450
Say, did the Gods take pity on thy vows?
Or have they given to Pyrrhus Hector's Spouse?"

Then she with downcast look, and voice subdu'd;
"Thrice happy Virgin, thou of Priam's blood,
Who, in the front of Troy by timely doom,   455
Did'st pour out life before a hostile tomb;
And, slaughter'd thus, wert guarded from the wrong
Of being swept by lot amid a helpless throng!
O happiest above all who ne'er did press
A conqùering Master's bed, in captive wretchedness!   460
I, since our Ilium fell, have undergone
(Wide waters cross'd) whate'er Achilles' Son
Could in the arrogance of birth impose,
And faced in servitude a Mother's throes.
Hereafter, he at will the knot unty'd,   465
To seek Hermione a Spartan Bride;
And me to Trojan Helenus he gave—
Captive to Captive—if not Slave to Slave.
Whereat, Orestes with strong love inflam'd
Of her now lost whom as a bride he claim'd,   470
And by the Furies driv'n, in vengeful ire
Smote Pyrrhus at the Altar of his Sire.
He, by an unexpected blow, thus slain,
On Helenus devolv'd a part of his Domain,
Who call'd the neighbouring fields Chaonian ground,   475
Chaonia named the Region wide around,
From Trojan Chaon,—chusing for the site
Of a new Pergamus yon rocky height.
But thee a Stranger in a land unknown
What Fates have urg'd ? What winds have hither blown ?   480
Or say what God upon our coasts hath thrown ?
Survives the Boy Ascanius ? In his heart
Doth his lost Mother still retain her part ?
What, Son of great Æneas, brings he forth
In emulation of his Father's worth ?   485
In Priam's Grandchild doth not Hector raise
High hopes to reach the virtue of past days ?"

Then follow'd sobs and lamentations vain;
But from the City, with a numerous train,
Her living Consort Helenus descends;   490
He saw, and gave glad greeting to his Friends;
And tow'rds his hospitable palace leads
While passion interrupts the speech it feeds.
As we advance I gratulate with joy
Their dwindling Xanthus, and their little Troy;   495

470 bride] wife MS.

348   APPENDIX A

Their Pergamus aspiring in proud state,
As if it strove the old to emulate;
And clasp the threshold of their Scaean Gate.
Nor fails this kindred City to excite
In my Associates unreserv'd delight;   500
And soon in ample Porticos the King
Receives the Band with earnest welcoming;
Amid the Hall high festival we hold,
Refresh'd with viands serv'd in massy gold
And from resplendent goblets, votive wine   505
Flows in libations to the Powers divine.

Two joyful days thus past, the southern breeze
Once more invites my Fleet to trust the Seas;
To Helenus this suit I then prefer:
"Illustrious Trojan! Heaven's interpreter!   510
By prescient Phoebus with his spirit fill'd,
Skill'd in the tripod, in the Laurel skill'd;
Skill'd in the stars, and what by voice or wing
Birds to the intelligence of mortals bring;
Now mark:—to Italy my course I bend   515
Urged by the Gods who for this aim portend,
By every sign they give, a happy end.
The Harpy Queen, she only doth presage
A curse of famine in its utmost rage;
Say thou what perils I am first to shun,   520
What course for safe deliverance must be run?"

Then Helenus (the accustom'd Victims slain)
Invoked the Gods their favour to obtain.
This done, he loos'd the fillets from his head,
And took my hand; and, while a holy dread   525
Possess'd me, onward to the Temple led,
Thy Temple, Phoebus!—from his lip then flow'd
Communications of the inspiring God.—
"No common auspices (this truth is plain)
Conduct thee, Son of Venus! o'er the Main;   530
The high behests of Jove this course ordain.
But, that with safer voyage thou may'st reach
The Ausonian harbour, I will clothe in speech
Some portion of the future; Fate hath hung
Clouds o'er the rest, or Juno binds my tongue.   535
And first, *that* Italy, whose coasts appear,
To thy too confident belief, so near,
With havens open for thy sails, a wide
And weary distance doth from thee divide.
501 Soon in a spacious Portico MS.

Trinacrian waves shall bend the pliant oar;   540
Thou, thro' Ausonian gulphs, a passage must explore,
Trace the Circean Isle, the infernal Pool,
Before thy City rise for stedfast rule.
Now mark these Signs, and store them in thy mind;⎫
When, anxiously reflecting, thou shalt find   ⎬   545
A bulky Female of the bristly Kind   ⎭
On a sequester'd river's margin laid,
Where Ilex branches do the ground o'ershade,
With thirty young ones couch'd in that Recess,
White as the pure white Dam whose teats they press,   550
There found thy City;—on *that* soil shall close
All thy solicitudes, in fixed repose.
Nor dread Celaeno's threat, the Fates shall clear
The way, and at thy call Apollo interfere.
But shun those Lands where our Ionian sea   555
Washes the nearest shores of Italy.
On all the coasts malignant Greeks abide;
Narycian Locrians there a Town have fortified;
Idomeneus of Crete hath compassed round
With soldiery the Sallentinian ground;   560
There, when Thessalian Philoctetes chose
His resting-place, the small Petilia rose.
And when, that sea past over, thou shalt stand
Before the Altars, kindled on the strand,
While to the Gods are offer'd up thy vows,   565
Then in a purple veil enwrap thy brows,
And sacrifice thus cover'd, lest the sight
Of any hostile face disturb the rite.
Be this observance kept by thee and thine,
And this to late posterity consign!   570
But when by favouring breezes wafted o'er
Thy Fleet approaches the Sicilian shore,
And dense Pelorus gradually throws
Its barriers open to invite thy prows,
That passage shunn'd, thy course in safety keep   575
By steering to the left, with ample sweep.

" 'Tis said when heaving Earth of yore was rent
This ground forsook the Hesperian Continent;
Nor doubt, that power to work such change might lie
Within the grasp of dark Antiquity.   580

543 stedfast] settled MS.   548 On ground which Ilex branches
overshade MS.   552 Thy cares and labours in assured repose MS.
554 . . . and Phoebus at thy call appear MS.   566 Then cast a purple
amice o'er MS.

Then flow'd the sea between, and, where the force
Of roaring waves establish'd the divorce,
Still, thro' the Straits, the narrow waters boil,
Dissevering Town from Town, and soil from soil.
Upon the right the dogs of Scylla fret;   585
The left by fell Charybdis is beset;
Thrice tow'rds the bottom of a vast abyss
Down, headlong down the liquid precipice
She sucks the whirling billows, and, as oft,
Ejecting, sends them into air aloft.   590
But Scylla, pent within her Cavern blind,
Thrusts forth a visage of our human kind,
And draws the Ship on rocks; She, fair in show,
A woman to the waist, is foul below;
A huge Sea-Beast—with Dolphin tails, and bound   595
With water Wolves and Dogs her middle round!
But Thou against this jeopardy provide
Doubling Pachynus with a circuit wide;
Thus shapeless Scylla may be left unseen,
Unheard the yelling of the brood marine.   600
But, above all if Phoebus I revere
Not unenlighten'd, an authentic Seer,
Then, Goddess-born, (on this could I enlarge
Repeating oft and oft the solemn charge)
Adore imperial Juno, freely wait   ⎫   605
With gifts on Juno's Altar, supplicate   ⎬
Her potent favour, and subdue her hate;   ⎭
So shalt thou seek, a Conqueror at last,
The Italian shore, Trinacrian dangers past!
Arrived at Cumae and the sacred floods   610
Of black Avernus resonant with woods,
Thou shalt behold the Sybil where She sits ⎫
Within her cave, rapt in extatic fits,   ⎬
And words and characters to leaves commits.⎭
The prophecies which on those leaves the Maid   615
Inscribes, are by her hands in order laid
'Mid the secluded Cavern, where they fill
Their several places, undisturb'd and still.
But if a light wind entering thro' the door
Scatter the thin leaves on the rocky floor,   620
She to replace her prophecies will use
No diligence; all flutter where they chuse,
In hopeless disconnection loose and wild;

608-9 So shalt thou reach (Sicilian limits past)
      The Italian shore, a conqueror at last. MS. D. W.

And they, who sought for knowledge, thus beguil'd
Of her predictions, from the cave depart,   625
And quit the Sybil with a murmuring heart.
But thou, albeit ill-dispos'd to wait,
And prizing moments at their highest rate,
Tho' Followers chide, and ever and anon
The flattering winds invite thee to be gone,   630
Beg of the moody Prophetess to break
The silent air, and for thy guidance speak.
She will disclose the features of thy doom,
The Italian Nations, and the Wars to come;
How to escape from hardships, or endure,   ⎫   635
And make a happy termination sure;   ⎬
Enough—chains bind the rest, or clouds obscure.   ⎭
Go then, nor in thy glorious progress halt,
But to the stars the Trojan name exalt!"

So spake the friendly Seer, from hallow'd lips,   640
Then orders sumptuous presents to the Ships;
Smooth ivory, massy gold, with pond'rous store
Of vases fashion'd from the paler ore;
And Dodonaean Cauldrons, nor withholds
The golden halberk, knit in triple folds,   645
That Neoptolemus erewhile had worn;
Nor his resplendent crest which waving plumes adorn.
Rich offerings also grace my Father's hands;
Horses he adds with Equerries, and Bands
Of Rowers, and supply of Arms commands.   650
—Meanwhile Anchises bids the Fleet unbind
Its sails for instant seizure of the wind.
The Interpreter of Phoebus then address'd
This gracious farewell to his ancient Guest;
"Anchises! to celestial honors led,   655
Beloved of Venus, whom she deign'd to wed,
Care of the Gods, twice snatch'd from Ilium lost,
Now for Ausonia be these waters cross'd!
Yet must thou only glide along the shores
To which I point; far lies the Land from ours   660
Whither Apollo's voice directs your powers:
Go, happy Parent of a pious Son,
No more—I baulk the winds that press thee on."

638-9 Go then; and high as heaven's ethereal vault
      The Trojan name by glorious deeds exalt. MS. D. W.
641   . . . orders Presents to our parting Ships. MS. D. W.   659 Yet
only hope to MS. D. W.

Nor less Andromache, disturb'd in heart
That parting now, we must for ever part,   665
Embroider'd Vests of golden thread bestows;
A Phrygian Tunic o'er Ascanius throws;
And studious that her bounty may become
The occasion, adds rich labours of the loom;
"Dear Child," she said, "these also, to be kept   670
As the memorials of my hand, accept!
Last gifts of Hector's Consort, let them prove
To thee the symbols of enduring love;
Take what Andromache at parting gives,
Fair Boy!—sole Image that for me survives   675
Of my Astyanax,—in whom his face,
His eyes are seen, his very hands I trace;
And now, but for obstruction from the tomb,
His years had open'd into kindred bloom."
To these, while gushing tears bedew'd my cheek,   680
Thus in the farewell moment did I speak:
"Live happy Ye, whose race of fortune run
Permits such life; from trials undergone
We to the like are call'd, by you is quiet won.
No seas have Ye to measure, nor on you   685
Is it impos'd Ausonia to pursue,
And search for fields still flying from the view.
Lo Xanthus here in miniature!—there stands
A second Troy, the labour of your hands,
With happier auspices—in less degree   690
Exposed, I trust, to Grecian enmity.
If Tiber e'er receive me, and the sod
Of Tiber's meadows by these feet be trod,
If e'er I see our promis'd City rise,
These neighbouring Nations bound by ancient ties   695
Hesperian and Epirian, whose blood came
From Dardanus, whose lot hath been the same,
Shall make one Troy in spirit. May that care
To our Descendants pass from heir to heir!"

We coast the high Ceraunia, whence is found   700
The shortest transit to Italian ground;

678-9 And his unfolding youth with thine kept pace MS. D. W.
683-4   *one* peril if we shun
       'Tis but to meet a worse: by you is Quiet won. MS. D. W.
688-9 Before your sight a mimic Xanthus flows;
       By your own hands the Troy that guards you rose MS. D. W.
694-5 If e'er our destined City I behold,
       Then neighbouring Towns, and Tribes akin of old MS. D. W.

Meanwhile the sun went down, and shadows spread
O'er every mountain dark'ned to its head.
Tired of their oars the Men no sooner reach
Earth's wish'd-for bosom than their limbs they stretch   705
On the dry margin of the murmuring Deep,
Where weariness is lost in timely sleep.
Ere Night, whose Car the Hours had yok'd and rein'd,
Black Night, the middle of her orbit gain'd,
Up from his couch did Palinurus rise,   ⎫   710
Looks to the wind for what it signifies,   ⎬
And to each breath of air a watchful ear applies.   ⎭
Next all the Stars gliding thro' silent Heaven
The Bears, Arcturus, and the cluster'd Seven,
Are noted,—and his ranging eyes behold   715
Magnificent Orion arm'd in gold.
When he perceives that all things low and high
Unite to promise fix'd serenity,
He sends the summons forth; our Camp we raise,—
Are gone,—and every Ship her broadest wings displays.   720

  Now, when Aurora redden'd in a sky   ⎫
From which the Stars had vanish'd, we descry   ⎬
The low faint hills of distant Italy.   ⎭
"Italia!" shouts Achates; round and round   ⎫
"Italia" flies with gratulant rebound,   ⎬   725
From all who see the coast, or hear the happy sound. ⎭
Not slow is Sire Anchises to entwine
With wreaths a goblet, which he fill'd with wine,
Then, on the Stern he took his lofty stand,
And cried, "Ye Deities of sea and land   730
Thro' whom the Storms are govern'd, speed our way
By breezes docile to your kindliest sway!"
—With freshening impulse breathe the wish'd-for gales,
And, as the Ships press on with greedy sails,
Opens the Port; and, peering into sight,   735
Minerva's Temple tops a craggy height.
The Sails are furl'd by many a busy hand;
The veering prows are pointed to the Strand.
Curved into semblance of a bow, the Haven
Looks to the East; but not a wave thence driven   740

704–7 Eased of the oar, upon earth's wished-for breast
        We seek refreshment and prepare for rest MS. D. W.
        We press the bosom of the wished for land;
        And, as we lay dispers'd along the Strand,
        Our bodies we refresh and dewy sleep
        Fell upon weary limbs beside the lulling deep. MS. W.W.

Disturbs its peacefulness; their foamy spray
Breaks upon jutting rocks that fence the Bay.
Two towering cliffs extend with gradual fall
Their arms into the Sea, and frame a wall
In whose embrace the harbour hidden lies; }   745
And, as its shelter deepens on our eyes,
Back from the shore Minerva's Temple flies.

   Four snow-white Horses, grazing the wide fields,
Are the first omen which our landing yields;
Then Sire Anchises—"War thy tokens bear   750
O Hospitable land! The Horse is arm'd for war;
War do these menace, but as Steed with Steed
Oft joins in friendly yoke, the sight may breed
Fair hope that peace and concord will succeed."
To Pallas then in clanking armour mail'd,   755
Who hail'd us first, exulting to be hail'd,
Prayers we address—with Phrygian amice veil'd;
And, as by Helenus enjoin'd, the fire
On Juno's Altar fumes—to Juno vows aspire.
When we had ceas'd this service to present   760
That instant, seaward are our Sail-yards bent,
And we forsake the Shore—with cautious dread
Of ground by Native Grecians tenanted.

   The Bay is quickly reach'd that draws its name
From proud Tarentum, proud to share the fame   765
Of Hercules tho' by a dubious claim:
Right opposite we ken the Structure holy
Of the Lacinian Goddess rising slowly;
Next the Caulonian Citadel appear'd
And the Scylacian bay for Shipwrecks fear'd;   770
Lo, as along the open Main we float,
Mount Etna, yet far off! and far remote
Groans of the Sea we hear;—deep groans and strokes
Of angry billows beating upon rocks;
And hoarse surf-clamours,—while the flood throws up   775
Sands from the depths of its unsettled cup.
My Sire exclaim'd, "Companions, we are caught
By fell Charybdis,—flee as ye were taught;
These, doubtless, are the rocks, the dangerous shores
Which Helenus denounc'd—away—with straining oars."   780
Quick, to the left the Master Galley veers
With roaring prow, as Palinurus steers;
And for the left the bands of Rowers strive,
While every help is caught that winds can give.

The whirlpool's dizzy altitudes we scale,   785
For ghastly sinking when the waters fail.
The hollow rocks thrice gave a fearful cry ;   ⎫
Three times we saw the clashing waves fling high   ⎬
Their foam dispers'd along a drizzling sky.   ⎭
The flagging wind forsook us with the sun,   790
And to Cyclopian shores a darkling course we run.

  The Port, which now we chance to enter, lies
By winds unruffl'd tho' of ample size ;
But all too near is Etna, thundering loud ;
And ofttimes casting up a pitchy cloud   795
Of smoke—in whirling convolutions driven,
With weight of hoary ashes, high as heaven,
And globes of flame ; and sometimes he gives vent
To rocky fragments, from his entrails rent ;
And hurls out melting substances—that fly   800
In thick assemblage, and confound the sky ;
While groans and lamentations burthensome
Tell to the air from what a depth they come.
The enormous Mass of Etna, so 'tis said,
On lightening-scorch'd Enceladus was laid ;   805
And ever pressing on the Giant's frame,
Breathes out, from fractur'd chimneys, fitful flame,
And, often as he turns his weary side   ⎫
Murmuring Trinacria trembles far and wide,   ⎬
While wreaths of smoke ascend and all the welkin hide. ⎭   810
We, thro' the night, enwrapp'd in woods obscure,
The shock of those dire prodigies endure,
Nor could distinguish whence might come the sound ;
For all the stars to ether's utmost bound
Were hidden or bedimm'd, and Night withheld   815
The Moon, in mist and lowering fogs conceal'd.
                    [*Desunt* ll. 588–706]
Those left, we harbour'd on the joyless coast
Of Drepanum, here harass'd long and toss'd,
And here my Sire Anchises did I lose,
Help in my cares, and solace of my woes.   820
Here, O best Father ! best beloved and best
Didst thou desert me when I needed rest,
Thou, from so many perils snatch'd in vain :
Not Helenus, though much in doleful strain
He prophesied, this sorrow did unfold,   825
Not dire Celaeno this distress foretold.
This trouble was my last ; Celestial Powers
O Queen, have brought me to your friendly shores."

—Sole speaker, thus Æneas did relate
To a hush'd audience the decrees of Fate,   830
His wandering course remeasur'd, till the close
Now reach'd, in silence here he found repose.

IV. 688-92

SHE who to lift her heavy eyes had tried
Faints while the deep wound gurgles at her side
Thrice on her elbow propp'd she strove to uphold
Her frame—thrice back upon the couch was roll'd,
Then with a wandering eye in heaven's blue round
She sought the light and groaned when she had found.

VIII. 337-66

THIS scarcely utter'd they advance, and straight
He shews the Altar and Carmental Gate,
Which (such the record) by its Roman name
Preserves the nymph Carmenta's ancient fame,
Who first the glories of the Trojan line   5
Predicted, and the noble Pallantine.
Next points he out an ample sylvan shade
Which Romulus a fit asylum made,
Turns thence, and bids Æneas fix his eyes ⎫
Where under a chill rock Lupercal lies   ⎬   10
Named from Lycaean Pan, in old Arcadian guise. ⎭
Nor left he unobserv'd the neighbouring wood
Of sacred Argiletum, stained with blood.
There Argos fell, his guest—the story told,
To the Tarpeian Rock their way they hold   15
And to the Capitol now bright with gold,—
In those far-distant times a spot forlorn
With brambles choked and rough with savage thorn.
Even then an influence of religious awe
The rustics felt, subdued by what they saw,   20
The local spirit creeping thro' their blood,
Even then they fear'd the rocks, they trembled at the wood.
"This grove (said he) this leaf-crown'd hill—some God
How nam'd we know not, takes for his abode,
The Arcadians think that Jove himself aloft   25
Hath here declared his presence oft and oft,
Shaking his lurid Ægis in their sight
And covering with fierce clouds the stormy height.
Here also see two mouldering towns that lie
Mournful remains of buried ancestry ;   30
That Citadel did father Janus frame,
And Saturn this, each bears the Founder's name.

Conversing thus their onward course they bent
To poor Evander's humble tenement;
Herds range the Roman Forum; in the street   35
Of proud Carinae bellowing herds they meet;
When they had reach'd the house, he said "This gate
Conquering Alcides enter'd, his plain state
This palace lodg'd; O guest, like him forbear
To frown on scanty means and homely fare;   40
Dare riches to despise; with aim as high
Mount thou, and train thyself for Deity."

This said, thro' that low door he leads his guest,
The great Æneas, to a couch of rest.
There propp'd he lay on withered leaves, o'erspread   45
With a bear's skin in Libyan desarts bred.

Georgic IV. 511–15

Even so bewails, the Poplar groves among,
Sad Philomela her evanished young;
Whom the harsh Rustic from the nest hath torn,
An unfledged brood; but on the bough forlorn   50
She sits, in mournful darkness all night long;
Renews, and still renews, her doleful song,
And fills the leafy grove, complaining of her wrong.

APPENDIX B

POEMS EITHER NEVER PRINTED BY WORDSWORTH
OR NOT INCLUDED IN THE EDITION 1849–50

(Poems to which no date of first printing is prefixed are here given for the first time)

I. FROM THE ALFOXDEN NOTEBOOK

[Composed 1798 ?]

AWAY, away, it is the air
That stirs among the wither'd leaves;
Away, away, it is not there,
Go, hunt among the harvest sheaves.
There is a bed in shape as plain   5
As from a hare or lion's lair
It is the bed where we have lain
In anguish and despair.

Away, and take the eagle's eye,
The tyger's smell,   10

I. 6 lair] lare MS.

Ears that can hear the agonies
And murmurings of hell;
And when you there have stood
By that same bed of pain,
The groans are gone, the tears remain.   15
Then tell me if the thing be clear,
The difference betwixt a tear
Of water and of blood.

CHAUCER MODERNISED

II. THE MANCIPLE

From *The Prologue.*

[Translated December, 1801.]

A MANCIPLE there was, one of a Temple
Of whom all caterers might take example
Wisely to purchase stores, whate'er the amount,
Whether he paid, or took them on account.
So well on every bargain did he wait,   5
He was beforehand aye in good estate.
Now is not that of God a full fair grace
That one man's natural sense should so surpass
The wisdom of a heap of learned men ?

Of masters he had more than three times ten   10
That were in law expert and curious,
Of which there was a dozen in that house
Fit to be steward over land and rent
For any Lord in England, competent
Each one to make him live upon his own   15
In debtless honour, were his wits not flown;
Or sparely live, even to his heart's desire;
Men who would give good help to a whole Shire
In every urgent case that might befal,
Yet could this Manciple outwit them all.   20

THE MANCIPLE'S TALE

When Phoebus took delight on earth to dwell
Among mankind, as ancient stories tell,
He was the blithest bachelor, I trow,
Of all this world, and the best archer too.
He slew the serpent Python as he lay   5
Sleeping against the sun upon a day,

II. 8 mother-wit *corr. to text* MS.   13 All worthy to be stewards *corr. to
text* MS.

THE MANCIPLE'S TALE

1-2 When Phoebus here below on earth did dwell
    As ancient histories to us do tell MS. 1

And many another noble worthy deed
Wrought with his bow as men the same may read.
He played, all music played on earthly ground,
And 'twas a melody to hear the sound   10
Of his clear voice, so sweetly would he sing.
Certes Amphion, that old Theban king
Who wall'd a city with his minstrelsy,
Was never heard to sing so sweet as he.
Therewith this Phoebus was the seemliest man   15
That is or hath been since the world began.
His features to describe I need not strive;
For in this world is none so fair alive.
He was moreover, full of gentleness,
Of honour and of perfect·worthiness.   20

This Phoebus, flower in forest and in court,
This comely Bachelor for his disport
And eke in token of his victory earned
Of Python, as is from the story learned,
Was wont to carry in his hand a bow.   25
Now had this Phoebus in his house a Crow
Which in a cage he fostered many a day
And taught to speak as men will teach a jay.
White was this Crow as is a snow-white Swan,
And counterfeit the speech of every man   30
He could, when he had mind to tell a tale;
Besides, in all the world no Nightingale
Could ring out of his heart so blithe a peal;
No, not a hundred thousandth part as well.

Now had this Phoebus in his house a Wife   35
Whom he loved better than he loved his life;
And, night and day, he strove with diligence
To please her, and to do her reverence,
Save only, for 'tis truth, the noble Elf
Was jealous, and would keep her to himself.   40
For he was loth a laughing stock to be,
And so is every wight in like degree;
But all for nought, for it availeth nought,
A good Wife that is pure in deed and thought
Should not be kept in watch and ward,—and, do   45
The best you may, you cannot keep a Shrew.
It will not be—vain labour is it wholly;
Lordings, this hold I for an arrant folly

36 And her he loved better than his life MS. 1   42 in like degree]
as loth as he MS. 1

Labour to waste in custody of wives;
And so old Clerks have written in their lives.   50

But to my purpose as I first began.
This worthy Phoebus doeth all he can
To please her, weening that through such delight
And of his government and manhood's right
No man should ever put him from her grace,   55
But Man's best plans, God knoweth, in no case
Shall compass to constrain a thing which nature
Hath naturally implanted in a creature.

Take any bird and put it in a cage
And wait upon this bird as nurse or page   60
To feed it tenderly with meat and drink
And every dainty whereof thou canst think,
And also keep it cleanly as thou may;
Altho' the cage of gold be never so gay
Yet hath the Bird by twenty thousand fold   65
Rather in forest that is wild and cold
Go feed on worms and such like wretchedness,
For ever will this Bird do more or less
To escape out of his cage whene'er he may;
His liberty the Bird desireth aye.   70

Go take a Cat and nourish her with milk
And tender flesh, and make her couch of silk,
And let her see a mouse go by the wall,
Anon she waiveth milk and flesh and all
And every dainty which is in the house,   75
Such appetite hath she to eat the mouse.
Behold the domination here of kind,
Appetite drives discretion from her mind.

A she-wolf also in her kind is base;
Meets she the sorriest wolf in field or chase   80
Him will she take—what matters his estate
In time when she hath liking to a mate?

Examples all for men that are untrue.
With women I have nothing now to do:
For men have still a wayward appetite   85
With lower things to seek for their delight

54 of] for MS. 1   56 But no man in good truth in any case MS. 1
60 And to this little bird thyself engage MS. 1   66 Lever MS. 1
77–8 Lo! here the domination of her kind,
        And appetite drives judgement from her mind. MS. 1
85 wayward] liquorish *corr. to* froward MS. 1   86 seek for] accomplish MS. 1

Than with their wives, albeit women fair
Never so true, never so debonnair.
All flesh is so newfangled, plague upon't
That are we pleased with aught on whose clear front　　90
Virtue is stampt, 'tis but for a brief while.

This Phoebus, he that thought upon no guile,
Deceived was for all his jollity;
For under him another one had she,
One of small note and little thought upon,　　95
Nought worth to Phoebus in comparison.
The more harm is, it happeneth often so
Of which there cometh mickle harm and woe.

And so befel as soon as Phoebus went
From home, his wife hath for her lemman sent,　　100
Her Lemman, certes that's a knavish speech;
Forgive it me and that I you beseech.

Plato the wise hath said, as ye may read,
The word must needs be suited to the deed;
No doubtful meanings in a tale should lurk,　　105
The word must aye be cousin to the work;
I am a bold blunt man, I speak out plain
There is no difference truly, not a grain,
Between a wife that is of high degree
(If of her body she dishonest be)　　110
And every low-born wench no more than this
(If it so be that both have done amiss)
That, as the gentle is in state above,
She shall be called his Lady and his Love
And that the other a poor woman is　　115
She shall be called his harlot and his miss.
And yet, in very truth, mine own dear brother,
Men lay as low that one as lieth that other.
Right so betwixt a haughty tyrant chief
And a rough outlaw or an errant thief,　　120

90-2 That when we might be happy, then we won't,
　　(That with plain virtue and her open front
　　We can take pleasure only a short while *deleted*)
　　But to my tale which I have left a while.
　　This worthy Phoebus, thinking of no guile　MS. 1
94 one] choice　MS. 1
99-100 . . . when Phoebus was from home
　　　　His Wife anon hath bid her Lemman come　MS. 1
105-6 Tell a thing rightly, Englishman or Turk,
　　In things told rightly no vague meanings lurk　MS. 1
107 bold blunt] boistrous　MS. 1　　　117 in God's good truth　MS. 1
119 . . . an outlaw, Robber chief,
　　Untitled tyrant, and an errant thief　MS. 1

The same I say, no difference I hold,
(To Alexander was this sentence told)
But, for the Tyrant is of greater might
By force of multitudes to slay downright
And burn both house and home, and make all plain,   125
Lo! therefore Captain is he called; again
Since the other heads a scanty company
And may not do so great a harm as he,
Or lay upon the land such heavy grief
Men christen him an Outlaw or a Thief.   130

But I'm no man of texts and instances,
Therefore I will not give you much of these
But with my tale go on as I was bent.

When Phoebus' wife had for her lemman sent
In their loose dalliance they anon engage;   135
This white Crow, that hung alway in the cage,
Beheld the shame, and did not say one word;
But soon as home was come Phoebus, the Lord,
The Crow sang Cuckow, Cuckow, Cuckow, "How
What! Bird", quoth Phoebus, "what song singst thou now,
Wert thou not wont to sing as did rejoice   141
My inmost heart, so merrily thy voice
Greeted my ear, alas, what song is this?"
"So help me Gods, I do not sing amiss,
Phoebus," quoth he, " for all thy worthiness,   145
For all thy beauty and all thy gentleness,
For all thy song and all thy minstrelsy,
For all thy waiting, hoodwinked is thine eye
By one we know not whom, we know not what,
A man to thee no better than a gnat,   150
For I full plainly as I hope for life
Saw him in guilty converse with thy wife."

What would you more, the Crow when he him told
By serious tokens and words stout and bold
How that his wife had played a wanton game   155
To his abasement, and exceeding shame,

133–4 I to my tale will go as I began.
    When Phoebus' wife had sent for her Lemman MS. 1
135 They took their fill of love and lover's rage MS. 1 *corr. to* To love's
delights themselves they did engage
137 Beheld their work MS. 1
141–3 Whilom thou wont so merrily to sing
    That to my heart it should great gladness bring
    To hear thy voice MS. 1
144 By all the Saints MS. 1   156 Him to abase, and cover with great
shame MS. 1

And told him oft he saw it with his eyes,
Then Phoebus turned away in woeful guise
Him thought his heart would burst in two with sorrow,
His bow he bent, and set therein an arrow,   160
And in his anger he his wife did slay;
This is the effect, there is no more to say.
For grief of which he brake his minstrelsy
Both lute and harp, guitar and psaltery,
And also brake his arrows and his bow   165
And after that thus spake he to the Crow.

"Thou Traitor! with thy scorpion tongue," quoth he,
"To my confusion am I brought by thee.
Why was I born, why have I yet a life
O wife, O gem of pleasure, O dear wife,   170
That wert to me so stedfast and so true,
Now dead thou liest with face pale of hue
Full innocent, that durst I swear, I wis.
O thou rash hand that wrought so far amiss,
O reckless outrage, O disordered wit   175
That unadvised didst the guiltless smite,
What in my false suspicion have I done,
Why thro' mistrust was I thus wrought upon?

"Let every Man beware and keep aloof
From rashness, and trust only to strong proof;   180
Smite not too soon before ye have learnt why,
And be advised well and stedfastly,
Ere ye to any execution bring
Yourselves from wrath or surmise of a thing.
Alas! A thousand folk hath ire laid low   185
Fully undone and brought to utter woe,
Alas for sorrow I myself will slay."

And to the Crow, "O vile wretch," did he say,
"Now will I thee requite for thy false tale.
Whilom thou sang like any Nightingale,   190
Henceforth, false thief, thy song from thee is gone
And vanished thy white feathers, every one.
In all thy life thou nevermore shalt speak
Thus on a traitor I men's wrongs do wreak.

159–60 Him thought his woeful heart would burst in two,
    His bow he took, an arrow forth he drew MS. 1
174 thou rash] senseless MS. 1   178 Where was my wit? Why was
I wrought upon? MS. 1   180 From rashness trusting nought without ... MS. 1   184 Yourselves upon your anger at the thing MS. 1
187 sorrow] anger MS. 1   194 do I vengeance wreak MS. 1

Thou and thy offspring ever shall be black,   195
Never again sweet noises shall ye make,
But ever cry against the storm and rain
In token that through thee my Wife is slain."

And to the Crow he sprang and that anon
And plucking his white feathers left not one   200
And made him black, and took from him his song,
And eke his speech, and out of doors him flung
Unto perdition, whither let him go
And for this very reason, you must know,
Black is the colour now of every Crow.   205

Lordings, by this example you I pray
Beware and take good heed of what you say,
Nor ever tell a man in all your life
That he hath got a false and slippery wife;
His deadly hatred till his life's last day   210
You will provoke. Dan Solomon, Clerks say,
For keeping well his tongue hath rules good store,
But I'm no textman, as I said before,
Nathless this teaching had I from my Dame.
My son, think of the Crow in God's good name.   215
My son, full often times hath mickle speech
Brought many a man to ruin, as Clerks teach,
But 'tis not often words bring harm to men
Spoken advisedly, and now and then.
My son be like the wise man who restrains   220
His tongue at all times, save when taking pains
To speak of God in honour, and in prayer.
'Tis the first virtue, and the one most rare,
My son, to keep the tongue with proper care.
Wouldst thou be told what a rash tongue can do,   225
Right as a sword cutteth an arm in two
So can a tongue, my child, a friendship sever,
Parted in two to be disjoined for ever.
A babbler is to God abominable.
Read Solomon so wise and honourable,   230
Read Seneca, the Psalms of David read,
Speak not, dear son, but beckon with thy head,
Make show that thou wert deaf if any prater
Do in thy hearing touch a perilous matter;

200 And stripp'd off his white feathers every one MS. 1
203 perdition] the devil MS. 1   210 deadly] mortal MS. 1
218 often] oft that MS. 1   229 babbler] Jangler MS. 1

The Fleming taught, and learn it if thou list,   235
That little babbling causeth mickle rest.
My son, if thou no wicked word have said
Then need'st thou have no fear to be betrayed,
But who misspeaks, whatever may befal,
Cannot by any means his word recal.   240
Thing that is said, *is* said, goes forth anon,
Howe'er we grieve repenting, it is gone,
The tale-bearer's his slave to whom he said
The thing for which he now is fitly paid.
My son, beware, and be not Author new   245
Of tidings, whether they be false or true.
Where'er thou travel, among high or low,
Keep well thy tongue, and think upon the Crow.

III.   FRAGMENTS FROM MS. M

[Composed 1802.]

(i)

I HAVE been here in the Moon-light,
I have been here in the Day,
I have been here in the Dark Night,
And the Stream was still roaring away.

(ii)

These Chairs they have no words to utter,
No fire is in the grate to stir or flutter,
The cieling and floor are mute as a stone,
My chamber is hush'd and still,
     And I am alone,
     Happy and alone.

Oh who would be afraid of life,
The passion the sorrow and the strife,
     When he may be
     Shelter'd so easily ?
May lie in peace on his bed
Happy as they who are dead.

Half an hour afterwards

I have thoughts that are fed by the sun.
     The things which I see
     Are welcome to me,
     Welcome every one:

239 But he that hath mis-said whate'er befal MS. 1

I do not wish to lie
　　Dead, dead,
Dead without any company;
　　Here alone on my bed,
With thoughts that are fed by the Sun,
And hopes that are welcome every one,
　　Happy am I.

O Life, there is about thee
A deep delicious peace,
I would not be without thee,
　　Stay, oh stay!
Yet be thou ever as now,
Sweetness and breath with the quiet of death,
Be but thou ever as now,
　　Peace, peace, peace.

IV. THE TINKER

[Composed April 27–9, 1802.—First printed in 1897.]

Who leads a happy life
If it's not the merry Tinker,
Not too old to have a Wife;
Not too much a thinker?
Through the meadows, over stiles,　　　　5
Where there are no measured miles,
Day by day he finds his way
Among the lonely houses:
Right before the Farmer's door
Down he sits; his brows he knits;　　　　10
Then his hammer he rouzes;
Batter! batter! batter!
He begins to clatter;
And while the work is going on
Right good ale he bouzes;　　　　15
And, when it is done, away he is gone;
　　And, in his scarlet coat,
　　With a merry note,
　　He sings the sun to bed;
　　And, without making a pother,　　　　20
Finds some place or other
For his own careless head.

When in the woods the little fowls
Begin their merry-making,
Again the jolly Tinker bowls　　　　25
Forth with small leave-taking:

Through the valley, up the hill;
He can't go wrong, go where he will:
   Tricks he has twenty,
    And pastimes in plenty;   30
He's the terror of boys in the midst of their noise;

When the market Maiden,
Bringing home her lading,
Hath pass'd him in a nook,
With his outlandish look,   35
And visage grim and sooty,
Bumming, bumming, bumming,
What is that that's coming?
Silly maid as ever was!
She thinks that she and all she has   40
Will be the Tinker's booty;
At the pretty Maiden's dread
The Tinker shakes his head,
Laughing, laughing, laughing,
As if he would laugh himself dead.   45
And thus, with work or none,
The Tinker lives in fun,
With a light soul to cover him;
And sorrow and care blow over him,
Whether he's up or a-bed.   50

V. TRANSLATION OF ARIOSTO

[*Orlando Furioso*, i. 5–14]

[Translated November 1802.]

ORLANDO who great length of time had been
Enamour'd of the fair Angelica;
And left for her beyond the Indian sea,
In Media, Tartary and lands between
Infinite trophies to endure for aye,   5
Now to the west with her had bent his way
Where, underneath the lofty Pyrenees,
With might of French and Germans, Charlemagne
Had pitch'd his tents upon the open plain.

To make Marsilius and king Agramont   10
Each for his senseless daring smite his head,
The one for having out of Afric led
As many as could carry spear or lance,
Th'other for pushing all Spain militant

To overthrow the beauteous realm of France;   15
Thus in fit time Orlando reach'd the tents
But of his coming quickly he repents.

For there to him was his fair Lady lost,
Taken away! how frail our judgments are
She who from western unto eastern coast   20
[   ]¹ with so long a war
Was taken from him now 'mid such a band
Of his own friends and in his native land,
Not one sword drawn to help the thing or bar!
'Twas the sage Emperor wishing much to slake   25
A burning feud who did the Lady take.

For quarrels had sprung lately and yet were
Twixt Count Orlando and Rinaldo: wroth
Were the two kinsmen, for that beauty rare
With amorous desire had mov'd them both.   30
The Emperor Charles who look'd with little favour
On such contention, to make fast the aid
The two Knights ow'd him, took away the Maid
And to Duke Namo he in wardship gave her,

Promising her to him who of the two,   35
During that contest on that mighty day,
The greatest host of Infidels should slay
And most excelling feats in battle do;
But the baptiz'd, who look'd not for such fate,
On that day's conflict fled their foes before;   40
The Duke a prisoner was with many more
And the Pavillion was left desolate.

Wherein, the Lady (as it were in thrall
Remaining there to be the Victor's prize)
Mounted, to meet such chance as might befall,   45
Her courser, and at length away she flies.
Presaging Fortune would the Christian faith
Disown that day, into a wood she hies,
Where she a knight on foot encountered hath
Who was approaching on a narrow path.   50

Helmet on head and cuirass on his back,
Sword by his side and on his arm his shield,
He ran more lightly on the forest track
Than swain half naked racing in the field;

¹ MS. defective.

Never did Shepherdess when she hath spied 55
A snake turn round so quickly in her fear
As drew Angelica the rein aside
When she beheld the knight approaching near.

This was that doughty Paladin, the Son
Of Amon Lord of Montalban in France, 60
From whom his steed Bayardo, by strange chance,
Had slipp'd not long before and loose had run.
Soon as he to the Lady turn'd his eyes,
Though distant, he that mien angelical
And that fair countenance did recognize, 65
Whereby his knightly heart was held in thrall.

The affrighted Lady turn'd her Horse around
And drove him with loose bridle through the wood,
Nor e'er in rough or smooth did she take thought
If safer way or better might be found; 70
But pale, and trembling, taking her of nought
She left the horse to find what way he could;
Now up now down along the forest fast
She drove, and to a river came at last.

There was Ferráno on the river brink 75
All overspread with dust and faint with heat;
Who thither from the fight had come to drink
And to repose himself in this retreat;
And there, though loth, he was compelled to stay;
His helmet, while with thirst he drank amain, 80
Had slipp'd into the river where it lay,
Nor could he yet recover it again.

VI. TRANSLATIONS FROM METASTASIO
[Composed after 1802.]

    i. To the grove, the meadow, the Well
        I will go with the flock I love;
        By the Well, in the meadow, the grove
        My Goddess will find with me
        Whatever shed or cell
        Shall to us a cover be
        That there with pleasure and glee
        Innocence will dwell.

    ii. The Swallow that hath lost
         His Mate and Lover
         Flies from coast to coast
         All the country over

Nor finds rest on earth beneath him
Pastime in heaven above:
Chrystal fountain, sunny river
Seeks no more, forsakes the daylight
And in his lonesome life he ever
Remembers his first love.

iii. Oh bless'd all bliss above
Innocent shepherdesses
Whom in love no law distresses
Who have no law but love,
Could I as ye may do
Who conceald adore him
Tell what love I have for him
Bless'd were I too
All bliss above.

iv. I will be that fond Mother
Who her Babe doth threaten
Yet is it never beaten
Never at all.
She lifts her hand to strike it
But the blow intended
By Love is suspended
When it would fall.

v. Gentle Zephyr
If you pass her by
Tell her you're a sigh
But tell her not from whom.
Limpid streamlet
If you meet her ever
Say with your best endeavour
That swoln with tears you come
But tell her not of whom.

VII. TRANSLATIONS FROM MICHELANGELO

I. A FRAGMENT

[Composed 1806 ? First printed in R. Duppa's *Life of Michel Angelo*, 1807.]

*　　*　　*　　*　　*

AND sweet it is to see in summer time
The daring goats upon a rocky hill
Climb here and there, still browzing as they climb,
While, far below, on rugged pipe and shrill
The master vents his pain ; or homely rhyme   5

He chaunts; now changing place, now standing still;
While his beloved, cold of heart and stern!
Looks from the shade in sober unconcern.

Nor less another sight do I admire,
   The rural family round their hut of clay;   10
Some spread the table, and some light the fire
   Beneath the household Rock, in open day;
The ass's colt with panniers some attire;
   Some tend the bristly hogs with fondling play;
This with delighted heart the Old Man sees,   15
   Sits out of doors, and suns himself at ease.

The outward image speaks the inner mind,
   Peace without hatred, which no care can fret;
Entire contentment in their plough they find,
   Nor home return until the sun be set: 20
No bolts they have, their houses are resign'd
   To Fortune—let her take what she can get:
A hearty meal then crowns the happy day,
   And sound sleep follows on a bed of clay.

In that condition Envy is unknown,   25
   And Haughtiness was never there a guest;
They only crave some meadow overgrown
   With herbage that is greener than the rest;
The plough's a sovereign treasure of their own;
   The glittering share, the gem they dream the best;   30
A pair of panniers serve them for buffette;
   Trenchers and porringers, for golden plate.
                           WORDSWORTH

II. MICHAEL ANGELO IN REPLY TO THE PASSAGE UPON HIS
STATUE OF NIGHT SLEEPING

[Composed 1806 ?—First printed 1883.]

Night Speaks.

GRATEFUL is Sleep, my life in stone bound fast
More grateful still: while wrong and shame shall last,
On me can Time no happier state bestow
Than to be left unconscious of the woe.
Ah then, lest you awaken me, speak low.
                       W. W.

GRATEFUL is Sleep, more grateful still to be
Of marble; for while shameless wrong and woe
Prevail, 'tis best to neither hear nor see:
Then wake me not, I pray you. Hush, speak low.

VIII. COME, GENTLE SLEEP

[Translation of Latin Verses.]

COME, gentle Sleep, Death's image tho' thou art,
Come, share my couch, nor speedily depart;
How sweet thus living without life to lie,
Thus without death how sweet it is to die.

IX. TRANSLATION OF THE SESTET OF A SONNET
BY TASSO

[Composed ?—First printed 1896.]

CAMOËNS, he the accomplished and the good,
Gave to thy fame a more illustrious flight
Than that brave vessel, though she sailed so far;
Through him her course along the Austral flood
Is known to all beneath the polar star,
Through him the Antipodes in thy name delight.

X. INSCRIPTION FOR THE MOSS–HUT
AT DOVE COTTAGE

[Composed December 1804.—First printed 1887.]

No whimsy of the purse is here,
No Pleasure-House forlorn,
Use, comfort, do this roof endear;
A tributary Shed to chear
The little Cottage that is near,
To help it and adorn.

XI. DISTRESSFUL GIFT!

[Composed 1805.]

DISTRESSFUL gift! this Book receives
Upon its melancholy leaves,
This poor ill-fated Book:
I wrote, and when I reach'd the end
Started to think that thou, my Friend,   5
Upon the words which I had penn'd
Must never, never look.

Alas, alas, it is a Tale
Of Thee thyself; fond heart and frail!
The sadly-tuneful line   10
The written words that seem to throng
The dismal page, the sound, the song,
The murmur all to thee belong,
Too surely they are thine.

And so I write what neither Thou   15
Must look upon, nor others now,
Their tears would flow too fast;
Some solace thus I strive to gain,
Making a kind of secret chain,
If so I may, betwixt us twain   20
In memory of the past.

Oft have I handled, often eyed,
This volume with delight and pride,
The written page and white;
Oft have I turn'd them o'er and o'er,   25
One after one and score by score,
All fill'd or to be fill'd with store
Of verse for his delight.

He framed the Book which now I see,
This book that rests upon my knee,   30
He framed with dear intent;
To travel with him night and day,
And in his private hearing say
Refreshing things, whatever way
His weary Vessel went.   35

And now—upon the written leaf
With heart oppress'd by pain and grief
I look, but, gracious God,
Oh grant that I may never find
Worse matter or a heavier mind,   40
Grant this, and let me be resign'd
Beneath thy chast'ning rod.

XI. 23 volume with delight] book with joyous glee S. H.   30 book that
rests] very book S. H.   36 And] But S. H.   37-8 With . . . look *etc.*]
I look indeed with pain and grief, I do S. H.   40/1 For those which
yet remain behind S. H.

XII.   ON SEEING SOME TOURISTS OF THE LAKES
PASS BY READING

A PRACTICE VERY COMMON

[Composed 1801-6.—First printed 1897.]

WHAT waste in the labour of Chariot and Steed!
For this came ye hither? is this your delight?
There are twenty-four letters and these ye can read;
But Nature's ten thousand are Blanks in your sight.
Then throw by your Books, and the study begin;
Or sleep, and be blameless, and wake at your Inn!

XIII.   THE ORCHARD PATHWAY

[Composed 1806.—First printed 1897.]

ORCHARD Pathway, to and fro,
Ever with thee, did I go,
Weaving Verses, a huge store!
These, and many hundreds more,
And, in memory of the same
This little lot shall bear *Thy Name!*

XIV.   ST. PAUL'S

[Composed March–April 1808.]

PRESS'D with conflicting thoughts of love and fear
I parted from thee, Friend, and took my way
Through the great City, pacing with an eye
Downcast, ear sleeping, and feet masterless
That were sufficient guide unto themselves,   5
And step by step went pensively. Now, mark!
Not how my trouble was entirely hush'd,
(That might not be) but how, by sudden gift,
Gift of Imagination's holy power,
My Soul in her uneasiness received   10
An anchor of stability.—It chanced
That while I thus was pacing, I raised up
My heavy eyes and instantly beheld,
Saw at a glance in that familiar spot
A visionary scene—a length of street   15
Laid open in its morning quietness,
Deep, hollow, unobstructed, vacant, smooth,
And white with winter's purest white, as fair,
As fresh and spotless as he ever sheds

XIV. 3 pacing] walking MS. A   11 stability] security MS. A

On field or mountain. Moving Form was none   20
Save here and there a shadowy Passenger
Slow, shadowy, silent, dusky, and beyond
And high above this winding length of street,
This moveless and unpeopled avenue,
Pure, silent, solemn, beautiful, was seen   25
The huge majestic Temple of St. Paul
In awful sequestration, through a veil,
Through its own sacred veil of falling snow.

XV. GEORGE AND SARAH GREEN

[Composed April 1808.—Published September 1839.]
(*Tait's Edinburgh Magazine*)

WHO weeps for strangers ? Many wept
   For George and Sarah Green ;
Wept for that pair's unhappy fate,
   Whose grave may here be seen.

By night, upon these stormy fells,   5
   Did wife and husband roam ;
Six little ones at home had left,
   And could not find that home.

For *any* dwelling-place of man
   As vainly did they seek.   10
He perish'd ; and a voice was heard—
   The widow's lonely shriek.

Not many steps, and she was left
   A body without life—
A few short steps were the chain that bound   15
   The husband to the wife.

22 silent] soundless MS. A   24 moveless] noiseless MS. A
XV. *Title.* Elegiac Stanzas composed in the Churchyard of Grasmere, Westmorland, a few days after the Interment there of a Man and his Wife,
Inhabitants of the Vale, who were lost upon the neighbouring Mountains,
on the night of the 19th of March last. MS.
5 fells] Heights MS.   7 at home] the Pair MS.   8 that] their MS.
12/13 Down the dark precipice he fell,
    And she was left alone
    Not long to think of her Children dear,
    Not long to pray or groan! MS.
13 A few wild steps, she too MS.
15–16 The chain of but a few wild steps
    To the Husband bound the Wife. MS.
16/17 Now lodge they in one Grave, this Grave
    A House with two-fold Roof,
    Two Hillocks but one Grave, their own.
    A covert tempest-proof.

Now do those sternly-featured hills
    Look gently on this grave;
And quiet *now* are the depths of air,
    As a sea without a wave.   20

But deeper lies the heart of peace
    In quiet more profound;
The heart of quietness is here
    Within this churchyard bound.

And from all agony of mind   25
    It keeps them safe, and far
From fear and grief, and from all need
    Of sun or guiding star.

O darkness of the grave! how deep,
    After that living night—   30
That last and dreary living one
    Of sorrow and affright!

O sacred marriage-bed of death,
    That keeps them side by side
In bond of peace, in bond of love,   35
    That may not be untied!

And from all agony of mind
It keeps them safe and far;
From fear, and from all need of hope,
From sun, or guiding Star.

Our peace is of the immortal Soul,
Our anguish is of clay;
Such bounty is in Heaven, so pass
The bitterest pangs away.

Three days did teach the Mother's Babe
Forgetfully to rest
In reconcilement how serene!
Upon another's breast.

The trouble of the elder Brood
I know not that it stay'd
So long—they seiz'd their joy, and they
Have sung, and danc'd, and play'd. MS.

19 are the depths] is the depth MS.   22 quiet] shelter MS.   24
bound] ground MS.   25–8 *v.* 16/17 (*second stanza*)   29 deep]
calm MS.   34 keeps] holds MS.   35 peace . . . love] love . . .
God MS.

XVI. TRANSLATION OF CHIABRERA'S EPITAPH ON TASSO

[Composed 1810.—First printed by Grosart 1876.]

TORQUATO TASSO rests within this tomb;
This figure weeping from her inmost heart
Is Poesy; from such impassioned grief
Let every one conclude what this man was.

XVII. THE SCOTTISH BROOM

[Composed 1818.—First printed 1891.]

THE Scottish Broom on Birdnest brae
Twelve tedious years ago,
When many plants strange Blossoms bore
That puzzled high and low,
A not unnatural longing felt,   5
What longing would ye know?
Why, friend, to deck her supple twigs
With *yellow* in full blow.

To Lowther Castle she addressed
A suit both bold and sly,   10
(For all the Brooms on Birdnest brae
Can talk and speechify)
That flattering breezes blowing thence
Their succour might supply,
And she would instantly hang out   15
A flag of *yellow* dye.

But from the Castle's turrets blew
A chill forbidding blast,
Which the poor Broom no sooner felt
Than she shrank up as fast;   20
Her wished-for yellow she forswore,
And since that time has cast
Fond looks on colours three or four
And put forth Blue at last.

But now, my friends, the Election comes   25
In June's sunshiny hours,
When every bush in field and brae
Is clad with yellow flowers.
While faction's Blue from shop and booth
Tricks out her blustering powers,   30
Lo! smiling Nature's lavish hand
Has furnished wreaths for ours.

XVII. 27 every field and bank MS.

XVIII. PLACARD FOR A POLL BEARING AN OLD SHIRT

[Composed 1818.—First printed 1896.]

IF money's slack,
The shirt on my back
Shall off, and go to the hammer;
Though I sell shirt and skin
By Jove I'll be in,
And raise up a radical clamor!

XIX. TWO EPIGRAMS ON BYRON'S *CAIN*

[Composed 1827.—First printed 1896.]

i

CRITICS, right honourable Bard, decree
Laurels to some, a night-shade wreath to thee,
Whose muse a sure though late revenge hath ta'en
Of harmless Abel's death, by murdering Cain.

ii

A German Haggis from receipt
Of him who cooked the death of Abel,
And sent "warm-reeking, rich" and sweet,
From Venice to Sir Walter's table.

XX. EPITAPH

(*In Grasmere Church*)

[Composed 1822.]

THESE vales were saddened with no common gloom
When good Jemima perished in her bloom;
When (such the awful will of heaven) she died
By flames breathed on her from her own fireside.
On Earth we dimly see, and but in part   5
We know, yet Faith sustains the sorrowing heart;
And she, the pure, the patient and the meek,
Might have fit epitaph could feelings speak;
If words could tell and monuments record,
How treasures lost are inwardly deplored,   10
No name by Grief's fond eloquence adorn'd
More than Jemima's would be praised and mourn'd.
The tender virtues of her blameless life,
Bright in the Daughter, brighter in the Wife,
And in the cheerful Mother brightest shone,—   15
That light hath past away—the will of God be done.

XXI. IN THE FIRST PAGE OF AN ALBUM BY ONE WHOSE HANDWRITING IS WRETCHEDLY BAD

[Composed 1824.]

FIRST flowret of the year is that which shows
Its rival whiteness 'mid surrounding snows;
To guide the shining Company of Heaven,
Brightest as first, appears the star of Even;
Upon imperial brows the richest gem   5
Stands ever foremost in the Diadem—
How then could mortal so unfit engage
To take his Station in this leading page?
For others marshall with his pen the way
Which shall be trod in many a future day?   10
Why was not some fair Lady called to write
Dear words for memory, "characters of light"?
Lines which enraptured fancy might explore
And thence create her Image? but no more;
Strangers! forgive the deed, an unsought task,   15
For what you look on Friendship deigned to ask.

XXII. PRITHEE, GENTLE LADY, LIST

[Composed 1826.—First printed 1896.]

PRITHEE, gentle Lady, list
To a small Ventriloquist:
I whose pretty voice you hear
From this paper speaking clear
Have a Mother, once a Statue!   5
I, thus boldly looking at you,
Do the name of Paphus bear,
Famed Pygmalion's son and heir,
By that wondrous marble wife
That from Venus took her life.   10
Cupid's nephew then am I,
Nor unskilled his darts to ply;
But from him I crav'd no warrant
Coming thus to seek my parent;
Not equipp'd with bow and quiver   15
Her by menace to deliver,
But resolv'd with filial care
Her captivity to share.
Hence, while on your Toilet, she
Is doom'd a Pincushion to be,   20

By her side I'll take my place,
As a humble Needlecase
Furnish'd too with dainty thread
For a Sempstress thoroughbred.
Then let both be kindly treated   25
Till the Term for which she's fated
Durance to sustain, be over:
So will I ensure a Lover,
Lady! to your heart's content;⎫
But on harshness are you bent?⎬   30
Bitterly shall you repent   ⎭
When to Cyprus back I go
And take up my Uncle's bow.

XXIII. THE LADY WHOM YOU HERE BEHOLD

[Composed 1826.]

THE Lady whom you here behold
Was once Pygmalion's Wife,
He made her first from marble cold
And Venus gave her life.

When fate remov'd her from his arms   5
Thro' sundry Forms she pass'd;
And conquering hearts by various charms
This shape she took at last.

We caught her, true tho' strange th' account,
Among a troop of Fairies,   10
Who nightly frisk on our green Mount
And practise strange vagaries.

Her raiment then was scant, so we
Bestowed some pains upon her;
Part for the sake of decency   15
And part to do her honour.

But as, no doubt, 'twas for her sins
We found her in such plight,
She shall do penance stuck with pins
And serve you day and night.   20

XXIV. COMPOSED WHEN A PROBABILITY EXISTED OF OUR BEING OBLIGED TO QUIT RYDAL MOUNT AS A RESIDENCE

[Composed 1826.—First printed 1889.]

THE doubt to which a wavering hope had clung
Is fled; we must depart, willing or not;
Sky-piercing Hills! must bid farewell to you
And all that ye look down upon with pride,
With tenderness imbosom; to your paths,   5
And pleasant Dwellings, to familiar trees
And wild-flowers known as well as if our hands
Had tended them: and O pellucid Spring!
Insensibly the foretaste of this parting
Hath ruled my steps, and seals me to thy side,   10
Mindful that thou (ah! wherefore by my Muse
So long unthank'd) hast cheared a simple board
With beverage pure as ever fix'd the choice
Of Hermit, dubious where to scoop his cell;
Which Persian kings might envy; and thy meek   15
And gentle aspect oft has minister'd
To finer uses. They for me must cease;
Days will pass on, the year, if years be given,
Fade,—and the moralizing mind derive
No lesson from the presence of a Power   20
By the inconstant nature we inherit
Unmatch'd in delicate beneficence;
For neither unremitting rains avail
To swell Thee into voice; nor longest drought
Thy bounty stints, nor can thy beauty mar,   25

XXIV. 1–14 Pellucid Spring, unknown beyond the verge
        Of a small Hamlet, there, from ancient time
    Not undistinguish'd (for, [of?] Wells that ooze
    Or Founts that gurgle from this cloud-capp'd hill,
    Their common Sire, thou only bear'st his name)
    One of my last fond looks is fix'd on Thee
    Who with the comforts of my simple board
    Hast blended, thro' the space of twice seven years,
    Beverage as choice as ever Hermit prized B
8 and Thou, pellucid Spring corr. to text A
8/9   Unheard of, save in one small hamlet, here
    Not undistinguish'd, for of Wells that ooze
    Or founts that gurgle from yon craggy Steep,
    Their common Sire, thou only bear'st his name. A, but marked 'out'.
15 thy meek] whose pure B   20 thy Presence, Gracious Power, B
24–36   . . . nor hottest drouth
    Can stint thy bounty, nor thy beauty mar.

Beauty not therefore wanting change to please
The fancy, for in spectacles unlook'd for,
And transformations silently fulfill'd,
What witchcraft, meek Enchantress, equals thine?
   Not yet, perchance, translucent Spring, had toll'd   30
The Norman curfew bell when human hands
First offered help that the deficient rock
Might overarch thee, from pernicious heat
Defended, and appropriate to man's need.
Such ties will not be sever'd: but, when We   35
Are gone, what summer Loiterer, with regard
Inquisitive, thy countenance will peruse,
Pleased to detect the dimpling stir of life,
The breathing faculty with which thou yield'st
(Though a mere goblet to the careless eye)   40
Boons inexhaustible? Who, hurrying on
With a step quicken'd by November's cold,
Shall pause, the skill admiring that can work
Upon thy chance-defilements—wither'd twigs
That, lodg'd within thy crystal depths, seem bright,   45
As if they from a silver tree had fallen;
And oaken leaves that, driv'n by whirling blasts,
Sank down, and lay immers'd in dead repose
For Time's invisible tooth to prey upon.
Unsightly objects and uncoveted,   50
Till thou with crystal bead-drops didst encrust
Their skeletons, turned to brilliant ornaments.
But, from thy bosom, would some venturous hand
Abstract those gleaming Relics, and uplift them,
However gently, tow'rd the vulgar air,   55
At once their tender brightness disappears,
Leaving the Intermeddler to upbraid
His folly. Thus (I feel it while I speak),
Thus, with the fibres of these thoughts it fares;

Such calm attraction have I found in thee,
My private treasure, while the neighbouring stream
Fam'd through the land for turbulent cascades
Not seldom forfeits his dependent praise
And disappoints the Stranger lured from far.
Henceforth, what summer Loiterer *etc.* B
26-7   ... to stir
The fancy pleased by spectacles unlook'd for A (*corr. to text*)
48 Have sunk, and lain B
51-2 ... with crust of liquid beads dost turn
Their skeletons to *etc.* B
53 covetous *corr. to* venturous A, B

And oh! how much, of all that love creates   60
Or beautifies, like changes undergoes,
Suffers like loss when drawn out of the soul,
Its silent laboratory! Words should say
(Could they depict the marvels of thy cell)
How often I have marked a plumy fern   65
From the live rock with grace inimitable
Bending its apex tow'rd a paler self
Reflected all in perfect lineaments—
Shadow and substance kissing point to point
In mutual stillness; or, if some faint breeze   70
Entering the cell gave restlessness to One,
The Other, glass'd in thy unruffled breast,
Partook of every motion, met, retired,
And met again; such playful sympathy,
Such delicate caress as in the shape   75
Of this green Plant had aptly recompens'd
For baffled lips and disappointed arms
And hopeless pangs, the Spirit of that Youth,
The fair Narcissus by some pitying God
Changed to a crimson Flower; when he, whose pride   80
Provoked a retribution too severe,
Had pin'd; upon his watery Duplicate
Wasting that love the Nymphs implored in vain.
    Thus while my Fancy wanders, Thou, clear Spring,
Mov'd (shall I say?) like a dear Friend who meets   85
A parting moment with her loveliest look,
And seemingly her happiest, look so fair
It frustrates its own purpose, and recals
The griev'd One whom it meant to send away—
Dost tempt me by disclosures exquisite   90
To linger, bending over Thee: for now,
What witchcraft, mild enchantress, may with thee

92–9 Eager as one who on some pleasant day
Peers from a headland searching the sea clouds
For coming sails, or as an earnest child,
While deaf to plaudits that proclaim the joy
Of all around him, sits by some new charm
Of scenic transmutation, wonder-bound.
Where is thy earthy floor? from keenest sight
That obstacle is vanished; and slant beams B
92–117 B *has another version of these lines:*
A subtler operation may withdraw
From sight the solid floor that limited
The nice communion, but that barrier gone
Nought checks nor intercepts the downward shew
Created for the moment, flowerets, plants,
And the whole body of the wall they deck,

Compare! thy earthy bed a moment past
Palpable unto sight as the dry ground,
Eludes perception, not by rippling airs   95
Concealed, nor through effect of some impure
Upstirring; but, abstracted by a charm
Of thy own cunning, earth mysteriously
From under thee hath vanished, and slant beams
The silent inquest of a western Sun,   100
Assisting, lucid Well-Spring! Thou reveal'st
Communion without check of herbs and flowers
And the vault's hoary sides to which they clung,
Imag'd in downward show; the flower, the herbs,
These not of earthly texture, and the vault   105
Not *there* diminutive, but through a scale
Of Vision less and less distinct, descending
To gloom impenetrable. So (if truths
The highest condescend to be set forth
By processes minute), even so—when thought   110
Wins help from something greater than herself—
Is the firm basis of habitual sense
Supplanted, not for treacherous vacancy
And blank dissociation from a world
We love, but that the residues of flesh,   115
Mirror'd, yet not too strictly, may refine
To Spirit; for the Idealizing Soul
Time wears the features of Eternity;
And Nature deepens into Nature's God.
    Millions of kneeling Hindoos at this day   120
Bow to the watery Element, adored
In their vast Stream, and if an age hath been
(As Books and haply votive Altars vouch)
When British floods were worshipped, some faint trace
Of that idolatry, through monkish rites   125
Transmitted far as living memory,

Reflected but not there diminutive,
These of etherial texture, and thro' scale
Of vision less and less distinct descending
To gloom impenetrable. So in moods
Of thought pervaded by supernal grace
Is the firm base of ordinary sense
Supplanted, and the residues of flesh
Are linked with spirit, shallow life is lost
In being; to the idealizing Soul . . .

93   earthy] pebbly A *corr. to text*
101 lucid Well-Spring] air propitious, B   108–10 truths . . . when]
not in B   112 firm basis] coarse texture A *corr. to text*

Might wait on Thee, a silent Monitor,
On thee, bright Spring, a bashful little-one,
Yet to the measure of thy promises
True, as the mightiest; upon thee, sequestered   130
For meditation, nor inopportune
For social interest such as I have shared.
Peace to the sober Matron who shall dip
Her Pitcher here at early dawn, by me
No longer greeted—to the tottering Sire,   135
For whom like service, now and then his choice,
Relieves the tedious holiday of age—
Thoughts raised above the Earth while here he sits
Feeding on sunshine—to the blushing Girl
Who here forgets her errand, nothing loth   140
To be waylaid by her Betrothed, peace
And pleasure sobered down to happiness!
    But should these hills be ranged by one whose Soul
Scorning love-whispers shrinks from love itself
As Fancy's snare for female vanity,   145
Here may the aspirant find a trysting-place
For loftier intercourse. The Muses crowned
With wreaths that have not faded to this Hour
Sprung from high Jove, of sage Mnemosyne
Enamour'd, so the fable runs; but they   150
Certes were self-taught Damsels, scattered Births
Of many a Grecian Vale, who sought not praise,
And, heedless even of listeners, warbled out
Their own emotions given to mountain air
In notes which mountain echoes would take up   155
Boldly, and bear away to softer life;
Hence deified as Sisters they were bound
Together in a never-dying choir;
Who with their Hippocrene and grottoed fount
Of Castaly, attest that Woman's heart   160
Was in the limpid age of this stained world
The most assured seat of [fine ecstasy,]
And new-born waters, deemed the happiest source
Of Inspiration for the conscious lyre.
    Lured by the crystal element in times   165
Stormy and fierce, the Maid of Arc withdrew
From human converse to frequent alone
The Fountain of the Fairies. What to her,

120–45 *A page missing from* B   162 The most rever'd seat of
fine ecstasy. B   165–6 In harsher times the Maid of Arc would
steal B

917.17 IV   C c

Smooth summer dreams, old favors of the place,
Pageant and revels of blithe Elves—to her   170
Whose country groan'd under a foreign scourge?
She pondered murmurs that attuned her ear
For the reception of far other sounds
Than their too-happy minstrelsy,—a Voice
Reached her with supernatural mandates charged   175
More awful than the chambers of dark earth
Have virtue to send forth. Upon the marge
Of the benignant fountain, while she stood
Gazing intensely, the translucent lymph
Darkened beneath the shadow of her thoughts   180
As if swift clouds swept over it, or caught
War's tincture, mid the forest green and still,
Turned into blood before her heart-sick eye.
Erelong, forsaking all her natural haunts,
All her accustomed offices and cares   185
Relinquishing, but treasuring every law
And grace of feminine humanity,
The chosen Rustic urged a warlike Steed
Tow'rd the beleaguer'd city, in the might
Of prophecy, accoutred to fulfil,   190
At the sword's point, visions conceived in love.
     The cloud of Rooks descending through mid air
Softens its evening uproar towards a close
Near and more near; for this protracted strain
A warning not unwelcome. Fare thee well   195
Emblem of equanimity and truth,
Farewell—if thy composure be not ours,

169–70   Were the reputed doings of the Elves,
              Their merryment and revelries; to her B
173–9   . . . reception of a deeper voice
              And holier listenings, the translucent lapse B
183–4   Then tinkled audibly the fairy fount,
              Till haply that mysterious voice again
              Roused her, and, from the injuries of France
              Sucking resentment, the moist eye took fire.
              Her outstretch'd arms, as if in midnight dreams,
              Petition'd the blank air for spear and shield;
              And her breast heaved, labouring beneath a soul
              Wild as the wind; and, when the fit was past,
              Not less determin'd than a torrent stream
              That, having smooth'd its brow on some dread brink
              Drops headlong, resolute to find or make
              A Gulph of rest, deep as the height it falls from. B, *but deleted*
184–6   Erelong, her lowly tasks and natural haunts
              Relinquishing B

Yet as Thou still when we are gone wilt keep
Thy living Chaplet of fresh flowers and fern,
Cherished in shade tho' peeped at by the sun;   200
So shall our bosoms feel a covert growth
Of grateful recollections, tribute due
To thy obscure and modest attributes
To thee, dear Spring, and all-sustaining Heaven!

XXV.   WRITTEN IN MRS. FIELD'S ALBUM

OPPOSITE A PEN-AND-INK SKETCH IN THE MANNER OF A
REMBRANDT ETCHING DONE BY EDMUND FIELD

[Composed 1828–9.]

THAT gloomy cave, that gothic nich,
Those trees that forward lean
As if enamoured of the brook—
How soothing is the scene!

No witchery of inky words
Can such illusions yield;
Yet all (ye Landscape Poets blush!)
Was penned by Edmund Field.

XXVI.   WRITTEN IN THE STRANGERS' BOOK AT "THE STATION," OPPOSITE BOWNESS

[Composed 1829 ?—First printed 1889.]

MY Lord and Lady Darlington,
I would not speak in snarling tone;
Nor to you, good Lady Vane,
Would I give a moment's pain;
Nor Miss Taylor, Captain Stamp,   5
Would I your flights of *memory* cramp.
Yet, having spent a summer's day
On the green margin of Loch Tay,
And doubled (prospect ever bettering)
The mazy reaches of Loch Katerine,   10
And more than once been free at Luss,
Loch Lomond's beauties to discuss,
And wished, at least, to hear the blarney
Of the sly boatmen of Killarney,
And dipped my hand in dancing wave   15
Of Eau de Zurich, Lac Genève,

202/3 (Not less than to wide lake and foaming rill) B

And bowed to many a major-domo
On stately terraces of Como,
And seen the Simplon's forehead hoary,
Reclined on Lago Maggiore,   20
At breathless eventide at rest
On the broad water's placid breast,—
I, not insensible, Heaven knows,
To all the charms this Station shows,
Must tell you, Captain, Lord and Ladies,   25
For honest worth one poet's trade is,
That your praise appears to me
Folly's own hyperbole.

XXVII.   TO THE UTILITARIANS

[Composed May, 1833.—First printed 1885.]

AVAUNT this œconomic rage!
What would it bring ?—an iron age,
When Fact with heartless search explored
Shall be Imagination's Lord,
And sway with absolute controul   5
The god-like Functions of the Soul.
Not *thus* can Knowledge elevate
Our Nature from her fallen state.
With sober Reason Faith unites
To vindicate the ideal rights   10
Of Human-kind—the true agreeing
Of objects with internal seeing,
Of effort with the end of Being.

XXVIII.   EPIGRAM

[Composed 1836.—First printed 1889.]

ON AN EVENT IN COL. EVANS'S REDOUBTED PERFORMANCES IN SPAIN

THE Ball whizz'd by,—it grazed his ear,
    And whispered as it flew,
'I only touch—not take—don't fear,
For both, my honest Buccaneer!
    Are to the Pillory due.'

XXIX. [A SQUIB ON COLONEL EVANS]

[Composed March 1838.—First printed 1889.]

SAID red-ribbon'd Evans:
"My legions in Spain
Were at sixes and sevens;
Now they're famished or slain!
But no fault of mine,   5
For, like brave Philip Sidney,
In campaigning I shine,
A true Knight of his Kidney.
Sound flogging and fighting
No Chief, on my troth,   10
E'er took such delight in
As I in them both.
Fontarabbia can tell
How my eyes watched the foe,
Hernani knows well   15
That our feet were not slow;
Our hospitals, too,
They are matchless in story;
Where her thousands Fate slew,
All panting for glory."   20
Alas for this Hero!
His fame touched the skies,
Then fell below Zero,
Never, never to rise!
For him to Westminster   25
Did Prudence convey,
There safe as a Spinster
The Patriot to play.
But why be so glib on
His feats, or his fall?   30
He's got his red ribbon,
And laughs at us all.

XXX. INSCRIPTION ON A ROCK AT RYDAL MOUNT

[Composed 1838.—First printed 1851.]

WOULDST thou be gathered to Christ's chosen flock,
Shun the broad way too easily explored,
And let thy path be hewn out of the Rock,
The living Rock of God's eternal Word.

XXX. 2 way] path MS.
3-4 And hew thy way from out the living Rock,
Established upon Earth, the eternal Word. MS.

XXXI. LET MORE AMBITIOUS POETS

[Composed 1841 ?]

LET more ambitious Poets take the heart
By storm, my Verse would rather win its way
With gentle violence into minds well pleased
To give it welcome with a prompt return
Of their own sweetness, as March flowers that shrink   5
From the sharp wind do readily yield up
Their choicest fragrance to a southern breeze,
Ruffling their bosoms with its genial breath.

XXXII. WITH A SMALL PRESENT

[Composed 1841 ?]

A PRIZED memorial this slight work may prove
As bought in charity and given in Love.

XXXIII. THOUGH PULPITS AND THE DESK
MAY FAIL

THOUGH Pulpits and the Desk may fail
To reach the hearts of worldly men ;
Yet may the grace of God prevail
And touch them through the Poet's pen.
                                        WM. WORDSWORTH
BATH, *April 28th*, 1841.

XXXIV. THE EAGLE AND THE DOVE

[Composed 1842 ?—Published 1842.]

SHADE of Caractacus, if spirits love
The cause they fought for in their earthly home,
To see the Eagle ruffled by the Dove
May soothe thy memory of the chains of Rome.

These children claim thee for their sire ; the breath   5
Of thy renown, from Cambrian mountains, fans
A flame within them that despises death
And glorifies the truant youth of Vannes.

With thy own scorn of tyrants they advance,
But truth divine has sanctified their rage,   10
A silver cross enchased with Flowers of France
Their badge, attests the holy fight they wage.

XXXI. 3–5 By gentle force into the Mind that yields
          With glad compliance, as March flowers that shrink *1st draft*
6 sharp . . . yield up] fierce . . . give out *1st draft*   7 choicest]
     sweetest *1st draft*

The shrill defiance of the young crusade
Their veteran foes mock as an idle noise;
But unto Faith and Loyalty comes aid   15
From Heaven, gigantic force to beardless boys.

XXXV. LINES

INSCRIBED IN A COPY OF HIS POEMS SENT TO THE QUEEN
FOR THE ROYAL LIBRARY AT WINDSOR

[Composed January 9, 1846.—First printed 1876.]

DEIGN, Sovereign Mistress! to accept a lay,
    No laureate offering of elaborate art;
But salutation taking its glad way
    From deep recesses of a loyal heart.

Queen, Wife and Mother! may All-judging Heaven   5
    Shower with a bounteous hand on Thee and Thine
Felicity that only can be given
    On earth to goodness blest by grace divine.

Lady! devoutly honoured and beloved
    Through every realm confided to thy sway;   10
May'st thou pursue thy course by God approved,
    And He will teach thy people to obey.

As thou art wont, thy sovereignty adorn
    With woman's gentleness, yet firm and staid;
So shall that earthly crown thy brows have worn   15
    Be changed for one whose glory cannot fade.

And now by duty urged, I lay this Book
    Before thy Majesty, in humble trust
That on its simplest pages thou wilt look
    With a benign indulgence more than just.   20

Nor wilt thou blame the Poet's earnest prayer
    That issuing hence may steal into thy mind
Some solace under weight of royal care,
    Or grief—the inheritance of humankind.

For know we not that from celestial spheres,   25
    When Time was young, an inspiration came
(Oh were it mine!) to hallow saddest tears,
    And help life onward in its noblest aim.

your Majesty's
devoted Subject and Servant
William Wordsworth

XXXVI

ODE ON THE INSTALLATION OF HIS ROYAL HIGHNESS PRINCE ALBERT AS CHANCELLOR OF THE UNIVERSITY OF CAMBRIDGE, JULY, 1847

[Composed 1847.—Published 1847.]

FOR thirst of power that Heaven disowns,
For temples, towers, and thrones
Too long insulted by the Spoiler's shock,
Indignant Europe cast
Her stormy foe at last   5
To reap the whirlwind on a Libyan rock.
War is passion's basest game
Madly played to win a name:
Up starts some tyrant, Earth and Heaven to dare,
The servile million bow;   10
But will the Lightning glance aside to spare
The Despot's laurelled brow?

War is mercy, glory, fame,
Waged in Freedom's holy cause,
Freedom, such as man may claim   15
Under God's restraining laws.
Such is Albion's fame and glory,
Let rescued Europe tell the story.
But lo! what sudden cloud has darkened all
The land as with a funeral pall?   20
The Rose of England suffers blight,
The Flower has drooped, the Isle's delight;
Flower and bud together fall;
A Nation's hopes lie crushed in Claremont's desolate Hall.

Time a chequered mantle wears—   25
Earth awakes from wintry sleep:
Again the Tree a blossom bears;
Cease, Britannia, cease to weep!
Hark to the peals on this bright May-morn!
They tell that your future Queen is born.   30
A Guardian Angel fluttered
Above the babe, unseen;
One word he softly uttered,
It named the future Queen;

And a joyful cry through the Island ràng,   35
As clear and bold as the trumpet's clang,
    As bland as the reed of peace:
        "VICTORIA be her name!"
    For righteous triumphs are the base
Whereon Britannia rests her peaceful fame.   40

Time, in his mantle's sunniest fold
Uplifted in his arms the child,
And while the fearless infant smiled,
Her happier destiny foretold:—
    "Infancy, by Wisdom mild,   45
    Trained to health and artless beauty;
    Youth, by pleasure unbeguiled
    From the lore of lofty duty;
    Womanhood in pure renown,
    Seated on her lineal throne;   50
    Leaves of myrtle in her Crown,
    Fresh with lustre all their own.
    Love, the treasure worth possessing
    More than all the world beside,
    This shall be her choicest blessing,   55
    Oft to royal hearts denied."

That eve, the Star of Brunswick shone
        With steadfast ray benign
On Gotha's ducal roof, and on
        The softly flowing Leine,   60
Nor failed to gild the spires of Bonn,
        And glittered on the Rhine.
Old Camus, too, on that prophetic night
        Was conscious of the ray;
And his willows whispered in its light,   65
        Not to the Zephyr's sway,
But with a Delphic life, in sight
        Of this auspicious day—
This day, when Granta hails her chosen Lord,
        And, proud of her award,   70
        Confiding in that Star serene,
Welcomes the Consort of a happy Queen.

    Prince, in these collegiate bowers,
    Where science, leagued with holier truth,
    Guards the sacred heart of youth,   75
    Solemn monitors are ours.

These reverend aisles, these hallowed towers,
Raised by many a hand august,
Are haunted by majestic Powers,
The Memories of the Wise and Just,   80
Who, faithful to a pious trust,
Here, in the Founder's Spirit sought
To mould and stamp the ore of thought
In that bold form and impress high
That best betoken patriot loyalty.   85
Not in vain those Sages taught,—
True disciples, good as great,
Have pondered here their country's weal,
Weighed the Future by the Past,
Learned how social frames may last,   90
And how a Land may rule its fate
By constancy inviolate,
Though worlds to their foundations reel
The sport of factious Hate or godless Zeal.

Albert, in thy race we cherish   95
A Nation's strength that will not perish
While England's sceptred Line
True to the King of Kings is found;
Like that wise ancestor of thine
Who threw the Saxon shield o'er Luther's life   100
When first, above the yells of bigot strife,
The trumpet of the Living Word
Assumed a voice of deep portentous sound,
From gladdened Elbe to startled Tiber heard.
What shield more sublime   105
E'er was blazoned or sung?
And the PRINCE whom we greet
From its Hero is sprung.
Resound, resound the strain
That hails him for our own!   110
Again, again, and yet again,
For the Church, the State, the Throne!
And that Presence fair and bright,
Ever blest wherever seen,
Who deigns to grace our festal rite,   115
The Pride of the Islands, VICTORIA THE QUEEN!

NOTES

EVENING VOLUNTARIES

The first eight of these Poems were printed, under this title, in *Yarrow Revisited and other Poems* (1835). Only one of them (No. VIII) had appeared before. To these was added a ninth, never reprinted, on which *v.* note to No. VIII *infra*. Nos. IX, XII, and XIII were added to the series in 1837, Nos. X and XI in 1845, and the rest in 1850.

p. 1. I. It will be noted, from the *app. crit.*, that the first version of the poem (a fair copy written by Dora W.) was much shorter. The added lines W. wrote several times—in one copy of them, after ll. 20, 21 in their final form, occurs the couplet:

> While the Rooks homeward wend,—compact yet spread,
> Like a large cloud they cross the mountain's head.

p. 2. II. On a High Part of the Coast of Cumberland: "The lines were composed on the road between Moresby and Whitehaven while I was on a visit to my Son, then Rector of the former place. This [and some other Voluntaries] originated in the concluding lines of the last paragraph of this Poem. With this coast I have been familiar from my earliest childhood, and remember being struck for the first time by the town and port of Whitehaven, and the white waves breaking against its quays and piers, as the whole came into view from the top of the high ground down which the road (it has since been altered) then descended abruptly. My sister, when she first heard the voice of the sea from this point, and beheld the scene spread before her, burst into tears. Our family then lived at Cockermouth, and this fact was often mentioned among us as indicating the sensibility for which she was so remarkable."—I. F.

p. 3. III. By the Seaside: The statement in the MS. that the poem was written at Moresby after a storm enables us to date it March–April, for in March 1833 W. was on a visit to his son there (*v. L.Y.*, pp. 644–7).

39. "our thoughts are *heard* in heaven": From Young, *Night Thoughts*, ii. 95.

p. 4. IV. *Not in the lucid intervals of life*: "The lines following 'nor do words' [l. 7] were written with Lord Byron's character, as a Poet, before me, and that of others, his contemporaries, who wrote under like influences."—I. F.

It will be noted that in the first version (MS. 1) of the poem there is nothing to correspond with ll. 7–19.

17–23. O Nature ... pensive hearts ... every charm] Reminiscent of Burns, *To William Simpson*, xiii, xiv: cf. especially the couplet

> O Nature, a' thy shows an' forms
> To feeling, pensive hearts hae charms,

which W. quotes in his letter on the Kendal and Windermere Railway (Grosart, ii. 331).

20–31. *app. crit. v.* note to VII, *infra.*

p. 7. VI. **1–4.** *Soft as a cloud*: What looks like a first draft of these lines occurs in a MS. among other scraps:

> No cloud seems softer than yon pale blue hill,
> The gleaming waters how profoundly still

p. 8. VII. *The leaves that rustled on this oak-crowned hill*: "Composed by the side of Grasmere Lake. The mountains that enclose the vale, especially towards Easedale, are most favourable to the reverberation of sound. There is a passage in *The Excursion*, towards the close of the fourth Book, where the voice of the raven in flight is traced through the modifications it undergoes, as I have often heard it in that vale and others of this district.

> 'Often, at the hour
> When issue forth the first pale stars, is heard,
> Within the circuit of this fabric huge
> One voice—the solitary raven.' "—I. F.

1–13. In one MS. these lines form the first part of a poem headed *Twilight*, of which the last lines are a first draft of IV, *supra*, ll. 20–31; *v. app. crit.*

p. 9. VIII. *The sun has long been set*: In 1807 one of the *Moods of my own Mind*. W. (*edd.* 1845, 1850) misdated the poem 1804, the correct date is given in D. W.'s *Journals*. "Reprinted at the request of my Sister, in whose presence the lines were thrown off."—I. F. In 1835 the note prefixed to this poem ran: "The *former* of the two following Pieces appeared, many years ago, among the Author's poems, from which, in subsequent editions, it was excluded. It is here reprinted, at the request of a friend who was present when the lines were thrown off as an impromptu.

"For printing the *latter*, some reason should be given, as not a word of it is original: it is simply a fine stanza of Akenside, connected with a still finer from Beattie, by a couplet of Thomson. This practice, in which the author sometimes indulges, of linking together, in his own mind, favourite passages from different authors, seems in itself unobjectionable: but, as the *publishing* such compilations might lead to confusion in literature, he should deem himself inexcusable in giving this specimen, were it not from a hope that it might open to others a harmless source of *private* gratification."

The poem referred to, not republished after the 1835 ed., ran:

> Throned in the Sun's descending car
> What Power unseen diffuses far
> This tenderness of mind ?
> What Genius smiles on yonder flood ?
> What God in whispers from the wood   5
> Bids every thought be kind ?

O ever pleasing Solitude,
Companion of the wise and good,
Thy shades, thy silence, now be mine,
  Thy charms my only theme ;   10
My haunt the hollow cliff whose Pine
  Waves o'er the gloomy stream ;
Whence the scared Owl on pinions grey
  Breaks from the rustling boughs,
And down the lone vale sails away   15
  To more profound repose !

ll. 1–6 are from Akenside's Ode *Against Suspicion*, viii ; ll. 7, 8 from the opening of Thomson's *Hymn on Solitude*, 1, 2 ; ll. 9–16 from Beattie's *Retirement*, 41–8. All three passages are included in the *Poems and Extracts chosen by W. W. for an Album presented to Lady Mary Lowther, Christmas*, 1819.

10–11. "Parading" . . . "masquerading"] From Burns, *The Two Dogs*, 124–5 :

    At operas an' plays parading
    Mortgaging, gambling, masquerading.

13/14. *app. crit.* W. used the last two of these lines in IV, *supra*, ll. 20, 21.

p. 10. IX. COMPOSED UPON AN EVENING OF EXTRAORDINARY SPLENDOUR AND BEAUTY: "Felt and in a great measure composed upon the little mount in front of our abode at Rydal. In concluding my notices of this class of Poems it may be as well to observe that among the 'Miscellaneous Sonnets' are a few alluding to morning impressions which might be read with mutual benefit in connection with these 'Evening Voluntaries'. See, for example, that one on Westminster Bridge, that 1st on May, 2nd on the song of the Thrush, and the one beginning—'While beams of orient light etc.' "—I. F. Before 1837 this poem was placed among *Poems of the Imagination*.

49. Wings at my shoulder seem to play] In these lines I am under obligation to the exquisite picture of "Jacob's Dream", by Mr. Alstone, now in America. It is pleasant to make this public acknowledgment to a man of genius, whom I have the honour to rank among my friends.—W.

p. 13. X. COMPOSED BY THE SEASHORE: "These lines were suggested during my residence under my Son's roof at Moresby, on the coast near Whitehaven, at the time when I was composing those verses among the 'Evening Voluntaries' that have reference to the sea. It was in that neighbourhood I first became acquainted with the ocean and its appearances and movements. My infancy and early childhood were passed at Cockermouth, about eight miles from the coast, and I well remember that mysterious awe with which I used to listen to anything said about storms and shipwrecks. Sea-shells of many descriptions were common in the town; and I was not a little surprised when I heard that Mr. Landor had denounced me as a plagiarist from himself for having described a boy applying a sea-shell to his ear and listening to it for intimations of what was going on in its native element. This I had done myself scores of times, and it was a belief among us that we could know from the sound whether the tide was ebbing or flowing."—I. F. Cf. note to III, *supra*.

p. 14. XI. *The Crescent Moon, etc.*: The date of composition is given on the MS.

p. 14. XII. To THE MOON: An early draft is preserved in the Crabb Robinson Collection at Dr. Williams's Library, of which the following is a transcription *v.* E. Morley, *M.L.R.* XIX, 211–14:

What fond affections on the name attend
Which calls thee, gentle Moon! *the Sailor's Friend*!
So calls thee not alone for what the sky
Through mist or cloud permits thee to supply
(As from a moving watchtower) of wan light   5
To guide his Bark through perils of the night,
But for thy private bounties; for that meek
And tender influence of which few will speak
Though it can wet with tears the hardiest cheek.
Say, is there One (Breathes there a Man) of all whose business lies
On the great deep cut off (waters far) from household ties,   11
A Man endowed with human sympathies,
Who has not felt the fitness of thy sway
To cherish thoughts that shun the blaze of day,
The soft (true) accordance of thy placid chear   15
With all that pensive memory holds most dear
Or Fancy pictures forth to soothe a breast
(That asks not happiness but longs for rest!)
Tired with its daily share of ea[rth's unrest ?]
And [? as] the lifelong wanderer o'er the seas   20
Steers his [?] ship (Runs a smooth course) before a steady breeze
While he keeps watch in some far distant clime,
Dull darkness (Thy absence) adding to the weight of time,
Oft does thy image with his memory blend
And thou art still, O Moon, the *Sailor's* (Poet's) *Friend*. 25
Who when he marks thee bright as when of yore
Whole nations knelt thy presence to adore
Beholds the[e] (girt) crossed by clouds that slowly move
Catching the lustre they in part reprove
Nor felt the fitness of thy modest sway   30
To cherish the thought that shuns the blaze of day.

1–2 Cf. XII. 11–12   5–7 Cf. ib. 15–17   15–18, 29–30 ib. 56–9
24–5 ib. 70–3   26–7 Cf. *app. crit.* of XIII. 1–4   28–9 Cf.
XII. 35–6

10–11. on this sea-beat shore Sole-sitting] Cf. *Poems on Naming of Places*, iv. 38. Sole-sitting by the shores of old romance.

63–4. And when thy beauty . . . monthly grave] Cf. *Written in a Grotto*, 4, "When thou art hidden in thy monthly grave," and note Vol. III, pp. 413 and 575.

K. gives some lines as "written by W. in a copy of his works after the lines *To the Moon*, XIII. They may have been intended as a sequel to them":

> And O dear soother of the pensive breast,
> Let homelier words without offence attest
> How where on random topics as they hit
> The moment's humour, rough Tars spend their wit,
> Thy changes, which to wiser Spirits seem   5
> Dark as a riddle, prove a favorite theme;
> Thy motions intricate and manifold
> Oft help to make bold fancy's flights more bold,
> Beget strange theories and to freaks give birth
> Of speech as wild as ever heightened mirth.   10

The lines are to be found in C., Lord Coleridge's copy of *Wordsworth's Poems* 1836, written by M. W. in the blank space after XIII *To the Moon*, but clearly intended by the tally-mark to follow the close of XII.

p. 16. XIII. To THE MOON (RYDAL): The variant of ll. 1–4, given in the *app. crit.*, is a passage deleted from the draft of the previous poem (*v. supra*).

50. To look on tempests, *etc.*] Shakespeare, *Sonnets*, cxvi. 6.

p. 18. XIV. To LUCCA GIORDANO: Lucca Giordano (1632–1705) of Naples, one of the most prolific of artists, of no originality, but great imitative and mechanical skill. The picture, brought by the poet's eldest son from Italy, hung on the staircase at Rydal Mount, *v.* M: i. 28. *v. Addenda*, p. 468.

p. 18. XIV and XV. The dates of these sonnets are given on the MSS.

p. 19. XVI. *Where lies the truth, etc.*] Suggested, as W. told Professor Reed in a letter dated Jan. 23, 1846 (*v.* M. ii. 423), by the deaths of his grandson and his nephew John, and the imminent death of his brother Christopher.

7–8. Larks . . . bid the Sun good morrow] An obvious reminiscence of *L'Allegro*, 41, 46.

POEMS COMPOSED OR SUGGESTED DURING A TOUR,
IN THE SUMMER OF 1833

In *Yarrow Revisited* (1835), in which this series was first printed, Nos. XI and XLVI were placed in another part of the volume, and XXVII and XLIII, which had been published in the 1827 ed., were omitted. *Fancy and Tradition* (Vol. III, p. 277), originally XXXVI of the series, was in 1837 transferred to its present place. "My companions were H. C. Robinson and my son John."—I. F.

p. 20. II. **3–8.** Cf. *Guide to the Lakes* (ed. E. de S.), p. 74: "Antiquity . . . may be styled the co-partner or sister of Nature . . . I have already spoken of the beautiful forms of the ancient mansions of this country, and of the happy manner in which they harmonize with the forms of Nature." For W.'s ideas about the laying-out of grounds cf. his letter to Sir G. Beaumont, *E. L.*, p. 522.

14. The final reading was adopted on the suggestion of Barron Field in a letter dated Nov. 21, 1839.

p. 21. IV. To the River Greta: **7.** But if thou, like Cocytus] Many years ago, when I was at Greta Bridge, in Yorkshire, the hostess of the inn, proud of her skill in etymology, said that "the name of the river was taken from the *bridge*, the form of which, as every one must notice, exactly resembled a great A". Dr. Whitaker has derived it from the word of common occurrence in the North of England, "*to greet*"; signifying to lament aloud, mostly with weeping, a conjecture rendered more probable from the stony and rocky channel of both the Cumberland and Yorkshire rivers. The Cumberland Greta, though it does not, among the country people, take up *that* name till within three miles of its disappearance in the River Derwent, may be considered as having its source in the mountain cove of Wythburn, and flowing through Thirlmere, the beautiful features of which lake are known only to those who, travelling between Grasmere and Keswick, have quitted the main road in the vale of Wythburn, and, crossing over to the opposite side of the lake, have proceeded with it on the right hand.

The channel of the Greta, immediately above Keswick, has, for the purposes of building, been in a great measure cleared of the immense stones which, by their concussion in high floods, produced the loud and awful noises described in the sonnet.

"The scenery upon this river," says Mr. Southey in his *Colloquies*, "where it passes under the woody side of Latrigg, is of the finest and most rememberable kind:—

————ambiguo lapsu refluitque fluitque,
Occurrensque sibi venturas aspicit undas.—W."

Dowden compares a letter from Coleridge to Humphry Davy of Oct. 9, 1800: "Greta, or rather Grieta, is exactly the Cocytus of the Greeks; the word, literally rendered in modern English, is 'The Loud Lamenter'; to griet, in the Cumbrian dialect, signifying to roar aloud for grief or pain, and it does *roar* with a vengeance."

p. 22. V. To the River Derwent: This sonnet has already appeared in several editions of the author's poems; but he is tempted to reprint it in this place, as a natural introduction to the **two that** follow it.—W. 1835. It first appeared, in 1819, with *The Waggoner*, and was republished in the 1820–32 editions, among the *Miscellaneous Sonnets*.

1–4.] Cf. *Prelude*, i. 269–81.

10. Nemean] The Nemean games were held in alternate years in the grove surrounding the temple of Zeus Nemea, which was situated in the valley of Nemea in Argolis, celebrated as the place where Hercules slew the lion.

p. 22. VI. In Sight of the Town of Cockermouth: **2.** my buried Little-ones] Catharine (died June 4, 1812) and Thomas (died Dec. 1, 1812), buried in Grasmere churchyard.

p. 23. VIII. Nun's Well, Brigham: "So named from the Religious House which stood close by. I have rather an odd anecdote to relate of the Nun's Well. One day the Landlady of a public-house, a field's length from the well, on the road side, said to me—'You have been to see the Nun's Well, Sir ?'—'The Nun's Well! what is that ?' said the Postman, who in his royal livery stopt his Mail-car at the door. The Landlady and I explained to him what the name meant, and what sort of people the Nuns were. A countryman who was standing by, rather tipsy, stammered out—'Aye, those Nuns were good people ; they are gone ; but we shall soon have them back again.' The Reform mania was just then at its height."—I. F.

11. By hooded Votaresses] Attached to the church of Brigham was formerly a chantry, which held a moiety of the manor ; and in the decayed parsonage some vestiges of monastic architecture are still to be seen.—W.

14. "too soft a tear"] Pope, *Eloise to Abelard*, 270 :

> Thy voice I seem in ev'ry hymn to hear ;
> With ev'ry bead I drop too soft a tear.

p. 24. IX. To a Friend: "Pastor and Patriot", "My son John, who was then building a Parsonage on his small living at Brigham."—I. F. "Were you ever told that my Son is building a parsonage house upon a small Living, to which he was lately presented by the Earl of Lonsdale ? The situation is beautiful, commanding the windings of the Derwent both above and below the site of the House ; the mountain Skiddaw terminating the view one way, at a distance of 6 miles—and the ruins of Cockermouth Castle appearing nearly in the centre of the same view. In consequence of some discouraging thoughts—expressed by my Son when he had entered upon this undertaking, I addressed to him the following Sonnet, which you may perhaps read with some interest at the present crisis."—W. to Lady Beaumont (*L.Y.* pp. 690–1). And Dora W. wrote to E. Q. in Feb. 1834, sending him the sonnet: "addressed to John whose spirit failed him somewhat on finding he should be obliged to lay out so much money on his parsonage which might be taken from him any day by the reformed Parliament; but it will do for any poor parson who is building for his parish."

p. 24. X. MARY QUEEN OF SCOTS: "The fears and impatience of Mary were so great," says Robertson, "that she got into a fisherboat, and with about twenty attendants landed at Workington, in Cumberland; and thence she was conducted with many marks of respect to Carlisle." The apartment in which the Queen had slept at Workington Hall (where she was received by Sir Henry Curwen as became her rank and misfortunes) was long preserved, out of respect to her memory, as she had left it; and one cannot but regret that some necessary alterations in the mansion could not be effected without its destruction.—W.

5. "Bright as a Star" (*v. app. crit.*). "I will mention for the sake of the Friend who is writing down these notes, that it was among the fine Scotch firs near Ambleside, and particularly those near Green Bank, that I have over and over again paused at the sight of this image. Long may they stand to afford a like gratification to others!—This wish is not uncalled for, several of their brethren having already disappeared."—I. F.

p. 25. XI. STANZAS SUGGESTED IN A STEAMBOAT OFF SAINT BEES' HEADS: St. Bees' Heads, anciently called the Cliff of Baruth, are a conspicuous sea-mark for all vessels sailing in the N.E. parts of the Irish Sea. In a bay, one side of which is formed by the southern headland, stands the village of St. Bees; a place distinguished, from very early times, for its religious and scholastic foundations.

"St. Bees," say Nicholson and Burns, "had its name from Bega, an holy woman from Ireland, who is said to have founded here, about the year of our Lord 650, a small monastery, where afterwards a church was built in memory of her.

"The aforesaid religious house, being destroyed by the Danes, was restored by William de Meschiens, son of Ranulph, and brother of Ranulph de Meschiens, first Earl of Cumberland after the Conquest; and made a cell of a prior and six Benedictine monks to the Abbey of St. Mary at York."

Several traditions of miracles, connected with the foundation of the first of these religious houses, survive among the people of the neighbourhood; one of which is alluded to in these Stanzas; and another, of a somewhat bolder and more peculiar character, has furnished the subject of a spirited poem by the Rev. R. Parkinson, M.A., late Divinity Lecturer of St. Bees' College, and now Fellow of the Collegiate Church of Manchester.

After the dissolution of the monasteries, Archbishop Grindal founded a free school at St. Bees, from which the counties of Cumberland and Westmoreland have derived great benefit; and recently, under the patronage of the Earl of Lonsdale, a college has been established there for the education of ministers for the English

Church. The old Conventual Church has been repaired under the superintendence of the Rev. Dr. Ainger, the Head of the College; and is well worthy of being visited by any strangers who might be led to the neighbourhood of this celebrated spot.

The form of stanza in this Poem, and something in the style of versification, are adopted from the "St. Monica", a poem of much beauty upon a monastic subject, by Charlotte Smith: a lady to whom English verse is under greater obligations than are likely to be either acknowledged or remembered. She wrote little, and that little un-ambitiously, but with true feeling for rural nature, at a time when nature was not much regarded by English Poets; for in point of time her earlier writings preceded, I believe, those of Cowper and Burns. —W.

The poem was printed with F. W. Faber's·Life of St. Bega in *Lives of the English Saints,* 1844 (edited by J. H. Newman) with a prefatory note by Faber: "By the kind permission of the author, we are allowed to reprint entire Mr. W.'s beautiful stanzas on St. Bees, written, be it observed, so long ago as 1833. The date is noticed as giving a fresh instance of the remarkable way in which his poems did in divers places anticipate the revival of catholic doctrines among us. When anyone considers the tone of sneering which was almost universal in English authors when treating of a religious past with which they did not sympathize, the tone of these verses is very striking indeed, the more striking since Mr. W.'s works prove him to be very little in sympathy with Roman doctrine on the whole. Yet the affectionate reverence for the catholic past, the humble consciousness of a loss sustained by ourselves, the readiness to put a good construction on what he cannot wholly receive, are in this poem in very edifying contrast with even the half irreverent sportiveness of Mr. Southey's pen when employed on similar subject-matters. . . . The reader acquainted with Mr. W.'s poems will find an alteration in the last stanza; it has been printed as it is here given at the request of the author himself." For the letter to Faber, dated 6 Aug. 1844, in which W. made this request *v. L.Y.,* p. 1218. For the alteration *v. app. crit.* 156–9.

37. Cruel of heart, *etc.*] Cf. *King Lear,* III. iv. 95, "false of heart, light of ear, bloody of hand".

73. Are not, in sooth, *etc.*] I am aware that I am here treading upon tender ground; but to the intelligent reader I feel that no apology is due. The prayers of survivors, during passionate grief for the recent loss of relatives and friends, as the object of those prayers could no longer be the suffering body of the dying, would naturally be ejacu-lated for the souls of the departed; the barriers between the two worlds dissolving before the power of love and faith. The ministers of religion, from their habitual attendance upon sick-beds, would be daily witnesses of these benign results, and hence would be strongly tempted to aim at giving to them permanence, by embodying them in rites and ceremonies, recurring at stated periods. All this, as it was in course of nature, so was it blameless, and even praiseworthy; since some of its effects, in that rude state of society, could not but be salutary. No reflecting person, however, can view without sorrow the abuses which rose out of thus formalising sublime instincts, and disinterested movements of passion, and perverting them into means of gratifying the ambition and rapacity of the priesthood. But, while we deplore and are indignant at these abuses, it would be a great mistake if we imputed the origin of the offices to prospective selfishness on the part of the monks and clergy: *they* were at first sincere in their sympathy, and in their degree dupes rather of their own creed, than artful and designing men. Charity is, upon the whole, the safest guide that we can take in judging our fellow-men, whether of past ages, or of the present time.—W.

94. Staff and cockle hat and sandal shoon] From Ophelia's song, *Hamlet*, IV. v. 26.

108/9 and **159/60.** (*app. crit.*) "When the poem was first printed two of the stanzas exceeded the others in length—a fault which was afterwards corrected in the edition of 1837."—W. in letter to Faber, *v. supra*.

118–26. W. spent much pains on this stanza, first printed in 1845. C shows nine successive drafts, of which the first is as follows:

> Less than the abundant means and patient skill
> Of cloistered architects, men free to fill
> Their souls with love of (Jesus) God could ne'er have raised
> Churches whereon the rudest Peasant gazed
> With reverence, the mail-clad chief with awe,   5
> As at this day we seeing what they saw
> Humble our hearts before those sanctities
> In field or town 'mid mountain fastnesses
> Or on wave-beaten shores like thine, St. Bees.

136. (*app. crit.*) Mountains of Caupland] Copeland Forest is the district between Ennerdale and Eskdale. The name belongs to the ancient Barony (*Cauplandia* of medieval documents).

158–9. (*app. crit.*) For MS. Letter 1842 *v. L.Y.*, p. 1138.

162. The reference in W.'s note is to *Excursion*, vii. 1008–57.

p. 30. XII. Cf. *Epistle to Sir George H. Beaumont*, 77–88 and note.

p. 31. XIV. **12.** Of Power, *etc.*] This reading was adopted on the suggestion of Barron Field, who pointed out that the "superfluous syllables" in the earlier reading "were not warranted". (Letter to W., Dec. 17, 1836.)

p. 32. XV. On Entering Douglas Bay: Dignum laude, *etc.*] The reference is to Horace, *Odes*, IV. viii. 28.

1. Cohorn] Menno Baron Van Coehorn or Cohorn, the Dutch military engineer, known as "the Dutch Vauban" (1641–1704). He fortified Namur and other Dutch towns. W. visited Namur in 1820. Both M. W. and D. W. mention the fortifications in their Journals; *v. Memorials of a Tour on the Continent*, 1820, VI, ll. 9–14, *supra*, Vol. III, pp. 167–8 and note, pp. 468–9. Coehorn was one of the authorities on military architecture read by Uncle Toby (*v. Tristram Shandy*, Bk. II, ch. iii.). W. was familiar with Uncle Toby's obsession with the Siege of Namur: *v. The Waggoner*, ii. 128–34, note, Vol. II, pp. 498–9.

14. noble Hillary] The Tower of Refuge, an ornament to Douglas Bay, was erected chiefly through the humanity and zeal of Sir William Hillary; and he also was the founder of the lifeboat establishment at that place; by which, under his superintendence, and often by his exertions at the imminent hazard of his own life, many seamen and passengers have been saved.—W.

D. W. records in her *Journal*, July 3, 1828, at Douglas: "Sir Wm. Hilary saved a boy's life today in harbour." The Tower of Refuge was built in 1832.

p. 33. XVII. ISLE OF MAN: "My son William is here the person alluded to as saving the life of the youth, and the circumstances were as mentioned in the sonnet."—I. F. But, as Dowden points out, John and not William was the poet's companion in the Isle of Man. William, however, was in the Isle of Man, with his aunt D. W. in 1828, and the incident may have occurred then.

p. 34. XIX. BY A RETIRED MARINER: This unpretending sonnet is by a gentleman nearly connected with me, and I hope, as it falls so easily into its place, that both the writer and the reader will excuse its appearance here.—W. "Mary's brother Henry."—I. F. He is the subject of the previous sonnet.

p. 34. XX. AT BALA-SALA. " 'A thankful Refugee,' supposed to be written by a friend, Mr. H. Cookson, who died there a few years after."—I. F. Actually, he died later in the same year (*v. L.Y.*, p. 673). He was not, as sometimes stated, a relative of Mrs. W.'s nor of her cousin Canon Cookson, but one of the Cooksons of Kendal; his son Strickland acted as W.'s executor.

10–12. Cf. letter in which W. describes his visit to the Cooksons at Bala-Sala July 17, 1833: "the upper part of the old Tower is overgrown with a yellow Lychen which has the appearance of a gleam of perpetual evening sunshine" (*L.Y.*, p. 659).

p. 35. XXI. TYNWALD HILL: "Mr. Robinson and I walked the greater part of the way from Castle-town to Peel, and stopped some time at Tynwald Hill. One of my companions was an elderly man, who in a muddy way (for he was tipsy) explained and answered, as far as he could, my enquiries about this place and the ceremonies held here. I found more agreeable company in some little children; one of whom, upon my request, recited the Lord's Prayer to me, and I helped her to a clearer understanding of it as well as I could; but

I was not at all satisfied with my own part; hers was much better done, and I am persuaded that, like other children, she knew more about it than she was able to express, especially to a Stranger."—I. F. Cf. also W.'s letter of July 17, 1833, quoted *supra*.

9. old Snafell] The summit of this mountain is well chosen by Cowley as the scene of the "Vision", in which the spectral angel discourses with him concerning the government of Oliver Cromwell. "I found myself", says he, "on the top of that famous hill in the Island Mona, which has the prospect of three great, and not long since most happy, kingdoms. As soon as ever I looked upon them, they called forth the sad representation of all the sins and all the miseries that had overwhelmed them these twenty years." It is not to be denied that the changes now in progress, and the passions, and the way in which they work, strikingly resemble those which led to the disasters the philosophic writer so feelingly bewails. God grant that the resemblance may not become still more striking as months and years advance!—W.

p. 36. XXIII. IN THE FRITH OF CLYDE: "The morning of the eclipse was exquisitely beautiful while we passed the Crag as described in the sonnet. On the deck of the steamboat were several persons of the poor and labouring class, and I could not but be struck by their cheerful talk with each other, while not one of them seemed to notice the magnificent objects with which we were surrounded; and even the phenomenon of the eclipse attracted but little of their attention. Was it right not to regret this? They appeared to me, however, so much alive in their own minds to their own concerns that I could not look upon it as a misfortune that they had little perception for such pleasures as cannot be cultivated without ease and leisure. Yet if one surveys life in all its duties and relations, such ease and leisure will not be found so enviable a privilege as it may at first appear. Natural Philosophy, Painting, and Poetry, and refined taste, are no doubt great acquisitions to society; but among those who dedicate themselves to such pursuits it is to be feared that few are as happy, and as consistent in the management of their lives, as the class of persons who at that time led me into this course of reflection. I do not mean by this to be understood to derogate from intellectual pursuits, for that would be monstrous: I say it in deep gratitude for this compensation to those whose cares are limited to the necessities of daily life. Among them, self-tormentors, so numerous in the higher classes of society, are rare."—I. F.

p. 36. XXIV. ON THE FRITH OF CLYDE (In a steamboat): "The mountain outline on the north of this Island, as seen from the Frith of Clyde, is much the finest I have ever noticed in Scotland or elsewhere."—I. F.

p. 37. XXV. ON REVISITING DUNOLLY CASTLE: This ingenious piece of workmanship, as I afterwards learned, had been executed for their own amusement by some labourers employed about the place.—W.

11. And of the towering courage, *etc.*] The reading of the text was due to Barron Field's objection that he "did not understand 'That towering courage, *etc.*' till [he] read it *Of* the blind courage, *etc.*"

p. 37. XXVI. THE DUNOLLY EAGLE: **7.** The MS. reading "Villatic fowl" is a reminiscence of *Samson Agonistes*, 1695.

p. 38. XXVII. WRITTEN IN A BLANK LEAF OF MACPHERSON'S OSSIAN: **47-8.** "The verses—

'Or strayed
From hope and promise, self-betrayed,'

were, I am sorry to say, suggested from apprehensions of the fate of my friend, H. C., the subject of the verses addressed to 'H. C. when six years old.' The piece to 'Memory' arose out of similar feelings."
—I. F.

Before 1845 this poem was placed among *Poems of Sentiment and Reflection*. For W.'s opinion of Macpherson's *Ossian* cf. Essay Supplementary to the Preface of 1815, *supra*, Vol. II, p. 423, and letter to E. H. Barker (*L.Y.*, p. 382).

39-40. Musaeus, *etc.*] Nowell Smith compares Virgil, *Aeneid*, vi. 667:

Musaeum ante omnes (medium nam plurima turba
Hunc habet atque humeris exstantem suscipit altis).

57-60. W. writes to T. N. Talfourd: "The leading interest attached to the name of Ossian is connected with grey hairs, infirmity and privation" (*L.Y.*, p. 817).

p. 40. XXIX. CAVE OF STAFFA: The reader may be tempted to exclaim, How came this and the two following sonnets to be written, after the dissatisfaction expressed in the preceding one? In fact, at the risk of incurring the reasonable displeasure of the master of the steamboat, I returned to the cave, and explored it under circumstances more favourable to those imaginative impressions which it is so wonderfully fitted to make upon the mind.—W.

6. "the high embowed roof" Milton, *Il Penseroso*, 157.

p. 41. XXXI. FLOWERS ON THE TOP OF THE PILLARS, *etc.*: Upon the head of the columns which form the front of the cave, rests a body of decomposed basaltic matter, which was richly decorated with that large bright flower, the ox-eyed daisy. I had noticed the same flower growing with profusion among the bold rocks on the western coast of the Isle of Man, making a brilliant contrast with their black and gloomy surfaces.—W.

p. 42. XXXIII. IONA, upon Landing: The four last lines of this sonnet are adopted from a well-known sonnet of Russel, as conveying my feeling better than any words of my own could do.—W. The sonnet from which W. borrows is No. X ("Could, then, the Babes") in the *Sonnets and Miscellaneous Poems* by the Rev. Thomas Russell, Fellow of New College, Oxford, 1789. For W.'s admiration of Russell's sonnets, particularly this one and that on Philoctetes (*Supposed to be written at Lemnos*), v. *L.Y.*, pp. 70, 652–3.

p. 43. XXXIV. THE BLACK STONES OF IONA: Martin's Voyage, *etc.*] i.e. *Description of the Western Islands of Scotland: including an account of the Manners, Customs, Religion, Language, Dress etc. of the inhabitants*, by M. Martin, 1703.

p. 43. XXXV. *Homeward we turn. Isle of Columba's cell*: Columba, an Irish saint born A.D. 521. In Ireland he founded two monasteries; then, with twelve disciples, he went to Scotland and was given the Island of Iona, where he built a church and monastery, and was largely instrumental in the conversion of the Picts.

p. 44. XXXVI. GREENOCK: Per me si va, *etc.* Dante, *Inferno*, iii. 1.

p. 44. XXXVII. *"There!" said a Stripling*: "Mosgiel was thus pointed out to me by a young man on the top of the coach on my way from Glasgow to Kilmarnock. It is remarkable that, though Burns lived some time here, and during much the most productive period of his poetical life, he nowhere adverts to the splendid prospects stretching towards the sea and bounded by the peaks of Arran on one part, which in clear weather he must have had daily before his eyes. Yet this is easily explained. In one of his poetical effusions he speaks of describing 'fair Nature's face' as a privilege on which he sets a high value; nevertheless, natural appearances rarely take a lead in his poetry. It is as a human being, eminently sensitive and intelligent, and not as a Poet, clad in his priestly robes and carrying the ensigns of sacerdotal office, that he interests and affects us. Whether he speaks of rivers, hills, and woods, it is not so much on account of the properties with which they are absolutely endowed, as relatively to local patriotic remembrances and associations, or as they ministered to personal feelings, especially those of love, whether happy or otherwise;—yet it is not *always* so. Soon after we had passed Mosgiel Farm we crossed the Ayr, murmuring and winding through a narrow woody hollow. His line—'Auld hermit Ayr strays through his woods'— came at once to my mind with Irwin, Lugar, Ayr, and Doon,— Ayrshire streams over which he breathes a sigh as being unnamed in song; and surely his own attempts to make them known were as successful as his heart could desire."—I. F.

9. "the random *bield* of clod or stone"] From Burns, *To a Mountain Daisy*, iv.:

> But thou beneath the random bield
> O' clod or stone. ·

"Bield" is the dialect word for shelter, often found in place-names in the Lake District. *v.* note to *Epistle to Sir G. H. Beaumont*, l. 175 (p. 147). Cf. *The Shepherd of Bield Crag*: Note to *Exc.* vi. 1114, Vol. V.

p. 45. XXXVIII. THE RIVER EDEN: It is to be feared that there is more of the poet than the sound etymologist in this derivation of the name Eden. On the western coast of Cumberland is a rivulet which enters the sea at Moresby, known also in the neighbourhood by the name of Eden. May not the latter syllable come from the word Dean, *a valley*? Langdale, near Ambleside, is by the inhabitants called Langden. The former syllable occurs in the name Emont, a principal feeder of the Eden; and the stream which flows, when the tide is out, over Cartmel sands, is called the Ea—eau, French— aqua, Latin.—W.

2-3. verse of mine the . . . Repeats but once] i.e. in *Song at the feast of Brougham Castle*, 46-7.

6-7. Nature gives thee flowers *etc.*] "This can scarcely be true to the letter; but, without stretching the point at all, I can say that the soil and air appear more congenial with many upon the banks of this river, than I have observed in any other parts of Great Britain."—I. F.

p. 45. XXXIX. MONUMENT OF MRS. HOWARD: "Before this monument was put up in the Chapel at Wetheral I saw it in the Sculptor's studio. Nollekens, who, by the bye, was a strange and grotesque figure that interfered much with one's admiration of his works, showed me at the same time the various models in clay which he had made, one after another, of the Mother and her Infant: the improvement on each was surprising; and how so much grace, beauty, and tenderness had come out of such a head I was sadly puzzled to conceive. Upon a window-seat in his parlour lay two casts of faces, one of the Duchess of Devonshire, so noted in her day; and the other of Mr. Pitt, taken after his death, a ghastly resemblance, as these things always are, even when taken from the living subject, and more ghastly in this instance from the peculiarity of the features. The heedless and apparently neglectful manner in which the faces of these two persons were left—the one so distinguished in London Society, and the other upon whose counsels and public conduct, during a most momentous period, depended the fate of this great Empire and perhaps of all Europe—afforded a lesson to which the dullest of casual visitors could scarcely be insensible. It touched me the more because I had so often seen Mr. Pitt upon his own ground at Cambridge and upon the floor of the House of Commons."—I. F. *v.* W.'s letter to Allan Cunningham (*L.Y.*, p. 708).

p. 46. XLI. NUNNERY: "I became acquainted with the walks of Nunnery when a boy; they are within easy reach of a day's pleasant excursion from the town of Penrith, where I used to pass my summer holidays under the roof of my maternal Grandfather. The place is well worth visiting; though, within these few years its privacy, and therefore the pleasure which the scene is so well fitted to give, has been injuriously affected by walks cut in the rocks on that side the stream which had been left in its natural state."—I. F.

14. Canal, and Viaduct, and Railway] At Corby, a few miles below Nunnery, the Eden is crossed by a magnificent viaduct; and another of these works is thrown over a deep glen or ravine, at a very short distance from the main stream.—W. *v. Addenda*, p. 468.

p. 47. XLIII. THE MONUMENT COMMONLY CALLED LONG MEG AND HER DAUGHTERS: The daughters of Long Meg, placed in a perfect circle eighty yards in diameter, are seventy-two in number above ground; a little way out of the circle stands Long Meg herself, a single stone, eighteen feet high. When I first saw this monument, as I came upon it by surprise, I might over-rate its importance as an object; but, though it will not bear a comparison with Stonehenge, I must say I have not seen any other relique of those dark ages which can pretend to rival it in singularity and dignity of appearance.—W.

The sonnet was probably written in January 1821. On Jan. 6 of that year he wrote to Sir George Beaumont: "My road brought me suddenly and unexpectedly upon that ancient monument called by the country people Long Meg and her Daughters. Everybody has heard of it, and so had I from very early childhood, but had never seen it before. Next to Stonehenge it is, beyond dispute, the most noble relic of the kind that this or probably any other country contains. Long Meg is a single block of unhewn stone, eighteen feet high, at a small distance from a vast circle of other stones, some of them of huge size, though curtailed of their stature by their having sunk into the ground by their own incessant pressure upon it" (*L.Y.*, p. 6).

The sonnet was first published in W.'s *Guide to the Lakes*, third edition, 1822 (*v.* edition by E. de S., London, 1906, p. 53), in 1827 and 1832 among the *Miscellaneous Sonnets*. It took its present position in 1837. Three manuscripts are known to me—one in the W. Museum at Grasmere, the other two in the Cornell Library, among the drafts of the *Ecclesiastical Sonnets* (*v. Ecclesiastical Sonnets*, ed. Potts, pp. 104 and 105).

p. 48. XLIV. LOWTHER: "Cathedral pomp. It may be questioned whether this union was in the contemplation of the Artist when he planned the Edifice. However this might be, a Poet may be excused for taking the view of the subject presented in this sonnet."—I. F.

p. 49. XLV. TO THE EARL OF LONSDALE: This sonnet was written immediately after certain trials, which took place at the Cumberland Assizes, when the Earl of Lonsdale, in consequence of repeated and long-continued attacks upon his character, through the local press, had thought it right to prosecute the conductors and proprietors of three several journals. A verdict of libel was given in one case; and, in the others, the prosecutions were withdrawn, upon the individuals retracting and disavowing the charges, expressing regret that they had been made, and promising to abstain from the like in future.—W.

p. 49. XLVI. THE SOMNAMBULIST: "This poem might be dedicated to my friends Sir G. Beaumont and Mr. Rogers, jointly. While we were making an excursion together in this part of the Lake District we heard that Mr. Glover, the Artist, while lodging at Lyulph's Tower, had been disturbed by a loud shriek, and upon rising he had learnt that it had come from a young woman in the house who was in the habit of walking in her sleep: in that state she had gone downstairs, and, while attempting to open the outer door, either from some difficulty or the effect of the cold stone upon her feet, had uttered the cry which alarmed him. It seemed to us all that this might serve as a hint for a poem, and the story here told was constructed, and soon after put into verse by me as it now stands."—I. F. In ed. 1837 W. dated the poem 1833, but he wrote of it to Rogers in July 1830 as written more than a year ago, and it is found in a manuscript with other work of 1828. Sir George Beaumont died in Feb. 1827, and he and Rogers had spent some time with W. in the Lake country during the previous summer.

84–5. that pale Queen] Lady Macbeth. (*Macbeth* v. 1.)

150. From vain temptations free] Cf. *Ode to Duty* (early draft).

p. 54. XLVII. To CORDELIA M——: i.e. Cordelia Marshall, daughter of D. W.'s great friend, Jane Marshall. In 1841 she married William Whewell, who succeeded W.'s brother as Master of Trinity, Cambridge, in that year.

POEMS OF SENTIMENT AND REFLECTION

p. 56. I. EXPOSTULATION AND REPLY: "This poem is a favourite among the Quakers, as I have learnt on many occasions. It was composed in front of the house at Alfoxden in the spring of 1798."—I. F.

Hutchinson points out that the friend alluded to in the *Advertisement* to *L.B.* 1798 [the two poems "arose out of a conversation with a friend who was somewhat unreasonably attached to modern books of Moral Philosophy"] was Hazlitt, who visited W. at Alfoxden in May–June 1798. Hazlitt was at the time busy over his *Essay on the Principles of Human Action*, and later, in his essay *On my First Acquaintance with Poets*, he relates that one evening "I got into a metaphysical argument with W. while Coleridge was explaining the different notes of the nightingale to his sister, in which we neither of us succeeded in making ourselves perfectly clear and intelligible".

15. For Matthew v. X, *infra*.

p. 58. III. LINES WRITTEN IN EARLY SPRING: "1798. Actually composed while I was sitting by the side of the brook that runs down from the Comb, in which stands the village of Alford, through the grounds of Alfoxden. It was a chosen resort of mine. The brook fell down a sloping rock so as to make a waterfall considerable for that country, and across the pool below had fallen a tree, an ash, if I

rightly remember, from which rose perpendicularly boughs in search
of the light intercepted by the deep shade above. The boughs bore
leaves of green that for want of sunshine had faded into almost lily-
white; and from the underside of this natural sylvan bridge depended
long and beautiful tresses of ivy which waved gently in the breeze
that might poetically speaking be called the breath of the waterfall.
This motion varied of course in proportion to the power of water in
the brook. When, with dear friends, I revisited this spot, after an
interval of more than forty years, this interesting feature of the scene
was gone. To the owner of the place I could not but regret that the
beauty of this retired part of the grounds had not tempted him to
make it more accessible by a path, not broad or obtrusive, but
sufficient for persons who love such scenes to creep along without
difficulty."—I. F.

p. 58. IV. A CHARACTER: "The principal features are taken from
that of my friend Robert Jones."—I. F. For Jones v. Vol. III,
Sonnets, pp. 41 and 110 and Notes. *A Character* was omitted from
edd. 1802–32. In 1800 it had the title *A Character, in the Antithetical
Manner.*

p. 59. V. TO MY SISTER: "Composed in front of Alfoxden House.
My little boy-messenger on this occasion was the son of Basil Montagu.
The larch mentioned in the first stanza was standing when I revisited
the place in May, 1841, more than forty years after. I was disappointed that it had not improved in appearance as to size, nor had it
acquired anything of the majesty of age, which, even though less
perhaps than any other tree, the larch sometimes does. A few score
yards from this tree grew, when we inhabited Alfoxden, one of the
most remarkable beech-trees ever seen. The ground sloped both
towards and from it. It was of immense size, and threw out arms
that struck into the soil, like those of the banyan tree, and rose again
from it. Two of the branches thus inserted themselves twice, which
gave to each the appearance of a serpent moving along by gathering
itself up in folds. One of the large boughs of this tree had been torn
off by the wind before we left Alfoxden, but five remained. In 1841
we could barely find the spot where the tree had stood. So remarkable
a production of nature could not have been wilfully destroyed."—I. F.

p. 60. VI. SIMON LEE: "This old man had been huntsman to the
Squires of Alfoxden, which, at the time we occupied it, belonged to
a minor. The old man's cottage stood upon the common, a little way
from the entrance to Alfoxden Park. But it had disappeared. Many
other changes had taken place in the adjoining village, which I could
not but notice with a regret more natural than well-considered.
Improvements but rarely appear such to those who, after long intervals of time, revisit places they have had much pleasure in. It is
unnecessary to add, the fact was as mentioned in the poem; and I
have, after an interval of 45 years, the image of the old man as fresh

before my eyes as if I had seen him yesterday. The expression when the hounds were out, 'I dearly love their voices' was word for word from his own lips."—I. F.

On the text of no other short poem did W. expend so much labour as on *Simon Lee*. As Dowden has pointed out, "the first seven stanzas are found in different texts and different sequence in 1798, 1802, 1820, 1827, 1832. Words and lines were altered, stanzas shifted in position, and new stanzas constructed by connecting the halves of certain stanzas with the halves of others." The object, as Hutchinson suggests, was probably "to broaden and emphasize the contrast between Simon's radiant youth and decrepit age. In 1798 contrasted traits of youth and age jostle each other throughout the several stanzas . . . in 1832 the traits and evidences of Simon's early vigour are concentrated within stanzas 1–3, while those of his sad decline are brought together in stanzas 4–7, the contrast being marked by the phrase 'But oh, the heavy change!' " I have given in the *app. crit.* the text of 1798; the later progress of the text was as follows: [a = ll. 1–4; b = ll. 5–8 of each stanza].

In 1800, the only change was in 5. l. 2 little *to* dwindled.

In 1802–15 stanzas 4, 5, 6 are transposed to the order 5, 6, 4.

In 1820 the order becomes 1a 2b, 3, 4a 5b, 6, 5a 4b, 7, 8, 9.

In 1827 the order becomes 1a 2b, 4a 3b, 3a 5b, 6, 5a 4b, 8, 7, 9.

In 1832 the order becomes 1a 2b, 3a 5b, 6, 4a 3b, *etc.* as 1827.

These changes in order were accompanied by some changes in the text. The final reading of ll. 7–8 dates from 1820, as also does that of ll. 27–9 (*but with* And *for* Old) and of l. 35. The final reading of ll. 4–5 and 13–16 dates from 1827. In 1827 also ll. 25–6 read:

> Worn out by hunting feats—bereft
> By time of friends and kindred, see!

The final reading dates from 1832. Lines 47–8 reached their final stage only in 1845.

> "But what," saith he, "avails the land,
> Which I can till no longer ?" 1827.
> But what avails it now, the land,
> Which he can till no longer ? 1832.
> 'Tis his, but what avails the land,
> Which he can till no longer ? 1837.
> The time alas! is come, when he
> Can till the land no longer. 1840.
> A sad possession now, for he
> Can till the land no longer. C.

> For 1798–1820 *v. app. crit.*

The final reading of ll. 55–6 dates from 1840.

25. But, oh the heavy change] From *Lycidas*, 37.

p. 64. VII. WRITTEN IN GERMANY: "1798 and 1799. A bitter winter it was when these verses were composed by the side of my Sister, in our lodgings at a draper's house in the romantic imperial town of Goslar, on the edge of the Hartz Forest. In this town the German emperors of the Franconian line were accustomed to keep their court, and it retains vestiges of ancient splendour. So severe was the cold of this winter, that when we passed out of the parlour warmed by the stove, our cheeks were struck by the air as by cold iron. I slept in a room over a passage which was not ceiled. The people of the house used to say, rather unfeelingly, that they expected I should be frozen to death some night; but, with the protection of a pelisse lined with fur, and a dog's-skin bonnet, such as was worn by the peasants, I walked daily on the ramparts, or in a sort of public ground or garden, in which was a pond. Here, I had no companion but a kingfisher, a beautiful creature, that used to glance by me. I consequently became much attached to it. During these walks I composed the poem that follows, *The Poet's Epitaph*."—I. F.

p. 65. VIII. THE POET'S EPITAPH: Mr. T. E. Casson (*Times Lit. Suppl.*, Sept. 11, 1937) calls attention to the parallel between this poem, especially the last couplet, and Theocritus, *Epigram* XIX:

'Ο μουσοποιὸς ἐνθάδ' 'Ιππῶναξ κεῖται.
εἰ μὲν πονηρός, μὴ ποτέρχευ τῷ τύμβῳ·
εἰ δ' ἐσσὶ κρήγυός τε καὶ παρὰ χρηστῶν,
θαρσέων καθίζευ, κὴν θέλῃς, ἀπόβριξον.

(Here lies the poet Hipponax! If thou art a sinner draw not near this tomb, but if thou art a true man, and the son of righteous sires, sit boldly down here, yea, and sleep if thou wilt. Trs. Lang.) It is noteworthy that in the February of the year in which the poem was composed W., in writing to Coleridge, refers to Theocritus. Cf. also Burns, *A Bard's Epitaph*.

24. (*App. crit.*) Lamb wrote in a letter, 1801: "*The Poet's Epitaph* is disfigured, to my taste, by the common satire upon parsons and lawyers in the beginning, and the coarse epithet of 'pin-point' in the sixth stanza."

p. 67. IX. TO THE DAISY: "This and the other poems addressed to the same flower were composed at Town-end, Grasmere, during the earlier part of my residence there. I have been censured for the last line but one—'thy function apostolical'—as being little less than profane. How could it be thought so? The word is adopted with reference to its derivation, implying something sent on a mission; and assuredly this little flower, especially when the subject of verse, may be regarded, in its humble degree, as administering both to moral and to spiritual purposes."—I. F.

Placed among *Poems of the Fancy*, 1815–32.

21–4. *v. The Simpliciad*:

Of Apostolic daisies learn to think,
Draughts from their urns of true devotion drink.

p. 68. X. MATTHEW: "Such a Tablet as is here spoken of continued to be preserved in Hawkshead School, though the inscriptions were not brought down to our time. This and other poems connected with Matthew would not gain by a literal detail of facts. Like the Wanderer in 'The Excursion', this Schoolmaster was made up of several both of his class and men of other occupations. I do not ask pardon for what there is of untruth in such verses, considered strictly as matters of fact. It is enough if, being true and consistent in spirit, they move and teach in a manner not unworthy of a Poet's calling."—I. F. Cf. Note to *Address to the Scholars of the Village School of* ——, p. 451 *infra*.

p. 73. XIII. PERSONAL TALK: "Written at Town-end. The last line but two stood, at first, better and more characteristically thus:

'By my half-kitchen and half-parlour fire.'

My Sister and I were in the habit of having the tea-kettle in our little sitting-room; and we toasted the bread ourselves, which reminds me of a little circumstance not unworthy of being set down among these minutiæ. Happening both of us to be engaged a few minutes one morning when we had a young prig of a Scotch lawyer to breakfast with us, my dear Sister, with her usual simplicity, put the toasting-fork with a slice of bread into the hands of this Edinburgh genius. Our little book-case stood on one side of the fire. To prevent loss of time, he took down a book, and fell to reading to the neglect of the toast, which was burnt to a cinder. Many a time we laughed at this circumstance, and other cottage simplicities of that day. By the bye, I have a spite at one of this series of Sonnets (I will leave the reader to discover which) as having been the means of nearly putting off for ever our acquaintance with dear Miss Fenwick, who has always stigmatised one line of it as vulgar, and worthy only of having been composed by a country Squire."—I. F.

6. maidens withering on the stalk] The line "stigmatised" by Miss Fenwick; but it is a reminiscence of the speech of Theseus to Hermia in *A Midsummer-Night's Dream*, I. i. 76–8.

> But earthlier happy is the rose distilled
> Than that which withering on the virgin thorn
> Grows, lives, and dies, in single blessedness;

Cf. also *Comus*, 743:

> If you let slip time, like a neglected rose
> It withers on the stalk with languished head.

25–6. sweetest melodies . . . sweet] From Collins, *Ode, The Passions*, 60:

> In notes by distance made more sweet.

W. had already borrowed the phrase in *An Evening Walk*, 237.

32. with the lofty sanctifies the low] Cf. *Prelude*, xiv. 271, and

Epitaphs translated from Chiabrera, iv. 24, p. 250 *supra*, and *Excursion*, vii. 1047. All go back to Isaiah ii. 12.

41–2. W. told R. P. Graves that "the Tragedy of *Othello*, Plato's record of the last scenes of the career of Socrates, and Isaac Walton's *Life of George Herbert*, were in his opinion the most pathetic of human compositions". For his love of the first book of the *Faerie Queene v.* dedication to *The White Doe of Rylstone*.

44–5. remote . . . thought] On this rhyme *v.* Vol. I, p. 367.

p. 75. XIV. ILLUSTRATED BOOKS AND NEWSPAPERS: K. notes that "*The Illustrated London News*—the pioneer of illustrated news-papers—was first issued on 14th May 1842".

p. 75. XV. TO THE SPADE OF A FRIEND: "This person was Thomas Wilkinson, a quaker by religious profession; by natural con-stitution of mind, or shall I venture to say, by God's grace, he was something better. He had inherited a small estate, and built a house upon it near Yanwath, upon the banks of the Emont. I have heard him say that his heart used to beat, in his boyhood, when he heard the sound of a drum and fife. Nevertheless, the spirit of enterprise in him confined itself to tilling his ground, and conquering such obstacles as stood in the way of its fertility. Persons of his religious persuasion do now, in a far greater degree than formerly, attach themselves to trade and commerce. He kept the old track. As represented in this poem, he employed his leisure hours in shaping pleasant walks by the side of his beloved river, where he also built something between a hermitage and a summer-house, attaching to it inscriptions after the manner of Shenstone at his Leasowes. He used to travel from time to time, partly from love of nature, and partly with religious friends in the service of humanity. His admiration of genius in every department did him much honour. Through his connection with the family in which Edmund Burke was educated, he became acquainted with that great man, who used to receive him with great kindness and consideration; and many times have I heard Wilkinson speak of those interesting interviews. He was honoured also by the friendship of Elizabeth Smith, and of Thomas Clarkson and his excellent wife, and he was much esteemed by Lord and Lady Lonsdale, and every member of that family. Among his verses (he wrote many) are some worthy of preservation—one little poem in particular upon disturbing, by prying curiosity, a bird while hatching her young in his garden. The latter part of this innocent and good man's life was melancholy. He became blind, and also poor by becoming surety for some of his relations. He was a bachelor. He bore, as I have often witnessed, his calamities with unfailing resigna-tion. I will only add that, while working in one of his fields, he un-earthed a stone of considerable size, then another, then two more, and, observing that they had been placed in order as if forming the segment of a circle, he proceeded carefully to uncover the soil, and brought into view a beautiful Druids' temple of perfect though small dimensions. In order to make his farm more compact, he exchanged this field for another; and, I am sorry to add, the new proprietor destroyed this interesting relic of remote ages for some vulgar purpose. The fact, so far as concerns Thomas Wilkinson, is mentioned in the note on a Sonnet on Long Meg and her Daughters."—I. F.

For Wilkinson v. also note to *The Solitary Reaper* (Vol. III, pp. 444–5).

28. For the change in text from the reading of 1807 (*v. app. crit.*) v. note to XVIII, *infra*.

p. 77. XVI. A NIGHT THOUGHT: "These verses were thrown off extempore upon leaving Mrs. Luff's house at Fox-Ghyll, one evening. The good woman is not disposed to look at the bright side of things, and there happened to be present certain ladies who had reached the point of life where *youth* is ended, who seemed to contend with each other in expressing their dislike of the country and climate. One of them had been heard to say she could not endure a country where there was 'neither sunshine nor cavaliers'."—I. F. On Mrs. Luff v. *E.L.*, pp. 277–8.

p. 77. XVII. INCIDENT CHARACTERISTIC OF A FAVOURITE DOG: "This Dog I knew well. It belonged to Mrs. Wordsworth's brother, Mr. Thomas Hutchinson, who then lived at Sockburn on the Tees, a beautiful retired situation where I used to visit him and his sisters before my marriage. My Sister and I spent many months there after our return from Germany in 1799."—I. F.

p. 79. XVIII. TRIBUTE TO THE MEMORY OF THE SAME DOG: The changes introduced into the text (*v. app. crit.*) were perhaps due to the contemptuous reference in *The Simpliciad* to poets who "Pray for their spaniels, consecrate their spades".

p. 80. XIX. FIDELITY: "The young man whose death gave occasion to this poem was named Charles Gough, and had come early in the spring to Patterdale for the sake of angling. While attempting to cross over Helvellyn to Grasmere he slipped from a steep part of the rock where the ice was not thawed, and perished. His body was discovered as is told in this poem. Walter Scott heard of the accident, and both he and I, without either of us knowing that the other had taken up the subject, each wrote a poem in admiration of the dog's fidelity. His contains a most beautiful stanza:—

'How long didst thou think that his silence was slumber?
When the wind waved his garment how oft didst thou start?'
        [*v.* note to *Musings near Aquapendente*, Vol. III, pp. 490–1.]

I will add that the sentiment in the last four lines of the last stanza in my verses was uttered by a shepherd with such exactness, that a traveller, who afterwards reported his account in print, was induced to question the man whether he had read them, which he had not."—I. F.

The lines (*v. app. crit.*) which W. omitted from the printed (1807) version of *Fidelity* are preserved in two manuscripts, one at Coleorton and the other, in the hand of S. H., at Grasmere.

p. 83. XX. ODE TO DUTY: "This Ode, written 1805, is on the model of Gray's Ode to Adversity which is copied from Horace's Ode to Fortune; [but is not the first stanza of Gray's from a Chorus of Æschylus ? and is not Horace's Ode also modelled on the Greek ?] Many and many a time have I been twitted by my wife and sister for having forgotten this dedication of myself to the stern lawgiver. Transgressor indeed I have been, from hour to hour, from day to day ; I would fain hope, however, not more flagrantly nor in a worse way than most of my tuneful brethren. But these last words are in a wrong strain. We should be rigorous to ourselves, and forbearing if not indulgent to others, and if we make comparisons at all it ought to be with those who have morally excelled us."—I. F. (The passage in square brackets written in, in pencil, in E. Q.'s hand.)

W.'s dating of the poem has been proved to be inaccurate. On April 7, 1805, Coleridge entered in a note-book: "I remember having written a strong letter to my most dear and honoured W. in consequence of his Ode to Duty." It is obvious, from his wording, that C. refers to a more or less distant date ; further, in writing to Stuart, April 20, he says he has had no letter from W. since one dated the previous September. It seems highly probable, as Nowell Smith suggests in *Times Lit. Suppl.*, June 20, 1935, that the ode was written soon after Coleridge left Grasmere in Jan. 1804, and was sent on to him to take with him to Malta. Its presence in MS. M corroborates this. In addition to MS. M two manuscripts are known to be extant, the *Longman* MS., and a transcript in the Beaumont collection at Coleorton. They are referred to in the *app. crit.* as M, L, and B.

While the debt to Gray's Ode to Adversity is obvious enough, it is interesting to note how W. had Milton at the back of his mind as he wrote. *v.* notes *infra*.

The motto is adapted from Seneca, *Moral Epistles*, cxx. 10 ; it was suggested to W. by Barron Field in a letter dated Dec. 17, 1836.

1. daughter of the voice of God] Cf. *Paradise Lost*, ix. 652–3 :

> God so commanded, and left that Command
> Sole Daughter of his voice.

31. (*app. crit.*) shoved away] Cf. *Lycidas*, 118 : "And shove away the worthy bidden guest."

38. I feel the weight *etc.*] Cf. *Misc. Sonnets*, i. 13.

41–8. This stanza was omitted from the text after 1807, but, following Hutchinson, I venture to restore it as a valuable link in the thought. The quotation in it is from Milton : Dedication to the Parliament of England of *The Doctrine and Discipline of Divorce* : "to enslave the dignity of Man, to put a garrison upon his neck of empty and over-dignified precepts."

55–6. These two lines, the most imaginative in the poem, were denounced by the *Edinburgh Review* as "utterly without meaning; we have no sort of conception in what sense *Duty* can be said to keep the old skies *fresh*, and the stars from wrong" (Oct. 1807).

61. lowly wise] Cf. *Paradise Lost*, viii. 173:

> Be lowly wise;
> Think only what concerns thee and thy being.

63. confidence of reason]: Professor Beatty points out that W. owed this phrase to Johnson's *Life of Addison*: "Truth . . . sometimes attracts regard in the robes of fancy, and sometimes steps forth in the confidence of reason."

p. 86. XXI. CHARACTER OF THE HAPPY WARRIOR: The above verses were written soon after tidings had been received of the Death of Lord Nelson, which event directed the Author's thoughts to the subject. His respect for the memory of his great fellow-countryman induces him to mention this; though he is well aware that the Verses must suffer from any connection in the Reader's mind with a Name so illustrious.—W. 1807.

"The course of the great war with the French naturally fixed one's attention upon the military character, and, to the honour of our country, there were many illustrious instances of the qualities that constitute its highest excellence. Lord Nelson carried most of the virtues that the trials he was exposed to in his department of the service necessarily call forth and sustain, if they do not produce the contrary vices. But his public life was stained with one great crime, so that, though many passages of these lines were suggested by what was generally known as excellent in his conduct, I have not been able to connect his name with the poem as I could wish, or even to think of him with satisfaction in reference to the idea of what a warrior ought to be. For the sake of such of my friends as may happen to read this note I will add, that many elements of the character here portrayed were found in my brother John, who perished by shipwreck as mentioned elsewhere. His messmates used to call him the Philosopher, from which it must be inferred that the qualities and dispositions I allude to had not escaped their notice. He often expressed his regret, after the war had continued some time, that he had not chosen the Naval, instead of the East India Company's service, to which his family connection had led him. He greatly valued moral and religious instruction for youth, as tending to make good sailors. The best, he used to say, came from Scotland; the next to them, from the North of England, especially from Westmoreland and Cumberland, where, thanks to the piety and local attachments of our ancestors, endowed, or, as they are commonly called, free, schools abound."—I. F.

It is probable that W. was also influenced in writing the poem by his memories of Beaupuy (*v. Prelude*, ix) and by Daniel's *Funerall Poem Upon the Earl of Devonshire*.

6–34. Cf. passages in W.'s letters to Sir G. Beaumont on his brother John (*E.L.*, pp. 452, 462): "Of all human beings whom I ever knew, he was the man of the most rational desires, the most sedate habits, and the most perfect self-command." "I will here transcribe a passage which I met with the other day . . . from Aristotle's *Synopsis of the Virtues and Vices*. 'It is,' says he, 'the property of fortitude not to be easily terrified by the dread of things pertaining to death; to possess good confidence in things terrible, and presence of mind in dangers; rather to prefer to be put to death worthily, than to be preserved basely; and to be the cause of victory. Moreover, it is the property of fortitude to labour and endure, and to make valorous exertion an object of choice. Further, presence of mind, a well-disposed soul, confidence and boldness are the attendants on fortitude; and, besides these, industry and patience.' Except in the circumstance of making valorous exertion 'an object of *choice*' (if the philosopher alludes to general habits of character), my brother might have sat for this picture; but he was of a meek and retired nature, loving all quiet things."

33–44. Cf. Daniel's *Funerall Poem Upon the Earl of Devonshire*, 139–45:

> For that which many, whom ambition foyles
> And tortures with their hopes, hardly attaine
> With all their thrusts, and shouldring plots, and wiles
> Was easily made thine, without thy paine.
> And without any private malicing
> Or publique greevance, every good man joy'd
> That vertue could come cleere to any thing.

48–60. Cf. ib. 107–14:

> Although in peace, thou seem'dst to be all peace
> Yet being in warre, thou wert all warre, and there
> As in thy spheere thy spirits did never cease
> To move with indefatigable care,
> And nothing seem'd more to arride thy heart
> Nor more inlarge thee into jollity,
> Then when thou sawest thy selfe in armour girt,
> Or any act of armes like to be nye.

75–6. persevering to the last From well to better]

> "For Knightes ever should be persevering
> To seek honour without feintise or slouth
> Fro well to better in all manner thing."
>
> CHAUCER.—*The Floure and the Leafe*: W. 1807.

p. 88. XXII. THE FORCE OF PRAYER: "An Appendage to *The White Doe*. My friend, Mr. Rogers, has also written on the subject.

The story is preserved in Dr. Whitaker's 'History of Craven'—a topographical writer of first-rate merit in all that concerns the past; but such was his aversion from the modern spirit, as shown in the spread of manufactures in those districts of which he treats, that his readers are left entirely ignorant both of the progress of these arts and their real bearing upon the comfort, virtues, and happiness of the inhabitants. While wandering on foot through the fertile valleys and over the moorlands of the Apennine that divides Yorkshire from Lancashire, I used to be delighted with observing the number of substantial cottages that had sprung up on every side, each having its little plot of fertile ground won from the surrounding waste. A bright and warm fire, if needed, was always to be found in these dwellings. The father was at his loom; the children looked healthy and happy. Is it not to be feared that the increase of mechanic power has done away with many of these blessings, and substituted many evils? Alas! if these evils grow, how are they to be checked, and where is the remedy to be found? Political economy will not supply it; that is certain, we must look to something deeper, purer, and higher."
—I. F.

For date of composition *v.* D. W.'s Letter to Jane Marshall, Oct. 18, 1807 (*M.Y.*, p. 146).

39–40. (*app. crit.*) "Alluding to a Ballad of Logan's. W. W., 1807" K. (referring one must suppose to a manuscript). Lines 39–46 of the poem clearly recall Logan's *The Braes of Yarrow*.

p. 91. XXIII. A FACT, AND AN IMAGINATION: "The first and last fourteen lines of this Poem each make a sonnet, and were composed as such; but I thought that by intermediate lines they might be connected so as to make a whole. One or two expressions are taken from Milton's *History of England*."—I. F.

The last fourteen lines of the poem are printed by K. and N. C. Smith, but with opening line, 'My son, behold the tide already spent', as an unpublished sonnet found in the same MS. as "Through Cumbrian Wilds". *v.* Appendix III, Vol. III, *supra*, p. 409.

On Canute and Alfred W. also wrote two *Ecclesiastical Sonnets* I. xxvi and xxx.

1–14. "He caused his royal seat to be set on the shore, while the tide was coming in; and with all the state that royalty could put into his countenance, said thus to the sea: 'Thou, Sea, belongest to me, and the land whereon I sit is mine; nor hath any one unpunished resisted my commands; I charge thee come no further upon my land, neither presume to wet the feet of thy sovereign lord.' *But the sea, as before, came rolling on,* and without reverence both wet and dashed him. Wherat *the King quickly rising* wished all about him to behold and consider the weak and frivolous power of a King, and that none indeed *deserved the name of King, but he whose eternal laws both heaven, earth, and sea obey.*"—Milton, *History of Britain*, bk. vi.

p. 92. XXIV. "*A little onward lend thy guiding hand.*" "The complaint in my eyes which gave occasion to this address to my daughter first showed itself as a consequence of inflammation, caught at the top of Kirkstone, when I was over-heated by having carried up the ascent my eldest son, a lusty infant [in Jan. 1805: *v. E.L*, p. 433]. Frequently has the disease recurred since, leaving my eyes in a state which has often prevented my reading for months, and makes me at this day incapable of bearing without injury any strong light by day or night. My acquaintance with books has therefore been far short of my wishes; and on this account, to acknowledge the services daily and hourly done me by my family and friends, this note is written."—I. F.

1–2. From *Samson Agonistes, init.*

11. The reference, in the early text, to Antigone alludes to her guidance of her blind father Oedipus from Thebes to Attica.

31. "abrupt abyss"]: From *Paradise Lost*, ii. 405, "The dark, unbottomed, infinite Abyss", and ii. 409, "the vast Abrupt".

32. plumy vans]: From *Paradise Regaind*, iv. 583.

49–55. (*app. crit.*) everlasting gates . . . portals!] reminiscent of *Paradise Lost*, vii. 565–76. *v. Addenda*, p. 468.

p. 94. XXV. ODE TO LYCORIS: " The discerning reader, who is aware that in the poem of 'Ellen Irwin' I was desirous of throwing the reader at once out of the old ballad, so as, if possible, to preclude a comparison between that mode of dealing with the subject and the mode I meant to adopt—may here perhaps perceive that this poem originated in the four last lines of the first stanza. Those specks of snow, reflected in the lake and so transferred, as it were, to the subaqueous sky, reminded me of the swans which the fancy of the ancient classic poets yoked to the car of Venus. Hence the tenor of the whole first stanza, and the name of Lycoris, which—with some readers who think mythology and classical allusion too far-fetched and therefore more or less unnatural and affected—will tend to unrealize the sentiment that pervades these verses. But surely one who has written so much in verse as I have done may be allowed to retrace his steps in the regions of fancy which delighted him in his boyhood, when he first became acquainted with the Greek and Roman Poets. Before I read Virgil I was so strongly attached to Ovid, whose Metamorphoses I read at school, that I was quite in a passion whenever I found him, in books of criticism, placed below Virgil. As to Homer, I was never weary of travelling over the scenes through which he led me. Classical literature affected me by its own beauty. But the truths of scripture having been entrusted to the dead languages, and these fountains having been recently laid open at the Reformation, an importance and a sanctity were at that period attached to classical literature that extended, as is obvious in Milton's "Lycidas", for example, both to its spirit and form in a degree that can never be

revived. No doubt the hackneyed and lifeless use into which mythology fell towards the close of the seventeenth century, and which
continued through the eighteenth, disgusted the general reader with
all allusion to it in modern verse; and though, in deference to this
disgust, and also in a measure participating in it, I abstained in my
earlier writings from all introduction of pagan fable—surely, even
in its humble form, it may ally itself with real sentiment—as I can
truly affirm it did in the present case."—I. F. W. took the name
Lycoris from Virgil, *Eclogue*, x: it has no special significance for him.

p. 96. XXVI. To THE SAME: "This as well as the preceding and
the two that follow were composed in front of Rydal Mount and
during my walks in the neighbourhood. Nine-tenths of my verses
have been murmured out in the open air; and here let me repeat
what I believe has already appeared in print. One day a stranger
having walked round the garden and grounds of Rydal Mount asked
one of the female servants who happened to be at the door, permission to see her master's study. 'This', said she, leading him forward,
'is my master's library, where he keeps his books, but his study is
out of doors.' After a long absence from home it has more than once
happened that some one of my cottage neighbours has said—'Well,
there he is; we are glad to hear him *booing* about again.' Once more,
in excuse for so much egotism, let me say, these notes are written for my
familiar friends, and at their earnest request. Another time a gentleman whom James had conducted through the grounds asked him
what kind of plants throve best there: after a little consideration he
answered—'Laurels.' 'That is', said the stranger 'as it should be;
don't you know that the Laurel is the emblem of Poetry, and that the
Poets used on public occasions to be crowned with it?' James stared
when the question was first put, but was doubtless much pleased
with the information."—I. F.

Though the date of this poem as a whole is doubtless 1817, ll. 41
ff. have a much earlier source, and some of them seem to have
haunted W.'s mind for nearly twenty years. In the draft of *Nutting*
written in 1798 (*v.* Vol. II, p. 504) is found a form of ll. 42–45, and in
MS. M (1803–4) are the following verses under the title *Travelling*:

> This is the spot:—how mildly does the sun
> Shine in between the fading leaves! the air
> In the habitual silence of this wood
> Is more than silent; and this bed of heath—
> Where shall we find so sweet a resting-place?
> Come, let me see thee sink into a dream
> Of quiet thoughts, protracted till thine eye
> Be calm as water when the winds are gone
> And no one can tell whither. My sweet Friend,
> We two have had such happy hours together
> That my heart melts in me to think of it.

This is the poem to which D. W. refers in her *Journal*, May 4, 1802: "I repeated verses to William while he was in bed; he was soothed and I left him. 'This is the spot' over and over again."

And at the close of a note-book containing the *Duddon* Sonnets is the following:

> Here let us rest,—here, where the gentle beams
> Of noontide stealing in between the boughs
> Illuminate their faded leaves; the air
> In the habitual silence of this wood
> Is more than silent, and this tuft of heath
> Decked with the fulness of its (bloom) flowers presents
> As beautiful a couch as ere was framed.
> Come let us venture to exchange the pomp[1]
> Of wide-spread landscape for the internal wealth
> Of quiet thought, protracted *etc. as text* 43–51, *but in* l. 46

blissful *for* happy.

p. 98. XXVII and XXVIII. *v.* I. F. note to XXVI, and for the redbreast's autumn song cf. *Prelude*, vii. 18–31.

p. 99. XXVIII. 14. my leaf is sere] *Macbeth*, v. iii. 23.

42. fierce vindictive song] H. T. Rhoades has suggested that here, perhaps, W. was recalling Horace, *Odes*, IV. ix. 7, "Alcaei minaces Camenae."

43–8. A reference to Sappho's ode to Aphrodite.

50. The wreck of Herculanean lore] K. notes that during the excavations in Herculaneum in 1752, 1,800 charred rolls of papyri were discovered, and it was hoped that they would add greatly to the *corpus* of classical literature. Simonides, born in Ceos, 556 B.C., one of the most celebrated of Greek lyric poets, was endeared to W. by the story told of him to which W. refers in his sonnet, "I find it written of Simonides" (*v.* Vol. III, p. 408, and note, p. 573), and in his *Essay on Epitaphs*.

p. 101. XXIX. MEMORY: *v.* I. F. note to *Written in a Blank Leaf of Macpherson's Ossian* (p. 38), p. 407 above.

p. 102. XXX. *This Lawn, a carpet all alive*: "This Lawn is the sloping one approaching the kitchen-garden, and was made out of it. Hundreds of times have I watched the dancing of shadows amid a press of sunshine, and other beautiful appearances of light and shade, flowers and shrubs. What a contrast between this and the Cabbages and Onions and Carrots that used to grow there on a piece of ugly-shaped unsightly ground! No reflection, however, either upon Cabbages or Onions; the latter we know were worshipped by the Egyptians, and he must have a poor eye for beauty who has not observed how much of it there is in the form and colour which Cabbages and

---

[1] *Corr. to* Come, thus invited, venture to exchange
      The pomp of wide-spread landscape for a mood.

plants of that genus exhibit through the various stages of their growth and decay. A richer display of colour in vegetable nature can scarcely be conceived than Coleridge, my Sister, and I saw in a bed of Potato-plants in blossom near a hut upon the moor between Inversneyd and Loch Katrine. These blossoms were of such extraordinary beauty and richness that no one could have passed them without notice. But the sense must be cultivated through the mind before we can perceive these inexhaustible treasures of Nature, for such they really are, without the least necessary reference to the utility of her productions, or even to the laws whereupon, as we learn by research, they are dependent. Some are of opinion that the habit of analysing, decomposing, and anatomizing is inevitably unfavourable to the perception of beauty. People are led into this mistake by over-looking the fact that such processes being to a certain extent within the reach of a limited intellect, we are apt to ascribe to them that insensibility of which they are in truth the effect and not the cause. Admiration and love, to which all knowledge truly vital must tend, are felt by men of real genius in proportion as their discoveries in natural Philosophy are enlarged; and the beauty in form of a plant or an animal is not made less but more apparent as a whole by more accurate insight into its constituent properties and powers. A *Savant* who is not also a Poet in soul and a religionist in heart is a feeble and unhappy Creature."—I. F.

6. strenuous idleness] A phrase already used by W. in *Prelude*, iv. 378. W. owed it to Horace, *Epistles*, I. xi. 28, "strenua nos exercet inertia". *v.* also *E.L.*, p. 48.

p. 102. XXXI. HUMANITY: Note under heading: "... at this day". "There is a remarkable one upon a Moorland Eminence overlooking the Vale of the Nid in Yorkshire", MS. "These verses and those entitled *Liberty* were composed as one piece, which Mrs. Wordsworth complained of as unwieldy and ill-proportioned; and accordingly it was divided into two on her judicious recommendation."—I. F.

32. Descending to the worm in charity] I am indebted, here, to a passage in one of Mr. Digby's valuable works—W. (i.e. Kenelm Digby, 1800–80, author of *The Broadstone of Honour*, 1822, enlarged 1827–8.)

78. Stone-walls a prisoner make] Lovelace, *To Althea from Prison*, 25.

77–94. Cf. Exc. VIII and IX, 113–28.

83. "Slaves cannot breathe in England"] From Cowper, *The Task*, ii. 40.

89–90. Idol, falsely called "the Wealth of Nations"] Cf. *Prelude*, xiii. 77.

p. 106. XXXII. *The unremitting voice of nightly streams*: In one manuscript this poem is headed *Introduction to the Somnambulist* (*v.* p. 49).

5. (*app. crit.*) at dewy eve the shutting flowers] Cf. *Paradise Lost*, ix. 278, "at shut of evening flowers".

10–17. (*app. crit.*) "The Hermit's Cell, nr. Knaresboro." MS. marginal note.

p. 107. XXXIII. THOUGHTS ON THE SEASONS: "Written at Rydal Mount, 1829."—I. F. *v. Addenda*, p. 468.

p. 107. XXXIV. To ——: "*To I—— W—— on the birth of her first child*. Written at Moresby near Whitehaven, when I was on a visit to my son, then Incumbent of that small living.

"While I am dictating these notes to my Friend, Miss Fenwick, January 24, 1843, the Child upon whose birth these verses were written is under my roof, and is of a disposition so promising that the wishes and prayers and prophecies which I then breathed forth in verse are, through God's mercy, likely to be realized."—I. F. Isabella (née Curwen), wife of John W. The quotation that heads the poem is from Lucretius *De Rerum Natura*, v. 223.

p. 110. XXXV. THE WARNING: "These lines were composed during the fever spread through the Nation by the Reform Bill. As the motives which led to this measure, and the good or evil which has attended or has risen from it, will be duly appreciated by future Historians, there is no call for dwelling on the subject in this place. I will content myself with saying that the then condition of the people's mind is not, in these verses, exaggerated."—I. F.

In a letter to his family W. spoke of this poem as "a sober and sorrowful sequel to [XXXIV] which I fear none of you will like" (*L.Y.*, p. 645). It represents, indeed, the lowest depths of depression to which W. sank in his poetry, though it can be paralleled by many places in his letters of the period.

The MS. copy of the Postscript at the end of the volume of 1835, sent to the Printer, contains the following opening paragraphs, afterwards cancelled:

"It has from time to time been the practice of the Author of this volume, since he was first interested in public affairs, to express in verse the feelings with which he regarded them. Accordingly it is known to all who have read his poems, that he rejoiced in the opening of the French Revolution; and it will appear hereafter, from his unpublished works, how deeply he deplored the excesses into which the French people were betrayed in its progress. His *Excursion*, Sonnets and other Pieces afford abundant evidence how he abhorred the abuses of Power that Buonaparte fell into; how he sympathized with the Nations that suffered from the Despot's reckless ambitions; and how he exalted in their deliverance. After the battle of Waterloo, the course of public events, however interesting to an observing and thoughtful Mind, was of a less exciting and therefore of a less poetic character, and he confined himself to subjects not so discordant in their elements. The lines, however, in the present volume entitled 'The Warning', both by the occasion that suggested them, and the manner in which the subject is treated, show that recent events have intimately touched his affections, and thrown him back upon sensations akin to those he was troubled with in the early period of his life. That Poem is indeed so little in harmony with the general tenor of his writings and with the contents of this volume in particular, that it seems to require from him some notice in plain prose. It was written for one of the best reasons which in a poetical case can be given, viz. that the author could not help writing it; and it is published because, if there ever was a time when such a warning could be of the least 'service to any portion of his Countrymen, that time is surely not passed away.

"The agitation attendant upon the introduction, and carrying of the Reform Bill has there called forth a strain of reprehension, which as far as concerns the Leaders of that agitation requires neither explanation nor apology; they are spoken of with a warmth of indignant reproof which no man free in spirit will condemn, if it will appear that the feeling has been kindled by reflective patriotism: but as to the misled multitude, if there be a word that bears hard upon them, the Author would find a difficulty in forgiving himself; for even the *semblance* of such a thought would be a deviation from his habitual feelings towards the poor and humbly employed; the greater part of his life has been passed among them, he has not been an unthinking observer of their condition, and from the strongest conviction that so many of that Class are seeking their happiness in ways which cannot lead to it those admonitions proceeded."

In the same MS. a Note following the text of the poem has likewise been cancelled:

"Aware that expressions of regret for the past are seldom of much use as a preventive of future evils, the Author has not admitted without reluctance the above into a Collection of Poems so different from it in character. But it was poured out in sincerity of heart—and the heart of a Poet may in some cases be trusted, where the opinion of a practical Statesman is erroneous: at all events, the Verses, however profitless or insignificant they may appear to many, could not have been suppressed, without shrinking from what the Writer felt (and he hopes without presumption) to be a duty to his Country in the present peril of her social Institutions."

H. C. R. was perhaps instrumental in making W. withdraw both these paragraphs. He was acting as his amanuensis in March 1835 for the Notes to the volume of 1835, and writes: "My interference was not always in vain. W. will aggravate antipathies by his polemical notes" (*H. C. R. on Books and their Writers*, ed. E. Morley, pp. 458-9).

20-1. "*The Warning* was composed on horseback while I was riding from Moresby in a snowstorm. Hence [the] simile." W. (*quoted* M. ii. 476).

23. Lay,] This emendation from the Lay. of the texts was suggested by Mr. Nowell C. Smith.

95. If to expedience principle must bow] "Sound minds find their expediency in principles; unsound their principles in expediency." W. to J. K. Miller, Dec. 1831 (*L.Y.*, p. 591).

p. 114. XXXVI. *If this great world of joy and pain*: Another reflection on the state of the country at the time of the Reform Bill. *v.* W.'s letter, Dec. 5, 1833, where the poem is quoted under the heading "Addressed to Revolutionists of All Classes" (*L.Y.*, p. 680).

p. 115. XXXVII. THE LABOURER'S NOON-DAY HYMN: "Bishop Ken's 'Morning and Evening Hymns' are, as they deserve to be, familiarly known. Many other hymns have also been written on the same subject; but, not being aware of any being designed for Noonday, I was induced to compose these verses. Often one has occasion to observe Cottage children carrying, in their baskets, dinner to their Fathers engaged with their daily labours in the fields and woods. How gratifying would it be to me could I be assured that any portion of these stanzas had been sung by such a domestic concert under such circumstances. A friend of mine has told me that she introduced this Hymn into a Village-school which she superintended, and the stanzas in succession furnished her with texts to comment upon in a way which without difficulty was made intelligible to the children, and in which they obviously took delight, and they were taught to sing it to the tune of the old 100th Psalm."—I. F.

p. 116. XXXVIII. ODE COMPOSED ON MAY MORNING: "This and the following poem originated in the lines 'How delicate the leafy veil', etc. [To MAY XXXIX, l. 81]—My daughter and I left Rydal Mount upon a tour through our mountains with Mr. and Mrs. Carr in the month of May, 1826, and as we were going up the vale of Newlands I was struck with the appearance of the little Chapel gleaming through the veil of half-opened leaves; and the feeling which was then conveyed to my mind was expressed in the stanza that follows. As in the case of 'Liberty' and 'Humanity', my first intention was to write only one poem, but subsequently I broke it into two, making additions to each part so as to produce a consistent and appropriate whole."—I. F.

An early draft in D. W.'s hand with additions by W. W. contains stanzas from both this poem and the next.

p. 118. XXXIX. To MAY: "As I passed through the tame and manufacture-disfigured country of Lancashire I was reminded by the faded leaves, of Spring, and threw off a few stanzas of an ode to May." W. to W. R. Hamilton, Nov. 1830 (*L.Y.*, p. 538).

59. rathe primrose] *Lycidas*, 142.

78–80. gentle mists *etc.*] Cf. *Anacreon*, 37–45 (Vol. I, p. 262) and note (p. 366).

p. 120. XL. LINES SUGGESTED BY A PORTRAIT, *etc.*: "This portrait has hung for many years in our principal sitting-room, and represents J. Q. [Jemima Quillinan] as she was when a girl. The picture, though it is somewhat thinly painted, has much merit in tone and general effect; it is chiefly valuable, however, from the sentiment that pervades it. The Anecdote of the saying of the Monk in sight of Titian's picture was told in this house by Mr. Wilkie, and was, I believe, first communicated to the Public in this Poem, the former portion of which I was composing at the time. Southey heard the story from Miss Hutchinson, and transferred it to 'The Doctor'; but it is not easy to explain how my friend Mr. Rogers, in a note subsequently added to his 'Italy', was led to speak of the same remarkable words having many years before been spoken in his hearing by a Monk or Priest in front of a picture of the Last Supper, placed over a Refectory-table in a convent at Padua."—I. F.

"Talking of composition [Rogers] showed me a note to his 'Italy', which, he says, took him a fortnight to write. It consists of a very few lines. W. has amplified the idea of this note in his poem on the picture of Miss Quillinan, by Stone. Rogers says, and I think truly, that the prose is better than the poem. The thought intended to be expressed is, that the picture is the substance, and the beholders are the shadows." H. C. R., *Diary* for Feb. 23, 1837. Rogers's note runs: " 'You admire that picture,' said an old Dominican to me at Padua, as I stood contemplating a Last Supper in the Refectory of his Convent, the figures as large as the life. 'I have sat at my meals before it for seven and forty years; and such are the changes that have taken place among us—so many have come and gone in the time—that, when I look upon the company there—upon those who are sitting at that table, silent as they are—I am sometimes inclined to think that we, and not they, are the shadows.' "

The poem is headed in the MS. "Poem by W. on Mima's portrait by Stone." Appended to it is the following: "Wilkie was the painter to whom this affecting incident occurred (I know it is not proper to say 'incident occurred', but I know not what other word to use) and he told it to me when at Rydal the other day." There seems, therefore, little doubt that Rogers owed the story to Wordsworth.

p. 125. XLII. *So fair, so sweet, withal so sensitive*: The incident which gave rise to the composition of this poem has been recorded by several persons. R. P. Graves recalls the walk to Loughrigg Tarn with W., Professor Archer Butler, Sir William Hamilton, and Julius C. Hare: "The splendour of a July noon surrounded us, and lit up the landscape with the Langdale Pikes soaring above, and the bright Tarn shining beneath; and when the poet's eyes were satisfied with their feast on the beauties familiar to them, they sought relief in the search, to them a happy vital habit, for new beauty in the flower-enamelled turf at his feet. There his attention was arrested by a fair smooth stone, of the size of an ostrich's egg, seeming to imbed at its centre, and at the same time to display a dark star-shaped fossil of most distinct outline. Upon closer inspection this proved to be the shadow of a daisy projected upon it with extraordinary precision by the intense light of an almost vertical sun. The poet drew the attention of the rest of the party to the minute but beautiful phenomenon, and gave expression at the time to thoughts suggested by it." And on Sept. 14, 1844, J. C. Hare wrote to W.: "One of the brightest days in those happy three weeks was that on which we accompanied you to Loughrigg Tarn; for that walk bore its part in ripening our previous friendship, if I may not call it our fraternal affection, into something still dearer and better; nor shall I ever forget your stopping and drawing our attention to the exquisitely pencilled shadow the daisy cast upon a neighbouring stone. I remember saying at the time 'We shall have a sonnet upon it,' and this probably has been fulfilled, I rejoice to learn, save that, instead of the sonnet, you have adopted a new form of verse,—that is, new, I believe, in your writings, in composing the beautiful triplets you have had the kindness to send."

16. (*app. crit.*) K. misread "bond" for "bred".

p. 126. XLIII. Upon seeing a Coloured Drawing of the Bird of Paradise: "I cannot forbear to record that the last seven lines of this Poem were composed in bed during the night of the day on which my sister Sara Hutchinson died about 6 p.m., and it was the thought of her innocent and beautiful life that, through faith, prompted the words—

'On wings that fear no glance of God's pure sight,
No tempest from his breath.'

The reader will find two poems on pictures of this bird among my Poems. I will here observe that in a far greater number of instances than have been mentioned in these notes one Poem has, as in this case, grown out of another, either because I felt the subject had been inadequately treated, or that the thoughts and images suggested in course of composition have been such as I found interfered with the unity indispensable to every work of Art, however humble in character."—I. F. For the other poem on this subject *v.* Vol. II, p. 320. S. H. died on June 23rd, 1835.

SONNETS DEDICATED TO LIBERTY AND ORDER

These sonnets were first placed in one group in 1845.

p. 128. I. Composed after reading a Newspaper of the Day: In the 1835 volume this sonnet was placed after "If this great world of joy and pain", and the following note was appended: "This sonnet ought to have followed No. VII in the series of 1831 [i.e. Composed in the Glen of Loch Etive, *v.* vol. III, p. 268], but was omitted by mistake." In ed. 1837 it had that position.

p. 128. II. Upon the Late General Fast: In 1832 this sonnet was placed among *Epitaphs and Elegiac Pieces*, with the title *Sonnet on the late General Fast, March 21, 1832*, in 1837 with the *Miscellaneous Sonnets*, Part III. The "General Fast" was enjoined because of a serious epidemic of cholera which had broken out in the previous year (*v. L.Y.*, p. 585).

p. 129. III. *Said Secrecy to Cowardice and Fraud*: First published in the sonnet-volume of 1838 in a note to *Protest Against the Ballot*. (*v.* Vol. III, p. 411). It was preceded in the note by the following comment: "Having in this notice alluded only in general terms to the mischief which, in my opinion, the Ballot would bring along with it, without especially branding its immoral and anti-social tendency, (for which no political advantages, were they a thousand times greater than those presumed upon, could be a compensation) I have been impelled to subjoin a reprobation of it upon that score. In no part of my writings have I mentioned the name of any contemporary, that of Buonaparte only excepted, but for the purpose of eulogy; and therefore, as in the concluding verse of what follows there is a deviation from this rule (for the blank will be easily filled up) I have excluded the Sonnet from the body of the collection, and placed it here as a public record of my detestation, both as a man and a citizen, of the proposed contrivance."

A MS. copy of the sonnet, with "Grote" in place of the "——" in l. 14 is found in a letter of W. to Dora W., March 1838. On March 10, 1838, he sent it to John W., saying that he could not include it in the sonnet-volume, but suggesting that he might send it, anonymously, to the *Canterbury Chronicle* (*v. L.Y.*, p. 918).

George Grote (1794–1871), the historian of Greece, was one of the "philosophical Radicals". He was M.P. for London 1832–41. In politics he was especially associated with voting by ballot, on which he wrote a pamphlet in 1821, and which he advocated in the House in four motions (1833, 1835, 1836, 1839) and two bills (1836 and 1837). His cause was only gained shortly before his death.

p. 129. IV. *Blest Statesman he etc.*: **14.** (*v. app. crit.*) "All change is perilous and all chance unsound." Spenser.—W. (*F.Q.* v. ii. 36).

p. 130. V. In Allusion to various Recent Histories: Carlyle's *French Revolution* had appeared in 1837.

9–10. the wrath of Man Works not the righteousness of God] Epistle of St. James, i. 20.

p. 131. VIII. *Men of the Western World*: These lines were written several years ago, when reports prevailed of cruelties committed in many parts of America, by men making a law of their own passions. A far more formidable, as being a more deliberate mischief, has appeared among those States, which have lately broken faith with the public creditor in a manner so infamous. I cannot, however, but look at both evils under a similar relation to inherent good, and hope that the time is not distant when our brethren of the West will wipe off this stain from their name and nation.—W. 1842.

Additional Note: I am happy to add that this anticipation is already partly realised; and that the reproach addressed to the Pennsylvanians in the next sonnet is no longer applicable to them. I trust that those other States to which it may yet apply will soon follow the example now set them by Philadelphia, and redeem their credit with the world.—W. 1850. *v.* note to next sonnet. The MS. readings in *app. crit.* are from W.'s letter to H. Reed, Dec. 23, 1839.

5. (*app. crit.*) "altered . . . not in the hope of substituting a better verse, but merely to avoid the repetition of the word 'brook' which occurs as a Rhyme in the Pilgrim Fathers".—W. to H. Reed, Sept. 4, 1842.

13. Cf. Sonnet, Vol. III, p. 119. *England! the time is come . . .* l. 3. "The truth should now be better understood."

p. 132. IX. To the Pennsylvanians: Written at some date between 1841 and the end of Feb. 1845. W.'s correspondence with Henry Reed shows that during all this period he was much troubled by the stoppage of payment of Pennsylvanian Bonds, in which both his brother Christopher and Miss Fenwick had large holdings. His fears (encouraged by a rumour "from a private quarter", which he reported to Reed on Nov. 18, 1844) that the State of Pennsylvania would repudiate their obligations, proved groundless, for in Feb. 1845 payment was resumed and the note (*v. supra*) added to his ed. of 1850 was inserted at the request of Reed made in two letters dated April 2 and Dec. 10, 1849—that note was probably W.'s last composition for the press.

9. William Penn (1644–1718), Quaker and founder of Pennsylvania, the land for which was granted to him by the Duke of York in March 1680–1.

p. 132. X. At Bologna: "This and the following were suggested at Bologna, and other cities in the North of Italy." MS. note. In 1842 they were published among the *Memorials of a Tour in Italy, 1837*. For their significance in the history of W.'s political thought *v.* Batho, *The Later Wordsworth*, pp. 146–9.

p. 134. XIII. Young England: "W. was in excellent spirits, and repeated with a solemn beauty, quite peculiar to himself, a sonnet he had lately composed on 'Young England', and his indignant burst, 'Where, then, is *old*, our dear old England ?', was one of the finest bursts of nature and art combined that I ever heard." Lady Richardson, *Reminiscences*, Feb. 9, 1845.

p. 134. XIV. *Feel for the wrongs to universal ken*: "This sonnet is recommended to the perusal of the Anti-Corn Law Leaguers, the Political Economists, and of all those who consider that the Evils under which we groan are to be removed or palliated by measures ungoverned by moral and religious principles."—I. F.

SONNETS UPON THE PUNISHMENT OF DEATH

In a long review of W.'s *Sonnets*, 1838, in *The Quarterly* for Dec. 1841, Sir Henry Taylor included "a short series written two years ago, which we have been favoured with a permission to present to the public for the first time. It was suggested by the recent discussions in parliament and elsewhere on the subject of Punishment by Death."

In 1836 a report by the Commissioners on Criminal Law had been laid before Parliament, with the result that in July 1837 Acts were passed which removed the death penalty from about 200 offences (for most of which it was already in practice obsolete), and left it applicable only to high treason, murder and attempted murder, rape, arson with danger to life, piracies, burglaries, and robberies when aggravated by cruelty and violence. But some members of the House, who had a considerable backing in the country, had conscientious objections to the infliction of the death penalty for any crime, and as an instalment towards total abolition brought in a Bill to remove it from all offences except treason and murder; as a compromise the crime of rape was further omitted from the list. "Thus", says Taylor, "the broad question which is left for the country to look at, in respect to the punishment by death, is in effect its *abolition*. It is to this question that Mr. W.'s Sonnets refer; and the general drift of the sentiments which they express is that there is a deeper charity and a more enlarged view of religious obligations than that which would dictate such a measure in this country in the present state of society." The sonnets follow, with Taylor's running commentary upon them.

p. 135. I. **10.** pass'd] *v. app. crit.* Cf. Note to *Artegal and Elidure*, 195 (Vol. II, p. 469), and Duddon Sonnet XV. 14, past *corr. to* pass'd.

p. 136. III. **1.** The Roman Consul] Lucius Junius Brutus who incited the Romans to expel the Tarquins, and upon their banishment was elected first consul: he put to death his two sons who had attempted to restore the Tarquins.

p. 138. VIII. **14.** "wild justice of revenge"] Bacon's *Essays.* Cf. *Revenge, init.*: "Revenge is a kinde of Wilde Justice; which the more Man's Nature runs to, the more ought Law to weed it out."

MISCELLANEOUS POEMS

p. 142. I. Epistle to Sir George Howland Beaumont: "This poem opened, when first written, with a paragraph that has been transferred as an introduction to the first series of my Scotch Memorials. The journey, of which the first part is here described, was from Grasmere to Bootle on the south-west coast of Cumberland, the whole among mountain roads through a beautiful country, and we had fine weather. The verses end with our breakfast at the head of Yewdale in a yeoman's house, which, like all the other property in that sequestered vale, has passed or is passing into the hands of Mr. James Marshall of Monk Coniston,—in Mr. Knott's, the late owner's, time called Waterhead. Our hostess married a Mr. Oldfield, a Lieut. in the Navy: they lived together for some time at Hackett where she still resides as his widow. It was in front of that house, on the mountain side, near which stood the Peasant who, while we were passing at a distance, saluted us, waving a kerchief in her hand as described in the Poem. (This matron and her husband were then residing at the Hackett. The house and its inmates are referred to in the fifth book of the 'Excursion', in the passage beginning—

> 'You behold,
> High on the breast of yon dark mountain, dark
> With stony barrenness, a shining speck.'—J. C.[1])

The dog which we met with soon after our starting belonged to Mr. Rowlandson, who for forty years was curate of Grasmere in place of the rector, who lived to extreme old age in a state of insanity. Of this Mr. R. much might be said both with reference to his character, and the way in which he was regarded by his parishioners. He was a man of a robust frame, had a firm voice and authoritative manner, of strong natural talents, of which he was himself conscious, for he has been heard to say (it grieves me to add with an oath)—'If I had been brought up at college by — I should have been a Bishop.' Two vices used to struggle in him for mastery, avarice and the love of strong drink: but avarice, as is common in like cases, always got the better of its opponent; for, though he was often intoxicated, it was never, I believe, at his own expense. As has been said of one in a more exalted station, he would take any *given* quantity. I have heard a story of him which is worth the telling. One summer's morning, our Grasmere curate, after a night's carouse in the vale of Langdale, on his return home, having reached a point near which the whole of the vale of Grasmere might be seen with the lake immediately below him, stepped aside and sat down on the turf. After looking for some time at the landscape, then in the perfection of its morning beauty, he exclaimed—'Good God, that I should have led so long a life in such a place!'—This no doubt was deeply felt by him at the time, but I am not authorised to say that any noticeable amendment followed: penuriousness strengthened upon him as his body grew feebler with age. He had purchased property and kept some land in his own hands, but he could not find in his heart to lay out the necessary hire for labourers at the proper season, and consequently he has often been seen in half-dotage working his hay in the month of November by moonlight, a melancholy sight which I myself have witnessed. Notwithstanding all that has been said, this man, on account of his

---

[1] "J. C." *i.e.*, John Carter, Wordsworth's clerk, who saw the "I. F." notes through the press in 1857. The reference is to *Exc.* v. 670 ff.

talents and superior education, was looked up to by his parishioners, who, without a single exception, lived at that time (and most of them upon their own small inheritances) in a state of republican equality, a condition favorable to the growth of kindly feelings among them, and in a striking degree exclusive to temptations to gross vice and scandalous behaviour. As a Pastor their curate did little or nothing for them; but what could more strikingly set forth the efficacy of the Church of England through its Ordinances and Liturgy than that, in spite of the unworthiness of the Minister, his Church was regularly attended; and, though there was not much appearance in his flock of what might be called animated piety, intoxication was rare, and dissolute morals unknown? With the Bible they were for the most part well acquainted; and, as was strikingly shown when they were under affliction, must have been supported and comforted by habitual belief in those truths which it is the aim of the Church to inculcate.

"*Loughrigg Tarn.* This beautiful pool and the surrounding scene are minutely described in my little Book upon the Lakes. Sir G. H. B., in the earlier part of his life, was induced, by his love of Nature and the art of painting, to take up his abode at Old Brathay, about three miles from this spot, so that he must have seen it under many aspects; and he was so much pleased with it that he purchased the Tarn with a view to build, near it, such a residence as is alluded to in this Epistle. Baronets and knights were not so common in that day as now, and Sir Michael le Fleming, not liking to have a rival in this kind of distinction so near him, claimed a sort of Lordship over the Territory, and showed dispositions little in unison with those of Sir. G. Beaumont, who was eminently a lover of peace. The project of building was in consequence given up, Sir G. retaining possession of the Tarn. Many years afterwards a Kendal tradesman born upon its banks applied to me for the purchase of it, and accordingly it was sold for the sum that had been given for it, and the money was laid out under my direction upon a substantial oak fence for a certain number of yew trees to be planted in Grasmere churchyard; two were planted in each enclosure, with a view to remove, after a certain time, the one which throve the least. After several years, the stouter plant being left, the others were taken up and placed in other parts of the same churchyard, and were adequately fenced at the expense and under the care of the late Mr. Barber, Mr. Greenwood, and myself: the whole eight are now thriving, and are already an ornament to a place which, during late years, has lost much of its rustic simplicity by the introduction of iron palisades to fence off family burying-grounds, and by numerous monuments, some of them in very bad taste; from which this place of burial was in my memory quite free. See the lines in the sixth book of 'The Excursion' beginning—'Green is the churchyard', —The 'Epistle' to which these notes refer, though written so far back as 1804 [1811—ED.], was carefully revised so late as 1842, previous to its publication. I am loth to add, that it was never seen by the person to whom it is addressed. So sensible am I of the deficiencies in all that I write, and so far does everything that I attempt fall short of what I wish it to be, that even private publication, if such a term may be allowed, requires more resolution than I can command. I have written to give vent to my own mind, and not without hope that, some time or other, kindred minds might benefit by my labours: but I am inclined to believe I should never have ventured to send forth any verses of mine to the world if it had not been done on the pressure of personal occasions. Had I been a rich man, my productions, like this 'Epistle', the tragedy of 'The Borderers', etc., would most likely have been confined to manuscript."—I. F.

For the delay in publishing the *Epistle v.* Note to *Misc. Sonnets,* Part I. IV (Vol. III, p. 419).

There are four manuscripts of the poem, the copy used for press, and three others very little earlier in date: that no one of them goes back to the date of composition is shown by the absence of the lines utilized for the introductory poem to the Scottish Tour of 1803. (*v.* Vol. III, p. 64.)

5. Black Comb] *v. Poems of Imagination,* xxxviii (Vol. II, p. 289), *Itinerary Poems of 1833,* XII. *supra,* p. 30, and *Inscriptions,* VI, *supra,* p. 199.

40–1. Phoebus . . . attendant on Thessalian flocks] Apollo, condemned by Zeus to serve a mortal for a year, as a punishment for having slain the Cyclops, pastured the flocks of Admetus on the banks of the river Amphrysus.

66. House of Keys] The Manx House of Commons, said to be so called because its twenty-four members are the keepers of the liberties of the people.

77–88. Cf. W. W.'s letter to Sir G. B. of Aug. 28, 1811 (*M.Y.,* p. 469).

84. telegraph] the name first applied to a device for signalling, an upright post with movable arms, invented by Chappe in France in 1792.

111. Gowdar] Gowdar Crag is by Lodore Falls in Borrowdale, not, therefore, on the route of the travellers, but merely referred to as the scene of their charioteer's girlhood.

113. those Infants dear] Catharine and Thomas; they both died in the following year (1812). (*v.* Epilogue to the poem.)

153. Archimago] The false enchanter of the *Faerie Queene;* there is no reference to any specific incident in the poem.

161. wild Arden's brakes] W. is probably thinking of the song of Amiens, "Under the green wood tree", in *As You Like It,* II. v.

246–7. butter fit to lie Upon a lordly dish] A reference to the story of Jael and Sisera in the *Song of Deborah* (Judges v. 25). In one Manuscript "lordly dish" is put in italics.

p. 151. II. GOLD AND SILVER FISHES IN A VASE: "They were a present from Miss Jewsbury, of whom mention is made in the note at the end of the next poem. The fish were healthy to all appearance for a long time, but at last, for some cause we could not make out, they languished, and, one of them being dead, they were taken to the pool under the Pollard-oak. The apparently dying one lay on its side unable to move. I used to watch it, and about the tenth day it began to right itself, and in a few days was able to swim about with its companions. For many months they continued to prosper in their new place of abode; but one night by an unusually great flood they were swept out of the pool, and perished to our great regret."—I. F. On Miss Maria Jane Jewsbury v. L.Y., pp. 198 and 398, and *Misc. Sonnets*, III. xiii. A copy of the poem sent by Dora W. to E. Q. on Dec. 19, 1829, is headed with the motto

"O mutis quoque piscibus
Donaturi cycni, si libeat, sonum!"

From 1837 to 1843 it was placed among *Poems of Sentiment and Reflection*.

1–2. lark ... at heaven's gate] From the song in *Cymbeline*, II. iii. 22.

7–8. something more than dull content] From the Countess of Winchelsea, v. *Misc. Sonnets, Dedication*, Vol. III, p. 1, and W.'s note, p. 418.

p. 153. III. LIBERTY: "The connection of this with the preceding Poem is sufficiently obvious."—I. F. and v. I. F. note to *Humanity*, p. 425. The motto is taken from the opening sentences of Cowley's *Essay on Liberty*.

2. Anna: Mrs. Fletcher, *née* Jewsbury.

8. living well] from Spenser, *F.Q.*, I. ii. 43.

60–5. Is there a cherished bird etc.] *The Squieres Tale*, 603–9.

91. the path that winds by stealth] Mr. Nowell Smith notes the reminiscence of Horace, *Epistles*, I. xviii. 103: "An secretum iter et fallentis semita vitae." For "the Sabine farm he loved so well" (103) v. *Odes*, II. xviii, "Satis beatus unicis Sabinis", and for Blandusia (104) v. note to *Musings near Aquapendente*, 255–62, Vol. III, p. 492.

111–19. In a deep vision's intellectual scene] This passage on the "melancholy Cowley" is obviously reminiscent of Cowley's poem *The Complaint*, especially ll. 1–7:

In a deep Vision's intellectual scene
Beneath a Bow'r for sorrow made,
Th' uncomfortable shade,
Of the black Yew's unlucky green,
Mixt with the mourning Willow's careful gray,
Where reverend *Cham* cuts out his famous way,
The Melancholy *Cowley* lay.

p. 158. IV. POOR ROBIN: "I often ask myself what will become

of Rydal Mount after our day. Will the old walls and steps remain in front of the house and about the grounds, or will they be swept away with all the beautiful mosses and ferns and wild Geraniums and other flowers which their rude construction suffered and encouraged to grow among them ?—This little wild flower—'Poor Robin'—is here constantly courting my attention, and exciting what may be called a domestic interest with the varying aspects of its stalks and leaves and flowers. Strangely do the tastes of men differ according to their employment and habits of life. 'What a nice well would that be,' said a labouring man to me one day, 'if all that rubbish was cleared off.' The '*rubbish*' was some of the most beautiful mosses and lichens and ferns and other wild growths that could possibly be seen. Defend us from the tyranny of trimness and neatness showing itself in this way! Chatterton says of freedom—'Upon her head wild weeds were spread;' and depend upon it if 'the marvellous boy' had undertaken to give Flora a garland, he would have preferred what we are apt to call weeds to garden-flowers. True taste has an eye for both. Weeds have been called flowers out of place. I fear the place most people would assign to them is too limited. Let them come near to our abodes, as surely they may without impropriety or disorder."
—I. F. One Manuscript gives the title: *Ragged Robin* (more commonly called Poor Robin).

p. 159. V. THE GLEANER: "This poem was first printed in the Annual called the 'Keepsake'. The Painter's name I am not sure of, but I think it was Holmes."—I. F. James Holmes (1777–1860), water-colourist and miniature-painter; several of his pictures were engraved in *Miscellanies* such as the "Amulet" and "Literary Souvenir". But the poem was not exclusively inspired by the picture, for in March 1828 W. wrote to M. and Dora W.: "I have written one little piece, 34 lines, on the Picture of a beautiful Peasant Girl bearing a Sheaf of Corn. The Person I had in mind lives near the Blue Bell, Fillingham—a sweet Creature, we saw her going to Hereford" (*L.Y.*, p. 295). Before 1845 the poem was placed among *Poems of Sentiment and Reflection*.

p. 160. VI. To A REDBREAST: "Almost the only verses by our lamented Sister, S. H."—I. F.

p. 160. VII. *I know an aged Man*: The Manuscript is dated Jan. 1846.

p. 162. IX. FLOATING ISLAND: "My poor Sister takes a pleasure in repeating these verses which she composed not long before the beginning of her sad illness."—I. F.

p. 163. XI. *Once I could hail*: **3–4.** No faculty yet given me to espy The dusky Shape] "Afterwards, when I could not avoid seeing it, I wondered at this, and the more so because, like most children, I had been in the habit of watching the Moon through all her changes, and had often continued to gaze at it while at the full, till half blinded."

—I. F. Before 1845 this poem was placed among *Epitaphs and Elegiac Poems*.

p. 165. XII. To the Lady Fleming: "After thanking in prose Lady Fleming for the service she had done to her neighbourhood by erecting this Chapel, I have nothing to say beyond the expression of regret that the Architect did not furnish an elevation better suited to the site in a narrow mountain-pass, and, what is of more consequence, better constructed in the interior for the purposes of worship. It has no chancel; the altar is unbecomingly confined; the pews are so narrow as to preclude the possibility of kneeling; there is no vestry; and what ought to have been first mentioned, the font, instead of standing at its proper place at the Entrance, is thrust into the farther end of a little Pew. When these defects shall be pointed out to the munificent Patroness, they will, it is hoped, be corrected."—I. F.

W. dated the poem 1823, and on the second MS. is written Jan. 24, 1823; but on Dec. 21, 1822, D. W. writes of it to H. C. R. as "just written". But as she speaks of it as "about eighty Lines" and says that William will "send it hereafter" (instead of enclosing it with her letter) we may assume that at that date it was only in rough draft. MS. 1, in S. H.'s hand, which has 80 lines, is dated January. Before 1845 this and the following poem were placed among *Poems of Sentiment and Reflection*.

59-60. Cf. *Ode: Intimations of Immortality*, 196–7.

81. "bold bad" men] *Faerie Queene*, i. i. 37.

83. "dark opprobrious den"] *Paradise Lost*, ii. 58.

p. 168. XIII. On the Same Occasion: **4.** The Mother Church is St. Oswald's, Grasmere.

27. The day-spring from on high] St. Luke i. 78.

p. 169. XIV. The Horn of Egremont Castle: The Story is a Cumberland tradition; I have heard it also related of the Hall of Hutton John, an antient residence of the Huddlestones, in a sequestered Valley upon the River Dacor.—W. 1807. "A tradition transferred from the ancient mansion of Hutton John, the seat of the Huddlestones, to Egremont Castle."—I. F. From 1815 to 1843 placed among *Poems of the Imagination*, in 1815 with the note: "This poem and the Ballad which follows it [i.e. *Goody Blake*], as they rather refer to the imagination than are produced by it, would not have been placed here but to avoid a needless multiplication of the Classes."

p. 173. XV. Goody Blake and Harry Gill: "Written at Alfoxden. The incident from Dr. Darwin's *Zoonomia*."—I. F. i.e. *Zoonomia, or the Laws of Organic Life*, by Erasmus Darwin, 2 vols., 1794–6. W. borrowed the book from Cottle in 1797 (*v. E.L.*, p. 169). The passage on which the poem is founded runs:—"I received good information of the truth of the following case, which was published a few years ago in the newspapers. A young farmer in Warwickshire, finding his hedges broke, and the sticks carried away during a frosty season, determined to watch for the thief. He lay many cold hours under a haystack, and at length an old woman, like a witch in a play, approached, and began to pull up the hedge; he waited till she had tied up her bottle of sticks, and was carrying them off, that he might convict her of the theft, and then springing from his concealment, he seized his prey with violent threats. After some altercation, in which her load was left upon the ground, she kneeled upon her bottle of sticks, and raising her arms to Heaven beneath the bright moon then at the full, spoke to the farmer already shivering with cold, 'Heaven grant that thou mayest never know again the blessing to be warm.' He complained of cold all the next day, and wore an upper coat, and in a few days another, and in a fortnight took to his bed, always saying nothing made him warm; he covered himself with many blankets, and had a sieve over his face as he lay; and from this one insane idea he kept his bed above twenty years for fear of the cold air, till at length he died." From 1815 to 1843 the poem was placed among *Poems of the Imagination. v.* W.'s reference to the poem in his *Preface*, 1800–5 (Vol. II, p. 401).

p. 176. XVI. PRELUDE: "These verses were begun while I was on a visit to my son John at Brigham, and finished at Rydal. As the contents of the volume, to which they are now prefixed [*Poems chiefly of Early and Late Years*, 1842], will be assigned to their respective classes when my Poems shall be collected in one volume, I should be at a loss where with propriety to place this Prelude, being too restricted in its bearing to serve for a Preface for the whole. The lines towards the conclusion allude to the discontents then fomented through the country by the agitators of the Anti-Corn-Law League: the particular causes of such troubles are transitory, but disposition to excite and liability to be excited are nevertheless permanent, and therefore proper objects for the Poet's regard."—I. F. In ed. 1842 dated by W. March 26, 1842.

p. 178. XVII. TO A CHILD: "This quatrain was extempore on observing this image, as I had often done, on the lawn of Rydal Mount. It was first written down in the Album of my God-daughter, Rotha Quillinan."—I. F. In the Album it is dated Rydal Mount, 3rd July 1834. In 1837 included under *Inscriptions*.

p. 178. XVIII. LINES WRITTEN IN THE ALBUM OF THE COUNTESS OF LONSDALE: "This is a faithful picture of that amiable Lady, as she then was. The youthfulness of figure and demeanour and habits, which she retained in almost unprecedented degree, departed a very few years after, and she died without violent disease by gradual decay before she reached the period of old age."—I. F. In 1837 included under *Inscriptions*.

8. *v.* Sonnet *To The Earl of Lonsdale, supra,* p. 49.

p. 180. XIX. GRACE DARLING: wrongly dated by W. 1842; sent by him in a letter to Henry Reed of March 27, 1843, as "the last poem from my pen. I threw it off two or three weeks ago, being in a great measure impelled to it by the desire I felt to do justice to the memory of a heroine, whose conduct presented some time ago a striking contrast to the inhumanity with which our countrymen shipwrecked lately upon the French coast have been mistreated." Grace Darling's father was lighthouse-keeper on the Farne Islands, off Northumberland; in Sept. 1838 she went with him in a small boat to the rescue of some survivors from a wreck. She died in October, 1842. The poem was privately printed, in March 1843, at Carlisle, "at the office of Charles Thurnam".

p. 183. XX. THE RUSSIAN FUGITIVE: "Peter Henry Bruce, having given in his entertaining Memoirs the substance of this Tale, affirms that, besides the concurring reports of others, he had the story from the lady's own mouth.

The Lady Catherine, mentioned towards the close, is the famous Catherine, then bearing that name as the acknowledged Wife of Peter the Great.—W.

"Early in life this story had interested me, and I often thought it would make a pleasing subject for an Opera or Musical drama."—I. F. Bruce's *Memoirs, containing an account of his travels in Germany, Russia, Tartary, Turkey, and the West Indies; as also several anecdotes of the Czar, Peter I of Russia*, was published in 1782. W. dated the poem 1830, but a letter written to G. H. Gordon on Jan. 19, 1829, states that it had been "lately" composed.

179–80. The leaves . . . hair] In 1835 W. placed these two lines in inverted commas, with the footnote "From Golding's Translation of Ovid's *Metamorphoses*. See also his Dedicatory Epistle prefixed to the same work". The passages are as follows:

There was not any wheare
As yet a Bay; by meanes whereof was Phebus faine to weare
The leaves of every pleasant tree about his goolden heare.

Metamorphoses, Bk. I.

As for example, in the tale of Daphnee turned to Bay
A myrror of virginitee appeare unto us may,
Which yielding neither unto feare, nor force, nor flatterye,
Doth purchace everlasting fame and immortalitye.

Epistle to the Earle of Leycester.

INSCRIPTIONS

p. 195. I. IN THE GROUNDS OF COLEORTON, *etc.*: "In the Grounds of Coleorton these verses are engraved on a stone placed near the Tree, which was thriving and spreading when I saw it in the summer of 1841."—I. F. Dated by W. 1808, but sent by him to Sir G. B. in Nov. 1811 with Nos. II and III, and if it had been written three years before it is unlikely that it would not have been sent at that time. It is true that W. says in a letter dated Nov. 20, 1811, that "the thought of writing" it "occurred to me many years ago", but "the thought of writing" is very different from actual composition.

17. the haunt of him]: Sir John Beaumont (1583–1627), born at Grace Dieu, the original family seat of the Beaumonts, and the author of *Bosworth Field*. In 1806 W. had proposed to Sir G. B. to edit Sir John B.'s poems. "I like your ancestor's verses the more, the more I see of them; they are manly, dignified, and extremely harmonious. I do not remember in any author of that age such a series of well-tuned [or turned ?] couplets" (*M.Y.*, p. 64); in Nov. 1811 he wrote that the composition of this inscription had "brought Sir J. B. and his brother Francis so livelily to my mind, that I recur to the plan of republishing the former's poems".

19. that famous Youth]: Francis Beaumont (1584–1616) the dramatist. On *Inscriptions* I–IV v. *M.Y.*, pp. 470–7.

p. 195. II. IN A GARDEN OF THE SAME: "This Niche is in the sandstone-rock in the winter-garden at Coleorton, which garden, as has been elsewhere said, was made under our direction out of an old unsightly quarry. While the labourers were at work, Mrs. Wordsworth, my Sister, and I used to amuse ourselves occasionally in scooping this seat out of the soft stone. It is of the size, with something of the appearance, of a Stall in a Cathedral. This inscription is not engraven, as the former and the two following are, in the grounds." —I. F.

p. 197. IV. FOR A SEAT IN THE GROVES OF COLEORTON: "The following I composed yesterday morning, in a walk from Brathay, whither I had been to accompany my sister".—W. to Lady Beaumont, Nov. 20, 1811. Despite this, W. dated the poem 1808. Cf. D. W. to Lady B., Nov. 16, 1806: "William and I went to Grace Dieu last week. We were enchanted with the little valley, and its rocks, and the rocks of Charnwood upon the hill, on which we rested for a long time" (*M.Y.*, p. 83).

18. And things of holy use unhallowed lie]: "I ought to mention that the line is taken from the following of Daniel:

Strait all that holy was unhallowed lies."—W. to Sir G. B., Nov. 20, 1811. The line is from *Musophilus*, st. 46.

p. 199. VI. WRITTEN WITH A SLATE PENCIL, *etc.*: "The circumstance alluded to at the conclusion of these verses was told me by Dr. Satterthwaite, who was Incumbent of Bootle, a small town at the foot of Black Comb. He had the particulars from one of the engineers who was employed in making trigonometrical surveys of that region." —I. F.

Black Comb stands at the southern extremity of Cumberland; its base covers a much greater extent of ground than any other Mountain in these parts; and, from its situation, the summit commands a more extensive view than any other point in Britain.—W. 1815–20. Cf. *View from the Top of Black Comb* (Vol. II, p. 289).

4. This speculative Mount] (*app. crit.*) Cf. Cowper, *The Task*, i. 289, "posted on this speculative height", and Note to *Exc.* V. 489.

p. 200. VII. WRITTEN . . . UPON A STONE . . . AT RYDAL: **27–31**. On W.'s objection to a glaring white for buildings in a mountainous district *v.* the Section of his *Guide to the Lakes* on "Colouring of Buildings" (reprint of 5th Ed., 1906, pp. 77–81). This would be Sir William Fleming of Rydal Hall, the first Baronet, *died* 1736.

p. 201. VIII. *In these fair Vales:* "Engraven, during my absence in Italy, upon a brass plate inserted in the Stone."—I. F. MS. 1 is inscribed "June 26, 1830, dictated by W. W. to D. W. senior". MS. 2 "recopied August 2, 1832".

p. 201. IX. *The massy Ways*: "The walk is what we call the *Far-Terrace* beyond the summer-house at Rydal Mount. The lines were written when we were afraid of being obliged to quit the place to which we were so much attached."—I. F. Cf. Appendix XXIV. The variant readings are quoted by K. I have not been able to discover the MS.

p. 204. XI. INSCRIBED UPON A ROCK: "The monument of ice here spoken of I observed while ascending the middle road of the three ways that lead from Rydal to Grasmere. It was on my right hand, and my eyes were upon it when it fell, as told in these lines."—I. F.

p. 205. XII. *Hast thou seen, with flash incessant*: "Where the second quarry now is, as you pass from Rydal to Grasmere, there was formerly a length of smooth rock that sloped towards the road, on the right hand. I used to call it Tadpole Slope, from having frequently observed there the water-bubbles gliding under the ice, exactly in the shape of that creature."—I. F.

p. 206. XV. FOR THE SPOT WHERE THE HERMITAGE STOOD, *etc.*: In 1815 placed among *Poems referring to the Period of Old Age*. The MS. readings are from two letters to Sir George and Lady Beaumont, dated Nov. 16 and Nov. 20, 1811. It is clear that the changes in the 1815 text date from about this time, when W. was at work on Inscriptions I–IV. But note that later he reverted to his original opening.

SELECTIONS FROM CHAUCER, MODERNISED

Wordsworth was occupied with translating Chaucer in 1801: *v.* D. W.'s *Journals*, Dec. 2, 4, 5, 6, 7, 8, 9. The text which he used is that of Anderson's *Works of the British Poets* (hereafter referred to as Anderson). John W. left his set of Anderson with W. W. when he left Grasmere in Sept. 1800. "Through these Volumes I became first familiar with Chaucer." I. F. to *Yarrow Visited*, vol. III, p. 450, *q.v.* *The Prioress's Tale* was published in ed. 1820; *The Cuckoo and The Nightingale* and the extract from *Troilus and Cressida* were his contribution to the volume edited by Thomas Powell, *The Poems of Geoffrey Chaucer, modernised*, 1841. He offered also, but later withdrew, his translation of *The Manciple's Tale, v.* Appendix, p. 358, and note, p. 470; and letters to Powell (*L.Y.*, pp. 992, 998, 1001, 1024).

p. 209. THE PRIORESS' TALE: The evidence of date is supplied in D. W.'s *Journal*, Dec. 4, 1801, "Wm translating *The Prioress's Tale*"; Dec. 5, "Wm finished *The Prioress's Tale*, and after tea Mary and he wrote it out." Their copy is quoted in *app. crit.* as MS. The motto is from *Il Penseroso*, 109–10.

51. scholar] Chaucer has "clergeon", which should be rendered "chorister".

61. Sweet is the holiness of youth] This line is not in Chaucer, and in order to introduce it W. added an extra line to his stanza. But in *Ecclesiastical Sonnets*, II, xxxi he quotes it as though it were Chaucer's and not his own.

66. with an earnest cheer] Not in Chaucer; W.'s first reading (*v. app. crit.*) is closer to the original.

113. our] so Anderson; but the better Chaucerian MSS. read "your", which is clearly right.

231. uncorrupted] This word is not in Chaucer, whose text is correctly represented in W.'s early reading (*v. app. crit.*). It is difficult to see why he made this change for the worse.

233–9. In this last stanza W. departs from the correct metrical scheme of the poem, and, moreover, leaves his second line unrhymed.

p. 217. THE CUCKOO AND THE NIGHTINGALE: Date supplied by D. W.'s *Journal*, Dec. 7, 1801, "Wm at work with Chaucer, *The God of Love*"; Dec. 8, "Wm. worked at *The Cuckoo and the Nightingale* till he was tired"; Dec. 9, "Wm writing out his alteration of Chaucer's *Cuckoo and Nightingale*." This poem, now attributed to Sir Thomas Clanvowe, was in W.'s day thought to be Chaucer's. Anderson's inferior text led him into several errors.

20. sheds] The correct text of his original is "And most his might he sheweth ever in May", but Anderson reads "shedith".

39. and heart-aches] The correct text of the original reads "an access", but Anderson had "and axis", which might mean anything.

64. Tall were the flowers, the grave a lofty cover] W.'s attempt to make sense of the corrupt text before him, "The flouris and the grevis alike hie"; the correct reading is "The floures and the gras ilike al hie".

67. birds come tripping from their bowers] Dowden notes that the text of the original reads "And saw the briddes crepe out of her boures" and comments on W.'s departure from it. But Anderson's text reads "trippe".

99. made a loud rioting] An addition of W.'s to the text before him, which read: That with her clere voice she maden ringe
Echoing through al the grene wode wide.
Cf. W.'s *O Nightingale*, Vol. II, p. 214.

103. *app. crit.* had 1842: heard MS., 1841. Anderson reads "For here hath ben the leude sory Cuckow".

180. He may full soon go with an old man's hair] W.'s rendering of the text before him "He maie full sone of age yhave his haire." But the correct text reads "heyr", meaning that very soon his heir will come of age.

185. raise a clamour] W. misses the point here. The text reads "thou shalt yhotin as do I", i.e. cry "cuckoo", a pun on the cry of the cuckoo and "cuckold".

270. Of that false Bird whom Love cannot abide] W.'s rendering of "Of that foule and false, and unkinde bride".

283. well-beseen] For the original "faire and grene".

p. 228. III. TROILUS AND CRESSIDA: i.e. Chaucer's T. AND C., v. 519–686.

8. to cover his intent] Chaucer has "his meine for to blend", i.e. to hoodwink the members of his household. W. evidently takes "meine" to mean "meaning" "purpose".

21. continuance] Chaucer has "countenance", spelt "countinaunce" in Anderson. W. must have misread the word.

104–5. Chaucer has

And al this nas but his melancolie
That he had of hymselfe such fantasie.

Dowden notes that W. introduces into his rendering an echo of *Hamlet*, II. ii. 638, "Out of my weakness and my melancholy".

118. With a soft voice] The reading of 1842–50, "With a soft night voice", can only be explained as an uncorrected printer's error.

123. I steer and sail] so Anderson; the correct text reads "in stere I sayle", i.e. "upon my rudder".

138. *app. crit.* above] Chaucer has "about", and so has Anderson. Possibly "about" was what W. first wrote, and "above" a slip in transcription.

POEMS REFERRING TO THE PERIOD OF OLD AGE

The class of Beggars, to which the Old Man here described belongs, will probably soon be extinct. It consisted of poor, and, mostly, old and infirm persons, who confined themselves to a stated round in their neighbourhood, and had certain fixed days, on which, at different houses, they regularly received alms, sometimes in money, but mostly in provisions.—W.

p. 234. THE OLD CUMBERLAND BEGGAR: "Observed, and with great benefit to my own heart, when I was a child: written at Racedown and Alfoxden in my 28th[1] year. The political economists were about that time beginning their war upon mendicity in all its forms, and by

[1] Written 23ᵈ in Dora and E. Q.'s copy of I. F.—an obvious error in transcription.

implication, if not directly, on Almsgiving also. This heartless process has been carried as far as it can go by the AMENDED poor-law bill, though the inhumanity that prevails in this measure is somewhat disguised by the profession that one of its objects is to throw the poor upon the voluntary donations of their neighbours; that is, if rightly interpreted, to force them into a condition between relief in the Union poor-house, and Alms robbed of their Christian grace and spirit, as being *forced* rather from the benevolent than given by them; while the avaricious and selfish, and all in fact but the humane and charitable, are at liberty to keep all they possess from their distressed brethren."—I. F.

At least five MSS. of fragments, or the whole, of this poem are extant: (1) a folio sheet with watermark 1795; (2) in the Pierpont Morgan Library at New York, a folio sheet, headed *Description of a Beggar*; (3) in D. W.'s note-book which also contains the first transcript of *Christabel* and MS. 2 of *Guilt and Sorrow, v.* Vol. I, p. 331; (4) in the Alfoxden note-book (*v. Prelude, Introd.*); (5) in note-book U (*v. Prelude*, p. xxii). All but No. 2 are in the Wordsworth Museum at Grasmere. No. 5 alone has a complete copy of the poem. No. 4 originally contained it, but some of its pages have been cut out.

The title of the poem—"The Old *Cumberland* Beggar"—shows it to be a recollection of W.'s Cockermouth days.

For the relation of this poem to *Animal Tranquillity and Decay v.* note to that poem *infra*, p.447.

48–50. (*app. crit.*) A reminiscence of *Paradise Lost*, vi. 640–1:

For earth hath this variety from Heaven
Of pleasure situate in hill and dale.

61. The cottage curs] "The cottage curs at early pilgrim bark", Beattie, *Minstrel*, i. 39.

88. This old man creeps] In the Alfoxden MS. are these lines, unused in the poem, but obviously another draft of the passage given in the *app. crit.*:

in this aged wretch
Their forlorn brother, banished as he is
By nature's self [?] from concerns
Business and reciprocities of life.
He has no suppliant voice for those who pass
No suppliant attitude, he has forgot (survived)
His occupation, 'tis enough for him
If he receive his dole, and when received
Repay [it] with a blessing, on he creeps

127. In MS. 3, after "exemption", we have the lines:

and blest are they
Who by whatever process have been taught
To look with holy reverence and with fear

Upon this intricate machine of things.
They touch not rashly neither in contempt
Nor hatred, for to them a voice hath said
When ye despise ye know not what ye do.

p. 240. II. THE FARMER OF TILSBURY VALE: With this picture, which was taken from real life, compare the imaginative one of 'The Reverie of Poor Susan', and see (to make up the deficiencies of this class) 'The Excursion', passim.—W.

"The character of this man was described to me, and the incident upon which the verses turn was told me, by Mr. Poole of Nether Stowey, with whom I became acquainted through our common friend, S. T. C. During my residence at Alfoxden I used to see much of him and had frequent occasions to admire the course of his daily life, especially his conduct to his Labourers and poor neighbours: their virtues he carefully encouraged, and weighed their faults in the scales of Charity. If I seem in these verses to have treated the weaknesses of the farmer, and his transgression, too tenderly, it may in part be ascribed to my having received the story from one so averse to all harsh judgment. After his death, was found in his escritoire a lock of grey hair carefully preserved, with a notice that it had been cut from the head of his faithful Shepherd, who had served him for a length of years. I need scarcely add that he felt for all men as his brothers. He was much beloved by distinguished persons—Mr. Coleridge, Mr. Southey, Sir H. Davy, and many others; and in his own neighbourhood was highly valued as a Magistrate, a man of business, and in every other social relation. The latter part of the poem, perhaps, requires some apology as being too much of an echo to the 'Reverie of Poor Susan'."—I. F.

p. 244. III. THE SMALL CELANDINE: Cf. *Poems of the Fancy*, xi and xii (Vol. II, pp. 142 and 144).

p. 245. IV. THE TWO THIEVES: "This is described from the life as I was in the habit of observing when a boy at Hawkshead School. Daniel was more than 80 years older than myself when he was daily thus occupied, under my notice. No book could have so early taught me to think of the changes to which human life is subject, and while looking at him, I could not but say to myself—we may, any of us, I, or the happiest of my playmates, live to become still more the object of pity than this old man, this half-doating pilferer."—I. F.

1. Bewick] Thomas Bewick (1753–1828), artist and wood-engraver, said to have restored the art of wood-engraving in England. His most famous works were the illustrations to *Select Fables*, 1784, and *History of British Birds*, 1797, 1804, 8th ed., 1847. Doubtless he appealed specially to W. from his resolve "to stick to nature as closely as he could".

p. 247. V. ANIMAL TRANQUILLITY AND DECAY: "If I recollect right these verses were an overflowing from *The Old Cumberland*

Beggar."—I. F. Both the Dove Cottage and the Pierpont Morgan MSS. of *The Old Cumberland Beggar* corroborate this, for each contains the main part of the present poem. The opening phrase of the latter MS. (2), "He travels on" (cf. original title *Old Man Travelling*, and l. 3 of the present poem), is the burden of both poems: v. ll. 24 and 44 of *The Old Cumberland Beggar*. The present poem has split off as a study of the inward state of the Old Man expressed in his outward form: "resigned to quietness" in the margin of ll. 7–8 expresses the spiritual core of it.

After l. **14** (*app. crit.*). These lines in edd. 1798–1805, afterwards discarded, must have been added in 1798.

EPITAPHS AND ELEGIAC PIECES

"Those from Chiabrera were chiefly translated when Mr. Coleridge was writing his 'Friend', in which periodical my Essay on Epitaphs, written about that time, was first published. For further notice of Chiabrera, in connection with his Epitaphs, see 'Musings at Aquapendente.'"[1]—I. F. The essay, which appeared in *The Friend* of Feb. 22, 1810, was republished as a note to *Exc.* V. 978 but without the opening paragraph (which was preceded by W.'s translations of two of Chiabrera's Epitaphs: II, "Perhaps some needful service", and III, "O Thou who movest onward" . . .): "In this and the preceding Numbers has been given a selection of Epitaphs from the Italian Poet Chiabrera: in one instance imitated [S. T. C.'s *Tombless Epitaph v. infra*, note to Epitaph V] and in the others carefully translated. The perusal of the original collection afforded me so much pleasure that I was induced to think upon the nature of that species of composition with more care than I had previously bestowed upon the Subject": two further essays, written in continuation, did not appear in *The Friend*, which came to an end in the following March; they were first printed by Grosart in 1876 (*Prose Works*, ii. 41–75). The MS. is now lost. In Essay II W. states that Chiabrera's epitaphs "occasioned this dissertation", and in Essay III, after quoting Weever's definition of an epitaph, which "shews that in his conception an epitaph was not to be an abstract character of the deceased but an epitomized biography blended with description by which an impression of the character was to be conveyed", he goes on: "Bring forward the one incidental expression, a kind of commiseration, unite with it a concern on the part of the dead for the well-being of the living made known by exhortation and admonition, and let this commiseration and concern pervade and brood over the whole, so that what was peculiar to the individual shall still be subordinate to a sense of what he had in common with the species, our notion of a perfect epitaph would then be realized; and it pleases me to say that this is the very model upon which those of Chiabrera are for the most part framed."

[1] *Musings near Aquapendente*, 231–49, Vol. III, p. 209.

In this passage we have a statement of the principles which guided W. in writing the four original epitaphs that follow.

For W.'s translation of C.'s epitaph on Tasso, which he included in this essay, but did not publish among the poems, *v.* Appendix, p. 377.

p. 250. IV. **13** and **30** (*v. app. crit.*). W. alters "forty" to "fifty", following the Italian "cinquanta"; but "sixty" to "seventy" where the Italian reads "sessanta". It seems clear that Chiabrera must have written "settanta", which the sense requires, and that sessanta was a misprint in the first editions.

24. the lofty and the low] Cf. *Prelude*, xiv. 271, "To penetrate the lofty and the low", and *Personal Talk*, 32, "Which with the lofty sanctifies the low". *v.* note on *Personal Talk*, 32, p. 415, *supra.*

p. 250. V. True is it, *etc.*] "Coleridge was also interested in this epitaph of Chiabrera, and rendered some lines of it in *A Tombless Epitaph* [first published in *The Friend*, Nov. 23, 1809] where he makes an idealising study in verse of his own character."—Dowden. *v.* W.'s letter to H. C. R. on C.'s plagiarisms (*C.R.*, 402).

p. 252. VII. In his third essay on Epitaphs, *Celebrated Epitaphs Considered*, first printed by Grosart (*Prose Works of W. W.* ii. 70) W. gives an earlier version of this epitaph simpler in phrasing and closer to its original:

> O Lelius, beauteous flower of gentleness,
> The fair Aglaia's[1] friend above all friends:
> O darling of the fascinating Loves,
> By what dire envy moved did Death uproot
> Thy days ere[1] yet full blown, and what ill chance
> Hath robbed Savona of her noblest grace ?
> She weeps for thee and shall for ever weep,
> And if the fountain of her tears should fail
> She would implore Sebeto[1] to supply
> Her need: Sebeto, sympathizing stream,
> Who on his margin saw thee close thine eyes
> On the chaste bosom of thy Lady dear.
> Ah, what do riches, what does youth avail ?
> Dust are our hopes, I weeping did inscribe
> In bitterness thy monument, and pray
> Of every gentle spirit, bitterly
> To read the record with as copious tears.

W. prefaces it by speaking of it as in Chiabrera's "mixed manner, exemplifying some of the points in which he has erred", and concludes: "This epitaph is not without some tender thoughts, but a comparison of it with the one on the youthful Pozzobonnelli [i.e. VIII] will more clearly shew that Chiabrera has here neglected to ascertain whether the passions expressed were in kind and degree a

---

[1] Grosart, followed by K., misprints Anglaia, e'er, and Sabete.

G g

dispensation of reason, or at least commodities issued under her licence and authority."

p. 253. IX. In his third Essay on Epitaphs W. thus comments on this poem: "The subject of the epitaph is introduced entreating, not directly in his own person but through the mouth of the author, that according to the religious belief of his country a prayer for his soul might be preferred to the Redeemer of the world; placed in counterpoize with this right which he has in common with all the dead, his individual earthly accomplishments appear light to his funeral Biographer as they did to the person of whom he speaks when alive, nor could Chiabrera have ventured to touch upon them but under the sanction of this person's acknowledgment. He then goes on to say how various and profound was his learning, and how deep a hold it took upon his affections, but that he weaned himself from these things as vanities, and was devoted in later life exclusively to the divine truths of the Gospel as the only knowledge in which he could find perfect rest. Here we are thrown back upon the introductory supplication and made to feel its especial propriety in this case; his life was long, and every part of it bore appropriate fruits. Urbino his birthplace might be proud of him, and the passenger who was entreated to pray for his soul has a wish breathed for his welfare. This composition is a perfect whole, there is nothing arbitrary or mechanical, but it is an organized body, of which the members are bound together by a common life and are all justly proportioned."

1. Baldi] Balbi 1815–50. Mr. Nowell Smith was the first editor to point out and correct the misprint. The reference is to Bernardino Baldi of Urbino (1553–1617), mathematician, philosopher, historian, and poet.

p. 254. I. *By a blest Husband guided*: "This lady was named Carleton; she, along with a sister, was brought up in the neighbourhood of Ambleside. The epitaph, a part of it at least, is in the church at Bromsgrove, where she resided after her marriage."—I. F.

p. 254. II. *Six months to six years added, etc.*: Inscribed on the tombstone of W.'s son Thomas in Grasmere churchyard. He died on Dec. 1, 1812. *v.* W.'s letter to Haydon, *L.Y.*, p. 1368. *v. Addenda*, p. 468.

p. 255. III. CENOTAPH: "See Elegiac Stanzas. Addressed to Sir G. H. B. upon the death of his Sister-in-law" [p. 269].—I. F.

I am the way, *etc.*] "Words inscribed upon her Tomb at her own request." MS.

p. 255. IV. EPITAPH IN THE CHAPEL OF LANGDALE: "Owen Lloyd, the subject of this epitaph, was born at Old Brathay, near Ambleside, and was the son of Charles Lloyd and his wife Sophia (*née* Pemberton), both of Birmingham, who came to reside in this part of the country soon after their marriage. They had many children, both sons and daughters, of whom the most remarkable was the subject of this Epitaph. He was educated under Mr. Dawes, at Ambleside, Dr.

Butler, of Shrewsbury, and lastly at Trinity College, Cambridge, where he would have been greatly distinguished as a scholar but for inherited infirmities of bodily constitution, which, from early childhood, affected his mind. His love for the neighbourhood in which he was born, and his sympathy with the habits and characters of the mountain yeomanry, in conjunction with irregular spirits, that unfitted him for facing duties in situations to which he was unaccustomed, induced him to accept the retired curacy of Langdale. How much he was beloved and honored there, and with what feelings he discharged his duty under the oppression of severe malady, is set forth, though imperfectly, in this Epitaph."—I. F. *v. L.Y.*, p. 1086.

p. 256. V. ADDRESS TO THE SCHOLARS OF THE VILLAGE SCHOOL OF——: "Composed at Goslar in Germany."—I. F. The subject of the poem was clearly "the honoured teacher of my youth" whose death-bed W. recalls, *Prelude*, x. 534: "The Rev. William Taylor, headmaster of the Hawkshead School 1782–1786, was regarded by the Poet with much affection. Taylor died while W. was still at school: and just before his death, he sent for the upper boys into his chamber . . . and there took leave of them on his death-bed." *Mem.* i, p. 38.

In an early draft, in place of ll. 57–72, occurs this stanza, in a different metre:

[Elegy (left in a school room)]
Among the distant stars we view
The hand of God in rain and dew
    And in the summer heat;
Our Master's humble works we trace
All round his happy native place
    In every eye we meet.

48/9. (*app. crit.*) In a Manuscript probably written in 1800 this poem ends as follows:

He taught in this his humble state
What happiness a man of worth
A single mortal may create
Upon a single spot of earth.
Among the distant stars we view
The hand of God in rain and dew
And in the summer heat,
And Matthew's little works we trace
All round his happy native place
In every eye we meet.
The neat trim house, the cottage rude
All owed to Matthew gifts of gold,
Light pleasures every day renewed
Or blessings half a century old.
Here did he sit for hours and hours,
But then he saw the woods and plains,

He heard the wind and saw the showers
Come streaming down the streaming panes.
He lies beneath the grass-green mound
A prisoner of the silent ground.
He loved the breathing air,
He loved the sun—he does not know
Whether the sun be up or no,
He lies forever there.
If he to you did aught amiss
Forgive him now that he is dead,
Both in your sorrow and your bliss
Remember him and his grey head.

Two more Elegies on Matthew, clearly written at the same time, are found in a Note-book used by D. W. at Alfoxden in 1798.

i

Could I the priest's consent have gained
Or his who toll'd thy passing bell,
Then, Mathew, had thy bones remain'd
Beneath this tree we loved so well.

Yet in our thorn will I suspend   5
Thy gift this twisted oaken staff,
And here where trunk and branches blend
Will I engrave thy epitaph.

Just as the blowing thorn began
To spread again its vernal shade,   10
This village lost as good a man
As ever handled book or spade.

Then Traveller passing o'er the green,
Thy course a single moment stay,
Though here no mouldering heap be seen   15
To tell thee thou art kindred clay.

A schoolmaster by title known
Long Mathew penn'd his little flock
Within yon pile that stands alone
In colour like its native rock.   20

Learning will often dry the heart,
The very bones it will distress,
But Mathew had an idle art
Of teaching love and happiness.

The neat trim house, the cottage rude   25
All owed to Mathew gifts of gold,
Light pleasures every day renewed
Or blessings half a century old.

His fancy play'd with endless play
So full of mother wit was he,
He was a thousand times more gay   30
Than any dunce has power to be.

Yet when his hair was white as rime
And he twice thirty years had seen
Would Mathew wish from time to time   35
That he a graver man had been.

But nothing could his heart have bribed
To be as sad as mine is now,
As I have been while I inscribed
This verse beneath the hawthorn bough.   40

ii

Elegy written in the same place upon the same occasion

Remembering how thou didst beguile
With thy wild ways our eyes and ears,
I feel more sorrow in a smile
Than in a waggon load of tears;

I smile to hear the hunter's horn,   5
I smile at meadow rock and shore,
I smile too at this silly thorn
Which blooms as sweetly as before.

I think of thee in silent love
And feel just like a wavering leaf,
Along my face the muscles move,   10
Nor know if 'tis with joy or grief,

But oft when I look up and view
Yon huts upon the mountain-side
I sigh and say, it was for you   15
An evil day when Mathew died.

The neat trim house, the cottage rude . . . old *as* in i. 25–8 *supra*.

Then weep, ye Elves, a noisy race
Thoughtless as roses newly blown,
Weep Mathew with his happy face
Now lying in his grave alone.

Thou one blind Sailor, child of joy   25
Thy lonely tunes in sadness hum
And mourn, thou poor half-witted boy,
Born deaf and living deaf and dumb.

Mourn, Shepherd, near thy old grey stone,
Thou Angler by the silent flood,   30
And mourn when thou art all alone
Thou woodman in the lonesome wood.

Mourn sick man sitting in the shade
When summer suns have warmed the earth,
Ye saw the [   ] which Mathew made   35
And shook with weakness and with mirth.

Mourn reapers thirsting in a crew
Who rouse with shouts the evening vale,
Thou mower in the morning dew,
Thou milkmaid by thy evening pail.   40

Ye little girls, ye loved his name,
Come here and knit your gloves of yarn,
Ye loved him better than your dame
—The schoolmaster of fair Glencarn.

For though to many a wanton boy   45
Did Mathew act a father's part,
Ye tiny maids, *ye* were his joy,
Ye were the favourites of his heart.

Ye ruddy damsels past sixteen
Weep now that Mathew's race is run   50
He wrote your love-letters, I ween
Ye kiss'd him when the work was done.

Ye Brothers gone to towns remote,
And ye upon the ocean tost,
Ye many a good and pious thought   55
And many a [   ] have lost.

Staid men may weep, from him they quaff'd
Such wit as never failed to please,
While at his [   ] they laugh'd
Enough to set their hearts at ease.   60

Ye mothers who for jibe or jest
Have little room in heart or head,
The child that lies upon your breast
May make you think of Mathew dead.

Old women in your elbow chairs,   65
Who now will be your fence and shield,
When wintry blasts and cutting airs
Are busy in both house and field ?

And weep thou School of fair Glencarn,
No more shalt thou in stormy weather   70
Be like a play-house in a barn
Where Punch and Hamlet play together.

Ye sheep-curs, a mirth-loving corps!
Now let your tails lie still between
Your drooping hips—you'll never more   75
Bark at his voice upon the green.

Remembering how thou didst beguile
With thy wild ways our eyes and ears,
I feel more sorrow in a smile
Than in a waggon-load of tears.   80

p. 258. VI. ELEGIAC STANZAS, SUGGESTED BY A PICTURE OF
PEELE CASTLE: "Sir George Beaumont painted two pictures on this
subject one of which he gave to Mrs. Wordsworth saying she ought
to have it; but Lady B. interfered and after Sir George's death she
gave it to Sir Uvedale Price in whose house at Foxley I have seen it—
rather grudgingly, shown."—I. F.

It seems clear from W.'s letter to Sir George B. on Aug. 1, 1806,
that he saw the picture for the first time on his visit to Sir G. B. at
Grosvenor Square in the previous May. But it had been engraved as
early as 1783, and Sir G. B. may have given him a copy on one of his
visits to the Lakes before 1805. It was reproduced as a frontispiece
to Vol. II of the 1815 ed. of W.'s Poems.

Peele Castle is on a promontory opposite Rampside in N. Lancashire. W. stayed there with his cousin Mrs. Barker during the summer
of 1794. v. Prelude (ed. E. de S.), p. 581.

15–16. The original reading restored at the request of Barron Field
who wrote that the lines "have passed into a quotation; they are
ferae naturae now; and I don't see what right you have to reclaim and
clip the wings of the words and tame them thus".

p. 260. VII. TO THE DAISY: v. Vol. II, p. 135. This and the
following poem are preserved, together with a hitherto unpublished
poem given in Appendix xi, p. 372, in a booklet in the hand of
S. H., which probably dates from shortly after their composition.
The MS. readings given in the app. crit. are to be found there.

The news of John Wordsworth's death reached Grasmere on Feb.
11, 1805. W. sent the present poem to Lady Beaumont in a letter
written Aug. 7, 1805 (E.L., pp. 512–13), introducing it thus:

"The following was written in remembrance of a beautiful letter of
my Brother John, sent to us from Portsmouth, when he had left us
at Grasmere, and first taken the command of his unfortunate ship,
more than four years ago. Some of the expressions in the Poem are
the very words he used in his letter. N.B. I have written two Poems
to the same flower before—this is partly alluded to in the first
stanza.—W. Wordsworth." v. note to ll. 19–28 infra.

19–28. John W. to D. W. writing from Portsmouth, April 2, 1801:
"We are painting the Ship, and make all as smart—Never Ship was
like ours—indeed we are not a little proud. . . . I have been on shore

this afternoon to stretch my legs upon the Isle of White. The Primroses are beautiful and the daisy's after sunset are like little *white* stars upon the dark green fields." (Unpublished letter.)

p. 263. VIII. Elegiac Verses: **21.** Here did we stop, *etc.*] "The point is 2 or 3 yards below the outlet of Grisdale Tarn on a foot-road by which a horse may pass to Paterdale, a ridge of Helvellyn on the left, and the summit of Fairfield on the right."—I. F. Cf. D. W.'s *Journal*, Sept. 29, 1800: "John left us. Wm and I parted with him in sight of Ulswater" (*Journals*, i, p. 62). This poem was probably withheld from publication till 1842 because of its intimate personal character. **16.** Moss Campion (Silene acaulis): This most beautiful plant is scarce in England, though it is found in great abundance upon the mountains of Scotland. The first specimen I ever saw of it, in its native bed, was singularly fine, the tuft or cushion being at least eight inches in diameter, and the root proportionately thick. I have only met with it in two places among our mountains, in both of which I have since sought for it in vain.

Botanists will not, I hope, take it ill, if I caution them against carrying off, inconsiderately, rare and beautiful plants. This has often been done, particularly from Ingleborough and other mountains in Yorkshire, till the species have totally disappeared, to the great regret of lovers of nature living near the places where they grew.—W.

p. 266. IX. Sonnet: "On Christmas eve we received a letter from Mrs. John Wordsworth then and still at Rome, communicating the death of her youngest son, nearly five years old. . . . The child . . . was one of the noblest creatures both in mind and body I ever saw." —W. W. to a cousin, Jan. 2, 1846 (*L.Y.*, p. 1272). To Henry Reed, W. wrote on Jan. 23 saying that his "state of feeling" upon this and other recent bereavements "had vented itself" in this sonnet and that beginning "Where lies the Truth". *v.* p. 19 *supra.*

p. 266. X. Lines composed at Grasmere, *etc.*: Fox died on Sept. 13, 1806. W. admired Fox for "a constant predominance of sensibility of heart" in his public character, and for looking upon men as individuals, while necessarily having to do with them in bodies or classes. *v.* his letter to Fox sent with the two volumes of *Lyrical Ballads*, Jan. 14, 1801 (*E.L.*, p. 259).

1–8. Cf. lines quoted by K. from fragments in D. W.'s *Journals* (K. *Life*, iii, p. 389):

> The rains at length have ceas'd, the winds are still'd
> The stars shine brightly between clouds at rest,
> And as a cavern is with darkness fill'd
> The Vale is by a mighty sound possess'd.

p. 267. XI. Invocation to the Earth: "Composed immediately after the *Thanksgiving Ode*, to which it may be considered as a second part."—I. F.

p. 268. XII. Lines written on a Blank Leaf in . . the Excursion, *etc.*: The Rev. Matthew Murfitt, vicar of Kendal, died on Nov. 7, 1814.

p. 269. XIII. Elegiac Stanzas, *etc.*: "On Mrs. Fermor. This lady had been a widow long before I knew her. Her husband was of the family of the Lady celebrated in the 'Rape of the Lock', and was, I believe, a Roman Catholic. The sorrow which his death caused her was fearful in its character as described in this poem, but was subdued in course of time by the strength of her religious faith. I have been, for many weeks at a time, an inmate with her at Coleorton Hall, as were also Mrs. Wordsworth and my Sister. The truth in the sketch of her character here given was acknowledged with gratitude by her nearest relatives. She was eloquent in conversation, energetic upon public matters, open in respect to these, but slow to communicate her personal feelings; upon these she never touched in her intercourse with me, so that I could not regard myself as her confidential friend, and was accordingly surprised when I learnt she had left me a Legacy of £100, as a token of her esteem. See, in further illustration, the second stanza inscribed upon her Cenotaph in Coleorton church."
—I. F. [*v.* p. 255 *supra.*]

p. 270. XIV. Elegiac Musings in the Grounds of Coleorton Hall, *etc.*: "These verses were in fact composed on horseback during a storm whilst I was on my way from Coleorton to Cambridge—they are alluded to elsewhere. (My Father was on my pony which he rode all the way from Rydal to Cambridge that I might have the comfort and pleasure of a horse at Cambridge—the storm of wind and rain on this day was so violent that the coach in which my Mother and I travelled the same road was all but blown over, and had the coachman drawn up as he attempted to do at one of his halting places we must have been upset. My Father and his pony were several times actually blown out of the road. D. Q.)"—I. F. "Thirty-seven miles did I ride in one day through the worst of these storms. And what was my resource? Guess again: writing verses to the memory of my departed friend Sir George Beaumont, whose house I had left the day before." Letter to W. Rowan Hamilton. Nov. 26, 1830 (*L.Y.*, p. 538). Sir G. B. died on Feb. 7, 1827.

46–7. From Fairfax's translation of Tasso's *Godfrey of Bullogne*, ii. xviii, "The Rose within herself her sweetness closed."

p. 272. XV. Written after the Death of Charles Lamb: "Light will be thrown upon the tragic circumstance alluded to in this Poem when, after the death of Charles Lamb's Sister, his biographer, Mr. Sergeant Talfourd, shall be at liberty to relate particulars which could not, at the time his Memoir was written, be given to the public. Mary Lamb was ten years older than her brother, and has survived him as long a time. Were I to give way to my own feelings, I should dwell not only on her genius and intellectual powers, but upon the delicacy and refinement of manner which she maintained inviolable under most trying circumstances. She was loved and honoured by all her brother's friends; and others, some of them strange characters, whom his philanthropic peculiarities induced him to countenance. The death of C. Lamb himself was doubtless hastened by his sorrow for that of Coleridge, to whom he had been attached from the time of their being schoolfellows at Christ's Hospital. Lamb was a good Latin scholar, and probably would have gone to college upon one of the school foundations but for the impediment in his speech. Had such been his lot, he would probably have been preserved from the indulgences of social humours and fancies which were often injurious to himself, and causes of severe regret to his friends, without really benefiting the object of his misapplied kindness."—I. F.

On Nov. 20, 1835, W. wrote to Moxon: "On the other page you have the requested Epitaph. It was composed yesterday—and by sending it immediately, I have prepared the way, I believe, for a speedy repentance—as I do not know that I ever wrote so many lines without some retouching being afterwards necessary. If these verses should be wholly unsuitable to the end Miss Lamb had in view, I shall find no difficulty in reconciling myself to the thought of their not being made use of, though it would have given me great, *very* great pleasure to fulfil, in all points, her wishes.

"The first objection that will strike you, and every one, is its extreme length, especially compared with epitaphs as they are now written—but this objection might in part be obviated by engraving the lines in double column, and not in capitals.

"Chiabrera has been here my model—though I am aware that Italian Churches, both on account of their size and the climate of Italy, are more favourable to long inscriptions than ours. His epitaphs are characteristic and circumstantial—so have I endeavoured to make this of mine—but I have not ventured to touch upon the most striking feature of our departed friend's character and the most affecting circumstance of his life, viz. his faithful and intense love of his Sister. Had I been pouring out an Elegy or Monody, this would and must have been done; but for seeing and feeling the sanctity of that relation as it ought to be seen and felt, lights are required which could scarcely be furnished by an Epitaph, unless it were to touch on little or nothing else. The omission, therefore, in my view of the case, was unavoidable, and I regret it the less, you yourself having already treated in verse the subject with genuine tenderness and beauty."

Moxon seems to have printed off a copy of the Epitaph (ll. 1–38) immediately. *v.* W.'s letter to Moxon, Dec. 1835 (*L.Y.*, p. 768), where he refers to the italics *at the close*, which tally with those found in T. J. Wise's unique copy (1835), ll. 35–8; the rest of the poem, now conceived as "an elegy or monody", with its tribute to Lamb's love for his sister, was added in December and read to H. C. R. as recorded in his *Diary* on Jan. 3, 1836. Letters of W. to Moxon, Nov., Dec. 1835, and Jan. 1836 (*v. L.Y.*, pp. 760–4, 767–8, 771–2), make it clear that W. several times revised the verses and that Moxon continued to print off copies for his approval. Three of these are quoted in the *app. crit.*: a proof-copy now in Dove Cottage with corrections in M. W.'s hand, a version recorded by Knight, Dowden, and T. J. Wise (1836[1]), and a copy in Dove Cottage Museum inscribed by Dora Wordsworth (1836[2]). All these privately printed copies are without title, date, or imprint. *v. Addenda*, p. 468.

15–17, 20–21. (*app. crit.*) *v.* W.'s letter to Moxon, Dec. 1835, *L.Y.*, p. 763.

24. the name he bore] This way of indicating the *name of* my lamented friend has been found fault with; perhaps rightly so; but I may say in justification of the double sense of the word, that similar allusions are not uncommon in epitaphs. One of the best in our language in verse, I ever read, was upon a person who bore the name of Palmer; and the course of the thought, throughout, turned upon the Life of the Departed, considered as a pilgrimage. Nor can I think that the objection in the present case will have much force with any one who remembers Charles Lamb's beautiful sonnet addressed to his own name, and ending,

"No deed of mine shall shame thee, gentle name!"—W. 1837.

30, 31, and **38.** These lines form part of the inscription in the Memorial to Lamb in Edmonton Church.

50. a scorner of the fields] *v.* Lamb's famous letter to W. (p.m. Jan. 30, 1801) in which he declines an invitation to visit the W.s at Grasmere.

56. peculiar sanctity] A phrase previously used by W. in *Exc.* vii. 479.

66. Through God] Altered from the earlier reading, "By God", because "in the beginning of the line [it] gives them the appearance of an oath" (W. to Moxon, *L.Y.*, p. 771).

128. *dual* loneliness] Cf. Lamb, *Mackery End*: "We house together, old bachelor and maid, in a sort of double singleness."

p. 276. XVI. EXTEMPORE EFFUSION UPON THE DEATH OF JAMES HOGG: "These verses were written extempore, immediately after reading a notice of the Ettrick Shepherd's death in the Newcastle paper, to the Editor of which I sent a copy for publication. The persons lamented in these verses were all either of my friends or acquaintance. In Lockhart's Life of Sir Walter Scott an account is given of my first meeting with him in 1803. How the Ettrick Shepherd and I became known to each other has already been mentioned in these notes. He was undoubtedly a man of original genius, but of coarse manners and low and offensive opinions. Of Coleridge and

Lamb I need not speak here. Crabbe I have met in London at Mr.
Rogers's, but more frequently and favorably at Mr. Hoare's upon
Hampstead Heath. Every spring he used to pay that family a visit
of some length, and was upon terms of intimate friendship with Mrs.
Hoare, and still more with her daughter-in-law, who has a large
collection of his letters addressed to herself. After the Poet's decease,
application was made to her to give up these letters to his biographer,
that they, or at least part of them, might be given to the public. She
hesitated to comply, and asked my opinion on the subject. 'By no
means,' was my answer, grounded not upon any objection there
might be to publishing a selection from these letters, but from an
aversion I have always felt to meet idle curiosity by calling back the
recently departed to become the object of trivial and familiar gossip.
Crabbe obviously for the most part preferred the company of women
to that of men, for this among other reasons, that he did not like to
be put upon the stretch in general conversation: accordingly in
miscellaneous society his *talk* was so much below what might have
been expected from a man so deservedly celebrated, that to me it
seemed trifling. It must upon other occasions have been of a different
character, as I found in our rambles together on Hampstead Heath,
and not so much from a readiness to communicate his knowledge of
life and manners as of Natural History in all its branches. His mind
was inquisitive, and he seems to have taken refuge from a remembrance of the distresses he had gone through, in these studies and the
employments to which they led. Moreover, such contemplations
might tend profitably to counterbalance the painful truths which he
had collected from his intercourse with mankind. Had I been more
intimate with him, I should have ventured to touch upon his office
as a Minister of the Gospel, and how far his heart and soul were in it
so as to make him a zealous and diligent labourer. In poetry, though
he wrote much, as we all know, he assuredly was not so. I happened once to speak of pains as necessary to produce merit of a
certain kind which I highly valued: his observation was—'It is not
worth while.' You are quite right, thought I, if the labour encroaches
upon the time due to teach truth as a steward of the mysteries of God:
if there be cause to fear that, write less: but, if poetry is to be produced at all, make what you do produce as good as you can. Mr.
Rogers once told me that he expressed his regret to Crabbe that he
wrote in his later works so much less correctly than in his earlier.
'Yes,' replied he, 'but then I had a reputation to make; now I can
afford to relax.' Whether it was from a modest estimate of his own
qualifications, or from causes less creditable, his motives for writing
verse and his hopes and aims were not so high as is to be desired.
After being silent for more than twenty years, he again applied himself to poetry, upon the spur of applause he received from the
periodical publications of the day, as he himself tells us in one of his

prefaces. Is it not to be lamented that a man who was so conversant with permanent truth, and whose writings are so valuable an acquisition to our country's literature, should have *required* an impulse from such a quarter?[1] Mrs. Hemans was unfortunate as a Poetess in being obliged by circumstances to write for money, and that so frequently and so much, that she was compelled to look out for subjects wherever she could find them, and to write as expeditiously as possible. As a woman, she was to a considerable degree a spoilt child of the world. She had been early in life distinguished for talent, and poems of hers were published whilst she was a girl. She had also been handsome in her youth, but her education had been most unfortunate. She was totally ignorant of housewifery, and could as easily have managed the spear of Minerva as her needle. It was from observing these deficiencies that, one day while she was under my roof, I purposely directed her attention to household economy, and told her I had purchased Scales, which I intended to present to a young lady as a wedding present; pointed out their utility (for her especial benefit), and said that no *ménage* ought to be without them. Mrs. Hemans, not in the least suspecting my drift, reported this saying, in a letter to a friend at the time, as a proof of my simplicity. Being disposed to make large allowances for the faults of her education and the circumstances in which she was placed, I felt most kindly disposed towards her, and took her part upon all occasions, and I was not a little affected by learning that after she withdrew to Ireland, a long and severe sickness raised her spirit as it depressed her body. This I heard from her most intimate friends, and there is striking evidence of it in a poem entitled [   ][2] written and published not long before her death. These notices of Mrs. Hemans would be very unsatisfactory to her intimate friends, as indeed they are to myself, not so much for what is said, but what for brevity's sake is left unsaid. Let it suffice to add, there was much sympathy between us, and, if opportunity had been allowed me to see more of her, I should have loved and valued her accordingly; as it is, I remember her with true affection for her amiable qualities, and, above all, for her delicate and irreproachable conduct during her long separation from an unfeeling husband, whom she had been led to marry from the romantic notions

[1] "Daddy dear, I don't like this—think how many reasons there were to *depress* his Muse; to say nothing of his duties as a Priest, and probably he found poetry interfere with them; he did not *require* such praise to make him write, but it just put it into his heart to try again, and gave him the courage to do so."—*Note by Dora Q. in I. F.*

[2] "Do you mean A Sonnet entitled *Sabbath Sonnet* composed by Mrs. Hemans April 26th, 1835, a few days before her death.
       How many blessed groups. . . ." (*Pencil note by E. Q. in I. F.*)
   But W. probably means *Flowers and Music in a Room of Sickness* which he selects for praise in a letter to Mrs. Hemans, Sept. 1834 (*L.Y.*, p. 714).

of inexperienced youth. Upon this husband I never heard her cast the least reproach, nor did I ever hear her even name him, though she did not forbear wholly to touch upon her domestic position; but never so as that any fault could be found with her manner of adverting to it."—I. F.

Walter Scott	.	.	.	.	. died	21st Sept., 1832.
S. T. Coleridge	.	.	.	.	„	25th July, 1834.
Charles Lamb .	.	.	.	.	„	27th Dec., 1834.
Geo. Crabbe	.	.	.	.	„	3rd Feb., 1832.
Felicia Hemans	.	.	.	.	„	16th May, 1835.

—W.

Hogg died 21st Nov. 1835.

The extempore character of the verses is independently attested by the following record in the Diary of the Rev. Francis Kilvert, who met W.'s niece, Miss Hutchinson,[1] at Whitney in 1871: "Miss Hutchinson said that once when she was staying at the Wordsworths' the poet was much affected by reading in the newspaper the death of Hogg, the Ettrick Shepherd. Half an hour afterwards he came into the room where the ladies were sitting and asked Miss Hutchinson to write down some lines which he had just composed. She did so and these lines were the beautiful Poem called The Graves of the Poets." v. Addenda, p. 469.

p. 278. XVII. INSCRIPTION FOR A MONUMENT IN CROSTHWAITE CHURCH: Robert Southey died on March 21, 1843. For the pains which W. took to make his Inscription as good as he could v. his correspondence with John Taylor Coleridge (L.Y., pp. 1187–90, 1194), to whom he submitted his drafts and corrections. Cf. also "Reminiscences of Wordsworth by Lady Richardson", Grosart, iii. 438.

Before line 1 (app. crit.) added in response to J. T. Coleridge's criticism: "I desiderate some notice of the Lake—in the third line I could almost venture to turn 'ye loved Books' into 'thou loved Lake'—and end the 4th line with shore." Letter to W., 30 Nov. 1843.

13, 14. (app. crit.) Lady Richardson records that in Dec. 1843 W. read to them his Epitaph on Southey; her mother objected to "holier nest" as not being a correct union of ideas. . . . "He said there was yet time to change it, and that he should consult Judge Coleridge whether the line as he once had it

Did private feeling[s] meet in holier rest

would not be more appropriate to the simplicity of an epitaph where you con every word, and where every word is expected to bear an

[1] Elizabeth Hutchinson, daughter of M. W.'s brother, Thomas Hutchinson, and Mary, née Monkhouse. The Rector of Whitney, Mr. Dew, married the only daughter of Thomas Monkhouse.

exact meaning." The inscription on the monument, however, reads "find a holier nest".

17, 18. (*app. crit.*) The inscription on the monument reads: "Through a life long and pure ; and Christian faith", *etc. as text.* But an inspection of the stone shows that the last two lines have been partly erased and the above re-incised. Possibly the erased words may be as in MS. 1 (first reading). Cuthbert Southey in his *Life* of his father gives this version for the closing lines with "steadfast" for "Christian". W. also attempted a prose inscription, of which the first version contains the word "prematurely" to which J. T. C. objected (*v. L.Y.,* p. 1188): it was not used at Crosthwaite.

p. 279. ODE. INTIMATIONS OF IMMORTALITY FROM RECOLLECTIONS OF EARLY CHILDHOOD

"This was composed during my residence at Town-End, Grasmere ; two years at least passed between the writing of the four first stanzas and the remaining part. To the attentive and competent reader the whole sufficiently explains itself ; but there may be no harm in adverting here to particular feelings or *experiences* of my own mind on which the structure of the poem partly rests. Nothing was more difficult for me in childhood than to admit the notion of death as a state applicable to my own being. I have said elsewhere—

'A simple child,
That lightly draws its breath,
And feels its life in every limb,
What should it know of death !'—

But it was not so much from [feelings] of animal vivacity that *my* difficulty came as from a sense of the indomitableness of the spirit within me. I used to brood over the stories of Enoch and Elijah, and almost to persuade myself that, whatever might become of others, I should be translated, in something of the same way, to heaven. With a feeling congenial to this, I was often unable to think of external things as having external existence, and I communed with all that I saw as something not apart from, but inherent in, my own immaterial nature. Many times while going to school have I grasped at a wall or tree to recall myself from this abyss of idealism to the reality. At that time I was afraid of such processes. In later periods of life I have deplored, as we have all reason to do, a subjugation of an opposite character, and have rejoiced over the remembrances, as is expressed in the lines—

'Obstinate questionings
Of sense and outward things,
Fallings from us, vanishings ;' etc.

To that dream-like vividness and splendour which invest objects of sight in childhood, every one, I believe, if he would look back, could bear testimony, and I need not dwell upon it here: but having in the Poem regarded it as presumptive evidence of a prior state of existence, I think it right to protest against a conclusion, which has given pain to some good and pious persons, that I meant to inculcate such a belief. It is far too shadowy a notion to be recommended to faith, as more than an element in our instincts of immortality. But let us bear in mind that, though the idea is not advanced in revelation, there is nothing there to contradict it, and the fall of Man presents an analogy in its favor. Accordingly, a pre-existent state has entered into the popular creeds of many nations; and, among all persons acquainted with classic literature, is known as an ingredient in Platonic philosophy. Archimedes said that he could move the world if he had a point whereon to rest his machine. Who has not felt the same aspirations as regards the world of his own mind? Having to wield some of its elements when I was impelled to write this Poem on the 'Immortality of the Soul', I took hold of the notion of pre-existence as having sufficient foundation in humanity for authorizing me to make for my purpose the best use of it I could as a Poet."—I. F.

"The poem rests entirely upon two recollections of childhood, one that of a splendour in the objects of sense which is passed away, and the other an indisposition to bend to the law of death as applying to our particular case. A Reader who has not a vivid recollection of these feelings having existed in his mind cannot understand that poem." (W. to Mrs. Clarkson, Dec. 1814.)

The date at which W. composed his Ode *Intimations of Immortality*, is a matter of great interest and some controversy among students of the poet; Wordsworth himself assigned it to the years 1803–6, and, accepting these dates, critics (myself among the number, in my edition of *The Prelude*, Ed. 1) have regarded its later stanzas as influenced by the loss of his brother John in Feb. 1805. But further investigation has convinced me that, as often, Wordsworth's dating is inaccurate.

D. W.'s *Journal* for March 26, 1802, records that "he wrote the Rainbow" (i.e. "My heart leaps up", *etc.*), and, for March 27, "Wm. wrote part of an Ode"; on the 28th they were with Coleridge, and W. must then have recited to him the first four stanzas of the Ode, for on April 4 Coleridge wrote his *Dejection*, in which the lines "I too will crown me with a coronal" and "They are not to me now the things which once they were" are deliberate reminiscences of lines 40 and 9 of the Ode. *Dejection* is, indeed, C.'s counterpart of the Ode, and it is probable that, though W. had written only four stanzas at the time, he enlarged to C. upon that mood of meditative ecstasy in which his poem was to close.

The poem, says W., was completed "two years at least" after its inception (*v.* I. F. note *supra*) and this would hardly justify our acceptance of so late a date as 1806 for its downward limit, even if there were not other reasons against it. But Coleridge relates in *The Friend* (Section II, Essay xi) that "during my residence in Rome [i.e. January to May, 1806] I had the pleasure of reading this sublime Ode to the illustrious Baron von Humbolt" who "listened with evident delight . . . and wonder that so great and original a poet should have escaped his notice". C.'s statement does not admit the interpretation that he read only the first four stanzas, or, as has been suggested, an incomplete draft of the whole; if he had done so, von Humbolt is not likely to have been so deeply impressed. Now even if C. had received the poem by post, it must have been sent off by Sept., 1804; for he left Malta in Sept. 1805, and he could have received no letter from Wordsworth for six months before that. On Jan. 19, 1805, he had written to W.: "It is my fixed intention to leave this place in March"; W. received this letter on March 27, and, believing that C. was already on his way home, had no address to write to. Hence, as we know that for some time after his brother's death W.'s distress of mind made all poetic composition impossible to him, the date of the Ode must be put back at least to Jan. 1805. But on April 20 C. wrote to Stuart complaining of the non-arrival of letters from England, the last being from W., dated the previous September. This would normally have reached Malta in November or December at latest; of course, a letter written between September and the following February might have been so much delayed in transit as to reach Malta after April 20, but this is improbable; hence the conclusion that the Ode was finished at least by Sept. 1804.

But there is good reason for the belief that the poem was not sent by letter to Coleridge, but that it was completed before he left England. For it is found in MS. M, which contains the great majority of the poems, then unpublished, which we know to have been written by the early months of 1804; it contains no poem of an authenticated later date, and it concludes with the first five books of *The Prelude*, which were completed before C.'s departure for Malta in April 1804. Even if my assumption (*Prelude, Introd.*) is incorrect that M is a duplicate of the volume copied for Coleridge to take with him, the appearance of the Ode in it still favours the view that it was among the poems completed by that date. Wordsworth speaks of "two years at least" as separating the inception and the conclusion of the poem. It was begun in March 1802; it seems to have been finished in March 1804.

In addition to MS. M two other Manuscripts are known to exist, one a transcript, in an unknown hand, in the Beaumont collection at Coleorton, described by Professor Ifor Evans in the *T.L.S.* of June 13, 1938, and quoted in *app. crit.* as B, the other in the *Longman* MSS., quoted as L, for a careful transcript, and also for a sight of which I am indebted to Mr. E. H. W. Meyerstein.

917.17 IV H h

1–6. There was a time *etc.*] Both verbally and metrically reminiscent of Coleridge's *Mad Monk* (1801), 9–16:

> There was a time when earth, and sea, and skies,
> The bright green vale, and forest's dark recess,
> With all things, lay before mine eyes
> In steady loveliness;
> But now I feel, on earth's uneasy scene,
> Such sorrows as will never cease;—
> I only ask for peace;
> If I must live to know that such a time has been!

23–4. A timely utterance *etc.*] Professor Garrod suggests (*Words-worth*, p. 113) that the "timely utterance" was the Rainbow poem, written the day before the Ode was begun, the last three lines of which, from 1815 on, were printed as a motto to the poem.

36–40. Cf. *The Idle Shepherd Boys*, 27–30 (Vol. I, p. 239).

36–76. Many critics have noted the parallels between much of this passage and the poems of Vaughan, especially *Retreat* and *Corruption*, which W. certainly knew; but parallels even more striking are to be found in the writings of Traherne, which were not published until 1905–8.

51–2. a Tree . . . A single field] W. refers in *The Prelude* to two trees which had a deep and haunting influence upon him in his youth, the "tall ash" opposite his bedroom window at Hawkshead (*Prelude*, iv. 86–92) and the "single tree" in the college groves at Cambridge ibid. vi. 76–94, "William's ash tree", as D.W. calls it, (*M.Y.*, p. 388): he may here have been thinking of either of these. The "single field" is perhaps the "one green field" described in *Poems on the Naming of Places*, v (To M. H.), associated in his mind with the days of his betrothal.

69. But He] *app. crit.* I have accepted this division of the line as providing the reading which W. originally intended. He has with his own hand made this correction in the *Longman* MS. for the press. This gives a rhyme to infancy, l. 66, which otherwise would remain unrhymed.

86–90. Behold the Child *etc.*] W. is thinking in particular of Hartley Coleridge. Cf. *Christabel* 656–61:

> A little child, a limber elf,
> Singing dancing to itself, . . .
> Makes such a vision to the sight
> As fills a father's eyes with light.

104. "humorous stage"] From l. 1 of Daniel's Sonnet to Fulke Greville, in dedication of *Musophilus*.

109–21. Quoted by Coleridge (*Biog. Lit.*, ch. xxii) as an instance of "mental bombast or thoughts and images too great for the subject".

119–21. Cf. *Essay upon Epitaphs*: "If we look back upon the days of childhood, we shall find that the time is not in remembrance when, with respect to our own individual Being, the mind was without this assurance [that some part of our nature is imperishable]."

121/2. (1807–15.) These lines were omitted after ed. 1815 owing to Coleridge's objections (in *Biog. Lit.*, ch. xxii) to the "frightful notion of lying *awake* in the grave". But to W. and his sister the idea was evidently both happy and familiar. Cf. D. W.'s *Journal* for April 29, 1802: "We went to John's grove, sate a while at first. Afterwards William lay, and I lay, in the trench under the fence—he with his eyes shut, and listening to the waterfalls and the birds . . . we both lay still, and unseen by one another; he thought that it would be as sweet thus to lie so in the grave, to hear the *peaceful* sounds of the earth, and just to know that our dear friends were near." Cf. Poem in Appendix B. III. ii.

127–9. Cf. *Prelude*, xiv. 157.

144. Fallings from us, vanishings] "I remember Mr. Wordsworth saying that, at a particular stage of his mental progress, he used to be frequently so rapt into an unreal transcendental world of ideas that the external world seemed no longer to exist in relation to him, and he had to reconvince himself of its existence *by clasping a tree*, or something that happened to be near him." (R. P. Graves quoted M. ii. 480). Cf. also the letter from Professor Bonamy Price, quoted by K.: "The venerable old man raised his aged form erect; he was walking in the middle, and passed across me to a five-barred gate in the wall which bounded the road on the side of the lake. He clenched the top bar firmly with his right hand, pushed strongly against it, and then uttered these ever-memorable words: 'There was a time in my life when I had to push against something that resisted, to be sure that there was anything outside me. I was sure of my own mind; everything else fell away, and vanished into thought.' "

155. our noisy years] A reminiscence of lines in an *Address to Silence*, published in *The Weekly Entertainer*. Cf. *On the Power of Sound*, 217–18:

O Silence! are Man's noisy years

No more than moments of thy life ? (Vol. II, pp. 330 and note, 526).

161. abolish or destroy] Cf. *Paradise Lost*, ii. 92:

More destroyd then thus
We should be quite abolisht and expire.

182. primal sympathy] Cf. *Prelude*, i. 555–8.

203. the meanest flower that blows] Cf. Gray, *Ode on the Pleasure arising from Vicissitude*:

The meanest floweret of the vale,
The simplest note that swells the gale,
The common sun, the air, the skies
To him are opening Paradise.

ADDENDA TO NOTES

p. 399. Note, p. 18, XIV, To Lucca Giordano: *add*: Another sonnet to a picture by Lucca Giordano, 'in the Museo Borbonico at Naples', which appears to be by Wordsworth, was published in the *New York Home Journal*, 2 Oct. 1847:

> A sad and lovely face with upturn'd eyes
> Tearless yet full of grief—how heavenly fair,
> How saintlike is the look those features wear!
> Such sorrow is more lovely in its guise
> Than joy itself—for underneath it lies
> A calmness that betokens strength to bear
> Earth's petty grievances—its toil and care:—
> A spirit that can look through clouded skies,
> And see the blue beyond.—Type of that grace
> That lit Her holy features, from whose womb
> Issued the blest Redeemer of our race—
> How little dost thou speak of earthly gloom!
> As little as the unblemish'd Queen of Night,
> When envious clouds shut out her silver light.

> (WILLIAM WORDSWORTH, Rydal Mount, Westmorland,
> Oct. 23, 1839.)

Wordsworth was prevented by the cholera from visiting Naples in 1837, but he may have seen a copy of the picture in Rome or elsewhere. *v. L.Y.* 1274.

p. 410. Insert Note to p. 47, XLII: A copy of this sonnet, signed Wm. Wordsworth, Elton Rectory and dated 11 Novr 1844 (he was staying with F. W. Faber, Rector of Elton), is preserved in the Library of St. John's College, Cambridge. It contains the following variants: 1. 9, For *for* In; 1. 10, will *for* doth; 1. 13, Welcomes *for* Accepts.

p. 418. *Ode to Duty*, p. 83. W. J. B. Owen (*Notes and Queries*, July 1958) quotes from the incomplete MS. of Coleridge's *The Friend* in the Library of the Victoria and Albert Museum (48 G. 28) some readings from the *Ode to Duty* which may be genuine variants.
1. 39: name] aim *orig.*; 1. 40, long] look(?) *orig.*;
1. 43:   Of my own wish; and feel past doubt]
         Of my own inborn wish nor doubt   *undeleted.*

p. 422. *Add* Note to XXIV, 18–20: cf. *Hamlet*, III. i. 89.

p. 426. XXXIII: *add to* Note: A copy of the poem is found in W.W.'s letter to John Wordsworth (Brit. Mus. Add. MSS. 46136) with the following variants: 1. 3, genial *for* sprightly; 1. 6, meridian *for* solstitial; 1. 9, fields repay *for* earth repays; 1. 11, daily *for* ripening, finest *for* forest; 1. 13, pomp, what *for* pensive.

pp. 448–50. *Epitaphs from Chiabrera*, pp. 250–253. W. J. B. Owen (*Notes and Queries*, July 1958) notes interesting variants in the MS. of Coleridge's *The Friend* in the Library of the Victoria and Albert Museum (48 G. 28).

p. 450. II: *add to* Note: M. W. wrote to E. Q. 19 Sept. 1822: 'It took him [W.] years to produce those 6 simple lines at the head of the earthly remains of our own dear Boy.'

p. 459. l. 11: *after* imprint *add*: v. also B.M. MS. Ashley 4642, and a copy in Turnbull Library, Wellington, N.Z.

p. 462. l. 21: *after* ". . . Graves of the Poets" *add* **21.** Like clouds that rake the mountain-summits. This expression is borrowed from a Sonnet by Mr. G. Bell, the author of a small volume of Poems lately printed at Penrith. Speaking of Skiddaw he says—"Yon dark cloud 'rakes' and shrouds its noble brow". Henry Reed, 1837.

p. 477. *Add to* Note, p. 379, XXI. The Album is now in the hands of Messrs Raper, Solicitors, Chichester. The poem is there signed *Wm Wordsworth. Whitehaven Castle.* 1st Oct. 1823. O'Callaghan was evidently in Lord Lonsdale's circle: he is referred to familiarly in W.'s letter to Lord Lonsdale, 9 Nov. 1823.

p. 479. *Add to* Note, p. 391, XXXV: First published by Grosart in *Prose Works of Wordsworth*, 1876. T. J. Wise produced a forged copy "Printed for the Author by R. Branthwaite and Son, Kendal", 1846.

APPENDIX A. TRANSLATION OF VIRGIL'S *ÆNEID*

The following Manuscripts are extant: (i) a rough copy, much corrected, in the hands of W. W., M. W., D. W., and Dora W., preserved in a large leather-bound folio volume used by W. from about 1820 or earlier to 1846 for composition or transcription, MS. 101. This is the earliest of the Manuscripts, and the only one to contain the last eleven lines of Bk. III, Bk. IV. 688–92, and Bk. VIII. 337–66. (ii and iii) Fair copies of Bks. I and II carefully written by D. W. on quarto sheets stitched together; the paper has watermarks 1820 and 1822. Bk. II is interleaved, and contains some corrections in the hand of Christopher W. Though Wordsworth seems to have accepted them, I have not introduced them into my text, but have given them in the *app. crit.* (iv) A fair copy of III. 1–580 in a small octavo notebook, written by S. H.; the paper shows watermark 1821. (v) A fair copy of Bks. I and II in the hand of S. H., watermarks 1822–3; and of Bk. III. 289–536 by D. W. on octavo sheets (watermark 1823) stitched together in a cardboard cover; this copy has a few corrections by W. W. and C. W.

The chronology of W.'s composition of his translations is determined by the dates of the following letters to Lord Lonsdale. (I have corrected W. Knight's dating of the letters, often wildly astray, by consulting the letters themselves in Lord Lonsdale's collection.)

(1) Letter to Lord Lonsdale, 9 Nov. 1823, quoted in K.'s *Poetical Works of W.* 1896, vol. viii, p. 276: "I have just finished a Translation into English Rhyme of the first Aeneid. Would your Lordship allow me to send it to you at Cottesmore ? I should be much gratified if you would take the trouble of comparing some passages of it with the original. I have endeavoured to be much more literal than Dryden, or Pitt, who keeps much closer to the original than his Predecessor."

(2) Letter to Lord L., [? Dec. 1823], *M.Y.*, p. 836; *Mem.* ii. 69: "Many thanks for your obliging letter. I shall be much gratified if you happen to like my Translation, and thankful for any remarks with which you may honour me. I have made so much progress with the 2nd book, that I defer sending the former till that is finished."

(3) Letter to Lord L., 23 Jan. 1824, *L.Y.*, p. 161: "I am quite ashamed of being so long in fulfilling my engagement. But the promises of Poets are like the Perjuries of Lovers, things at which Jove laughs! At last, however, I have sent off the two first books of my Translations. . . ."

(4) Letter to Lord L., 5 Feb. [1824], *M.Y.*, p. 836: "I am truly obliged by your friendly and frank communication. May I beg that you would add to the favour, by marking with a pencil, some of the passages that are faulty in your view. . . . I do not think of going beyond the fourth book. [He implies that he has translated Book III: 'I will send it ere long.'] As to the MS., be so kind as to forward it at your leisure to me at Sir George Beaumont's, Coleorton Hall, near Ashby, whither I am going in about ten days."

(5) Letter to Lord L., 17 Feb. [1824], Coleorton Hall, *M.Y.*, p. 840: "I began my translation by accident. . . . In my last I troubled you with a quotation from my own translation" [He refers to a passage in letter (4)].

Three letters from other correspondents carry on the tale:

(6) Letter of S. T. C. to Mrs. Allsop, dated 8 April 1824. *Letters, Conversations and Recollections of S. T. Coleridge*, 1836, vol. i. 166–7. He asks for three rolls of paper in the sideboard drawer, "Mr. Words-worth's translation of the first, second and third books of the Æneid", to be given to the bearer. These would appear to be MSS. ii, iii, and iv.

(7) Letter of D. W. to H. C. R., Dec. 1824. H. C. R., i. 129: ". . . ask Charles [Lamb] if my Brother's translation of Virgil is in his possession."

(8) Letter of C. Lamb to W. W., May 1825: "Your Virgil I have lost sight of, but suspect it is in the hands of Sir G. Beaumont. . . . Will you write to him about it ? and your commands shall be obeyed to a tittle."

From these letters it is clear that W.'s translations of Books I and II

were finished and copied by 23 Jan. 1824, (1), (2), (3), and that by
5 Feb. (4) he had already completed a draft of III, of which S. T. C.
had a fair copy in his hands along with Books I and II before 8 Apr.
1824 (6). Knight had conjectured the date 1819 for letters (2), (4), (5)
on the grounds of Christopher Wordsworth's statement (*M*. ii. 68)
that "in preparing his son for his University career he reperused the
Latin poets" (D. W.'s letter of 1 Aug. 1819, *M.Y.*, p. 851 shows that
W. was then acting as John's tutor), and that "Among the fruits of
this course of reading was a translation of some of the earlier books
of Vergil's Aeneid." W. may have tried his hand at a translation of
Virgil as early as 1819, but I surmise that he settled down to it in
earnest in 1823, and pursued the work through the early months of
1824. S. T. C.'s verdict on it in a letter, conjecturally but I think
rightly, dated 1824 by E. H. C. (*Letters of S. T. C.* ii. 733), was not
encouraging and may have influenced W. against going farther. His
translation stops short at Bk. III, line 580. In Dec. 1827 W. writes
to Christopher W. Junior: "As to the Virgil I have no objection to its
being printed if two or three good judges would previously take the
trouble of looking it over . . ." (*L.Y.* 282).

A portion of his translation of Bk. I, ll. 657 to the end was in 1832
published in the *Philological Museum* prefaced by the following letter:

"To the Editors of the 'Philological Museum.'"

"Your letter reminding me of an expectation I some time since
held out to you of allowing some specimens of my translation from the
Æneid to be printed in the 'Philological Museum', was not very
acceptable; for I had abandoned the thought of ever sending into
the world any part of that experiment—for it was nothing more—
an experiment begun for amusement, and I now think a less fortunate
one than when I first named it to you. Having been displeased in
modern translations with the additions of incongruous matter, I
began to translate with a resolve to keep clear of that fault, by adding
nothing; but I became convinced that a spirited translation can
scarcely be accomplished in the English language without admitting
a principle of compensation. On this point, however, I do not wish
to insist, and merely send the following passage, taken at random,
from a wish to comply with your request. W. W."

APPENDIX B

p. 357. I. From the Alfoxden Notebook: This note-book (described in *Prelude, Introd.*) contains work written in the early months
of 1798; it is unlikely that these lines would be found in it unless they
were of that period, though they appear there as a curious survival
of W.'s earlier and more crudely "romantic" taste.

p. 358. II. Chaucer Modernised—The Manciple (from the
Prologue) and the Manciple's Tale: D. W. records in her *Journal*

of Dec. 2, 1801, "I read the Tale of Phoebus and the Crow, which [Wm.] afterwards attempted to translate, and did translate a large part of it to-day"; on April 28, 1802, she "wrote out *The Manciple's Tale*". In Dec. 1839 W. offered it to Powell for inclusion in his *Chaucer Modernised* (*v.* pp. 443–4 *supra*) and in the following February he was busy revising his version of it. But on May 1 he wrote to Powell: "You are welcome to my Cuckoo and Nightingale and to the small part of the Troilus and Cressida, and were my own judgment only to be consulted to the Manciple's Tale, but there is a delicacy in respect to this last among some of my Friends which though I cannot sympathize with it I am bound to respect. Therefore in regard to that piece you will consider my decision as at present suspended." W. never printed it. Two of these friends were certainly Miss Fenwick and Quillinan. To Quillinan he wrote: "I do not acknowledge the force of the objections made to my publishing the specimens of Chaucer, nevertheless I have yielded to the judgments of others," and, a little later, to Dora W.: "Tell Mr. Quillinan, I think he has taken rather a narrow view of the spirit of the Manciple's Tale, especially as concerns its *morality*. The formal prosing at the end and the selfishness that pervades it flows from the genius of Chaucer, mainly as characteristic of the narrator whom he describes in the Prologue as eminent for shrewdness and clever worldly Prudence. The main lesson, and the most important one, is inculcated as a Poet ought chiefly to inculcate his lessons, not formally, but by implication; as when Phoebus in a transport of passion slays a wife whom he loved so dearly. How could the mischief of telling truth, merely, because it *is* truth, be more feelingly exemplified? The Manciple himself is not, in his understanding, conscious of this; but his heart dictates what was natural to be felt and the moral, without being intended, forces itself more or less upon every Reader. Then how vividly is impressed the mischief of jealous vigilance, and how truly and touchingly in contrast with the world's judgements are the transgressions of a woman in a low rank of life and one in high estate placed on the same level, treated." To Miss Fenwick he wrote more generally. "Chaucer was one of the greatest poets the world has ever seen. He is certainly, at times, in his comic tales, indecent, but he is never, as far as I know, insidiously or openly voluptuous, much less would a stronger term, which would apply to some popular writers of our own day, apply to him. He had towards the female sex as exquisite and pure feelings as ever the heart of man was blessed with, and has expressed them as beautifully in the language of his age, as ever man did" (*v. L.Y.*, pp. 993, 1002, 1009, 1018, 1025).

The Manuscript is headed by the following lines, taken from Drayton's *Elegy*, "To my most dearly-loved friend Henry Reynolds Esquire, of *Poets and Poesie*:

That noble Chaucer, in those former times
The first enriched our English histories
And was the first of ours that ever brake
Into the Muses' treasure, and first spake
In weighty numbers, *delving in the mine*
Of perfect knowledge".

But the correct reading of l. 2 is "The first inrich'd our English with his rimes".

p. 365. III. FRAGMENTS FROM MS. M. (On MS. M *v. Prelude, Introd.*). The lines seem to have been written shortly before April 22, 1802. Cf. D. W.'s *Journal* for that day: "We walked into Easedale . . . the waters were high for there had been a great quantity of rain in the night. . . . I sate upon the grass till they [Wm. and C.] came from the waterfall . . . when they returned Wm. was repeating the poem 'I have thoughts that are fed by the sun'. It had been called to his mind by the dying away of the stunning of the waterfall when he came behind a stone."

p. 366. IV. THE TINKER: Preserved in MS. M and in the *Longman* MSS. Its presence in the latter suggests that W. intended to publish and then withdrew it. Cf. D. W.'s *Journal*, April 27, 1802, "In the evening Wm. began to write *The Tinker*." April 28, "He is working at *The Tinker*." April 29, ". . . I had written down *The Tinker*, which Wm. finished this morning."

p. 367. V. TRANSLATION OF ARIOSTO: Dated by an entry in D. W.'s *Journal* for Nov. 8, 1802: "W. is writing out his stanzas from Ariosto." According to a letter written to Sir G. Beaumont on Oct. 17, 1805 (*E.L.*, p. 529), W. translated two books of the *Orlando Furioso*, but this fragment, representing Canto I, v–xiv, and preserved on the back of a folio sheet, formerly used for a rough draft of *The Ruined Cottage*, is all that has survived.

p. 369. VI. TRANSLATIONS FROM METASTASIO: These translations are written into W.'s copy, presented by Mr. Gordon Wordsworth to the Fitzwilliam Museum, Cambridge, of *Pieces selected from the Italian Poets by Agostino Isola (Teacher of the Italian Language) and translated into English Verse by some of the Gentlemen of the University.* Cambridge 1784. i, iii, and v are in W.'s hand, ii and iv in D. W.'s. On the blank front page W. has written a list of fourteen of his sonnets (giving the opening words as titles), which were all composed between 1802 and 1806 and published in 1807: one of the titles, "There is a trickling . . .", gives an early reading of "There is a little unpretending Rill", *v.* Vol. III, p. 4. From the evidence of handwriting it would appear that the translations were written at the same time that the list was made, i.e. between 1802 and 1806, a time when D. W. was often his amanuensis. W. tells us that as an undergraduate he "read nothing but classic authors according to my fancy, and Italian poetry. My Italian master was named Isola. . . . As I took to these studies with much interest he was proud of my progress" (M. i, p. 14). He returned from time to time to the translation of Italian poetry: *v.* Translation of Ariosto, V *supra* (1802); of Chiabrera (1810), *v.* p. 248, *supra*; and in 1805–6 he was busied with translation from Michael Angelo, *v.* Vol. III, pp. 14–15 and 423. These translations from Metastasio are simpler, terser, and more faithful than the printed versions by Isola's pupils, which are tricked out in the literary style of the late eighteenth century.

p. 370. VII. TRANSLATIONS FOOM MICHAEL ANGELO. i. The translation appeared in R. Duppa's *Life and Literary Works of Michel Angelo*, 2nd edition, 1807; *v.* note to Misc. Sonnets Vol. III, p. 423. The stanzas by Michael Angelo are printed by Duppa among the poems he appends to his book, under the title, *Alcune stanze ritrovate tra altre composizioni di Michel Agnolo così senza cominciato*. There are nine stanzas, and in Duppa's third edition, 1816, the first four of the stanzas translated are attributed to Wordsworth, the last five to Southey.

ii. *Michael Angelo in reply to the passage upon his Statue of Night Sleeping*: These two versions (the first initialled W. W.) of Michael Angelo's quatrain are written into the blank pages at the front of vol. i of the copy, quoted by K. as C., of the 1836–7 edition of W.'s *Poems*. The original quatrain and the epigram which provoked it were printed in R. Duppa's *Life of M. A.*: "Riposta all'epigramma di Giovanni Strozzi sopra la Statua della notte, che è questo:

> La notte, che tu vedi in si dolci atti
> Dormir, fu da un Angelo scolpita.
> In questo sasso, e perche forme, ha vita;
> Destala se nol credi, e parleratti.
> Grato m'èl sonno, e più l'esser di sasso,
> Mentre che 'l danno, e la vergogna dura:
> Non veder, non sentir m'è gran ventura
> Però non mi destar, deh parla basso."

The date when W. made the translations is uncertain. K. assigned them to 1806, *v.* preceding note. But their appearance in the copy of the 1836–7 edition makes it equally likely that they were composed at the time of his later translations from Michael Angelo, during or just after his Italian tour of 1837.

p. 372. VIII. *Come, gentle Sleep, etc.*: This quatrain follows the above lines from Michael Angelo in C. and may have been written about the same time. Warton's Latin verses are as follows:

> "Somne veni! quamvis placidissima Mortis imago es,
> Consortem cupio te tamen esse tori;
> Huc ades, haud abiture citò! nam sic sine vita
> Vivere quam suave est, sic sine morte mori!"

first included in T. Warton's Poetical Works in the fifth edition, 1802, ed. by R. Mant, who refers to Headley's *Select Beauties of Ancient English Poetry*, 1787, where Headley says "they are written by the present Poet Laureate". The ascription is likely to be authentic since Headley was a friend and admirer of Warton, and a fellow member of Trinity College.

p. 372. IX. TRANSLATION OF THE SESTET OF A SONNET BY TASSO— (Vasco, le cui felici ardite antenne . . .). Written by W. on a sheet of Manuscript sold at Sotheby's in Dec. 1896, and printed by the late Mr. Garnett, who prefixed to them the following translation of the Octave:

> Vasco, whose bold and happy mainyard spread
> Sunward thy sails where dawning glory dyed
> Heaven's orient gate; whose westering prow the tide
> Clove, where the day-star bows him to his bed;
> Not sterner toil than thine, or strife more dread,
> Or nobler laud to nobler lyre allied—
> His, who did baffled Polypheme deride,
> Or his, whose soaring shaft the Harpy fled.

p. 372. X. INSCRIPTION FOR THE MOSS-HUT: On Dec. 25, 1804, W. wrote to Sir G. Beaumont: "We have lately built in our little rocky orchard a little circular Hut, lined with moss, like a wren's nest, and coated on the outside with heath, that stands most charmingly, with several views from the different sides of it, of the Lake, the Valley and the Church—the latter sadly spoiled lately by being white-washed. The little retreat is most delightful, and I am sure you and Lady Beaumont would be highly pleased with it. Coleridge has never seen it. What a happiness would it be for us to see him there, and entertain you all next Summer in our homely way under its shady thatch. I will copy a dwarf inscription which I wrote for it the other day, before the building was entirely finished, which indeed it is not yet.

p. 372. XI. DISTRESSFUL GIFT!: Preserved, together with *To the Daisy* and *Elegiac Verses* (pp. 260–5), in a booklet in the hand of S. H., probably copied soon after its composition in the spring of 1805. The Manuscript has corrections in pencil by W., which are incorporated in my text. The book referred to in the poem may, as Mr. Gordon W. suggested, have been that known as M; if not, it was a similar volume into which W.'s poems were copied for the benefit of his brother John.

p. 374. XII. ON SEEING SOME TOURISTS, *etc.*: Preserved in the *Longman* MSS., after the lines *To a young lady who had been reproached, etc.* The date may be any time between 1801 and 1806, when Longman received the Manuscripts for the volumes of 1807. Its inclusion in the *Longman* MSS. suggests that W. intended to publish, but cancelled it.

p. 374. XIII. THE ORCHARD PATHWAY: Preserved in the *Longman* MSS., preceded by the note "To the first division of the first Volume [i.e., as Hutchinson points out, pp. 1–74 of Vol. I of the 1807 volumes] you will prefix a separate Title Page thus *The Orchard Pathway* (and in the same page the following motto)." The lines were probably written shortly before sending the Manuscripts to the printer, i.e. in the autumn of 1806.

p. 374. XIV. ST. PAUL'S: The date of this poem is fixed by a letter to Sir G. Beaumont, April 8, 1808: "You will deem it strange, but really some of the imagery of London has, since my return hither, been more present to my mind than that of this noble vale. I left Coleridge at seven o clock on Sunday morning, and walked towards the city in a very thoughtful and melancholy state of mind. I had passed through Temple Bar and by St. Dunstan's, noticing nothing, and entirely occupied with my own thoughts, when, looking up, I saw before me the avenue of Fleet Street, silent, empty, and pure white, with a sprinkling of new-fallen snow, not a cart or carriage to obstruct the view, no noise, only a few soundless and dusky foot-passengers here and there. You remember the elegant line of the curve of Ludgate Hill in which this avenue would terminate, and beyond, towering above it, was the huge and majestic form of St. Paul's, solemnised by a thin veil of falling snow. I cannot say how much I was affected at this unthought-of sight in such a place, and what a blessing I felt there is in habits of exalted imagination. My sorrow was controlled, and my uneasiness of mind—not quieted and relieved altogether—seemed at once to receive the gift of an anchor of security." Two Manuscripts of the poem are extant, one in the first Manuscript copy of *Peter Bell* (which I quote as MS. A), the other (which I take for my text) in a note-book containing also *A Tuft of Primroses* and *To the Clouds*.

p. 375. XV. GEORGE AND SARAH GREEN: For the story of the tragedy of the Greens, and the interest which the W.s took in the welfare of their orphan children, *v. George and Sarah Green, A Narrative*, by D. W., Oxford, 1935, and *M.Y.*, pp. 178–210. De Quincey contributed to Tait's *Edinburgh Magazine* for Sept. 1839 a vivid but inaccurate account of the incident, under the title *Recollections of Grasmere*, into which he introduced the poem with the words "it may be proper to remind the reader of W.'s memorial stanzas", though in fact the stanzas had not before been published. De Q.'s text is here reproduced—the Manuscript readings are from W.'s letter to Coleridge dated April 19, 1808, just after the poem had been written. The date of W.'s revision of it is unknown.

p. 377. XVI. TRANSLATION OF CHIABRERA'S EPITAPH ON TASSO: From W.'s third *Essay on Epitaphs*, written, probably, early in 1810, for inclusion in *The Friend*, which, however, came to an end on March

15; before that date W.'s first *Essay on Epitaphs* had appeared in it.

   p. 377. XVII. THE SCOTTISH BROOM: A Manuscript in Dove Cottage in an unknown hand gives the title: *A Help for the Memory of the Grand Independent, A New Song* by W. W.; first printed in 1891 in *Annals of my Early Life*, by Charles Wordsworth, who states (p. 107): "While I was staying at Rydal Mount [in 1831] my cousin Dora gave me a copy of the following political squib, written by my uncle some years before on the occasion of a Westmorland election, when Brougham stood as the Radical candidate against Lord Lowther and his brother the Colonel. . . . It is interesting and deserves to be preserved, because it shows beyond question (as the writer, through his intimacy with Lord Lonsdale, could not have been mistaken upon the point) that there had been a time when Brougham would have been content to join the Tory ranks provided the proprietor of Lowther Castle would have taken him in hand." The verses must have been written at the time when W. took a prominent part in opposing Brougham's candidature for Westmorland in 1818 (*v. M.Y.*, pp. 804–16, 821). Birdnest was the name by which Brougham Hall was popularly known, from the Bird family to whom the Manor originally belonged (*v. D. W., Journal* for July 14, 1802).

   1. Scottish] "Because Mr. Brougham pretended that he was a native of England." Note by Charles Wordsworth. D. W. says he claimed to be a native of Westmorland (*M.Y* 814–15). He was born in Edinburgh.

   p. 378. XVIII. PLACARD FOR A POLL BEARING AN OLD SHIRT: Preserved in a Manuscript at Lowther Castle (K.), and probably written at the same date as the previous lines.

   p. 378. XIX. TWO EPIGRAMS ON BYRON'S "CAIN": Found by K. in a catalogue of Autograph Letters. It may be conjectured that as Byron's *Cain*, dedicated to Sir Walter Scott, was published late in Dec. 1821, these epigrams were written in the following year. On Gessner's *Tod Abels*, referred to in the second Epigram, *v. Prelude*, vii. 564, and note. The quotation (l. 3) is from Burns, *To a Haggis*:

> "O, what a glorious sight,
> Warm-reekin', rich!"

   p. 378. XX. EPITAPH: These lines are preserved in a large folio book, MS. 101, and written by M. W., headed "By W. W." and preceded by the note: "In the Burial ground of this Church are deposited the Remains of Jemima A. B. [should be A. D.] second daughter of Sir Egerton Brydges Bart. of Lee Priory, Kent, who departed this life at Rydal, May 25th, 1822, ag. 28 years. This memorial is erected by her afflicted husband Edwd. Quillinan." Above her transcript M. W. has written: "Mr. Quillinan's Sketch for his Wife's Epitaph (to be erected in Grasmere Church):

The good Jemima perished in her bloom
Her hapless fate o'erspread these vales with gloom.
The good, the kind, the lovely and the meek
Might have fit Epitaph *etc. as* 8–16, *but* l. 9 or marble could *for* monument, l. 10 by the heart *for* inwardly *and* l. 16 to heaven *for* away.''

The *Memoir* of W. (i. 444) states that the first six lines of the epitaph were composed by W. It seems likely, however, that W. took E. Q.'s Sketch and rewrote it as a whole. Jemima Anne Deborah Quillinan, wife of Edward Quillinan, was the Wordsworths' near neighbour at Ivy Cottage below Rydal Mount. D. W. attended her in her last illness, due to grievous burns—her clothes having accidentally taken fire. *v.* D. W.'s letter to J. Marshall, 13 June 1822. *L.Y.*, p. 79.

p. 379. XXI. IN THE FIRST PAGE OF AN ALBUM, *etc.*: Preserved in the Postscript to a letter from Dora W. to Edward Quillinan— "Trinity Lodge, Cambridge, May 16, 1824:—I transcribe what my Father wrote in O'Callaghan's Album.'' (*The poem follows.*) *v. Addenda*, p. 469 *supra*.

pp. 379–80. XXII and XXIII. PRITHEE, GENTLE LADY *and* THE LADY WHOM YOU HERE BEHOLD: Underneath the Manuscript copy of these two poems the Rev. Herbert Hill (*m.* Bertha Southey, 1839) has written: "The two poems above have the interest of being playful effusions of Mr. Wordsworth's Muse; they were written for two dolls dressed up by Edith Southey and Dora Wordsworth: the Papers remained as they were originally placed for some twenty years, which accounts for their brown or yellow tint: A published poem of Mr. W.'s on a Needle case in the form of a harp belongs to the same date.'' At the foot of the second poem is written: "Composed by Mr. Wordsworth, Written by E. M. Southey.'' Apparently the first of the two did duty for two dolls, for K. has printed it from another Manuscript, which, in place of the first four lines of my text, reads:

I, whose pretty Voice you hear,
Lady (you will think it queer)

and has the footnote: "*Composed*, and in part transcribed, for Fanny Barlow, by her affectionate Friend, Wm. Wordsworth. Rydal Mount, *Shortest Day*, 1826.'' K. has prefixed this note: "These lines were written for Miss Fanny Barlow of Middlethorpe Hall, York. She was first married to the Rev. E. Trafford Leigh, and afterwards to Dr. Eason Wilkinson of Manchester.''

p. 381. XXIV. COMPOSED WHEN A PROBABILITY EXISTED OF OUR BEING OBLIGED TO QUIT RYDAL MOUNT AS A RESIDENCE: There are several Manuscripts of this poem, on which W. seems to have expended much pains, though he was clearly dissatisfied with the result: he never published it. MS. A, which is complete, I take to be the final text; MS. B consists of two copies, neither of them complete, and other fragments, from which together the whole text can be constructed. Previously printed texts of the poem contain errors which I have not found in any Manuscript. It is dated 1826. Towards the end of 1825 W. was informed that in 1827 Lady le Fleming intended to let Rydal Mount to another tenant, and he bought "at an extravagant fancy price" a piece of ground just below the house and made preparations for building there for himself. But by the following October the notice to quit had been withdrawn, and a little later W. presented the ground to his daughter: it is now known as "Dora's field" (v. L.Y., pp. 232–3, 245–6, 256).

8/9. (*app. crit.*) The spring was called "the Nab Well" (*v. M. i. 23*). "yon craggy Steep" is Nab Scar.

24–36. (*app. crit.*) 'the neighbouring stream" is the Rydal Beck with its famous waterfalls. (*v. An Evening Walk*, ll. 53–65).

p. 387. XXV. Written in Mrs. Field's Album, *etc.*: On Dec. 24, 1828, Barron Field wrote to W. asking him to write in Mrs. Field's Album; on Feb. 26, 1829, he wrote: "Mrs. Field thanks you for writing in her Album, and my Brother is very proud of your praise." Underneath W.'s lines in the Album B. F. wrote:

Words inky! They're worth more than that,
I can't let that go forth;
The line that would detract from words
Itself shews a Word's-worth.

p. 387. XXVI. Written in the Strangers' Book at "The Station", opposite Bowness: dated by K. 1829. "The Strangers' Book at the Station", he writes, "contains the following: 'Lord and Lady Darlington, Lady Vane, Miss Taylor and Captain Stamp pronounce this Lake superior to Lac de Genève, Lago de Como, Lago Maggiore, L'Eau de Zurich, Loch Lomond, Loch Katerine, or the Lakes of Killarney'." On seeing the above W. wrote the lines in the text. The Station was a favourite viewpoint for Windermere on the hill above the Ferry, opposite Bowness (v. W.'s *Guide to the Lakes*, ed. E. de S., p. 5).

p. 388. XXVII. To the Utilitarians: Sent as a postscript to a letter to H. C. R., dated May 5, 1833, preceded by the words "To fill up the paper I [? send] these verses composed or rather thrown off this morning", and followed by "Is the above intelligible—I fear not— I know however my own meaning—and that's enough [?] on Manuscripts".

p. 388. XXVIII. Epigram on an Event in Col. Evans's Redoubted Performances in Spain: On Oct. 27, 1836, H. C. R. wrote to M. W.: "By the bye, could you answer me a question that has been put to me more than once? Did the author of *The Excursion* ever

write an Epigram ?" M. W. replied "To show you that *we* can write
an Epigram—we do *not say* a good one" [*Epigram follows*]. "The
Producer thinks it not amiss as being murmured between sleep and
awake over the fire while thinking of you last night!"

p. 388. XXIX. A SQUIB ON COL. EVANS: Sent in a letter from
W. W. to H. C. R., March 26, 1838: "You know of old my partiality
for Evans: the squib below I let off immediately upon reading his
modest self-defence speech the other day." George de Lacy Evans
(1787–1870) was a gallant and distinguished soldier who fought under
Wellington in Spain and at Waterloo, and later commanded a division
in the Crimea. In 1835 he took command of the British Legion raised
for the service of the Queen Regent of Spain against Don Carlos. He
was defeated at Fuentarabia in July 1836 and at Hernani in March
1837, but in the following July he retook them both; and in August
1837 obtained the red ribbon of a K.C.B. W. W.'s patently unjust
attacks upon him in this squib and in the previous epigram were
prompted by political prejudice. Evans was the radical member for
Westminster (elected 1833) and a strong supporter of the Reform
Bill. The lines were, of course, not written for publication, and were
probably inspired by the desire to score off H. C. R., who in politics
agreed with Evans.

p. 389. XXX. INSCRIPTION ON A ROCK AT RYDAL MOUNT. First
published in M, vol. i, p. 25. "The rock is situated in Dora's Field"
(*v.* note to XXIV *supra*). The inscription is still partly legible.

p. 390. XXXI and XXXII. LET MORE AMBITIOUS POETS, *and*
WITH A SMALL PRESENT: Both these poems are preserved in a note-
book of which the contents seem to belong to the years 1840–6. A
second copy "With a small Present" is found in another Manuscript
book, written just above "The Crescent Moon" (p. 14 *supra*) which is
dated Feb. 25, 1841. It is probably, therefore, of the same date.

p. 390. XXXIII. THOUGH PULPITS AND THE DESK MAY FAIL:
From a bookseller's Catalogue. Mr. Gordon Wordsworth inspected
the Manuscript, and guaranteed its genuineness. W. was at Bath on
the date recorded on the Manuscript (*v. L.Y.*, p. 1074).

p. 390. XXXIV. THE EAGLE AND THE DOVE: From a volume
entitled "*La Petite Chouannerie, ou Histoire d'un Collège Breton sous
l'Empire.* Par A. F. Rio. Londres: Moxon, Dover Street, 1842", and
probably written shortly before that date. Most of the contents of
the book are in French, but beside W.'s there were English verses by
Landor, Monckton Milnes, and others. Henry Reed tells us that the
book dealt with "the romantic revolt of the royalist students of the
college of Vannes in 1815, and their battles with the soldiers of the
French Republic". *v.* Letter to Moxon, 11 May 1842.

p. 391. XXXV. LINES INSCRIBED IN A COPY OF HIS POEMS, *etc.*:
Written for insertion in a presentation copy of the edition of 1845
(*v. L.Y.*, pp. 1271, 1274, 1277).

p. 392. XXXVI. ODE ON THE INSTALLATION OF HIS ROYAL HIGHNESS PRINCE ALBERT, *etc.*: "The plan and composition of this Ode was chiefly prepared by Mr. Quillinan, but carefully revised in MS. by Mr. Wordsworth, who, being in a state of deep domestic affliction, could not otherwise have been able to fulfil the engagement with Prince Albert, previously made, in time for the installation"— *note by M. W. in a copy of the Ode in the Wordsworth Museum.* The "affliction" was the last illness of his daughter Dora, who died on July 9, 1847.

INDEX OF TITLES AND FIRST LINES

Variants are shown by an asterisk or square brackets

Printed and bound by CPI Group (UK) Ltd, Croydon, CR0 4YY